Managing the Internet of Things (IoT) for Business Transformation and Consumer Adoption

Asa Romeo Asa
https://orcid.org/0000-0002-7549-2949
Namibia University of Science and Technology, Namibia

Johanna Pangeiko Nautwima
https://orcid.org/0009-0004-6153-5014
Namibia University of Science and Technology, Namibia

IGI Global
Scientific Publishing
Publishing Tomorrow's Research Today

Vice President of Editorial | Melissa Wagner
Director of Acquisitions | Mikaela Felty
Director of Book Development | Jocelynn Hessler
Production Manager | Mike Brehm
Cover Design | Jose Rosado

Published in the United States of America by
IGI Global Scientific Publishing
701 East Chocolate Avenue
Hershey, PA, 17033, USA
Tel: 717-533-8845 | Fax: 717-533-7115
Website: https://www.igi-global.com E-mail: cust@igi-global.com

Library of Congress Cataloging-in-Publication Data

Names: Asa, Asa Romeo, 1986- editor | Nautwima, Johanna, 1992- editor
Title: Managing the Internet of things (IOT) for business transformation and consumer adoption / [edited by] Asa Romeo Asa, Johanna Pangeiko Nautwima.
Description: Hershey, PA : IGI Global Scientific Publishing, [2026] | Includes bibliographical references and index. | Summary: "This book aims to critically examine the strategic integration of the Internet of Things (IoT) in contemporary business management, focusing on how organizations can leverage IoT to drive operational transformation and enhance consumer adoption. It aims to explore key challenges, strategic frameworks, and marketing innovations that contribute to IoT technologies' successful deployment and acceptance"-- Provided by publisher.
Identifiers: LCCN 2025018888 (print) | LCCN 2025018889 (ebook) | ISBN 9798337334417 hardcover | ISBN 9798337334424 paperback | ISBN 9798337334431 ebook
Subjects: LCSH: Technological innovations--Management | Internet of things
Classification: LCC HD45 .M3285 2026 (print) | LCC HD45 (ebook) | DDC 658.5/14--dc23/eng/20250627
LC record available at https://lccn.loc.gov/2025018888
LC ebook record available at https://lccn.loc.gov/2025018889

British Cataloguing in Publication Data
A Cataloguing in Publication record for this book is available from the British Library.

Table of Contents

Detailed Table of Contents

The Internet of Things (IoT) is reshaping consumer behavior, yet trust deficits remain a significant barrier to adoption. This chapter examines the psychological and behavioral economic factors that influence IoT acceptance, highlighting the centrality of perceived risk, trust heuristics, and emotional engagement. It explores strategies for building brand trust through transparency, ethical responsibility, and corporate accountability. Furthermore, the chapter analyzes how IoT brands can differentiate themselves through authentic digital storytelling, influencer partnerships, and omnichannel marketing. The role of real-time personalization and smart data-driven experiences is discussed alongside the ethical imperatives they entail. Drawing on cross-industry case studies, the chapter identifies key success factors in IoT branding and marketing. It concludes by outlining future trends that will shape consumer expectations and strategic responses in an increasingly connected marketplace.

This chapter employs a systematic review design a structured and replicable method for synthesizing existing research to address identified gaps in the literature. Additionally, by integrating insights from both consumer psychology and behavioural economics, the review aims to explore the complex, multidimensional factors that influence the adoption of IoT technologies. The paper relied exclusively on secondary sources to conduct the systematic review. Furthermore, this study employs a hybrid theoretical framework that integrates three well-established models to assess technological influences, evaluate risk and loss aversion from a behavioural economics perspective and to understand behavioural intention, social norms, and perceived control in technology adoption. When studied together, these three models provide a holistic context as to why consumers may embrace or reject technology. Understanding this, enables marketing experts to devise strategies that address factors that may deter consumers from embracing IoT technologies.

The Internet of Things (IoT) is revolutionizing industries by enhancing connectivity and consumer experiences. However, widespread adoption is hindered by concerns over consumer trust, primarily due to security vulnerabilities, data privacy issues, and ethical dilemmas. This chapter explores the foundational elements of trust in IoT environments, focusing on transparency, cybersecurity, regulatory compliance, and corporate digital responsibility. It examines how breaches and ethical lapses undermine user confidence and emphasizes the importance of transparent data practices and responsible AI use. Consumer psychology is also addressed, illustrating how perceptions of risk, control, and accountability shape trust. The chapter provides an in-depth analysis of security challenges inherent in interconnected IoT systems, highlighting vulnerabilities that cybercriminals exploit. Through case studies, it reviews common threats and presents best practices, including robust cybersecurity frameworks, encryption, and risk mitigation techniques.

The Internet of Things (IoT) is transforming business innovation and competitiveness, yet adoption across Africa remains uneven due to a deep digital divide. This review of 44 peer-reviewed studies (2015–2025) examined how digital readiness and organizational transformation shape IoT uptake. Results show that limited broadband, unstable electricity, and weak cloud systems constrain readiness, while skill shortages and poor digital leadership further slow progress. Many enterprises lack the technical capacity, managerial support, and flexibility required for IoT integration. External obstacles include fragmented regulation and scarce finance, though initiatives such as AfCFTA, the Smart Africa Alliance, and fintech programs offer new opportunities. Effective adoption depends not only on access to technology but also on firms' ability to sense, seize, and reconfigure resources. Building agility, leadership, innovation culture, and robust infrastructure, underpinned by coherent policy and academia-industry collaboration, is crucial for sustainable IoT-driven growth in Africa.

The rapid growth of the Internet of Things (IoT) brings both opportunities and cybersecurity challenges for businesses. This chapter examines the integration of cybersecurity frameworks within IoT ecosystems, highlighting their role in mitigating risks. It discusses frameworks like the NIST Cybersecurity Framework and ISO/IEC 27001 as essential tools for addressing vulnerabilities. Through qualitative analysis of case studies, the chapter assesses how organizations utilize these frameworks to identify risks, develop management strategies, and enhance security awareness. Findings reveal that adopting cybersecurity frameworks improves risk management and boosts consumer trust, enhancing operational resilience. The chapter concludes with recommendations for tailored frameworks, employee training, transparent consumer communication, and regular vulnerability assessments.

The Internet of Things (IoT) has emerged as a transformative force, reshaping industries by enabling smarter operations, data-driven decision-making, and enhanced consumer experiences. As businesses increasingly adopt IoT technologies, they face both opportunities and challenges in leveraging connected ecosystems for business transformation and consumer adoption. This paper explores the strategic management of IoT to drive organizational growth, operational efficiency, and market competitiveness while addressing barriers to widespread consumer acceptance. Key factors in successful IoT implementation include robust data security, seamless integration with existing systems, and scalable infrastructure. Businesses must navigate challenges such as interoperability, privacy concerns, and high deployment costs to fully capitalize on IoT's potential. Additionally, fostering consumer trust

like education campaigns, personalized messaging, and influencer engagement are discussed as means to address consumer fears and motivations. The chapter also identifies future directions including personalized marketing, gamification, and ethical considerations. By combining psychological understanding with targeted marketing and trust-building, IoT companies can better engage consumers and foster sustained adoption in a competitive and evolving market.

This chapter explores the transformative role of the Internet of Things (IoT) in shaping both business operations and consumer interactions. It examines how IoT technologies enable businesses to enhance operational efficiencies, create innovative consumer experiences, and develop new business models. Through strategic frameworks, IoT adoption is positioned as a key driver of digital transformation. The chapter further delves into the behavioral dimensions of consumer engagement with IoT, highlighting personalization and real-time data utilization. Additionally, it addresses the challenges of IoT integration, including technical barriers, data privacy concerns, and regulatory compliance. Lastly, the future of IoT is considered, with a focus on its convergence with emerging technologies, and its potential for fostering sustainability, inclusivity, and societal well-being.

This paradigm is rapidly revolutionizing the way businesses operate, governments function, and consumers engage with their environments. consumer environments, emphasizing the wide-ranging impact of this technology. Defining the Internet of

Preface

INTRODUCTION

How do organizations and consumers navigate an increasingly interconnected world shaped by intelligent devices, real-time data, and automated decision-making? Much like a compass guiding travelers toward their destination, the Internet of Things (IoT) offers direction for businesses and societies seeking transformation, efficiency, and innovation. Yet, as with any journey, the path toward widespread IoT adoption is neither linear nor without obstacles. Issues of trust, security, infrastructure, and human behavior complicate this navigation, requiring both strategic insight and ethical consideration.

Managing the Internet of Things (IoT) for Business Transformation and Consumer Adoption brings together a diverse collection of scholarly perspectives that examine IoT not only as a technological advancement but as a socio-economic and organizational phenomenon. Across global contexts—from emerging markets to advanced digital economies—this volume explores how IoT reshapes industries, influences consumer decision-making, and demands new approaches to governance, marketing, and innovation.

A central theme that emerges throughout the book is the critical role of trust. While IoT promises convenience, personalization, and efficiency, its adoption is often hindered by concerns surrounding data privacy, cybersecurity vulnerabilities, and ethical responsibility. Contributors in this volume collectively argue that successful IoT integration depends as much on human perception and institutional accountability as it does on technological capability. By integrating insights from consumer psychology, behavioral economics, cybersecurity frameworks, and organizational transformation, the chapters provide a comprehensive understanding of both the opportunities and challenges associated with IoT ecosystems.

Equally important is the recognition that IoT adoption is uneven across regions and sectors. Structural barriers such as limited infrastructure, regulatory fragmentation, and skill shortages highlight the need for context-sensitive strategies. At the same time, emerging technologies—including artificial intelligence, 5G connectivity, and data-driven analytics—are accelerating the evolution of IoT, opening new possibilities for innovation while intensifying existing risks. This volume therefore situates IoT within a broader trajectory of digital transformation, emphasizing adaptability, inclusivity, and sustainability.

CHAPTER OVERVIEW

Chapter 1: Examines branding in the IoT era, emphasizing the importance of trust-building, transparency, and emotional engagement in influencing consumer adoption. It highlights strategies such as digital storytelling, influencer partnerships, and personalized experiences.

Chapter 2: Provides a systematic review of consumer psychology and behavioral economics in IoT adoption, integrating multiple theoretical models to explain how risk perception, social norms, and behavioral intentions shape technology acceptance.

Chapter 3: Explores the interplay between consumer trust, security, and ethics, detailing how cybersecurity risks, data privacy concerns, and regulatory practices influence confidence in IoT systems.

Chapter 4: Investigates digital readiness and organizational transformation in African enterprises, identifying infrastructural, institutional, and leadership challenges that affect IoT adoption in developing contexts.

Chapter 5: Focuses on cybersecurity frameworks within IoT ecosystems, demonstrating how structured approaches to risk management enhance organizational resilience and consumer trust.

Chapter 6: Analyzes IoT as a driver of business innovation and competitive advantage, highlighting key success factors such as scalability, integration, and data security.

Chapter 7: Examines IoT's role in enabling scalable digital transformation, emphasizing real-time analytics, system architecture, and the alignment between enterprise goals and end-user needs.

Chapter 8: Discusses marketing strategies for IoT adoption, with a focus on consumer psychology, transparent communication, and targeted engagement techniques to overcome barriers to acceptance.

Chapter 9: Explores the strategic role of IoT in shaping business models and consumer experiences, addressing both operational benefits and integration challenges.

Chapter 10: Provides a forward-looking perspective on IoT systems, detailing their core components, functionalities, and the growing autonomy of interconnected devices.

Chapter 11: Concludes with an in-depth exploration of trust as the cornerstone of future IoT adoption, offering frameworks for building brand confidence through ethical and consumer-centric strategies.

CONCLUSION

As this volume demonstrates, the Internet of Things is far more than a network of connected devices—it is a transformative force redefining how businesses operate and how consumers interact with the world around them. However, its success depends on navigating a complex landscape shaped by technological innovation, human behavior, and ethical responsibility.

The chapters collectively underscore that trust is the linchpin of IoT adoption. Without transparent data practices, robust cybersecurity measures, and accountable governance, even the most advanced technologies risk rejection. At the same time, organizations must cultivate agility, invest in infrastructure and skills, and align technological capabilities with consumer expectations.

Looking ahead, the future of IoT will be shaped by its convergence with emerging technologies and its capacity to address global challenges in inclusive and sustainable ways. By offering interdisciplinary insights and practical frameworks, this book serves as both a guide and a compass—supporting scholars, practitioners, and policymakers as they navigate the evolving terrain of IoT-driven transformation.

Asa Romeo Asa
Namibia University of Science and Technology, Namibia

Johanna Pangeiko Nautwima
Namibia University of Science and Technology, Namibia

Chapter 1
Branding in the Age of IoT:
Building Trust and Driving Consumer Adoption

Md Mehedi Hasan Emon
http://orcid.org/0000-0002-6224-9552
American International University-Bangladesh, Bangladesh

ABSTRACT

The Internet of Things (IoT) is reshaping consumer behavior, yet trust deficits remain a significant barrier to adoption. This chapter examines the psychological and behavioral economic factors that influence IoT acceptance, highlighting the centrality of perceived risk, trust heuristics, and emotional engagement. It explores strategies for building brand trust through transparency, ethical responsibility, and corporate accountability. Furthermore, the chapter analyzes how IoT brands can differentiate themselves through authentic digital storytelling, influencer partnerships, and omnichannel marketing. The role of real-time personalization and smart data-driven experiences is discussed alongside the ethical imperatives they entail. Drawing on cross-industry case studies, the chapter identifies key success factors in IoT branding and marketing. It concludes by outlining future trends that will shape consumer expectations and strategic responses in an increasingly connected marketplace.

INTRODUCTION

The growing strength of IoT technology is radically changing the realm of consumer contact and is offering both opportunities and the challenges to the idea of

DOI: 10.4018/979-8-3373-3441-7.ch001

the contemporary branding high. The fear of lack of privacy and civilianization of information continues to haunt the customer and still makes the IoT solutions not more commonly used. As a result, customers address companies to employ advanced measures to foster trust and maintain ethical practices in addition to open communication. To start with, this chapter delves into the subject of behavioral economics and consumer psychology that contributes immensely towards the comprehension of the process of adoption of IoT. This paper is founded on incorporation of psychological identification of consumer anxiety of threats and privacy along with behavioral economics of how people perceive the use of technology. Information on the psychological dimensions is highly significant regarding branding since contemporary consumers rely on the psychological dimensions to meet their specific needs. The second half of this chapter demonstrates the ability of the IoT business to take advantage of reliable branding to make sure it is doing well in business. Developing credibility in the Internet of Things market entails accountability transparency and proper data handling above customary warranty operations. The review considers the correlation between ethical business conduct and branding and shows how social responsibility can lessen the doubt of customers and enhance trust and loyalty.

IoT companies require customized branding building models to be successful in the saturated market. Avoiding industry saturation and even more cutthroat rivalry, companies have-to go beyond technological innovation and build substantial emotional bonds and honest stories. The chapter examines the strategic nature of digital storytelling, although brand ambassadors are being used as significant streams to enhance consumer engagement and win consumer interest in the brand. The chapter examines how the shift in the touchpoints of the customers influences digital marketing initiatives and integration in the informational channels. One of the most prominent propositions put forward in the paper is the role of artificial intelligence (AI) marketing, predictive analytics, and interaction with social media in terms of promoting the IoT solutions. The unethical activities aim at building synergies on brand experiences across different channels in-order-to deliver brand unity and better customer relationships. The chapter demonstrates that the empowerment of the IoT technologies can bring about highly personalized interactions to users. The study examines superior data analytics in the creation of flexible and premium market categories in promotional approaches relying on data sources. Since this balance is very important to effective branding strategies, it is a significant issue. The chapter employs real-life examples of leaders in different industries to base theoretical concepts with practical components on the use of IoT. We can see that the core strategies of implementation and the key risks are crystallized in the real world as smart home objects, wearables gadgets and connected vehicles. The winning companies have sailed using the navigation of catering to the trust of the customers and enhancement of markets and technologies through strategic innovations. The chapter outlines three possible developments of IoT branding including converging with digital twins, advances in edge computing, and development of autonomous systems. To succeed in this highly dynamic IoT ecosystem, the brands should be creative but ethical at the same time and adaptive to dynamic expectations of customers so-as-to stay competitive. The chapter outlines a template of working with branding problems and opportunities according to the psychological knowledge, the focus on the formation of trust and the practical market strategies along with the interesting case-studies.

CONSUMER PSYCHOLOGY AND BEHAVIORAL ECONOMICS IN IOT ADOPTION

The aspect of customer acceptance is trust particularly when it comes to the system that gathers- much information and works with automation. The uncertainty regarding these threats may include illegal access to data, device malfunctioning, and the possibility to lose control, which could increase the vulnerability of customers in the IoT systems (Neal et al., 2022). Many find the market acceptance of the IoT devices a hard nut to crack, they are easy to use but carry with them threats to the personal freedoms that would be brought to extinction. According to scholarly findings of the last year, in all cases where sensitive personal data is involved, privacy security issues will always gain greater significance than perceived functionality of the system (Emon, 2025c; Palanisamy & Wu, 2021). The moving of the data led to confusion and significantly dared consumers to be more cautious in choosing when the convenience benefits and the safety are equal, and, therefore, reluctance or outright rejecting of the IoT solutions is a more probable case (Protick et al., 2024). It is often hard to explain customers how their information is stored on networked devices due to confusing privacy policies (Khan et al., 2024; Quach et al., 2022). Lack of knowledge among customers about the internal operation of their devices causes confusion and hence they cannot adopt the product even where they have real benefits. Consumers view control as a significant factor impacting the rates of up taking of the IoT devices and systems. Losing the sense of control over how devices work, protecting their data or upgrading their systems is a sign of the unwillingness of customers to be near their IoT devices as outlined by Rizi & Seno, (2022). Companies with brands that have exemplified clear control systems in the form of privacy controls built on user premises are likely to be positively adopted by consumers. Behavioral economics provides scholars with accurate information about the cognitive biases that influence consumer behavior in the adoption of IoT technologies. Status quo bias is a critical psychological tendency that proves that people have a natural inclination to stick to established habits rather than transition to new technologies that demand the acquisition of new behavioral patterns (Oschinsky et al., 2021; Xi, 2024). The issue is getting serious since the majority of IoT devices need adjustments to the current routines and user habits. According to Bouteska & Regaieg (2020), the sensation of potential losses is stronger than the satisfaction that would be obtained in the case of similar gain in what is termed as loss aversion. The IoT model prompts customers to highly emphasize the safety implications of security breaches and unwanted surveillance and technological failures at the expense of the convenience benefits and novel feature (Neal et al., 2022). Both the nature of customers and the imbalanced profit against the possible risks force companies to make proactive moves in the direction of mitigation of losses and observable security with privacy assurances. In situations of uncertainty customers put their confidence in instant emotional brand reliability judgments prior to performing detailed cognitive judgments (Hassan et al., 2025; Wang et al., 2023). There is increased acceptance of brands that are honest, behave ethically and socially responsibly as well as consistent in developing technological environments. The branding activities which are limited by the technological superiority will fail to succeed unless the emotional assurances concerning safety and integrity and the respect of customer autonomy are enhanced (Behera et al., 2024; Guido, 2025; Khan et al., 2025). Research has noted that human beings will exhibit various reactions based on the manner-in-which information is presented when embracing the IoT solutions. Research indicates that the aim to place customers to focus on the positive (lifestyle elevation and improved energy efficiency and improved security) significantly influences the purchasing decisions (Issock Issock et al., 2020; Ma et al., 2022). Social influence methods that primarily involve use of social proof and normative conformity are incredibly effective in influencing customer choice. This is because users can take away their doubts about adoption when they believe that their peers have confidence in and support technology (Lee et al., 2025; Norbu et al., 2024). The increasing popularity of the IoT products makes endorsements and peer-to-peer recommendations and product reviews of the user visible, which serves as an efficient strategy to address the barriers in the behaviors and mindset.

Table 1. Psychological and Behavioral Barriers to IoT Adoption

Barrier	*Description*
Trust Deficit	Anxiety about misuse of sensitive personal information, infringement of privacy and untrustworthiness of smart gadgets cause most people to decline innovative technology.
Technological Opacity	The enigmatic nature of how data is handled by IoT systems commonly makes users uncomfortable and uncertain.
Status Quo Bias	General adoption of new technologies for more convenience is not as appealing to consumers as their current norms.

continued on following page

Table 1. Continued

Barrier	*Description*
Loss Aversion	The fear of such risks has been known to weigh more than the value that may be added by IoT leading to a sluggish or resistant adoption of IoT.
Information Overload	When too much technical or marketing detail is involved, consumers are befuddled, losing interest and being unable to decide to purchase.
Perceived Complexity	Believing that IoT devices require a lot of set up, maintenance or knowledge makes those who are not technology savvy ignorant of using them.
Fear of Surveillance	The fear of constant monitoring using smart gadgets can cause discomforts to reduce the empowerment of using smart devices.
Lack of Social Proof	Lacking assurance from peer groups regarding consumption of IoT, new potential consumers may find themselves uncertain or apprehensive to embrace it as an early adopter.

BUILDING BRAND TRUST IN IOT PRODUCTS AND SERVICES

Development of the brand in the IoT setting requires a lot of consideration since security and privacy and transparency issues should be given priority as well as accountability and ethical principles in managing the corporate identity. Today, trust is a significant requirement of the interaction of customers in sensitive data settings (Luo et al., 2024; Sakib et al., 2023)

Addressing Security, Privacy, and Ethical Considerations

Effective branding of the IoT requires constant dedication to the matter of security and privacy, and ethics. The compliant organizations to both GDPR and CCPA must go beyond compliance good enough to be confident in attracting trust of their customers (Shandilya et al., 2024). Organizations have the responsibility to look after the interests of the users, and currently, the consumers demand more than just following the rules. This program is grounded in the privacy-by-design paradigm and has its priorities on securing and ensuring privacy by including security and privacy features in IoT hardware and applications (Bu et al., 2020; Butt et al., 2023). Firms make risk disclosures and reveal their risk management plans to customers, which gives them a chance to understand risks and get involved in storing their sensitive data. Reliability towards the consumer will be achieved through the adoption of the mechanisms that will enable the customers to manage their privacy settings by introducing adjustable control parameters and straightforward grant-of-access processes (Dehghanpouri et al., 2020; Panahi Rizi et al., 2022). In other words, besides merely addressing technical concerns, the ethics of IoT branding is also concerned with social justice issues, is more inclusive, and is more concerned with the overall impact of IoT implementation on society. The brands evaluation conducted by customers also includes the ethical aspects of algorithm prejudice and digital divide matters and related gadget environmental effects (Emon & Mazid-Ul-Haque, 2025; Shams et al., 2025). Companies that apply the ethical perspectives in their IoT strategies have increased ability to establish long-term customer relationships.

Transparency and Accountability

The positive attribute of transparency that was formerly beneficial has become a compulsory need. Companies that work with IoT environments must develop readable rules regarding the use of the data that must be elaborate and accessible when working with complex and often obscure data flow processes. The users must be completely knowledgeable about complicated technological processes by means of communication that presents the details about the acquired types of data as well as the purpose of collecting the data and the protection rules and access controls (Rosário & Dias, 2023). The empirical evidence shows that customers tend to trust business organizations that share their data Policies in an open and clear and meaningful manner (Hassan El-Annan & Hassoun, 2024; Willis et al., 2021; Zhang et al., 2023). The benefits offered to customers are the increase in transparency provided by privacy dashboards, which communicate with customers and data use alerts indicating data actions in real-time as vast and comprehensive cybersecurity educational campaigns illustrate these concepts. Transparency directly in its concept is related to accountability due to the development of trust among various parties. The audit conducted by external auditors helps brands to have external assurance on their privacy and security measures (Raji et al., 2022). A brand is willing to take responsibility for its actions by providing customers with care-giving intuitive and fast grievance resolution procedures which provide care and effective solutions to the customers. Transparency is an active continuous relationship when coupled with accountability and both involves responses and commitments.

Corporate Social Responsibility (CSR) and Ethical Branding

To mirror the dynamic Ness of the internet of things, the CSR model should be broadened to cover standard charity activity, safe information management, eco friendliness of business and marketing of fair technology distribution. Ethical branding is an important constituent of corporate identity, as observed in the newest fashionable market, which managed to unite more customers and, therefore, enhance brand awareness. Young consumers and the general audience are both concerned with the involvement of socially responsible companies and the community well-being program (Li et al., 2024; Narayanan & Singh, 2023). The privacy practices required of ethical data stewardship anticipate that an authenticated situation will occur when data management does not reinforce inequality or disadvantage marginalized or underrepresented populations. Consumers today are keen to monitor the way connected devices are manufactured and discarded both in the production side and in- regards to how they manage the entire life cycle of a product in a responsible manner. The brands enhance their credibility by creating IoT solutions that can be accessible to such different categories of people as seniors, the disabled, the low-income. Inclusive businesses have extensive market networks and great moral authority. To succeed, IoT brands must convince viewers to embrace an all-encompassing security investment of a brand as specified by the brand with privacy, openness, social integrity, and responsible stewardship as a core element of brand narrative. Fantasy-driven content is unable to build trust in a reality-driven uncertainty market, in which real customer satisfaction is the building block of establishing reliable connections across the supply chain (Emon, 2025a).

BRANDING AND POSITIONING STRATEGIES FOR IOT BUSINESSES

In-order-to succeed in the ever-competitive market situations, and in the ever-evolving development environments, IoT companies must embrace advanced positioning strategies beyond mere basic technical capabilities. A successful business in IoT will require full brand identities that establish emotional and moral and functional connections with the customers. To achieve long-term market positions, three essential components are needed that comprise uniqueness and digital narrative and involvement of influencers within this setting.

Differentiation Strategies

Long-term success in the growing IoT market cannot be achieved just by competition according to the traditional scheme of performance as the products of this kind become more-and-more common. The brands must create special value propositions that transcend beyond normal technical requirements, to satisfy deep emotional needs, social and ethical requirements of the customers. Several paths result in differentiation within the internet of things. Emotional branding comes in as a remedy by demonstrating to the customers that the products are there to bring about life aspirations and involvement of emotions (More, 2023). SMART home technology is currently being marketed as devices that improve the functionality and individual and family safety as well as greater relaxation. When the IoT companies are integrated into the everyday life of the customer, they are getting committed customers more than what they can offer them in a functional form. Daily life functional integration is one of the distinguishing factors of products. By including IoT products in known user behavior without requesting significant changes in behavior, brands will have higher acceptance rates and customer loyalty (Eslami et al., 2024; Ren et al., 2024). The correspondence of the health-related wearable technologies to the existing wellness and fitness trends allows maintaining prolonged contact with the end-users resulting in the reduction of barriers of usage and emotional reaction. Behavioral excellence is a strong argument in-order-to create uniqueness. Social awareness makes more customers buy products where data protection, environmental sustainability and inclusion of the audience have been given priority (Panahi Rizi et al., 2022). Companies that launch elaborate privacy controls and articulate data utilization rules alongside configurable user preferences generate better autonomy respect that enables them to establish archetypal values-based standings in the IoT marketplace.

Digital Storytelling

Digital storytelling as a practice is an effective means of making IoT business friendly and establishing deeper relationships between companies and consumers. With the best practices of digital storytelling, we start moving the weight off exaggerated stories and divert our attention towards real-life stories and technologies like Internet of Things, not in the traditional way of advertising based on product attributes. The accounts on the ways in which the IoT tools can make everyday life easier by offering security and health monitoring and energy management systems resonate with user goals and issues (Ahmad et al., 2021). Emotional reactions make brand loyalty more efficient because they further the guidelines of practical benefits beyond the intellectual benefits of intellectual motives. The core attribute of building strong digital stories is that they should have authentic content. The contemporary audience is now more sensitive to artificial brand messages, as corporate communication suffers more mistrust, therefore it is easy to see tale packs that appear to be fake. Narrative construction has to be based on real-life stories of customers with true testimonials and real-life scenario illustrations (Garczarek-Bak et al., 2024). Any information presented that is not authentic compromises the credibility of the brand besides depriving it of the ability to convince the audience successfully. The multimodality of digital platforms allows the creation of immersive experiences that perceive different sensory stimuli by the companies offering audiovisual content with elements of interaction and social media capabilities. Telling the brand story may become a major branding tool using realistic microsites as well as documentary techniques that include user participation paradigms (Emon & Chowdhury, 2025; Hay et al., 2022; Hossen et al., 2024).

Role of Brand Ambassadors and Influencer Marketing

The environment of IoT is trust-based, which implies that influencers and brand ambassadors play a vital role in it as trust intermediaries. Consumers rely on credible people such as those who are perceived to be informed and authenticated about their values to help them with the interpretation of difficult and ambiguous issues that revolve around new technology (Patwa et al., 2024). The solution to the question of how to implement the IoT in the market is reputable alliances with influencers. Cybersecurity and tech review as well as health and fitness domains specialists bolster brand narratives as they introduce credibility to demonstrate security functionality and features of products as well as ethics. The pieces of advice provided by influencers are used as social evidence to remove fears in consumers and stimulate trust in products (Emon, 2025b; Naeem, 2021). Brands and influencers must have real relationships and serve the corporate ethical values in business relations. This leads to disadvantaged consumer trust due to coercive and entirely commercial relations where sponsored content is not revealed to the masses. The long-term positive relations that the brand has with the authentic influencers who reflect their mission are more crucial than the short-term promotional agreements with influencers (Shams et al., 2025).

Brands provide added value to formal influence campaigns as they assist in achieving the promotion of their consumer brand ambassadors to promote company products naturally. Brands can get the best brand acceptance by using ambassador programs where the players will promote the brand in good faith and tell personal narratives as they connect with followers in a manner that will reduce the concerns of highly skeptical consumers. The IoT businesses must create brand and positioning solutions that eliminate the conventional marketing methods. The IoT corporate should strive to create emotional distance when applying authentic stories and creating reliable relationships with ambassadors and influencer programs. These actions are helpful to the IoT industry, as they establish strong relationships with customers who are moving beyond early fascination with the technical aspects and are changing their marketing strategy in response to the changing consumer attitudes in the digital market (Yerpude & Singhal, 2019).

EFFECTIVE DIGITAL MARKETING AND OMNICHANNEL STRATEGIES

Digital and omnichannel application to this market is important in ensuring robust brand success in IoT market. Organizations employ creative marketing strategy due-to the fact that IoT technology introduces more complexities and even uncertainties related to nature of IoT that require more awareness and trust and emotional connectivity. The use of marketing analytics through AI, strategic allocation of social media and management of omnichannel approach are all initiatives that are professionally fruitful.

AI-Driven Marketing and Predictive Analytics

With the development of AI, the digital sphere of marketing has changed radically, and the projects of IoT business have the chance to obtain knowledge about the behavior of customers and predict the responses of consumers guiding their actions. The market developers exploit predictive analytics to reduce segments of audiences with the help of the past and present information to define potential buyers who may be interested in the IoT technologies (Eslami et al., 2024; Khan & Emon, 2025). After the analysis of the historical data and the online trends and measure the social media sentiment, only potential customers of the IoT products can be customized by the marketers. The AI customer response is dynamic and provides the marketer with the capacity to deliver content that is highly relevant and well-adapted to ever-altering circumstances of customers. The customers who research smart house security regimes may expect receiving materials comprising useful product information and realistic case studies of community safety specific to the area. Relevant context adds to brand interaction with consumers advancing with the results immensely (Hassan et al., 2024; Santos et al., 2022).

Through the AI analysis, companies can determine the points at which customers will fall off and create interventions and attractive incentives that will keep them onboard. These attempts are indispensable in assisting customers in overcoming the obstacles to the adoption of IoT devices; since, the adoption process is often hindered by severe psychological barriers (Ahmed & Ahmed, 2026). The marketing methods that are backed by AI ought to be fashioned in a manner that upholds ethical values as its principal underpinning. A customer will also not react well when a company is asking to do more than is necessary or when privacy concerns have already been raised, and processes that appear to be too intrusive. Businesses must demonstrate their accountability in the way they use information and provide their clients the ability to decline and underline their freedom to maintain customer loyalty (Hassan El-Annan & Hassoun, 2024).

Social Media Engagement and Content Marketing

The synergy of social media sites acts as a short-cut mechanism where users get to know about the existence of IoT and eliminates misconceptions and creates confidence in each other. The consumer penetration of IoT technology in the mainstream is still at an early stage and therefore the direction of instructional content is of critical value. The success of implementation of IoT is based on the brands delivering resources that provide knowledge about the nature of IoT technology and concerns their security risks and longevity of the devices in addition to transparent illustrations of the meaningful customer advantages. Companies that work in the sphere of IoT obtain efficient content strategy by incorporating both the educational material and inspirational pieces and participative resources. Webinars and explainer videos, and blog articles and white papers can assist customers in their decision-making process that is founded on basic knowledge (Gilbert, 2024). The information contained in the messages should be simplified in such a way that complex information is not used but at the same time the language and the delivery must be understandable without the use of any specialized words. When individuals apply interactive forms, social media interaction becomes much more potent. Humanization of IoT enterprises happens by demonstrations of live devices alongside the live question and answer sessions between customers and cybersecurity experts and user-created content success stories that increase community involvement (Kingdon, 2024). When selling smart home technology to the customers, it is advised to promote the emotional bond building by marketing with a real-life testimonial that demonstrates the benefits of the technology in the house. Monitoring online conversations in-order-to conduct social listening aids organizations in gathering insights that can be used to develop their content strategy. Promotion of content that reacts fast to the current problems causes customers to view the brand as thoughtful besides alleviating the risk of misinformation that may compromise the acceptance of the brand. The development of collaboration with social media influencers may assist companies in reaching their maximum and enhancing their brand image. Through technical reviews, cybersecurity skills of proponents, and the lifestyle of influencers, companies in the IoT can showcase their products without any form of superficiality since they have trusted networks of individuals (Alqudhaibi et al., 2024).

Omnichannel Integration

The integration of the various points of touching to create a consistent brand experience is significant among the brands of IoT that are held in the dynamic purchasing landscape. The brands lose consumer trust and have a reduced adoption rate when they offer fragmented branding and inconsistency in the communication and the level of support they offer within the channels. A fundamental requirement is integration of digital software with physical equipment that is easy and effortless. Customers overall who begin interacting with a brand through targeted social media advertisements, they move to physical stores and require mobile applications assistance, they are supposed to always be the beneficiaries of the same quality of messages and services (Oncioiu et al., 2021). By regular communication, the brands would be known and trusted thus reducing the perception of their security issues related to the IoT technology. With the application of augmented reality technologies, the customers could observe the way smart thermostats could look in a real place and reduce the gaps between the research conducted online and the product experience. The product is at the control of the consumer by incorporation of mobile applications which provide information such as quick help and control of the device. In the current digital space, retailers are interested in offering in-store experiences (Quinones et al., 2023). The retail settings must have had their areas where the shoppers can feel the live demonstration of the IoT devices and how they can determine the value of IoT devices in an actual environment. The salespeople who are informed about IoT technology can boost customer confidence levels by being assured and honest regarding the issue with the customers. To ensure that the omnichannel operations are a success, the enterprises must have trustful backbone connectivity that will help to push seamless data flow among the different touchpoints so-as-to allow personalized and contextual customer interaction (Arafat et al., 2025). One of the difficulties of personalization and privacy is to set up the proper data governance policies that would safeguard the data and the trust of the customer simultaneously (Morić et al., 2024). An omnichannel system needs constant feedback systems to be incorporated in its operation. Implementation of the omnichannel strategy means the inclusion of feedback loops that have-to be continuous. The active feedback system applied on different platforms can assist consumers in impacting the quality of products and services and demonstrate the interest of the brand in consumer-centricity in the markets where it is possible to build trust (Šerić et al., 2024).

PERSONALIZED CUSTOMER EXPERIENCES ENABLED BY IOT

With the dynamic digital economy, personal expectations have been a necessity rather than a new factor in all brands. With the advent of the IoT, the brands have a rare chance to learn and satisfy individual needs of the customers as never before. Following the cascading outgrowth of IoT technologies, there has been paradigm shift where the experience of customers has changed to be generalized mass segments to very personal experience that is real time and contextual. Despite the abundance of opportunities, ethical issues that the networked world is founded on must be questioned.

Data Analytics for Customer Segmentation

A development of personalized customer experience in the IoT ecosystems is premised on state-of-the-art data analytics and sophisticated segmentation. Unlike traditional types of data source, IoT devices generate streams of granular real-time data of both transactional and situational contexts, usage behavior, emotional state and environmental conditions. With the help of this data exhaust, extremely advanced profiles of consumers can be constructed and do not end at their standard demographic due to psychographic ones (Panahi Rizi et al., 2022). With machine learning and AI-driven segmentation models, it is possible to analyze large and diverse data sets to identify the appearance of trends and classify consumers in micro segments and predict future behavior with man levels of accuracy (Hassan et al., 2025). As an example, wearable health devices would separate users not just by age or fitness, however, by specific health objectives, daily disciplines, motivational triggers and even sleep cycles. Likewise, smart home ecosystems will be able to distinguish among users with preferences that save energy or optimize comfort and prefers this than a specific brand can tailor its communications and products to suit the preferences (Korneeva et al., 2021). Of importance, the ability to identify and serve micro-audiences gives brands the skills to establish hyper-personalized value propositions with a high level of resonance at the individual level. Rather than using generic promotions, the importance of IoT-enabled segmentation will be that brands will offer offers, content, and experience that initially resonate with the context and needs of the user in question, thus establishing a connection with the user and creating a stronger emotional bond and loyalty (Masoodi et al., 2024).

Real-Time Personalization and Smart Recommendations

On top of the prosaic tier of the creation of the fixed segments, the radical aspect of the IoT is the possibility to enable personalization in real time. The IoT devices enable dynamically changing the product recommendations, marketing messages, and services delivery through unlimited sensing, evaluation, and response to consumer behaviors, environmental stimuli. Such a level of individualism enhances customer satisfaction and interaction perceived relevance of interactions and, in general, customer satisfaction. Smart home devices can even learn user routines and preference overtime, as an example; the lighting, temperature or entertainment settings will automatically adjust to the specific routine. Voice assistants such as Amazon Alexa or Google Assistant rely on real-time data so that they can offer personalized news updates or notifications or shopping recommendations based on previous interactions and situational prompts (Malodia et al., 2022). Connected cars are starting to be able to customize driving modes, suggest customized routes and even recommend maintenance decisions in the automotive industry, based on individual drivers and their behavior.

The other good examples of the power of real-time personalization are the fitness trackers and health monitoring devices. As biometric information is constantly monitored, these gadgets can present tailor-made plans of action, nutrition advice and even wellness tricks push them to their stage of health as it becomes increasingly dynamic. Not only do such on-the-spot, contextually relevant ideas provide a stronger user experience but also allow consumers to achieve more personal goals, which enhances greater brand identification. Marketing wise, dynamic personalization also enables brands to optimally execute customer journeys in the process. Indeed, an intelligent shopping application, when it realizes that a consumer spends more time window shoppers at a particular product line in a store, the application can issue promotions, reviews or recommendations on other products to complement the client smartphone or wearable device, on the fly. Timely intervention will improve the purchase intention and pleasurable and more enjoyable shopping experience (Dhaigude & Mohan, 2023). However, the application of real-time personalization must be applied seeing not to overdo it, otherwise the customers will feel estranged. Relevance should not only be exploited but be managed in a way that sums up exposing the user to a better rather than a worse experience.

Ethical Considerations

The world in which IoT-based personalization is highly a prospect also presents immense ethical innuendos particularly on the aspect of data privacy, autonomy and consumer well-being. The invasion, manipulation, or exploitation might ruin trust and provoke strong negative reactions and cancel the brand (Tiwari & Waoo, 2024). The positive sides of data collection in the context, predictive capabilities, and the IoT personalization, also render this personalization to abuses, or omissions. Without clear permission, clear data usage, and actual user control, personalization campaigns in the absence of explicit consent can easily revolve around transparency and surveillance and annoy the consumers with the sense of being violated at a personal level. Thus, compliance is not the issue, but it is a strategic necessity of transparency. The brands should be able to inform them properly of what data they gather, how they utilize it, with and without whom. Effective consent mechanisms should be explicit, granular and revisable and users of the system should have control over the degree in addition to the nature of their personalized experiences (Burkhardt et al., 2023).

Moreover, the strategy should focus on consumer welfare rather than short term commercial interests. As an illustration, a fitness tracker can encourage users to exercise more but should not force it and promote unhealthy behavior. Furthermore, despite the possibility of individual willingness to pay to change prices in dynamically-pricing algorithms, the ethical concerns must curb potentially exploitative, potentially unfair, or even discriminatory behavior (Seele et al., 2021). One emerging best practice is the application of the so-called privacy by design, ethics by design model in which ethical reasoning is built into the nature of IoT products and services. This implies systems design which minimize the data collection to what is expected, anonymization or pseudonymization of in place data where needed and default configurations to facilitate the authority of the user and their privacy (Khan & Hasan Emon, 2024; Sim et al., 2023). Lastly, the brands must understand that not all consumers want to be personalized. Some of them can become more homogeneous, with less personal on-line communication or more privacy conscious. Consumer diversity is acknowledged with the help of offering opt outs, personalization intensity controls, and alternate user choices, and brand integrity is improved.

CROSS-INDUSTRY INSIGHTS: LESSONS FROM SUCCESSFUL IOT ADOPTION CAMPAIGNS

The spread of IoT in industries has not only transformed the abilities to operate but has transformed branding and brand inclination approaches as well. The successful IoT adoption campaigns imply that branding IoT solutions cannot be achieved by simply demonstrating the superiority of the technology. Instead, it needs to have those lacking a soul, a conscience, and a conscience in society. The presence of state-of-the-art players such as Nest Labs, Fitbit and Tesla have paved new paths in streamlining the innovations in the IoT, have shown that successful branding links the technology with the narration of man of trust, empowerment and aspiration.

Case Studies of Leading Brands

Smart Home Technology: Nest Labs

Nest Labs was founded in 2010 and was subsequently acquired by Google; it redesigned the conventional narrative entirely in the smart homestay industry as far as thermostats are concerned. Nest did not sell the product as a technological device, but as a champion of the comforts of home and efficiency and combating the good fight against the environment. Its branding appreciated the ability to make it intuitive in design, user-friendly and ensure privacy so that the thermostat started being viewed as an intelligent caring home assistant rather than a mechanical one (Almusaed et al., 2023). The success of Nest was premised on its simplicity and sentimental inclination. Technical terms were not overloaded with the consumers, but instead, they were presented with the idea of a learning thermostat that will operate and adapt to the ways people live and conserve energy without compromising comfort. Focusing on the environmental responsibility the role that Nest could have in the context of energy conservation and reduced carbon footprint the company responded to the growing public attention to the issue of sustainability (Xiao et al., 2021). Moreover, Nest overspent on open communication regarding data privacy through providing explicit answers as to what data were gathered and their application, which had the side effect of creating confidence in a time where an increasing number of people were becoming skeptical of digital communication. The argument here on the part of the Nest is pretty-simple: IoT branding within the smart home area has-to become more humanized, it has-to be aligned with the societal values, and it must learn to handle consumer apprehensions of data security.

Wearables: Fitbit

The application of Fitbit around stimulants enabled it to become a market leader by altering the concept of a cold measuring unit of a fitness tracker to a device to promote communal and motivational health initiatives. The branding of Fitbit amplified the emotion of it all community, achievement, and transformation instead of making claims that can be done by the device alone (Kim & Cho, 2024). The Fitbit ecosystem had social support and allowed us to participate in challenges to celebrate successes and share them with friends and family. This was the strategy of generating emotional investment, thereby making fitness tracking a socially approved activity, which the people threw their joint will in support of. In addition, Fitbit gave specific insights and encouragement based on the information provided by consumers, therefore, creating a continuous dialogue between brand and customer, this reinforced loyalty and kept the interest going. Based on the path that Fitbit has taken, brands have seen that in the world of IoT product utility has to be supplemented with an emotional and social connection. Consumers want functionality; they want a brand that supports their ambition, one that cheers them on, one that embraces them with fellow like-minded folks.

Connected Vehicles: Tesla

Tesla is a pioneer on how to integrate IoT into the motor car industry, where connectivity will allow empowerment of the users, as well as adding value to the products once they are purchased. After the innovations of an over-the-air (OTA) type of software updates, Tesla changed the definition of what a vehicle is not just a fixed product but a platform that could be constantly updated and enhanced through innovations (Winkelhake, 2022). The branding process of Tesla easily linked the slickness of the technology to the user freedom. Comparisons, such as Autopilot, Smart Summon and customization allowed the Tesla car extension to turn out to be the whim of the user, which could learn, adjust and transform without any big effort. The emphasis on the ability of drivers to get real-time updates and advancements met the image of the next generation investments of Tesla as it united the technological advancements and the ability to control and empower the users. Switching to the topic of public stance, the public stance on such ethical issues as open patent policy and the mission to make the world convert to sustainable energy that Tesla has enhanced contributed to the enhancement of brand narrative by offering consumers the desire to join the larger movement of change (Palmié et al., 2024).

Key Takeaways

There are a number-of common patterns of IoT adoption as seen in the case studies. It needs to have technical know-how, but it must also have a significant emotional appeal. Consumers do not measure IoT products exclusively on what they can be useful in doing. Trust, identity and aspiration are among the emotional inclinations that are crucial in shaping their decisions (Xu & Mehta, 2022). Second, it should practice ethical transparency. The big data generated by IoT devices creates intense data that can be analyzed, which leads to open disclosure of data strategies and the possibility to assist consumers in the control of their data use, contributing to an attachment to the brand and preventing the likelihood of being hectored publicly (El-Afifi et al., 2024; Jamil et al., 2025). Third, adoption is enhanced by social validation. Through community development, social engagement, and alignment of their brand message with the greater social objectives in mind, the IoT companies can turn the decisions made by individual users into collective actions to ensure that they move quicker and more sustainably into new markets (Ahmed et al., 2026). Lastly, it is also important that the brands should learn the subtleties to emotional considerations in the adoption of technology. Individuals are typically a combination of good anticipations and internal fear toward bringing in new technology. Top brands are aware of and are-take action regarding the- underlying issues of the consumer. They do not completely shun these sentiments but rather touch them directly since security, privacy, reliability, and easy-to-use features are significant elements of their message.

Table 2. Comparative Analysis of IoT Branding Success Across Industries

Industry Sector	*Brand*	*Core Branding Message*	*Consumer Value Proposition*	*Key Adoption Driver*
Smart Home	Nest (Google)	Simplicity, security, sustainability	Comfort, automation, energy efficiency	Environmental responsibility and ease of use
Wearables	Fitbit	Health empowerment through connectivity	Personalized health tracking, community support	Social motivation and lifestyle integration
Automotive	Tesla	Innovation, control, and over-the-air convenience	Autonomous features, seamless updates	User empowerment and cutting-edge tech appeal
Retail & Logistics	Amazon Go	Frictionless shopping experience	No checkouts, personalized inventory interaction	Convenience and novelty
Healthcare	Philips Health	Smart care and remote diagnostics	Real-time monitoring, preventive care	Data-driven personalization and trust in tech

This table is an example of what major brands in various locations considered in their identification to increase the use of the IoT. The importance of consumer values in the message, which stimulates trust and contact, is demonstrated by the strategy of such a company like Nest that is oriented on simplicity and sustainability and the strategy of Tesla that is oriented on the control of the user. Emotional involvement normally contributes to creating adoption by hinting at the convenience and mass communications on technological processes. These examples show that the key to a successful brand in the field of IoT is not merely consistent with technical innovation, but with the possibility to find and fulfill the identity, lifestyle and ethical concerns that can be present in consumers.

Future Trends in IoT Branding and Adoption

The development of IoT systems is provoking the rise of new technological and sociological tendencies that can significantly change the way individuals see products and services and make brands reconsider their approaches. The digital copies of physical products or physical environments, which enable monitoring and simulating real-time and optimizing them, are one of the main developments of the digital twin. Taking the healthcare and manufacturing as examples, digital twins contribute to predictive maintenance, personalized care, and a platform that is easy to use (Haleem et al., 2023; van Dinter et al., 2022). In case of such brands that use digital twins, transparency and users control and the clearly generated benefits that combine the physical and the digital world are worth accentuating. The significant change is the growth of edge computing because the data processing is performed on the device instead of in-the cloud servers. The implementation of edge computing can increase the secrecy of data, decrease the time lag, and increase the immediate reactiveness of the devices of the IoT (Nain et al., 2022). Through edge computing, companies will be able to differentiate, providing enhanced privacy and increased responsiveness.

Also, Systems that accommodate autonomy, whether autonomous cars, sophisticated factories, etc., are shifting to implementation. The more autonomous IoT solutions are integrated, the more that brands should focus effort on trust-building, user protection, and ethical codes since more choice is being devolved to machines. With this ongoing shift in regulations (particularly in data protection and AI surveillance, e.g., GDPR, CCPA), IoT brands ought to become more verbose and adaptable. Regulatory compliance beyond the law necessitates an opportunity to brands to show their concern towards ethics and consumer protection. Such a situation has never demanded such agility in this ever-changing environment. To become trusted and relevant in the IoT setting, it is important to constantly review the problems faced by consumers, societal norms, regulatory changes, and frontier technology. IoT is not a single sale, it is a process and the firms that have the capability to follow this dynamic with actual interest, appreciation, and taking a step towards the future are pioneering ones.

The existence of advanced technology does not necessarily make success an assurance in the leadership of different industries in the use of IoT in their programs. To create a strong brand image of IoT technologies, companies should seek a comprehensive approach. coordination of technical expertise, emotional engagement, moral message, and social agreement. Marketers need to appeal to the emotional needs behind the usage of technologies and develop messages that touch on the wish/need of the consumer and assuage his fears. The focus enhancement of digital twins, edge computing, and autonomy demands rapid industrial progress along with investments in outstanding ethics and responsiveness to shifting consumer/ societal patterns. The milestones reached in this endeavor will not just drive the IoT industry, but the way humans will be dealing with technology in future will be influenced by this.

CONCLUSION

With the development of the IoT, brands must also alter their strategy, and trust, personalization, and emotional engagement are not only bonuses, but necessities.

This chapter emphasizes the fact that to be successful in the IoT industry firms must be highly knowledgeable in consumer psychology, behavioral sciences and even the more subtle understanding of technology and human sentiment. Oddly enough, the aspects that motivate people to utilize IoT are constructed through perspectives and practices relating to technology. The adoption of this connected device by consumers is not, therefore, dependent on utility and features. Finally, convenience and social identity, control and security are also influential in the decision of the consumers. The behavioral economic concepts, including loss aversion, trust asymmetry, and status-quo tendency largely condition the consumer response to the technological advances in this cluster. When such psychological considerations have been discovered, the brands will be better placed to apply persuasive communication in not only breaking the barriers to adoption, but more significantly developing a lasting customer engagement. Critical sectors of IoT like health and home care IoT solutions demand increased trust and acceptance of its users on adoption compared to other less dramatic technologies of consumption. The clarity of the manner-in-which the data will be handled, ethical aspects, a clear description of advantages and disadvantages, and a commitment to improve the empowered customers are very crucial components of branding strategy in the modern context. They are prerequisite requirements. The companies that do not follow these simple principles will face the threat of immediate market failure and ruined reputation. Theoretically, as far as IoT brands are concerned, there is a requirement to concentrate on the emotional needs, but not direct technical functionality. The customers seek the brands that have sound technology and the associated principles of sustainability, empowerment, protection, or innovation that resonate with the beliefs of the customer. Making complex technology simple, accessing the emotional element and utilizing real-life worth helps make brands of complex technology more persuasive to consumers, which makes them trust their products. In such a competitive IoT market, the excellence and achievement of the storytelling of each brand is what pushes winners above losers. It requires an omnichannel and full digital approach to marketing to achieve and sustain consumer interest with the IoT brands. In winning, the brands of IoT must assure perpetual and hassle-free user directions, including interaction with smart appliances, retail stores and the like of interaction with the service channels of customers. Though the AI and predictive analytics are helpful in the context of customizing targeted marketing strategies, therefore, they are honest and fitting, these methods remain critical. In addition, consumer educative messages that assuage consumer anxieties and create confidence are important in addressing the broader issues of privacy, complexity and security of which consumers are also anxious.

When used in the right way, the data provided by IoT devices can help businesses to provide highly personalized experiences that would greatly increase consumer loyalty and satisfaction. As soon as the customers are provided with personalized efforts in real time, which are accompanied by smart recommendations and adaptive options, they might significantly contribute to the enjoyment and total worth. Nevertheless, the more the brands develop their personalization strategies, the higher the level of ethical concerns. The decision to kill in the name of personalization and privacy will require companies to establish ease of use, non-enforceable, but permitting data management policies. Cleopatra instances on the revolutionary smart home inventions of Nest Labs, community-oriented approaches of Fitbit in terms of wearable products, and goals-oriented approaches of Tesla towards vehicles establishment provide exemplary examples of brands to follow in terms of IoT branding. The above brands demonstrate that technology innovation has a profound relation with emotional needs and societal perceptions, and therefore, the brands need to establish trust and possess a specific personality and embody aspirational values. IoT is an ever-changing environment with new trends that are bound to transform the pages of operation of our brands. With the advent of digital twins, edge computing, and autonomous systems, they are predicted to not only enhance brand-customer interactions but also provoke dilemmas of challenging strategic importance to brands. Conversely, the consumers will require technology companies to be more intelligent, more personalized, more ethically responsible, and more powerful in society. Thus, agile brands will be honest in their practices and proactive in matters related to ethics, which will make a difference in the scale of the IoT. It is those marketers who understand that branding is an element of their business goals that will tend to dazzle. When businesses concentrate on their fundamental values, duties and strong human relations, then it will be the ultimate success of businesses in the future. Brand identity in the era of sisterhood emphasizes credibility over complexity when it comes to searching for the most recent innovations as mandatory and achievable aspects of life.

REFERENCES

Ahmad, W., Rasool, A., Javed, A. R., Baker, T., & Jalil, Z. (2021). Cyber Security in IoT-Based Cloud Computing: A Comprehensive Survey. *Electronics (Basel)*, *11*(1), 16. DOI: 10.3390/electronics11010016

Ahmed, M., & Ahmed, M. J. (2026). Sustainable Industrial Operations Through IoT-Generated Big Data Insights. In *Sustainable Operations in the Age of AI and Big Data* (pp. 37–82). DOI: 10.4018/979-8-2600-0216-2.ch002

Ahmed, M., Al Amareen, O. S., & Arafat, Y. (2026). Harnessing Big Data for Reverse Logistics and Waste Management: Pathways to Sustainable Supply Chains. In *Enhancing Sustainability in Global Supply Chains With Big Data Analytics* (pp. 175–210). IGI Global Scientific Publishing. DOI: 10.4018/979-8-3373-6896-2.ch006

Almusaed, A., Yitmen, I., & Almssad, A. (2023). Enhancing Smart Home Design with AI Models: A Case Study of Living Spaces Implementation Review. *Energies*, *16*(6), 2636. DOI: 10.3390/en16062636

Alqudhaibi, A., Krishna, A., Jagtap, S., Williams, N., Afy-Shararah, M., & Salonitis, K. (2024). Cybersecurity 4.0: Safeguarding trust and production in the digital food industry era. *Discover Food*, *4*(1), 2. DOI: 10.1007/s44187-023-00071-7

Arafat, Y., Pk, M. K., Hossen, A., & Sarker, M. N. (2025). Adaptive Temporal Convolution Framework for Multi-Channel Sales Forecasting Through Dynamic EMA-XGBoost. *International Journal of Research. Innovation and Commercialisation*, *6*(1), 10073445. Advance online publication. DOI: 10.1504/IJRIC.2025.10073445

Behera, R. K., Bala, P. K., & Rana, N. P. (2024). Assessing the intention to adopt computational intelligence in interactive marketing. *Journal of Retailing and Consumer Services*, *78*, 103765. DOI: 10.1016/j.jretconser.2024.103765

Bouteska, A., & Regaieg, B. (2020). Loss aversion, overconfidence of investors and their impact on market performance evidence from the US stock markets. *Journal of Economics, Finance and Administrative Science*, *25*(50), 451–478. DOI: 10.1108/JEFAS-07-2017-0081

Bu, F., Wang, N., Jiang, B., & Liang, H. (2020). "Privacy by Design" implementation: Information system engineers' perspective. *International Journal of Information Management*, *53*, 102124. DOI: 10.1016/j.ijinfomgt.2020.102124

Burkhardt, G., Boy, F., Doneddu, D., & Hajli, N. (2023). Privacy Behaviour: A Model for Online Informed Consent. *Journal of Business Ethics*, *186*(1), 237–255. DOI: 10.1007/s10551-022-05202-1

Butt, U., & Gutappa, B. shaheer, Pendlebury, G., Hassan, B., Butt, W., & Davelis, A. (2023). *IoT Privacy by Design* (pp. 270–300). DOI: 10.4018/978-1-6684-6403-8.ch015

Dehghanpouri, H., Soltani, Z., & Rostamzadeh, R. (2020). The impact of trust, privacy and quality of service on the success of E-CRM: The mediating role of customer satisfaction. *Journal of Business and Industrial Marketing*, *35*(11), 1831–1847. DOI: 10.1108/JBIM-07-2019-0325

Dhaigude, S. A., & Mohan, B. C. (2023). Customer experience in social commerce: A systematic literature review and research agenda. *International Journal of Consumer Studies*, *47*(5), 1629–1668. DOI: 10.1111/ijcs.12954

El-Afifi, M. I., Sedhom, B. E., Padmanaban, S., & Eladl, A. A. (2024). A review of IoT-enabled smart energy hub systems: Rising, applications, challenges, and future prospects. *Renewable Energy Focus*, *51*, 100634. DOI: 10.1016/j.ref.2024.100634

Emon, M. M. H. (2025a). Digital transformation in emerging markets: Adoption dynamics of AI image generation in marketing practices. *Telematics and Informatics Reports*, *20*, 100267. DOI: 10.1016/j.teler.2025.100267

Emon, M. M. H. (2025b). Leveraging AI on Social Media & Digital Platforms to Enhance English Language Teaching and Learning. In *AI-Powered English Teaching* (pp. 211–238). IGI Global Scientific Publishing., DOI: 10.4018/979-8-3373-1952-0.ch007

Emon, M. M. H. (2025c). Navigating the Digital Labyrinth: Personal Data Privacy and Security at Individual and Organizational Levels. In *User-Centric Cybersecurity Implications for Sustainable Digital Transformation* (pp. 257–288). IGI Global Scientific Publishing. DOI: 10.4018/979-8-3373-3171-3.ch008

Emon, M. M. H., & Chowdhury, M. S. A. (2025). Safeguarding Student Data: Privacy and Security Challenges in AI-Powered Education Tools. In *Enhancing Student Support and Learning Through Conversational AI* (pp. 191–228). IGI Global Scientific Publishing. DOI: 10.4018/979-8-3373-3316-8.ch008

Emon, M. M. H., & Mazid-Ul-Haque, M. (2025). Balancing Usability and Security: Enhancing User Experience Without Compromising Privacy. In *User-Centric Cybersecurity Implications for Sustainable Digital Transformation* (pp. 309–342). IGI Global Scientific Publishing. DOI: 10.4018/979-8-3373-3171-3.ch010

Eslami, E., Razi, N., Lonbani, M., & Rezazadeh, J. (2024). Unveiling IoT Customer Behaviour: Segmentation and Insights for Enhanced IoT-CRM Strategies: A Real Case Study. *Sensors (Basel)*, *24*(4), 1050. DOI: 10.3390/s24041050

Garczarek-Bak, U., Szymkowiak, A., Jaks, Z., & Jansto, E. (2024). Impact of product vs brand storytelling on online customer experience. *International Journal of Wine Business Research, 36*(3), 370–405. DOI: 10.1108/IJWBR-07-2023-0041

Gilbert, M. A. (2024). *Disrupting Marketing*., DOI: 10.4018/979-8-3693-4361-6.ch002

Guido, G. (2025). Godfather Marketing: Offering favors before products. *Review of Managerial Science, 19*(4), 1095–1129. DOI: 10.1007/s11846-024-00785-7

Haleem, A., Javaid, M., Pratap Singh, R., & Suman, R. (2023). Exploring the revolution in healthcare systems through the applications of digital twin technology. *Biomedical Technology, 4*, 28–38. DOI: 10.1016/j.bmt.2023.02.001

Hassan, M. M., Fahim Abrar, M., Kakon, S., Hossen, A., & Arafat, Y. (2024). Improving Loan Approval Decisions: The Impact of Data Balancing on the Classifier's Performance in Predicting Borrower Reliability. *2024 27th International Conference on Computer and Information Technology (ICCIT)*, 1690–1695. DOI: 10.1109/ICCIT64611.2024.11022094

Hassan, M. M., Hossen, A., Arafat, Y., Sarker, M. N., Jamil, M. H., & Siddika, A. (2025). Exploratory Analysis of the Impact of Data Balancing on the Classifier's Performance in Predicting Creditworthiness Reliability. [IJEEI]. *Indonesian Journal of Electrical Engineering and Informatics, 13*(3). Advance online publication. DOI: 10.52549/ijeei.v13i3.6667

Hassan, M. M., Hossen, A., Sarker, M. N., Arafat, Y., Khan, A., Talukder, S. I., & Roy, B. K. S. (2025). An Empirical Analysis on Renewable Energy: Biogas Production Prediction Using Machine Learning. *Journal of Power and Energy Engineering, 13*(07), 40–59. DOI: 10.4236/jpee.2025.137002

Hassan El-Annan, S., & Hassoun, R. (2024). *Enhancing Consumer Trust Through Transparent Data Practices and Ethical Data Management in Business*., DOI: 10.4018/979-8-3693-8357-5.ch005

Hay, N. A., Chien, P. M., & Ruhanen, L. (2022). Tell me your story: Branding destinations through residents' (place) stories. *Journal of Vacation Marketing, 28*(3), 319–334. DOI: 10.1177/13567667211060567

Hossen, A., Arafat, Y., Sarker, M. N., Jamil, M. H., Islam, M. A., & Hasan, R. (2024). A Predictive Framework for Financial Crashes Using Advanced Time Series Techniques. *2024 International Conference on Progressive Innovations in Intelligent Systems and Data Science (ICPIDS)*, 476–483. DOI: 10.1109/ICPIDS65698.2024.00080

Issock Issock, P. B., Roberts-Lombard, M., & Mpinganjira, M. (2020). The importance of customer trust for social marketing interventions: A case of energy-efficiency consumption. *Journal of Social Marketing*, *10*(2), 265–286. DOI: 10.1108/JSOCM-05-2019-0071

Jamil, M. H., Hossen, A., Talukder, S. I., Arafat, Y., & Sozib, H. M. (2025). Big Data Analytics and Its Usage on Financial Fraud Detection in the USA. *Advances in Machine Learning IoT and Data Security*, *1*, amlid25001. Advance online publication. DOI: 10.63471/amlid25001

Khan, T., & Emon, M. M. H. (2025). The role of digital supply chain practices in enhancing firm performance: Insights from the manufacturing sector of Bangladesh. *Brazilian Journal of Operations & Production Management*, *22*(2), 2493. DOI: 10.14488/BJOPM.2493.2025

Khan, T., Emon, M. M. H., & Nath, A. (2024). Quantifying the Effects of AI-Driven Inventory Management on Operational Efficiency in Online Retail. *2024 27th International Conference on Computer and Information Technology (ICCIT)*, 2092–2097. DOI: 10.1109/ICCIT64611.2024.11021996

Khan, T., Emon, M. M. H., Rahman, K. M., Nipa, M. N., & Fuad, M. N. (2025). The Role of AI in Driving Customer Engagement Through Technological, Organizational and Environmental Enablers in E-Commerce. *2025 International Conference on Quantum Photonics, Artificial Intelligence, and Networking (QPAIN)*, 1–6. DOI: 10.1109/QPAIN66474.2025.11171949

Khan, T., & Hasan Emon, M. M. (2024). Determinants of AI Image Generator Adoption Among Marketing Agencies: The Mediating Effects of Perceived Usefulness. *2024 IEEE 3rd International Conference on Robotics, Automation, Artificial-Intelligence and Internet-of-Things (RAAICON)*, 177–182. DOI: 10.1109/RAAICON64172.2024.10928548

Kim, M., & Cho, I. (2024). Navigating user discontent in wearable tech: An in-depth study of Fitbit reviews. *Technology Analysis and Strategic Management*, •••, 1–15. DOI: 10.1080/09537325.2024.2408727

Kingdon, A. (2024). *Socio-Technical and Multi-stakeholder Approaches to Countering Online Propaganda.*, DOI: 10.1007/978-3-031-75393-0_8

Korneeva, E., Olinder, N., & Strielkowski, W. (2021). Consumer Attitudes to the Smart Home Technologies and the Internet of Things (IoT). *Energies*, *14*(23), 7913. DOI: 10.3390/en14237913

Lee, A. T., Ramasamy, R. K., & Subbarao, A. (2025). Understanding Psychosocial Barriers to Healthcare Technology Adoption: A Review of TAM Technology Acceptance Model and Unified Theory of Acceptance and Use of Technology and UTAUT Frameworks. *Healthcare (Basel), 13*(3), 250. DOI: 10.3390/healthcare13030250

Li, J.-Y., Lee, Y., Tao, W., Xu, D., & Dong, E. (2024). Organizations with True Heart: The Role of Organizational Identity in Shaping Consumer Attributions of Corporate Responsibility to Race (CRR) Motives. *Journal of Public Relations Research, 36*(4), 320–340. DOI: 10.1080/1062726X.2023.2298864

Luo, H., Luo, J., & Vasilakos, A. V. (2024). BC4LLM: A perspective of trusted artificial intelligence when blockchain meets large language models. *Neurocomputing, 599*, 128089. DOI: 10.1016/j.neucom.2024.128089

Ma, G., Ma, J., Li, H., Wang, Y., Wang, Z., & Zhang, B. (2022). Customer behavior in purchasing energy-saving products: Big data analytics from online reviews of e-commerce. *Energy Policy, 165*, 112960. DOI: 10.1016/j.enpol.2022.112960

Malodia, S., Kaur, P., Ractham, P., Sakashita, M., & Dhir, A. (2022). Why do people avoid and postpone the use of voice assistants for transactional purposes? A perspective from decision avoidance theory. *Journal of Business Research, 146*, 605–618. DOI: 10.1016/j.jbusres.2022.03.045

Masoodi, F. S., Bamhdi, A., Manocha, A., Teli, T. A., Masoodi, Z. S., & Reegu, F. A. (2024). *Internet of Things Applications and Technology*. Auerbach Publications., DOI: 10.1201/9781003458401

More, A. B. (2023). *Implementing Digital Age Experience Marketing to Make Customer Relations More Sustainable*., DOI: 10.1007/978-3-031-20443-2_5

Morić, Z., Dakic, V., Djekic, D., & Regvart, D. (2024). Protection of Personal Data in the Context of E-Commerce. *Journal of Cybersecurity and Privacy, 4*(3), 731–761. DOI: 10.3390/jcp4030034

Naeem, M. (2021). The role of social media to generate social proof as engaged society for stockpiling behaviour of customers during Covid-19 pandemic. *Qualitative Market Research, 24*(3), 281–301. DOI: 10.1108/QMR-04-2020-0050

Nain, G., Pattanaik, K. K., & Sharma, G. K. (2022). Towards edge computing in intelligent manufacturing: Past, present and future. *Journal of Manufacturing Systems, 62*, 588–611. DOI: 10.1016/j.jmsy.2022.01.010

Narayanan, S., & Singh, G. A. (2023). Consumers' willingness to pay for corporate social responsibility: Theory and evidence. *International Journal of Consumer Studies, 47*(6), 2212–2244. DOI: 10.1111/ijcs.12910

Neal Joshua, E. S., Bhattacharyya, D., & Rao, N. T. (2022). Managing information security risk and Internet of Things (IoT) impact on challenges of medicinal problems with complex settings. In *Multi-Chaos, Fractal and Multi-Fractional Artificial Intelligence of Different Complex Systems* (pp. 291–310). Elsevier. DOI: 10.1016/B978-0-323-90032-4.00007-9

Norbu, T., Park, J. Y., Wong, K. W., & Cui, H. (2024). Factors Affecting Trust and Acceptance for Blockchain Adoption in Digital Payment Systems: A Systematic Review. *Future Internet*, *16*(3), 106. DOI: 10.3390/fi16030106

Oncioiu, I., Căpu neanu, S., Topor, D., Tama , A., Solomon, A.-G., & Dănescu, T. (2021). Fundamental Power of Social Media Interactions for Building a Brand and Customer Relations. *Journal of Theoretical and Applied Electronic Commerce Research*, *16*(5), 1702–1717. DOI: 10.3390/jtaer16050096

Oschinsky, F. M., Stelter, A., & Niehaves, B. (2021). Cognitive biases in the digital age – How resolving the status quo bias enables public-sector employees to overcome restraint. *Government Information Quarterly*, *38*(4), 101611. DOI: 10.1016/j.giq.2021.101611

Palanisamy, R., & Wu, Y. (2021). Users' attitude on perceived security of enterprise systems mobility: An empirical study. *Information and Computer Security*, *29*(1), 159–186. DOI: 10.1108/ICS-05-2020-0069

Palmié, M., Miehé, L., Mair, J., & Wincent, J. (2024). Valuation entrepreneurship through product-design and blame-avoidance strategies: How Tesla managed to change the public perception of sustainable innovations. *Journal of Product Innovation Management*, *41*(3), 644–676. DOI: 10.1111/jpim.12732

Panahi Rizi, M. H., Hosseini Seno, S. A., Rizi, M. H. P., & Seno, S. A. H. (2022). A systematic review of technologies and solutions to improve security and privacy protection of citizens in the smart city. *Internet of Things : Engineering Cyber Physical Human Systems*, *20*, 100584. DOI: 10.1016/j.iot.2022.100584

Patwa, N., Gupta, M., & Mittal, A. (2024). Social proof: Empowering social commerce through social validation. *Global Knowledge, Memory and Communication*. Advance online publication. DOI: 10.1108/GKMC-06-2023-0188

Protick, T. I., Sabir, A., Abhinaya, S., Bartlett, A., & Das, A. (2024). Unveiling Users' Security and Privacy Concerns Regarding Smart Home IoT Products from Online Reviews. *ACM Journal on Computing and Sustainable Societies*, *2*(4), 1–41. DOI: 10.1145/3685929

Quach, S., Thaichon, P., Martin, K. D., Weaven, S., & Palmatier, R. W. (2022). Digital technologies: Tensions in privacy and data. *Journal of the Academy of Marketing Science*, *50*(6), 1299–1323. DOI: 10.1007/s11747-022-00845-y

Quinones, M., Gomez-Suarez, M., Cruz-Roche, I., & Díaz-Martín, A. M. (2023). Technology: A strategic imperative for successful retailers. *International Journal of Retail & Distribution Management*, *51*(4), 546–566. DOI: 10.1108/IJRDM-03-2022-0088

Raji, I. D., Xu, P., Honigsberg, C., & Ho, D. (2022). Outsider Oversight: Designing a Third Party Audit Ecosystem for AI Governance. *Proceedings of the 2022 AAAI/ACM Conference on AI, Ethics, and Society*, 557–571. DOI: 10.1145/3514094.3534181

Ren, G., Chen, Y., & Yang, M. (2024). Customer perception, integration behavior, and loyalty of internet of things enterprises. *Technology in Society*, *78*, 102600. DOI: 10.1016/j.techsoc.2024.102600

Rosário, A. T., & Dias, J. C. (2023). How has data-driven marketing evolved: Challenges and opportunities with emerging technologies. *International Journal of Information Management Data Insights*, *3*(2), 100203. DOI: 10.1016/j.jjimei.2023.100203

Sakib, N., Veeramalla, H. S. J., Naidu, N. A. R., Anik, F. I., Vanga, L. R., Valero, M., & Hossain, E. (2023). *Unpacking Privacy Calculus and Interplay of Data Privacy and Healthcare: Paths Towards Safeguarding Patient Empowerment* (pp. 137–171). DOI: 10.1007/978-3-031-42112-9_7

Santos, Z. R., Cheung, C. M. K., Coelho, P. S., & Rita, P. (2022). Consumer engagement in social media brand communities: A literature review. *International Journal of Information Management*, *63*, 102457. DOI: 10.1016/j.ijinfomgt.2021.102457

Seele, P., Dierksmeier, C., Hofstetter, R., & Schultz, M. D. (2021). Mapping the Ethicality of Algorithmic Pricing: A Review of Dynamic and Personalized Pricing. *Journal of Business Ethics*, *170*(4), 697–719. DOI: 10.1007/s10551-019-04371-w

Šerić, M., Vernuccio, M., & Pastore, A. (2024). Revising the basic principles of integrated marketing communications during a health-related crisis: The case of Croatian tourism and hospitality industry. *Corporate Communications*, *29*(2), 257–278. DOI: 10.1108/CCIJ-05-2023-0081

Shams, S. M. R., Brown, D. M., & Hardcastle, K. (2025). *Brand Management*. Marketing Communication, and Promotion Management for People, Planet, and Profit., DOI: 10.1007/978-3-031-79130-7_4

Shandilya, S. K., Datta, A., Kartik, Y., & Nagar, A. (2024). *Navigating the Regulatory Landscape*., DOI: 10.1007/978-3-031-53290-0_3

Sim, J., Kim, B., Jeon, K., Joo, M., Lim, J., Lee, J., & Choo, K.-K. R. (2023). Technical Requirements and Approaches in Personal Data Control. *ACM Computing Surveys, 55*(9), 1–30. DOI: 10.1145/3558766

Tiwari, M., & Waoo, A. A. (2024). *Transforming Healthcare: The Synergistic Fusion of AI and IoT for Intelligent*. Personalized Well-Being., DOI: 10.1007/978-3-031-65022-2_7

van Dinter, R., Tekinerdogan, B., & Catal, C. (2022). Predictive maintenance using digital twins: A systematic literature review. *Information and Software Technology, 151*, 107008. DOI: 10.1016/j.infsof.2022.107008

Wang, J., Shahzad, F., & Ashraf, S. F. (2023). Elements of information ecosystems stimulating the online consumer behavior: A mediating role of cognitive and affective trust. *Telematics and Informatics, 80*, 101970. DOI: 10.1016/j.tele.2023.101970

Willis, B., Jai, T., & Lauderdale, M. (2021). Trust and commitment: Effect of applying consumer data rights on U.S. Consumers' attitudes toward online retailers in big data era. *Journal of Consumer Behaviour, 20*(6), 1575–1590. DOI: 10.1002/cb.1968

Winkelhake, U. (2022). Vision Digitised Automotive Industry 2030. In *The Digital Transformation of the Automotive Industry* (pp. 85–145). Springer International Publishing. DOI: 10.1007/978-3-030-83826-3_5

Xi, Y. (2024). Navigating Technological Shifts: An Examination of User Inertia and Technology Prestige in Large-Language-Model AI Chatbot Transition. *International Journal of Human-Computer Interaction*, •••, 1–17. DOI: 10.1080/10447318.2024.2405786

Xiao, J., Zhen, Z., Tian, L., Su, B., Chen, H., & Zhu, A. X. (2021). Green behavior towards low-carbon society: Theory, measurement and action. *Journal of Cleaner Production, 278*, 123765. DOI: 10.1016/j.jclepro.2020.123765

Xu, L., & Mehta, R. (2022). Technology devalues luxury? Exploring consumer responses to AI-designed luxury products. *Journal of the Academy of Marketing Science, 50*(6), 1135–1152. DOI: 10.1007/s11747-022-00854-x

Yerpude, S., & Singhal, T. K. (2019). Custolytics. *International Journal of Emerging Markets, 16*(1), 92–112. DOI: 10.1108/IJOEM-05-2018-0250

Zhang, W., Siyal, S., Riaz, S., Ahmad, R., Hilmi, M. F., & Li, Z. (2023). Data Security, Customer Trust and Intention for Adoption of Fintech Services: An Empirical Analysis From Commercial Bank Users in Pakistan. *SAGE Open, 13*(3), 21582440231181388. Advance online publication. DOI: 10.1177/21582440231181388

KEY TERMS AND DEFINITIONS

Behavioral Economics: An academic field that asserts the impact of the psychological, emotional, and social factors on their economic and decision-making behavior and generation of new options independent of mainstreams of the traditional rational-choice models.

Brand Differentiation: The preconceived channels whereby a brand differentiates its products/services using atypical words, lovable feelings, or conscientious standpoints.

Consumer Trust: How the consumers are convinced of the assurance; the brand needs to be telling them about ensuring their data is safe, that they will deliver on the delivery service and that they will be ethical regarding the devices involved.

Digital Storytelling: Addition of narrative solution into online platforms in-order-to bring brands to life, create an emotional connection, and lure customers to technology-related material.

Ethical Data Stewardship: Adherence A framework that incorporates a balance of transparency, responsible use and respect for privacy, but all-of these together with verification data practices are in conformity with ethical and legal regulations.

Internet of Things (IoT): Intertwined objects that collaborate to collect, distribute and process data to offer responsive services and enrich the daily experience of a user.

Omnichannel Strategy: This is a comprehensive strategy that makes sure that consumers experience an attractive environment of your brand regardless of whether they experience it in a digital or physical avatar.

Real-Time Personalization: Revisiting the marketing content, lines, or service offerings that include up-to-the-minute consumer behavior, likes, and environmental data collected via IoT networks.

Chapter 2
Consumer Psychology and Behavioural Economics in the Adoption of Internet of Things (IoT) Technologies:
A Systematic Review

Petrina Patricia Louw
Namibia University of Science and Technology, Windhoek, Namibia

Tracy Schaller
Namibia University of Science and Technology, Windhoek, Namibia

Noble Pete-I Gotolph Eiaseb
http://orcid.org/0009-0002-0318-9761
University of Namibia, Namibia

ABSTRACT

This chapter employs a systematic review design a structured and replicable method for synthesizing existing research to address identified gaps in the literature. Additionally, by integrating insights from both consumer psychology and behavioural economics, the review aims to explore the complex, multidimensional factors that influence the adoption of IoT technologies. The paper relied exclusively on secondary sources to conduct the systematic review. Furthermore, this study employs a hybrid theoretical

DOI: 10.4018/979-8-3373-3441-7.ch002

framework that integrates three well-established models to assess technological influences, evaluate risk and loss aversion from a behavioural economics perspective and to understand behavioural intention, social norms, and perceived control in technology adoption. When studied together, these three models provide a holistic context as to why consumers may embrace or reject technology. Understanding this, enables marketing experts to devise strategies that address factors that may deter consumers from embracing IoT technologies.

1. INTRODUCTION

The rapid proliferation of the Internet of Things (IoT) has ushered in transformative changes across key sectors such as healthcare, retail, transportation, and home automation. IoT refers to an interconnected network of devices that collect, exchange, and analyse data to enhance operational efficiency and create intelligent user experiences (Mouha, 2021). Despite the promise of enhanced functionality and convenience, consumer adoption of IoT technologies has been inconsistent. Compared to 72% of families in developed economies, just 35% of households in developing nations use IoT devices as of 2023 (International Telecommunication Union, 2023). This adoption disparity suggests that technological innovation alone does not account for user engagement. Therefore, and inference could be drawn instead, psychological and behavioural economic factors are instrumental in shaping consumer decisions (Gerli et al. 2022).

Furthermore, while traditional economic models presume rationality and utility maximization, behavioural economics highlights how cognitive biases, heuristics, and emotional influences often lead to decisions that deviate from rational choice paradigms (Negm 2022; Kim & Wang, 2021). For example, concepts like loss aversion, perceived control, and the endowment effect have been shown to influence how consumers evaluate risk and benefit in the context of new technologies like IoT (Ladeira et al., 2024). Additionally, consumer psychology provides vital insights into user attitudes, motivations, and perceived barriers.

Factors such as trust in technology providers, perceived ease of use, social influence, and privacy concerns are consistently identified as key determinants of IoT adoption (Guhr et al., 2020; Kwakye, 2023; Aggarwal & Singh, 2025). Importantly, the privacy paradox where consumers express concerns about data privacy yet continue to adopt data-collecting technologies demonstrates the nuanced interplay between risk perception and behavioural intent (Guhr et al., 2020; Kwakye, 2023).

From a marketing perspective, IoT enables a shift from traditional mass communication to context-aware, real-time engagement driven by user behaviour and predictive analytics (Rane, 2023). This marks a transition from static demographic segmentation to dynamic personalization, with marketing strategies increasingly leveraging behavioural cues to deliver anticipatory and value-enhanced experiences (Chandra et al. 2022).

Given the convergence of behavioural economics, consumer psychology, and technology design, there is a need to synthesize empirical and theoretical developments in this interdisciplinary field. Therefore, this chapter presents a systematic review of literature published between 2015 and 2025 to examine how behavioural and psychological factors influence the adoption of IoT technologies. This integrative review aims to inform the development of consumer-centred IoT innovations and evidence-based marketing strategies.

1.1 Background of the Study

Digitalisation has brought with great innovative and creative strides to improve everyday living of ordinary citizens. Furthermore, the incorporation sensors in physical infrastructure by utilising digital twins and IoT has enabled many developing countries to create smart cities (Gerli et al., 2022). Aggarwal and Singh (2025) agree and argue that the IoT has rapidly transformed various sectors, including healthcare, retail, transportation, and home automation, by enabling devices to collect, exchange, and analyse data to enhance efficiency and user experiences. However, despite the technological advancements and the promise of improved user experiences, the adoption of IoT technologies remains inconsistent among consumers (Balaji et al., 2019).

Consequently, Govinda and Saravanaguru (2016) propound that this variability in adoption rates cannot be solely attributed to technological features but is significantly influenced by psychological and economic factors. Research indicates that consumer perceptions and behaviours play a pivotal role in determining the acceptance and usage of IoT devices (Aggarwal & Singh, 2025; Gerli et al. 2022). Rath et al. (2024) maintain that the emergence of IoT marks a new era in digital transformation, linking physical devices to digital networks to enhance efficiency, convenience, and personalization. From smart thermostats and wearables to precision agriculture and telehealth, IoT is embedded in modern life. Yet, its adoption hinges not only on technical advancement but on nuanced human behaviour (Vaikhandla et al., 2021).

In addition, Tripathy and Anuradha (2017) aver that IoT is a crucial component of digital transformation, enabling physical devices to link and share real time data over digital networks. Furthermore, the uses of IoT are extensive and include but are not limited to smart healthcare, home automation, logistics, and agriculture (Nizetic et al., 2020). Although IoT offers greater efficiency, convenience, and immediate insights, consumer acceptance is still uneven. As a result, this disparity increases the divide between developed countries and emerging economies on the digitalization and IoT development and implementation sphere (Muteba et al., 2019). For example, merely 35% of homes in developing nations have embraced IoT technologies, while the figure stands at 72% in advanced economies (ITU, 2023).

Consumer psychology and behavioural economics offer critical insights into how individuals perceive, evaluate, and decide to adopt these technologies. Factors such as perceived usefulness, trust, and privacy concerns have been identified as significant predictors of IoT adoption (Kwakye, 2023). For instance, studies have shown that consumers' trust in IoT providers and their perceptions of the usefulness of IoT devices are strong predictors of adoption intentions (Guhr et al., 2020). Additionally, privacy concerns, while often cited as barriers to adoption, do not always deter consumers, suggesting the presence of a privacy paradox where perceived benefits outweigh privacy risks (Guhr et al., 2020; Kwakye, 2023; Aggarwal & Singh, 2025).

According to Muteba et al. (2019), behavioural economics further demonstrate the complexities of consumer decision-making in the context of IoT adoption. Traditional economic models often assume rational decision-making processes. However, these models fall short in explaining the complexities of consumer behaviour in the context of IoT adoption (Ding et al., 2023). Behavioural economics, which integrates insights from psychology and economics, provides a more nuanced understanding by highlighting how emotions, cognitive biases, and social influences affect consumer choices (Aggarwal & Singh, 2025). For example, concepts like loss aversion, perceived control, and the endowment effect have been shown to influence how consumers evaluate risk and benefit in the context of new technologies like IoT (Kim & Wang, 2021).

In addition, understanding these psychological and behavioural determinants is crucial for effectively designing, marketing, and distributing IoT devices. Factors such as perceived usefulness, trust, privacy concerns, and social influence have been identified as significant predictors of IoT adoption (Kim & Wang, 2021). Moreover, (Guhr et al., 2020) agrees and proffers that the integration of behavioural economics into the study of IoT adoption offers valuable insights into the non-rational factors influencing consumer decisions. Therefore, this study aims to synthesize recent literature to explore how consumer psychology and behavioural economics intersect with IoT technology adoption, providing a comprehensive understanding of the factors influencing consumer decisions in the IoT domain (Aggarwal & Singh, 2025).

1.2 Problem Statement

Despite the transformative potential of the IoT in sectors such as healthcare, transportation, retail, and smart homes, consumer adoption remains inconsistent and, in some markets, unexpectedly slow (Kim & Wang, 2021). Furthermore, while

IoT technologies offer significant convenience, personalization, and efficiency. However, Negun (2022) argue that adoption is hindered not only by technological limitations or costs but also by human factors such as risk perception, psychological resistance, and behavioural uncertainty. Additionally, studies have shown that technological sophistication alone is insufficient to drive widespread adoption unless accompanied by consumer trust, perceived control, and emotional acceptance of such innovations (Negm, 2022).

Traditional models of technology acceptance, such as the Technology Acceptance Model (TAM) which was created by Davies et al. (1989), primarily emphasize rational decision-making based on perceived usefulness and ease of use. However, this model overlooks the psychological and behavioural dimensions that often deviate from rationality (Mortenson & Vidgen, 2016). Behavioural economics highlights the role of cognitive biases, social influence, heuristics, and emotional responses in shaping consumer decision-making, particularly in uncertain or novel contexts like IoT (Kim & Wang, 2021). For instance, privacy concerns, loss aversion, and ambiguity avoidance frequently complicate user willingness to adopt IoT technologies, even when the benefits are clear (Guhr et al., 2020). These non-rational factors remain insufficiently integrated into mainstream technology adoption frameworks.

Despite the growing scholarly interest in consumer-centric approaches to IoT, there is still a lack of comprehensive synthesis that brings together consumer psychology and behavioural economics in a unified framework to explain adoption behaviours (La Diega, 2023). Subsequently, Sheoran and Vij (2023) maintains that existing research is fragmented, often focusing on isolated variables or contexts without fully capturing the complex, multi-dimensional drivers of consumer decisions. Therefore, a systematic investigation is needed to consolidate current findings, identify key psychological and behavioural determinants (Sheoran & Vij, 2023). This could possibly provide a more holistic understanding of how and why consumers adopt or resist IoT technologies. Addressing this gap can support more effective policy formulation, product design, and marketing strategies aimed at accelerating consumer adoption.

1.3 Aim of the Study

This study aims to address the identified gaps by conducting a systematic review that integrates insights from both consumer psychology and behavioural economics to understand the multidimensional factors influencing the adoption of IoT technologies. Unlike prior research that often isolates technological or demographic variables, this study synthesizes empirical findings from 2015 to 2025. Furthermore, the rationale of the study is to explore how cognitive biases, emotional responses, trust, privacy perceptions, and social influence collectively shape consumer decision-making.

Moreover, by bridging theoretical frameworks from behavioural economics with psychological constructs such as perceived control, attitude, and motivation, the study provides a more comprehensive model of IoT adoption. Furthermore, this review seeks to inform both academia and industry by highlighting actionable insights for designing user-centric IoT solutions and marketing strategies that align with actual consumer behaviour, rather than idealized rational models.

1.4 Limitations of the Study

A key limitation of this study lies in its dependence on existing peer-reviewed literature published between 2014 and 2025, which inherently restricts the analysis to the scope, and geographical coverage of the selected studies. This reliance may overlook emergent behavioural trends, cultural nuances, or consumer attitudes evolving in real-time, especially in underrepresented regions such as parts of Africa, Latin America, or Southeast Asia, where IoT penetration is increasing but less frequently studied. Additionally, the heterogeneity in research designs, theoretical frameworks, and operational definitions of key constructs such as adoption, trust, or privacy, which may introduce inconsistencies that complicate comparative analysis and the generalization of findings. Some studies may also emphasize technological or economic variables while underexploring psychological or behavioural factors, leading to an imbalance in the reviewed literature. Furthermore, publication bias can skew the synthesis toward studies with statistically significant results, potentially overlooking valuable insights from null or mixed findings.

However, to mitigate these limitations, future research should complement systematic reviews with primary data collection, such as surveys, interviews, or ethnographic studies across diverse cultural and socioeconomic settings. This would allow for the validation and contextualization of synthesized findings in real-world environments. Employing a meta-analysis approach in future iterations of this study could also enhance the reliability of conclusions by quantifying effect sizes across studies and identifying statistically robust patterns. Additionally, incorporating literature, high-quality industry reports, and preprints, while maintaining academic rigor could possibly help capture emerging trends and underreported perspectives. Finally, using a transparent and replicable inclusion/exclusion protocol and critically assessing the methodological quality of included studies can further strengthen the reliability and applicability of the review's findings.

1.5 Delimitations of the Study

This study is delimited by its focus on peer-reviewed academic literature published between 2015 and 2025, which intentionally excludes older foundational works, non-peer-reviewed materials such as industry white papers, blogs, and studies not published in English. While this temporal and linguistic delimitation ensures relevance to recent technological developments and methodological rigor, it may omit valuable historical context or insights from non-English-speaking regions where IoT adoption dynamics differ. Furthermore, the review emphasizes consumer adoption in sectors such as smart homes, wearables, and personal devices, thereby excluding industrial, governmental, or Business-to-Business IoT applications that may operate under different psychological and economic paradigms. The study also focuses on behavioural economics and consumer psychology frameworks, deliberately limiting integration with adjacent fields like sociology, human-computer interaction, or cybersecurity studies that may offer complementary perspectives.

However, to mitigate the impact of these delimitations, future research could extend the review to include cross-disciplinary frameworks, enabling a richer understanding of adoption behaviours from multiple lenses. Expanding the temporal scope to include pre-2015 literature could provide a more comprehensive longitudinal analysis, highlighting how consumer behaviour has evolved over time with technological maturity. Additionally, incorporating multilingual studies and region-specific research in follow-up analyses would help contextualize findings across diverse cultural and socioeconomic settings. Researchers are also encouraged to explore the interplay between consumer-focused and industrial IoT adoption in hybrid environments, such as smart cities or connected vehicles, to build a more holistic picture of the IoT ecosystem.

1.6 Significance of the Study

This study is significant in advancing theoretical and practical understanding of how psychological and behavioural economic factors influence consumer adoption of Internet of Things (IoT) technologies. While prior models like the Technology Acceptance Model (TAM) and the Unified Theory of Acceptance and Use of Technology (UTAUT) provide useful frameworks, they often emphasize rational decision-making and technological attributes, overlooking the non-logical, emotional, and social dynamics that drive real-world consumer behaviour. Furthermore, by systematically reviewing recent literature through the lens of consumer psychology and behavioural economics, this study offers a more holistic perspective that accounts for cognitive biases, risk aversion, perceived control, trust, social influence, and the privacy paradox elements.

These aspects are therefore increasingly recognized as central to understanding technology adoption. This nuanced perspective contributes to academic literature by bridging a critical interdisciplinary gap between technology adoption studies and behavioural sciences. Practically, the insights generated from this review are valuable to IoT designers, marketers, and policy makers aiming to foster greater consumer engagement with connected technologies. Understanding the psychological and behavioural drivers of adoption can inform the development of more user-centric products and personalized marketing strategies that resonate with consumers' actual decision-making processes.

For instance, strategies that enhance perceived security, simplify user interfaces, or build trust through transparent data policies can directly address psychological adoption barriers. Furthermore, by recognizing that consumers do not always behave in economically rational ways, firms and governments can develop more effective interventions such as nudges, framing techniques, and behaviourally informed policies to encourage responsible and widespread adoption of IoT devices. As IoT technologies continue to evolve and permeate daily life, this study supports the creation of more inclusive, accessible, and psychologically attuned digital ecosystems.

1.7 Review Objectives

The objectives of this review are:

- To analyse the key psychological and behavioural economic factors influencing consumers' decisions to adopt IoT technologies;
- To identify and summarize empirical research on the role of consumer trust, risk perception, perceived value, and social influence in IoT adoption;
- To explore how behavioural biases, such as loss aversion, status quo bias, and herd behaviour, impact the adoption and usage of IoT products;
- To evaluate the effectiveness of current marketing strategies that leverage consumer psychology and behavioural insights to promote IoT technologies; and
- To provide practical implications recommendations in the areas of IoT product development, digital marketing, and consumer engagement.

2. SYSTEMATIC LITERATURE REVIEW

2.1 Definition of Key Terms

2.1.1 Internet of Things (IoT)

The Internet of Things (IoT) is an emerging concept. According to Berte (2018) IoT refers to the new phase in the internet development whereby computing devices are integrated in everyday objects and devices that are able to transmit data on their own. Mckinsey & Company (2024) states that any physical item having sensors embedded that has the potential to communicate with computers can be classified as IoT. Consequently, the digital monitoring and control of physical world has been enabled by IoT.

2.1.2 Consumer Psychology

Consumers are making purchasing decisions daily and now more than ever because they can purchase items from the comfort of their homes using smart devices. Consumer psychology can be defined as the study that explores reasons and motivations behind consumers purchasing decisions (University of Southern California, 2023). Evidently, the concept is derived from a multidisciplinary field that combines social psychology marketing and behavioural economics to understand consumer behaviour (Ladeira et al., 2025).

2.1.3 Behavioural Economics

Alam (2022) defines behavioural economics as a field of study that examines how psychological, cognitive, emotional, cultural, and social factors influence the decision-making processes of individuals and institutions. In the context of IoT, it entails how these factors influence the decision of customers when interacting with smart devices (Mohanty et al., 2022).

2.1.4 Technology Acceptance

Despite the widespread adoption of technology and the emergence of IoT, attaining technology acceptance remains a significant challenge (Nadal et al., 2020). The decision-making process by which consumers determine whether to adopt or to reject a technology is fundamentally influenced by the principles outlined in the Technology Acceptance Model as discussed in the next section (Negm, 2023).

2.2 Theoretical literature

2.2.1 Psychological and Behavioural Economic Factors Influencing IoT Adoption

Consumer decisions regarding the adoption of Internet of Things (IoT) technologies are significantly influenced by psychological and behavioural economic factors. Behavioural economics suggests that individuals often deviate from purely rational decision-making due to cognitive biases and emotional responses (AlHogail,

2018). For instance, the status quo bias leads consumers to prefer existing technologies over new IoT solutions, while loss aversion makes them more sensitive to potential losses than to equivalent gains, hindering adoption (Ladeira et al., 2024). Additionally, factors such as perceived usefulness, trust, and privacy concerns play pivotal roles in shaping consumer intentions. Perceived usefulness, for example, has been identified as a strong predictor of adoption intentions, as consumers are more likely to embrace technologies that they believe will enhance their daily lives (AlHogail, 2018).

2.2.2 Role of Trust, Risk Perception, Perceived Value, and Social Influence

Empirical research highlights the critical roles of trust, risk perception, perceived value, and social influence in IoT adoption. Trust in IoT providers is paramount as consumers are more inclined to adopt IoT devices when they trust that their data will be handled securely and responsibly (AlHogail, 2018). Risk perception, particularly concerning privacy and data security, can deter adoption, even when perceived benefits are substantial (Barth & de Jong, 2017). Perceived value, encompassing both functional and emotional benefits, also influences adoption decisions; consumers are more likely to adopt IoT technologies that offer clear value propositions (Okorie et al., 2024).

Social influence further impacts adoption, as individuals often look to peers and societal trends when making technology adoption decisions (Wang et al., 2023; Jayashankar, 2018). Confidence and Safety Trust is a crucial factor in the adoption of IoT, particularly in situations that involve personal data. Clarity, robust encryption, and external validations like UL 2900 greatly enhance trust and the probability of adoption (Yavari & Georgakopoulos, 2021; Torre et al, 2022). Consumers tend to prefer IoT products from trusted brands or platforms that transparently communicate their data practices.

The privacy paradox describes consumers who voice concerns but still utilize data-heavy technologies, which is evident in numerous IoT situations (Guhr et al., 2020). Madden (2014) states that 62% of users decline smart home gadgets because of worries about surveillance. These apprehensions are heightened by exaggerated media reporting and ambiguous regulations. Valued Expectations and Usefulness Perceived value encompasses utilitarian drivers such as financial savings and health benefits as well as hedonic elements such as enjoyment (Wang et al., 2023).

Lizhen et al (2022) discovered that perceived usefulness is highly linked to IoT adoption within the wearable technology industry. Nonetheless, if the apparent complexity surpasses the advantages, acceptance declines even for valuable devices. Social norms also play a vital role in influencing consumer perceptions. Dhanawade et al. (2024) discovered that interaction with peers who utilize IoT devices increased the adoption rate among young adults threefold.

2.2.3 Impact of Behavioural Biases on IoT Adoption

According to Rimbeck et al. (2024), behavioural biases such as loss aversion, status quo bias, and herd behaviour significantly affect consumer decisions regarding IoT products. Loss aversion leads consumers to perceive potential losses from adopting new technologies as more significant than potential gains, making them hesitant to switch to IoT solutions (Kahneman & Tversky, 1979). Status quo bias causes individuals to prefer maintaining their current situation, even when new technologies may offer improvements (Ladeira et al., 2024). Herd behaviour, where individuals mimic the actions of others, can accelerate adoption if peers are seen embracing IoT technologies, but may also impede adoption if there is a perception of widespread reluctance (Wang et al., 2023; Jayashankar, 2018).

Moreover, Caputo et al. (2018) maintains that aversion to Loss aversion causes consumers to shy away from new technologies because of perceived risks like financial loss, damage to reputation, or data breaches. This bias may be reduced by rephrasing marketing communications to highlight safety and loss prevention (Thaler & Sunstein, 2021). In addition, consumers frequently stick to familiar technologies, opposing change due to anxiety about the unfamiliar. In IoT environments, this is intensified by perceived learning difficulties, distrust in automation and the desire for eco-friendly technologies (Mansilla et al., 2019).

Furthermore, Collective Behaviour Herding is particularly common in emerging technologies. Individuals might embrace IoT devices simply because members of their community or social media circles have adopted them, irrespective of their personal risk-benefit evaluation (AsirT & Manohar 2023). The long-term benefits of IoT frequently conflict with present bias, as consumers prioritize immediate convenience or comfort over future advantages (Lin et al., 2016). Complimentary trials and immediate rewards can assist in closing this motivation gap.

2.2.4 Effectiveness of Marketing Strategies Leveraging Consumer Psychology

Current marketing strategies that incorporate consumer psychology and behavioural insights have shown effectiveness in promoting IoT technologies (Kumo, 2023). Brands that emphasize emotional benefits, such as convenience, security, and enhanced lifestyle, resonate more with consumers than those focusing solely on technical specifications (Okorie et al., 2024). The current IoT marketing strategies are effective in the sense that it provides marketers with up-to-minute data and insights about consumer behaviour and preferences which enables real-time decision making (Basu et al., 2023).

Businesses have found ways to connect online and in-person customer experiences, making it easier for people to move between different platforms without disruption (Dhanawade et.al., 2024). Utilizing social proof, such as testimonials and user reviews, alleviate perceived risks and build trust (Talib & Saat 2017). This is one of the most common digital marketing strategies that are employed across the various sectors and disciplines. A study conducted by Wang (2024) found that businesses leveraging IoT-driven emotional insights experienced a 35% increase in customer loyalty, as their campaigns were perceived as more relevant, empathetic, and emotionally engaging.

Influencing and contextualization behavioural nudges, like default opt-ins and social validation, can greatly enhance adoption. Mobile applications that incentivize users for utilizing IoT functionalities such as fitness monitoring, energy-saving suggestions, which can enhance user engagement (Wang, 2024). Liu et al. (2024) showed that gamified interfaces resulted in extended device usage and decreased churn rates. IoT marketing strategies that incorporate narratives that emphasize genuine transformations or the effect on communities elicits emotional reactions that encourage engagement (Kim et al., 2018).

2.2.5 Obstacles Related to Structure and Socio-Economic Factors That Hinder IoT Adoption

Structural and socio-economic obstacles hinder adoption of IoT technologies. When viewed through the lens of consumer psychology and behavioural economics, these barriers determine how consumers perceive and respond to IoT (Tewera et al., 2024). Consequently, it ultimately influences attitudes, beliefs, and the decision on whether consumers embrace and adopt these technologies (Padyab et al., 2019). Firstly, the digital divide, cost access, initial expenses and subscription services render IoT unapproachable for low-income groups. This is especially evident in developing nations, where cost and digital infrastructure continue to be significant obstacles (Kala, 2023).

Furthermore, gender inequalities and literacy deficiencies according to GSMA (2022) also affects adoption of IoT. GSMA (2022) highlights that women in developing nations are 23% less inclined to embrace IoT because of technophobia and insufficient exposure. Efforts to enhance digital literacy are crucial for bridging this divide. According to Kronlid et al. (2024), when consumers perceive any given technology to be complex for set up, use and integration in daily routine, it will discourage adoption. As behavioural economics suggests, people tend to shy away from choices that feel mentally or practically demanding (Kronlid et al., 2024).

2.2.6 Practical Implications for IoT Product Development and Marketing

According to Dhanawade et.al., (2024) IoT is playing a key role in making marketing strategies more efficient and data-driven, hence the need to leverage on these technologies to develop consumer-centric strategies. Therefore, Okorie et al. (2024) propound that it is imperative for marketers to understand the psychological and behavioural factors influencing IoT adoption provides valuable insights for product development and marketing strategies. Designing IoT devices with user-friendly interfaces, clear value propositions, and robust security features can enhance adoption rates (Okorie et al., 2024).

Marketing campaigns that highlight the emotional and practical benefits of IoT technologies, rather than just technical specifications, are more likely to resonate with consumers (Wang, 2024). Additionally, addressing privacy concerns through transparent policies and certifications can build trust and encourage adoption (Al-Hogail, 2018). Moreover, transparent communication regarding data usage and privacy policies mitigates concerns and foster a sense of security among potential adopters (AlHogail, 2018). Strengthening this is transparent privacy policies, full encryption, and adherence to regulations like GDPR which promote confidence. Certification logos can enhance perceived safety and trustworthiness (Madhavaram 2024).

Consumers final decision to adopt IoT is driven more by behaviour than by technology. Understanding the psychological and behavioural economic dimensions of IoT adoption offers valuable insights for accelerating uptake (Wang, 2024). Madhavaram (2024) asserts that consumers are not always rational actors they are driven by trust, peer influence, perceived value, and cognitive biases. Thus, effective IoT strategies must account for these dynamics through thoughtful design, inclusive pricing, robust data practices, and targeted education (AlHogail, 2018).

As the IoT landscape expands, human-centred approaches will be the key to unlocking its full potential. Grasping cognitive biases, emotional reactions, and socio-economic inequalities is vital for creating inclusive, ethical, and efficient IoT approaches (Okorie et al., 2024). Therefore, future studies ought to analyse long-term behaviour changes after adopting IoT; Create nudging frameworks that are culturally adaptable; Investigate IoT design and policy that is sensitive to gender issues. Integrating behavioural science within IoT ecosystems enables developers and marketers to connect innovation with daily utilization (Wang, 2024).

Table 1. To enhance consumer acceptance of IoT

Domain	Recommendation	Impact
Product Development	Simplify user interfaces and offer customization Reduce perceived complexity by offering intuitive interfaces and clear instructions.	Reduces perceived complexity
Marketing	Use behavioural nudges and trust symbols Highlight how IoT technologies can improve daily life, focusing on convenience, security, and lifestyle enhancements. Utilize testimonials, user reviews, and influencer partnerships to build credibility and encourage adoption.	Increases conversion
Consumer Engagement	Offer interactive onboarding and gamification	Encourages habit formation
Policy	Promote digital literacy and subsidize IoT access Implement transparent data usage policies, obtain relevant certifications, and communicate these clearly to consumers.	Addresses equity gaps and builds trust
Privacy Concerns	Adopt privacy-by-design principles and provide consumers with control over their data.	It builds trust and consumers are likely to adopt IoT if they feel their information and private data is protected.

Source: Authors (2025)

2.3 Empirical Literature Review

A comprehensive study by Zheng et al. (2018) explored user perceptions of smart home IoT privacy, revealing that convenience and connectedness often outweigh privacy concerns in consumer decision-making. Despite recognizing potential privacy risks, users frequently trust IoT device manufacturers to protect their data without verifying these protections (Amofah & Chai, 2022). This phenomenon underscores the complexity of consumer behaviour in the IoT landscape, where perceived benefits can overshadow privacy apprehensions. In a large-scale survey, a study by AlHogail (2018) examined the drivers of domestic IoT adoption. The research found that perceived usefulness and trust in the IoT provider were significant factors influencing adoption intentions.

Interestingly, while consumers expressed privacy concerns, these did not significantly affect their intention to use IoT devices, highlighting a privacy paradox where concerns do not always translate into avoidance behaviour. Amofah and Chai

(2022) investigated the role of trust and payment methods in sustaining e-commerce adoption in Sub-Saharan Africa, focusing on Ghana. Their study revealed that trust significantly mediates the relationship between the Unified Theory of Acceptance and Use of Technology (UTAUT) variables and e-commerce adoption (Van Den Wiele et al., 2025).

This finding suggests that enhancing consumer trust is crucial for the sustained adoption of digital technologies, including IoT, in the region. An assessment of IoT adoption readiness in Sub-Saharan Africa by Atayero et al. (2016) highlighted that while there is a growing interest in IoT technologies, challenges such as infrastructure deficits, high costs, and limited digital literacy impede widespread adoption. The study emphasizes the need for targeted interventions to address these barriers and facilitate the integration of IoT solutions across various sectors in the region (Atayero et al., 2016).

In South Africa, a study by Ngwenya and Ngoepe (2022) examined data trust in Consumer Internet of Things (CIoT) assemblages. The research found that consumers' trust in IoT systems increases with continuous interactions, suggesting that fostering long-term relationships and transparent data practices can enhance trust and adoption rates (Ngwenya & Ngoepe, 2022). Soeker et al. (2021) assessed the readiness of the South African agricultural sector to implement IoT technologies. Their findings indicated that factors such as technological infrastructure, access to the internet, and mobile technology position South Africa favourably for IoT adoption in agriculture. However, the study also noted the need for policy support and capacity building to fully leverage IoT's potential in the sector.

In Namibia, the Consumer IoT market is projected to reach US$12.00 million by 2024, with an annual growth rate of 0.25% from 2024 to 2029 (Statista, 2023). This growth is indicative of a gradual but steady adoption of IoT technologies in the country, influenced by factors such as increasing internet penetration and the availability of affordable smart devices. The Namibian government has been actively promoting digitalization, with initiatives aimed at improving internet infrastructure and digital literacy (Statistica, 2023). These efforts are expected to facilitate the adoption of IoT technologies by addressing key barriers such as limited connectivity and low digital skills among the population.

Despite the positive trends, challenges remain in Namibia's IoT adoption landscape. Issues such as high device costs, limited local content, and concerns over data privacy continue to hinder widespread adoption (Statista, 2023). Addressing these challenges will require coordinated efforts between the government, private sector, and consumers. A study by Kamutuezu et al. (2021) studying the adoption of ICT enabled entrepreneurship applications highlighted the importance of consumer education and awareness in promoting IoT adoption. The research found that many consumers are unaware of the benefits and functionalities of IoT devices, suggesting that targeted awareness campaigns could play a crucial role in increasing adoption rates (Kamutueza et al., 2021).

2.4 Theoretical Framework

This review is underpinned by two main academic disciplines: behavioural economics and consumer psychology. Additionally, while behavioural economics draws on psychological insights to understand why and how consumers deviate from rational decision-making models (Sahoo & Goswami, 2023; Kahneman & Tversky, 1979), consumer psychology focuses on the cognitive, emotional, and social mechanisms that influence consumer behaviour (Dirwan & Latief, 2023). The adoption of IoT technologies presents a multifaceted context involving risk perception, trust, usability, and social influence, making it imperative to use an interdisciplinary framework (Koohong et al., 2022).

This study employs a hybrid theoretical framework that integrates three well-established models: the Technology Acceptance Model (TAM) to assess technological influences, Prospect Theory to evaluate risk and loss aversion from a behavioural economics perspective, and the Theory of Planned Behaviour (TPB) to understand behavioural intention, social norms, and perceived control in technology adoption (Musa et al., 2024; Schorr, 2023; Hager et al., 2022; Leoneti & Gomes, 2021).

2.4.1 Technology Acceptance Model (TAM)

The Technology Acceptance Model (TAM), proposed by Davis (1985), stems from the Theory of Reasoned Action by Fishbein and Ajzen (1975). TAM posits that the perceived usefulness (PU) and perceived ease of use (PEOU) of a technology influence users' attitudes and intentions toward adopting it. In the context of IoT, TAM suggests that consumers are more inclined to adopt devices they find beneficial and easy to operate (Granić, 2022; Marikyan & Papagiannidis, 2024). With IoT being a technology-driven domain, consumer acceptance hinges on intuitive interfaces and clear value propositions. As such, device developers and marketers must emphasize functionality and ease-of-use to enhance adoption. TAM can be extended by incorporating constructs like trust, privacy concerns, and social influence to better predict user behaviour in IoT contexts.

2.4.2 Prospect Theory

Developed by Kahneman and Tversky (1979), Prospect Theory addresses the limitations of expected utility theory in explaining decision-making under risk and uncertainty. Central to this theory is loss aversion, where losses are psychologically more impactful than gains of equivalent value. This results in consumers often making irrational decisions that favour avoiding loss over acquiring benefits. In the realm of IoT, this translates into heightened concerns over privacy, data breaches, and the uncertainty of new technologies (Bedewy, 2024). Therefore, marketing strategies should underscore the tangible gains and address risk-related concerns to counteract consumers' natural aversion to loss and promote acceptance. Theory of Prospect Theory provides a behavioural perspective for comprehending consumer uncertainty. It recognizes multiple biases: Status quo bias: Favouring known technologies instead of new yet uncertain options (Rimbeck et al., 2024).

2.4.3 Theory of Planned Behaviour (TPB)

The Theory of Planned Behaviour (TPB), introduced by Ajzen (1991), expands upon the Theory of Reasoned Action by incorporating perceived behavioural control alongside attitudes and subjective norms. TPB asserts that these three factors influence behavioural intentions, which in turn drive actual behaviour (Ajzen, 2020). In IoT adoption, TPB helps explain the role of social influence, ease of access, and internal control in shaping an individual's intention to adopt emerging technologies. As technological advancement increases, consumers face both opportunities and challenges, including learning curves and privacy concerns (Ajzen, 2020). Hence, understanding user attitudes and behavioural drivers is key to shaping effective adoption strategies.

Figure 1. Conceptual framework for understanding the how behavioural economics and consumer psychology affect the adoption and use of IoT.

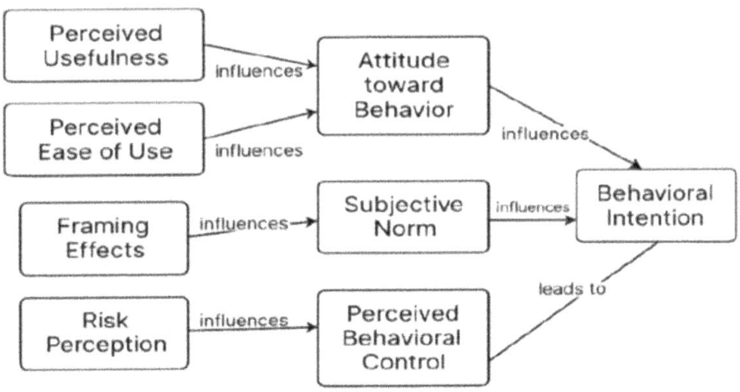

3. RESEARCH METHODOLOGY

3.1 Research Design

This study adopts a systematic review design, a structured and replicable approach to synthesizing existing research evidence. Systematic reviews are particularly effective for aggregating findings across diverse studies to answer specific research questions, especially in fields where empirical data is abundant but fragmented (Matos et al., 2023; Rashid et al., 2021). This design allows for a comprehensive assessment of the current state of knowledge regarding the influence of consumer psychology and behavioural economics on IoT adoption. According to Creswell and Creswell (2018), Paul and Barari (2022) systematic reviews are essential for identifying patterns, inconsistencies, and gaps in the literature, thereby providing a solid foundation for future research and practical applications.

3.2 Research Philosophy

The study is grounded in a pragmatic research philosophy, which emphasizes the practical application of research findings and the use of mixed methods to address research questions. This study agrees with De Waal (2021) maintains that pragmatism is particularly suited for interdisciplinary studies like this one, where the integration of psychological, economic, and technological perspectives is crucial. As Creswell and Creswell (2018), King (2022) note, pragmatism allows researchers to draw from both qualitative and quantitative data, facilitating a more comprehensive understanding of complex phenomena such as consumer behaviour in the context of IoT adoption.

3.3 Research Approach

A qualitative research approach is employed to explore the nuanced psychological and behavioural factors influencing consumer decisions regarding IoT technologies. Qualitative methods are adept at capturing the depth and complexity of human experiences, perceptions, and motivations, which are central to understanding the adoption process. As highlighted by Campell (2024), De Vaus (2014), qualitative research provides rich, detailed data that can reveal underlying themes and patterns, making it an appropriate choice for this study's objectives.

3.4 Time Frame

The study focuses on literature published between 2014 and 2025, encompassing a decade of research to ensure the inclusion of the most recent and relevant studies. This time frame allows for an examination of evolving trends and developments in consumer psychology, behavioural economics, and IoT adoption. As Saunders et al. (2019) suggest, selecting an appropriate time frame is crucial for capturing the dynamic nature of technological adoption and the factors influencing it.

3.5 Data Collection and Analysis

Data collection involves a comprehensive search of multiple scholarly databases, including Google Scholar, Scopus, Web of Science, and JSTOR, using keywords such as adoption, behavioural economics, consumer psychology, Internet of Things, and IoT technologies. The inclusion criteria focus on peer-reviewed articles, empirical research, and theoretical papers that address consumer behaviour and decision-making in relation to IoT adoption. Studies that concentrate solely on technical aspects of IoT without considering the consumer perspective are excluded. Data analysis follows a thematic synthesis approach, categorizing findings into key themes such as trust, risk perception, perceived value, social influence, and behavioural biases. This method allows for the identification of patterns and insights across studies, facilitating a comprehensive understanding of the factors influencing IoT adoption.

3.6 Justification for Methodological Choices

The chosen methodology aligns with established best practices for conducting systematic reviews. Fink (2019) emphasizes the importance of a clear and replicable process in systematic reviews, which this study adheres to by following the PRISMA guidelines. Additionally, the integration of a hybrid search strategy, combining database searches with snowballing techniques, enhances the comprehensiveness of the literature search and reduces the risk of missing relevant studies (Wohlin et al., 2023). Moreover, this study aims to provide a robust and comprehensive synthesis of the factors influencing consumer adoption of IoT technologies.

4. DISCUSSION AND FINDINGS

Literature highlights the importance of consumer psychology and behavioural economics in shaping how people adopt Internet of Things technologies. Consumer psychology and behavioural economics offer critical insights into how individuals perceive, evaluate, and decide to adopt these technologies. Key factors that encourage adoption include a positive attitude, perceived usefulness, personal innovativeness, and a sense of control over the technology. Concerns about security and perceived risks often hold users back. Social influence and emotional reactions also play a role, though their impact can vary depending on the context. As the field continues to evolve rapidly, there's a clear need for more research to explore these dynamics in greater depth and across different settings.

Therefore, based on the literature it is apparent that there is a need for businesses to create focused marketing strategies that address customer concerns, foster trust, and emphasize the emotional and social value of IoT products by comprehending the behavioural and psychological elements that affect consumer decisions in its quest to encourage and expediate adoption of IoT. Adoption can be accelerated, for instance, by highlighting the security and simplicity of IoT devices and utilizing peer endorsements and social proof.

In the context of Namibia, this study highlights the need to develop tailored IoT marketing strategies to cater for the unique psychological and socio-economic realities of the Namibian market. While global study highlights perceived usefulness, trust, security, privacy and ease of use as primary drivers of IoT adoption, the case may not be the same for the Namibian consumers. Namibian consumers may face additional challenges pertaining to digital literacy, accessibility, affordability, cultural and language barriers and lack of access to technological devices and infrastructure. These factors can influence how consumers perceive and engage with IoT technologies.

To address these challenges from a local perspective, marketers should develop culturally relevant messaging, invest in community-based education, expanding the digital infrastructure. Notwithstanding the importance of transparent communication and protection of privacy. In this context, the Namibian Government is moving in the right direction as it has allocated N$120 million for the 2024/25 to 2026/27 financial years to roll-out network transmission towers nationwide to bridge the digital divide. The initiatives from the central government and relevant stakeholders acknowledge that digital divide goes beyond the infrastructure and calls for development of digital skills (Gaiseb, 2025).

5. CONTRIBUTION

This paper offers a meaningful contribution to the field of IoT technologies by examining it through a marketing lens and enriching the existing body of literature. It also identifies key gaps in current research, providing a foundation for future studies. Importantly, the study delivers practical insights for marketing professionals, encouraging the integration of psychological and behavioural principles into strategy development – thus emphasising the need for consumer-centric strategies. These insights are especially valuable for effectively engaging consumers and maximizing the potential of the rapidly evolving IoT landscape. The unique contribution of this study is providing a Namibian context based on secondary data. Therefore, it points out the need for future research by collecting primary data to capture the voices and experiences of the Namibian consumer market to gain a deeper understanding of how cultural norms, economic realities and access to technology shapes the adoption of IoT in Namibia.

6. CONCLUSION

In conclusion, existing literature clearly demonstrates that consumer psychology and behavioural economics play a pivotal role in shaping individuals' decisions to adopt or reject IoT technologies. From a marketing perspective, this insight places increasing pressure on professionals to rethink traditional strategies. It is no longer sufficient to rely on conventional marketing approaches; instead, there is a growing need to integrate psychological and behavioural insights into marketing efforts. Emphasizing the practical benefits and convenience of IoT technologies can help drive adoption. Equally important is the need for transparent communication, along with robust security and privacy measures, to build consumer trust and confidence (Okorie et al., 2024; Wang 2024; Madhavaram 2024). Given that this study relied exclusively on secondary sources to conduct the systematic review, future research would benefit from incorporating primary data collection methods. This would provide a more grounded and nuanced understanding of IoT adoption behaviours. Additionally, while this paper focused specifically on frameworks rooted in behavioural economics and consumer psychology, future studies could expand the scope by integrating cross-disciplinary perspectives. Drawing from fields such as sociology, anthropology, and technology studies could offer a more holistic view of the factors influencing adoption and help uncover insights that may be overlooked within a single theoretical lens.

ACKNOWLEDGEMENT

During the preparing this work, the authors used AI-based tools to assist with proofreading. All content was carefully reviewed and edited afterward, and the authors take full responsibility for the final version of the publication. The theoretical framework conceptualized and thereafter developed with the assistance of AI generative tools.

REFERENCES

Aggarwal, N., & Singh, S. (2025). Embracing the future by unlocking the door to smart living: A systematic review of consumers' adoption and acceptance of smart home devices. *The Journal of Consumer Research*, *42*(3), 123–145. DOI: 10.1177/09711023241310286

Ajzen, I. (1991). The theory of planned behavior. *Organizational Behavior and Human Decision Processes*, *50*(2), 179–211. DOI: 10.1016/0749-5978(91)90020-T

Ajzen, I. (2020). The theory of planned behavior: Frequently asked questions. Human Behavior and Emerging Technologies. https://www.researchgate.net/publication/342077056

Alam, S. M. I. (2022). *Behavioral Economics: Concepts*. History, and Evolution.

AlHogail, A. (2018). Improving IoT technology adoption through improving consumer trust. *Technologies*, *6*(64), 64. Advance online publication. DOI: 10.3390/technologies6030064

Amofah, D. O., & Chai, J. (2022). Sustaining Consumer E-Commerce Adoption in Sub-Saharan Africa: Do Trust and Payment Method Matter? *Sustainability (Basel)*, *2022*(14), 8466. DOI: 10.3390/su14148466

Asir, T. R. G., & Manohar, H. L. (2023). Variations on Internet of Things adoption factors between India and the USA. *South African Journal of Business Management*, *54*(1), a3810. DOI: 10.4102/sajbm.v54i1.3810

Atayero, A. A., Oluwatobi, S. O., & Alege, P. O. (2016). An assessment of the Internet of Things (IoT) adoption readiness of Sub-Saharan Africa. *Journal of South African Business Research*, *2016*, 321563. Advance online publication. DOI: 10.5171/2016.321563

Balaji, S., Nathani, K., & Santhakumar, R. (2019). IoT technology, applications and challenges: A contemporary survey. *Wireless Personal Communications*, *108*(1), 363–388. DOI: 10.1007/s11277-019-06407-w

Barth, S., & de Jong, M. D. T. (2017). The privacy paradox – Investigating discrepancies between expressed privacy concerns and actual online behavior – A systematic literature review. *Telematics and Informatics*, *34*(7), 1038–1058. DOI: 10.1016/j.tele.2017.04.013

Basu, R., Lim, W. M., Kumar, A., & Kumar, S. (2023). Marketing analytics: The bridge between customer psychology and marketing decision-making. *Psychology and Marketing*, *40*(12), 2588–2611. DOI: 10.1002/mar.21908

Bedewy, S. F. (2024). The Impact of Data Security and Privacy Concerns on the Implementation of Integrated Systems in Smart Cities. https://www.intechopen.com/chapters/89615#:~:text=DOI%3A%2010.5772/intechopen.115076

Berte, D.-R. (2018). Defining the IoT. *Proceedings of the International Conference on Business Excellence*. 12. 118-128. DOI: 10.2478/picbe-2018-0013

Caputo, F., Scuotto, V., Carayannis, E., & Cillo, V. (2018). Intertwining the internet of things and consumers' behaviour science: Future promises for businesses. *Technological Forecasting and Social Change*, *136*, 277–284. DOI: 10.1016/j.techfore.2018.03.019

Chandra, S., Verma, S., Lim, W.M., Kumar, S. & Donthu, N. (2022). Personalization in personalized marketing: Trends and ways forward. DOI: DOI: 10.1002/mar.21670

Creswell, J. W., & Creswell, J. D. (2018). *Research design: Qualitative, quantitative, and mixed methods approaches* (5th ed.). SAGE Publications.

Davis, F. D. (1985). A technology acceptance model for empirically testing new end-user information systems: Theory and results [Doctoral dissertation, Massachusetts Institute of Technology]. MIT Libraries. http://hdl.handle.net/1721.1/15192

De Vaus, D. A. (2014). *Research design in social research*. SAGE Publications.

De Waal, C. (2021). *Introducing pragmatism: a tool for rethinking philosophy*. Routledge. DOI: 10.4324/9781003199731

Dhanawade, M., Nikam, P., & Mane, S. T. (2024). Role of Internet of Things (IOT) in Revolutionizing Digital Marketing. ShodhKosh. *Journal of Visual and Performing Arts*, *5*(6), 767–784.

Ding, S., Tukker, A., & Ward, H. (2023). Opportunities and risks of internet of things (IoT) technologies for circular business models: A literature review. *Journal of Environmental Management, 336*, 117662. DOI: 10.1016/j.jenvman.2023.117662

Dirwan, D., & Latief, F. (2023). Understanding the Psychology Behind Consumer Behavior. *Advances in Business & Industrial Marketing Research, 3*(1), 130–145. DOI: 10.60079/abim.v1i3.201

Fink, A. (2019). *Conducting research literature reviews: From the Internet to paper* (5th ed.). SAGE Publications.

Gaiseb, R. (2025) N$120m to bridge the digital divide. New Era Publication. https://neweralive.na/n120m-to-bridge-digital-divide/

Gerli, P., Clement, J., Esposito, G., Mora, L., & Crutzen, N. (2022). The hidden power of emotions: How psychological factors influence skill development in smart technology adoption. *Technological Forecasting and Social Change, 180*, 121721. Advance online publication. DOI: 10.1016/j.techfore.2022.121721

Govinda, K., & Saravanaguru, R. A. K. (2016). Review on IOT technologies. *International Journal of Applied Engineering Research: IJAER, 11*(4), 2848–2853.

Granić, A. (2022). Technology acceptance and adoption in education. In *Handbook of open, distance and digital education* (pp. 1–15). Springer Singapore. DOI: 10.1007/978-981-19-0351-9_11-1

GSMA. (2022). *The Mobile Gender Gap Report 2022*. GSMA.

Guhr, N., Werth, O., Blacha, P. P. H., & Breitner, M. H. (2020). Privacy concerns in the smart home context. *SN Applied Sciences, 2*(247), 247. Advance online publication. DOI: 10.1007/s42452-020-2025-8

International Telecommunication Union. (2023). Measuring digital development. https://demo.ifgict.org/wp-content/uploads/2024/09/ITU-Report-on-Measuring-digital-development.pdf

International Telecommunication Union (ITU). (2023). Measuring digital development: Facts and figures 2023.

Jayashankar, P., Nilakanta, S., Johnston, W. J., Gill, P., & Burres, R. (2018). IoT adoption in agriculture: The role of trust, perceived value and risk. *Journal of Business and Industrial Marketing, 33*(6), 804–821. Advance online publication. DOI: 10.1108/JBIM-01-2018-0023

Kahneman, D., & Tversky, A. (1979). Prospect theory: An analysis of decision under risk. *Econometrica, 47*(2), 263–291. DOI: 10.2307/1914185

Kala, E. (2023). Challenges of Technology in African Countries: A Case Study of Zambia. *Open Journal of Safety Science and Technology, 13*(4), 202–230. DOI: 10.4236/ojsst.2023.134011

Kamutuezu, E.U., Winschiers-Tehophilus, H. & Peters, A. (2021). AN exploration of factors influencing the adoption of ictenabled entrepreneurship applications in Namibian ruralcommunities.

Kim, H. J., Park, S. Y., & Park, H. Y. (2018). A study on the effect of storytelling marketing on brand image and brand attitude. *Journal of Economics, Marketing, and Management, 6*(4), 1–16. DOI: 10.20482/jemm.2018.6.4.1

Kim, K. J., & Wang, S. (2021). Understanding the acceptance of the Internet of Things: An integrative theoretical approach. *Aslib Journal of Information Management, 73*(5), 754–771. DOI: 10.1108/AJIM-03-2021-0073

King, R. (2022). The utility of pragmatism in educational research. *Creative Education, 13*(10), 3153–3161. DOI: 10.4236/ce.2022.1310199

Kronlid, C., Brantnell, A., Elf, M., Borg, J., & Palm, K. Sociotechnical analysis of factors influencing IoT adoption in healthcare: A systematic review. *Technology in Society* 78 (2024) 102675. ISSN 0160-791X, https://doi.org/DOI: 10.1016/j.techsoc.2024.102675

Kumo, W. (2023). Leveraging consumer behavior research for effective marketing strategies. *Advances in Business & Industrial Marketing Research, 1*(3), 117–129. DOI: 10.60079/abim.v1i3.196

Kwakye, E. (2023). Unraveling the Privacy Paradox: Smart Home IoT Adoption Dynamics in Saudi Arabia. DOI: 10.13140/RG.2.2.25471.21923

La Diega, N. (2023). *Internet of things and the law: legal strategies for consumer-centric smart technologies*. Taylor & Francis.

Ladeira, W. J., Lim, W. M., de Oliveira Santini, F., Rasul, T., Frantz, B., de Oliveira Rosa, J. C., & Azhar, M. (2025). Consumer adoption of internet of things. *Journal of Consumer Behaviour, 24*(2), 673–693. DOI: 10.1002/cb.2427

Ladeira, W. J., Lim, W. M., Santini, F. O., Rasul, T., Frantz, B., Rosa, J. C. O., & Azhar, M. (2024). Consumer Adoption of Internet of Things. *Journal of Consumer Behaviour, 24*(2), 673–693. DOI: 10.1002/cb.2427

Leoneti, A. B., & Gomes, L. F. A. M. (2021). A novel version of the TODIM method based on the exponential model of prospect theory: The ExpTODIM method. *European Journal of Operational Research, 295*(3), 1042–1055. DOI: 10.1016/j.ejor.2021.03.055

Lin, D., Lee, C. K. M., & Lin, K. (2016). Research on effect factors evaluation of internet of things (IOT) adoption in Chinese agricultural supply chain. *IEEE International Conference on Industrial Engineering and Engineering Management (IEEM)*, Bali, Indonesia, 2016, pp. 612-615, DOI: 10.1109/IEEM.2016.7797948

Liu, A., Urquía-Grande, E., López-Sánchez, P., & Rodríguez-López, Á. (2024). The power of play in microfinance: Examining the effect of gamification on customer relationship management performance. *Journal of Behavioral and Experimental Finance, 44*, 100972. Advance online publication. DOI: 10.1016/j.jbef.2024.100972

Lizhen, S.H.I, Huang, X., Abbas, S., Yang, Z. & Huang, L. (2022). The Relationships Between Perceived Usefulness and Fitness Wearable Technology User Adoption Mediated by Culture, Gender, and COVID-19: A Meta-Analysis. Quality in Sport. 2022;8(1):55-69. eISSN 2450-3118. DOI http://dx.doi.org/DOI: 10.12775/QS.2021.08.01.005

Madden, M. (2014), Public perceptions of privacy and security in the age of smart devices. Pew Research Center. https://www.pewresearch.org/internet/2014/11/12/public-privacy-perceptions/

Madhavaram, S. (2024). Chartering marketing strategy and marketing management research toward greater relevance and impact. *Journal of Business Research, 178*, 114667. Advance online publication. DOI: 10.1016/j.jbusres.2024.114667

Mansilla, D. C., Irizar, A. M., Garaizar, P., & Ipina, D. L. (2019). On the Side Effects of Automation in IoT: Complacency and Comfort vs. *Relapse and Distrust. CHI Workshop*, Glasgow, UK

Marikyan, D., & Papagiannidis, S. (2024). Technology Acceptance Model: A review. In Papagiannidis, S. (Ed.), *TheoryHub Book.*, Available at https://open.ncl.ac.uk /

Matos, J. F., Piedade, J., Freitas, A., Pedro, N., Dorotea, N., Pedro, A., & Galego, C. (2023). Teaching and learning research methodologies in education: A systematic literature review. *Education Sciences, 13*(2), 173. DOI: 10.3390/educsci13020173

Mckinsey & Company. (2024) What is the Internet of Things (IoT)? Accessed 27 April 2024, https://www.mckinsey.com/featured-insights/mckinsey-explainers/what-is-the-internet-of-things#/

Mohanty, S. N., Chatterjee, J. M., & Satpathy, S. (Eds.). (2022). *Internet of Things and Its Applications*. Springer. DOI: 10.1007/978-3-030-77528-5

Mortenson, M. J., & Vidgen, R. (2016). A computational literature review of the technology acceptance model. *International Journal of Information Management, 36*(6), 1248–1259. DOI: 10.1016/j.ijinfomgt.2016.07.007

Mouha, R. A. (2021). Internet of Things (IoT). *Journal of Data Analysis and Information Processing*, *9*(2), 77–101. https://www.scirp.org/journal/jdaip. DOI: 10.4236/jdaip.2021.92006

Musa, H. G., Fatmawati, I., Nuryakin, N., & Suyanto, M. (2024). Marketing research trends using technology acceptance model (TAM): A comprehensive review of researches (2002–2022). *Cogent Business & Management, 11*(1), 2329375. DOI: 10.1080/23311975.2024.2329375

Muteba, F., Djouani, K., & Olwal, T. (2019). A comparative survey study on LPWA IoT technologies: Design, considerations, challenges and solutions. *Procedia Computer Science, 155*, 636–641. DOI: 10.1016/j.procs.2019.08.090

Nadal, C., Sas, C., & Doherty, G. (2020). Technology Acceptance in Mobile Health: Scoping Review of Definitions, Models, and Measurement J Med. *Journal of Medical Internet Research, 22*(7), e17256. https://www.jmir.org/2020/7/e17256. DOI: 10.2196/17256

Negm, E. (2022). Internet of Things (IoT) acceptance model – assessing consumers'behavior toward the adoption intention of IoT. *Arab Gulf Journal of Scientific Research, 41*(4), 539–556. Advance online publication. DOI: 10.1108/AGJSR-09-2022-0183

Negm, E. (2023). Internet of Things (IoT) acceptance model–assessing consumers' behavior toward the adoption intention of IoT. *Arab Gulf Journal of Scientific Research, 41*(4), 539–556. DOI: 10.1108/AGJSR-09-2022-0183

Ngwenya, M., & Ngoepe, M. (2022). Data trust in Consumer Internet of Things assemblages in the mobile and fixed telecommunication operators in South Africa. *South African Journal of Information Management, 24*(1), a1426. DOI: 10.4102/sajim.v24i1.1426

Nizetic, S., Soli, P., & Patrono, L. (2020). Internet of Things (IoT): Opportunities, issues and challenges towards a smart and sustainable future. *Journal of Cleaner Production, 274*, 1–32. DOI: 10.1016/j.jclepro.2020.122877

Okorie, G. N., Egieya, Z. E., Ikwue, U., Udeh, C. A., & Adaga, E. M. (2024). Leveraging big data for personalized marketing campaigns: A review. *International Journal of Management & Entrepreneurship Research*, *6*(1), 216–242. DOI: 10.51594/ijmer.v6i1.778

Padyab, A., Habibipour, A., Rizk, A., & Ståhlbröst, A. (2019). Adoption barriers of IoT in large scale pilots. *Information (Basel)*, *11*(1), 23. DOI: 10.3390/info11010023

Paul, J., & Barari, M. (2022). Meta-analysis and traditional systematic literature reviews—What, why, when, where, and how? *Psychology and Marketing*, *39*(6), 1099–1115. DOI: 10.1002/mar.21657

Rane, N. L. (2023). Enhancing Customer Loyalty through Artificial Intelligence (AI), Internet of Things (IoT), and Big Data Technologies: Improving Customer Satisfaction, Engagement, Relationship, and Experience. http://dx.doi.org/DOI: 10.2139/ssrn.4616051

Rashid, A., Rasheed, R., Amirah, N. A., Yusof, Y., Khan, S., & Agha, A. A. (2021). A Quantitative Perspective of Systematic Research: Easy and Step-by-Step Initial Guidelines. *Turkish Online Journal of Qualitative Inquiry, 12*(9).

Rath, K. C., Khang, A., & Roy, D. (2024). The role of Internet of Things (IoT) technology in Industry 4.0 economy. In *Advanced IoT technologies and applications in the industry 4.0 digital economy* (pp. 1–28). CRC Press. DOI: 10.1201/9781003434269-1

Rimbeck, M., Stumpf-Wollersheim, J., & Richter, A. (2024). Unfolding IoT Adoption: A Status Quo Bias Perspective. *Business & Information Systems Engineering*. Advance online publication. DOI: 10.1007/s12599-024-00891-6

Rimbeck, M., Stumpf-Wollersheim, J., & Richter, A. (2024). Unfolding IoT Adoption: A status quo bias perspective. *Business & Information Systems Engineering*, •••, 1–18.

Sahoo, S. K., & Goswami, S. S. (2023). A comprehensive review of multiple criteria decision-making (MCDM) methods: Advancements, applications, and future directions. *Decision Making Advances*, *1*(1), 25–48. DOI: 10.31181/dma1120237

Saunders, M., Lewis, P., & Thornhill, A. (2019). *Research methods for business students* (8th ed.). Pearson Education.

Schorr, A. (2023). The technology acceptance model (TAM) and its importance for digitalization research: A review. *Proceedings TecPsy*, *2023*, 55–65. DOI: 10.2478/9788366675896-005

Sheoran, S., & Vij, S. (2023). A consumer-centric paradigm shifts in business environment with the evolution of the Internet of Things: A literature review. *Vision (Basel)*, *27*(4), 431–442. DOI: 10.1177/09722629211033944

Soeker, I., Lusinga, S., & Chigona, W. (2021). Readiness of the South African agricultural sector to implement IoT. *arXiv*. https://arxiv.org/abs/2108.10081

Statista. (2023). Consumer IoT - Namibia. https://www.statista.com/outlook/tmo/internet-of-things/consumer-iot/namibia

Talib, Y. Y. A., & Saat, R. M. (2017). Social proof in social media shopping: An experimental design research. SHS Web of Conferences 34, shsconf/20173402005

Tewera, D., Zhou, M., & Gavai, P. V. (2024, November). Enhancing IoT Security for Socio-Economic Development in the Mirror of Challenges, Emerging Technologies, and Holistic Solutions. In *2024 3rd Zimbabwe Conference of Information and Communication Technologies (ZCICT)* (pp. 1-8). IEEE.

Thaler, R. H., & Sunstein, C. R. (2021). *Nudge: The final edition*. Penguin Books.

Torre, D., Chennamaneni, A., & Rodriguez, A. (2022). *IoT security standards and certifications. Institute of Electrical and Electronics Engineers*. IEEE Transactions and Journals., DOI: 10.1109/ACCESS.2023.3245524

Tripathy, B. K., & Anuradha, J. (Eds.). (2017). *Internet of things (IoT): technologies, applications, challenges and solutions*. CRC press. DOI: 10.1201/9781315269849

University of Southern Califonia. (2024) What is Consumer Psychology https://app liedpsychologydegree.usc.edu/blog/what-is-consumer-psychology

VanDeWiele, M. D., Hastings, A. M., Evans, M. D., O'Connell, M. S., & Flynn, P. M. (2025). Using the Unified Theory of Acceptance and Use of Technology (UTAUT) to predict the behavioral intent of teledentistry utilization amongst United States adults. *Journal of Telemedicine and Telecare*, *31*(2), 286–296. DOI: 10.1177/1357633X231182405

Wang, S. (2024). The role of IoT in transforming marketing strategies for a connected era. *Journal of Business and Future Economy*, *1*(2), 41–49.

Wang, W. X., Kim, K. S., & Kim, J. K. (2023). Investigating the determinants of IoT device continuance intentions: An empirical study of smart speakers through the lens of expectation-confirmation theory. *SAGE Open*, *10*(3), 21582440231197067. DOI: 10.1177/21582440231197067

Wohlin, C., Kalinowski, M., Romero Felizardo, K., & Mendes, E. (2023). Successful combination of database search and snowballing for identification of primary studies in systematic literature studies. arXiv. https://arxiv.org/abs/2307.02612

Yavari, A., & Georgakopoulos, D. (2021). Privacy-preserving mechanisms for IoT data collection. *Future Generation Computer Systems*, *115*, 230–246.

Zheng, S., Apthorpe, N., Chetty, M., & Feamster, N. (2018). User perceptions of smart home IoT privacy. *arXiv*. https://arxiv.org/abs/1802.08182

Chapter 3

Consumer Trust, Security, and Ethical Considerations in IoT Markets

Nitika Malik
http://orcid.org/0009-0006-3991-9526
Maharshi Dayanand University, India

Shivangi Rapria
http://orcid.org/0009-0002-2778-8443
Institute of Management Studies and Research, India

Dinesh Aleria
http://orcid.org/0009-0006-1289-1850
Institute of Management Studies and Research, India

Mohit Sharma
http://orcid.org/0009-0007-2280-8077
Institute of Management Studies and Research, India

ABSTRACT

The Internet of Things (IoT) is revolutionizing industries by enhancing connectivity and consumer experiences. However, widespread adoption is hindered by concerns over consumer trust, primarily due to security vulnerabilities, data privacy issues, and ethical dilemmas. This chapter explores the foundational elements of trust in IoT environments, focusing on transparency, cybersecurity, regulatory compliance, and corporate digital responsibility. It examines how breaches and ethical lapses undermine user confidence and emphasizes the importance of transparent data practices

DOI: 10.4018/979-8-3373-3441-7.ch003

and responsible AI use. Consumer psychology is also addressed, illustrating how perceptions of risk, control, and accountability shape trust. The chapter provides an in-depth analysis of security challenges inherent in interconnected IoT systems, highlighting vulnerabilities that cybercriminals exploit. Through case studies, it reviews common threats and presents best practices, including robust cybersecurity frameworks, encryption, and risk mitigation techniques.

INTRODUCTION

The Internet of Things (IoT) has emerged as a transformative innovation across various industries, allowing interconnected devices to communicate, exchange data, and automate processes with remarkable efficiency. Its applications extend to diverse domains such as smart homes, healthcare, transportation, agriculture, and industrial automation, positioning IoT as a key driver of how societies function, how businesses create and deliver value, and how consumers engage with their surroundings. However, the widespread adoption and long-term success of IoT systems depend largely on one essential factor: consumer trust. In the absence of trust—particularly in the areas of data security, privacy, and ethical handling of information—consumers may hesitate to adopt or continue using IoT technologies, hindering the overall development and sustainability of this dynamic ecosystem (Lee & Lee, 2015; Roman et al., 2013). Consumer trust in IoT is influenced by a multifaceted combination of technological, psychological, legal, and ethical factors. While IoT promises enhanced convenience, personalization, and operational efficiency, it simultaneously introduces significant risks such as data breaches, unauthorized surveillance, algorithmic bias, and misuse of sensitive personal data (Weber, 2010; Zeng et al., 2017). These challenges are not hypothetical—real-world incidents, including the Mirai botnet attack that exploited security vulnerabilities in IoT devices, have demonstrated the fragility of existing systems and weakened public confidence in their safety (Antonakakis et al., 2017). As IoT technologies continue to integrate more deeply into daily life, establishing transparent, secure, and ethically responsible frameworks has become a critical imperative for ensuring both consumer protection and sustained technological progress.

The Evolution and Impact of IoT on Consumers

The proliferation of IoT has accelerated rapidly, with billions of devices currently connected worldwide and projections indicating exponential growth in the coming years. According to Statista (2023), the number of connected IoT devices is expected to surpass 30 billion by 2030. From wearable fitness trackers and voice assistants to smart thermostats and autonomous vehicles, IoT applications have become integral to modern living. These devices collect and transmit data to provide personalized services, optimize energy usage, monitor health, and enhance user convenience. However, this ubiquity also raises critical questions about the boundaries of data collection and the extent to which consumers are aware of or control the information being harvested from their daily routines. Research suggests that while consumers are generally enthusiastic about the benefits of IoT, many remain skeptical and cautious, particularly regarding data privacy, device reliability, and the trustworthiness of service providers (Park et al., 2017; Choe et al., 2018). A Gartner survey found that 63% of consumers are concerned about how companies use data collected from smart devices (Gartner, 2021). This discrepancy between technological innovation and consumer confidence underscores the importance of designing IoT ecosystems that prioritize trust as a foundational element.

Defining Consumer Trust in the IoT Context

Trust in the digital realm is often defined as a user's willingness to be vulnerable to technology or an organization based on the belief that it will act in a reliable, ethical, and secure manner (Mayer et al., 1995; Gefen et al., 2003). In the context of IoT, consumer trust extends beyond device functionality to include confidence in the broader ecosystem—manufacturers, service providers, cloud platforms, and regulatory bodies. It involves perceived competence (i.e., technological reliability), integrity (i.e., ethical behavior), and benevolence (i.e., prioritizing user interests) (McKnight & Chervany, 2002). When these elements are absent or compromised, consumers may feel exposed or manipulated, leading to hesitation in adopting new devices or even discontinuing existing usage. Furthermore, trust is fragile and context-dependent; it can be easily eroded by a single breach or unethical action and requires ongoing efforts to rebuild. In the dynamic and fast-evolving IoT market, maintaining trust demands a strategic and holistic approach that encompasses secure design, transparent policies, ethical governance, and proactive communication.

Security Vulnerabilities in IoT Ecosystems

One of the most significant barriers to consumer trust in IoT is the issue of security. IoT devices are often characterized by limited computing power, lightweight operating systems, and inconsistent security standards, making them susceptible to cyberattacks (Sicari et al., 2015). Unlike traditional computing systems, IoT devices are frequently deployed in uncontrolled or public environments, such as homes or cities, which further increases their exposure to threats. Security breaches in IoT can have far-reaching consequences beyond data theft. For instance, compromised medical devices could endanger patient health, hacked autonomous vehicles could cause accidents, and infiltrated smart home systems could lead to physical intrusions. The Mirai botnet incident in 2016, which hijacked thousands of unsecured IoT devices to launch distributed denial-of-service (DDoS) attacks, exemplifies the scale of risk associated with poor security design (Antonakakis et al., 2017). Many devices continue to ship with default credentials, unencrypted data transmissions, and outdated firmware, creating systemic vulnerabilities. Building consumer trust therefore necessitates robust cybersecurity practices, including device authentication, end-to-end encryption, firmware updates, anomaly detection, and secure cloud infrastructure (Alrawais et al., 2017). Additionally, adherence to security-by-design principles—embedding security throughout the product lifecycle—is essential to mitigate risks proactively.

Privacy and Ethical Considerations

Beyond security, IoT introduces complex privacy and ethical dilemmas. These devices often collect sensitive information, such as health metrics, location data, voice recordings, and behavioral patterns, raising concerns about data ownership, surveillance, and consent (Weber, 2010; Zeng et al., 2017). Many consumers are unaware of the extent of data collection or the ways in which their information is analyzed, shared, or monetized. This lack of transparency exacerbates feelings of vulnerability and distrust. Ethical challenges also arise from the use of AI and machine learning in IoT. Algorithmic decision-making can result in unintended biases, discrimination, or loss of human agency. For instance, smart insurance devices that monitor driving behavior could unfairly penalize users based on flawed data interpretation. Furthermore, consumer profiling for targeted advertising may cross ethical boundaries, especially when consumers are not fully informed or able to opt out. Responsible data governance frameworks must emphasize transparency, informed consent, user autonomy, and algorithmic accountability (Floridi et al., 2018). Companies that prioritize ethical practices not only comply with regulations but also strengthen brand reputation and consumer loyalty.

The Role of Corporate Digital Responsibility

Corporate Digital Responsibility (CDR) refers to the ethical and accountable use of digital technologies by organizations to benefit society while minimizing harm. In the IoT context, CDR includes commitments to ethical data use, consumer education, inclusivity, sustainability, and security. As consumers become more digitally aware, they increasingly expect companies to demonstrate social responsibility in their technological offerings (Accenture, 2020). Organizations that embrace CDR are better positioned to earn and maintain consumer trust. This includes transparency in privacy policies, rapid response to data breaches, active engagement with regulatory developments, and open dialogue with stakeholders. In fact, trust can become a competitive differentiator, with companies that consistently prioritize ethics and security gaining a loyal customer base and reputational advantage.

Psychological Drivers of Trust

Understanding the psychological underpinnings of consumer trust can further inform IoT strategies. Trust is influenced by perceived risk, perceived control, and familiarity (Gefen et al., 2003). When consumers feel that they have control over their data, such as the ability to configure privacy settings or revoke access, they are more likely to trust the technology. Similarly, familiarity with a brand, prior positive experiences, and third-party endorsements (e.g., certifications) enhance trustworthiness. Risk perception plays a pivotal role. Consumers assess both the likelihood of a negative event (e.g., hacking) and the severity of its consequences (e.g., identity theft). Efforts to reduce perceived risk—through clear explanations of security features, visible compliance badges, and user education—can significantly bolster trust (Beldad et al., 2010).

Future Outlook

Looking ahead, consumer trust in IoT will depend on continuous innovation in security and privacy, evolving ethical standards, and inclusive regulatory frameworks. Emerging solutions such as blockchain, federated learning, and Zero Trust Architecture offer new opportunities to enhance transparency and reduce risk. At the same time, cross-sector collaboration between governments, tech companies, researchers, and civil society will be essential to shape an IoT ecosystem that is not only intelligent but also trustworthy and equitable.

In conclusion, building consumer trust in the IoT era requires a multifaceted approach that aligns technological design, ethical principles, and legal accountability. By understanding the drivers of trust and addressing the barriers, stakeholders can foster a more secure, transparent, and responsible digital future.

BACKGROUND OF THE STUDY

The Internet of Things (IoT) represents a paradigm shift in the way technology interacts with human life, businesses, and the broader ecosystem. Defined as the networked interconnection of everyday objects, equipped with ubiquitous intelligence, IoT has significantly transformed industries, households, and public services by enabling real-time data collection, transmission, and analysis (Atzori, Iera, & Morabito, 2010). The rapid proliferation of IoT devices—ranging from smart home appliances and wearable fitness trackers to industrial sensors and autonomous vehicles—demonstrates its broad utility and disruptive potential. However, the expansion of IoT has also surfaced a spectrum of complex issues concerning consumer trust, data security, and ethical governance.

Evolution of the IoT Ecosystem

The roots of IoT can be traced to early developments in radio-frequency identification (RFID) and wireless sensor networks, which enabled the tracking and monitoring of physical items (Gubbi et al., 2013). Over the past decade, with advancements in cloud computing, machine learning, and 5G connectivity, IoT has evolved into a dynamic system that not only captures and transmits data but also processes it for intelligent decision-making. According to Statista (2023), the number of IoT devices globally surpassed 15 billion in 2022, and is projected to reach over 29 billion by 2030. This exponential growth is being driven by consumer demand for smart living, business needs for automation, and governmental ambitions for smart cities and efficient public infrastructure. This ecosystem is inherently complex, involving various stakeholders including consumers, device manufacturers, data aggregators, software developers, and regulatory bodies. The interaction among these entities necessitates robust frameworks that ensure transparency, accountability, and protection of consumer interests (Weber, 2010).

Consumer Trust as a Foundational Element

Trust is a critical factor that influences consumer acceptance and continued use of IoT technologies. Defined as the consumer's willingness to rely on the vendor's capability and integrity in the face of uncertainty (Gefen, 2000), trust in the IoT context encompasses perceptions about data handling, device reliability, responsiveness, and adherence to privacy norms. Unlike traditional digital services, IoT devices operate autonomously and often invisibly, which can intensify concerns about user control and informed consent (Zeng, Mare, & Roesner, 2017). Research indicates that consumer trust in IoT devices is shaped by multiple dimensions, including data security measures, reputation of the manufacturer, third-party endorsements, and the clarity of terms and conditions (Park, Chung, & Lee, 2021). A breach in any of these aspects—whether due to a cyberattack or unethical data monetization—can erode trust rapidly, leading to user attrition and reputational damage for businesses. For instance, in the infamous 2016 Mirai botnet attack, compromised IoT devices were used to launch one of the largest distributed denial-of-service (DDoS) attacks in history, targeting major internet infrastructure providers (Kolias et al., 2017). Such incidents have underscored the vulnerabilities in IoT networks and the dire need for resilient cybersecurity architectures.

Security Challenges in IoT Markets

Security remains one of the most pressing challenges in IoT deployment. The decentralized and heterogeneous nature of IoT devices complicates the establishment of standardized security protocols. Many consumer-grade devices are built with minimal computing resources, limiting their ability to support robust encryption and authentication mechanisms (Roman, Zhou, & Lopez, 2013). Additionally, frequent software updates—a cornerstone of cybersecurity—are often neglected in IoT devices due to hardware limitations or manufacturer oversight (Sicari et al., 2015). Compounding the problem is the fact that IoT devices often collect highly sensitive personal data such as location, biometric identifiers, and behavioral patterns. Without proper safeguards, this data can be intercepted, misused, or sold without consumer consent, resulting in severe breaches of privacy (Conti, Dehghantanha, Franke, & Watson, 2018). The lack of a global regulatory framework further exacerbates security concerns. While some regions have taken proactive steps—such as the European Union's General Data Protection Regulation (GDPR)—others lack comprehensive legislation to address the nuances of IoT data collection and usage. Even where laws exist, enforcement mechanisms are often weak or ambiguous, leaving consumers vulnerable (Alrawais et al., 2017).

Ethical Considerations in IoT Deployment

The ethical dimensions of IoT are multifaceted, involving data ownership, informed consent, algorithmic bias, and surveillance. As IoT devices become more integrated into personal and social spaces, they raise concerns about autonomy, dignity, and the right to privacy. For example, smart home assistants that continuously listen for voice commands may inadvertently capture private conversations, raising questions about whether users are truly informed about the extent of data collection (Lau, Zimmerman, & Schaub, 2018). Another ethical concern is the use of predictive analytics in IoT. While data-driven insights can enhance user experience and operational efficiency, they may also lead to discrimination or manipulation if not properly regulated. Consider health monitoring devices that share data with insurance companies—individuals may be penalized based on algorithmic interpretations that are neither transparent nor contestable (Mittelstadt et al., 2016). Additionally, ethical dilemmas emerge around surveillance. Governments and corporations are increasingly leveraging IoT for mass surveillance under the guise of security or efficiency. Smart city initiatives, while beneficial in terms of traffic control and energy management, also involve extensive monitoring of citizens' movements and activities (Van Zoonen, 2016). Without strict oversight, such practices risk transforming societies into surveillance states, compromising civil liberties. Ethical IoT deployment also requires inclusivity. Many current IoT designs fail to consider the needs of marginalized groups, elderly populations, or individuals with disabilities, thereby exacerbating the digital divide (Brinkley, 2020). An ethically responsible IoT ecosystem must prioritize universal accessibility, equitable benefits, and participatory governance.

Regulatory and Industry Responses

Recognizing the importance of trust, security, and ethics, governments and industry bodies are beginning to develop standards and frameworks for IoT governance. The National Institute of Standards and Technology (NIST) in the United States has issued guidelines for securing IoT devices, focusing on access control, data protection, and secure software updates (NIST, 2020). The International Organization for Standardization (ISO) has also introduced ISO/IEC 30141, a reference architecture for IoT systems. Private companies are also taking steps to enhance consumer trust. Some have started implementing "privacy by design" principles, where data protection is integrated into the development lifecycle of IoT products (Cavoukian, 2012). Others are promoting data transparency through user dashboards and consent management tools. However, such initiatives often lack consistency and enforcement. Industry self-regulation, while valuable, may not suffice in the absence of legal mandates. There is an urgent need for a collaborative global approach that involves public institutions, private enterprises, civil society, and academic researchers to develop ethical and secure IoT frameworks.

Role of Consumer Awareness and Education

Consumer education is a vital yet often overlooked aspect of IoT governance. Studies show that many users are unaware of how their data is being collected, stored, and shared by IoT devices (Zeng, Mare, & Roesner, 2017). This asymmetry of knowledge limits consumers' ability to make informed choices, weakening the foundation of trust. Educational initiatives must go beyond mere user manuals and include accessible, multimedia resources that explain data flows, risks, and protective actions in simple language. Programs promoting digital literacy should also emphasize critical thinking skills to help consumers assess product claims and identify misleading practices. Moreover, user-centric design can enhance awareness by embedding intuitive privacy controls within devices and applications. Interactive consent mechanisms, visual data-sharing indicators, and real-time alerts about potential threats can empower consumers to take control of their digital lives (Lee & Kobsa, 2016).

Emerging Technologies and Their Implications

The IoT landscape is being reshaped by emerging technologies such as artificial intelligence (AI), edge computing, and blockchain. These innovations offer both opportunities and challenges. AI can enable more responsive and personalized IoT applications, but it also raises issues of explainability and accountability in decision-making (Floridi et al., 2018). Edge computing can mitigate latency and enhance privacy by processing data locally, but it requires a robust infrastructure and new security models (Shi et al., 2016). Blockchain, with its decentralized ledger system, holds promise for secure IoT data exchanges but faces scalability and energy-efficiency concerns (Christidis & Devetsikiotis, 2016). Integrating these technologies into IoT must be accompanied by ethical foresight and regulatory agility. Policymakers need to stay ahead of the curve, anticipating future risks and setting proactive standards that ensure technology serves the public good.

Academic and Practical Relevance

From an academic perspective, understanding the interplay between consumer trust, security, and ethics in IoT markets is crucial for interdisciplinary research spanning information systems, behavioral science, law, and ethics. There is a growing body of literature examining specific facets of these themes, but integrated frameworks that address their interdependencies remain limited. Practically, this study is significant for business leaders, developers, regulators, and consumers alike. For businesses, trust and ethical conduct can become competitive differentiators in increasingly saturated IoT markets. For regulators, insights into consumer concerns can inform better policy design. For consumers, awareness of security and ethical practices can lead to more empowered usage of IoT technologies.

RESEARCH METHODOLOGY

This study adopts a qualitative research methodology to explore the multifaceted dimensions of consumer trust, security challenges, and ethical considerations in the Internet of Things (IoT) markets. The research is based on an integrative literature review approach, which involves a comprehensive synthesis of academic, industry, and policy-related sources published over the past decade. Key databases such as Scopus, Web of Science, IEEE Xplore, SpringerLink, and Google Scholar were utilized to gather peer-reviewed journal articles, conference proceedings, and white papers. To ensure relevance and rigor, inclusion criteria focused on publications that explicitly address themes related to consumer behavior, trust mechanisms, cybersecurity protocols, ethical implications, and regulatory frameworks in IoT contexts. Over 100 articles were initially identified, and a final sample of 60 high-impact sources was selected after a relevance and quality screening process. Thematic analysis was used to categorize insights into three core dimensions: (1) Consumer Trust and Perception, (2) Security and Data Protection Mechanisms, and (3) Ethical and Regulatory Challenges. This method allowed for the identification of patterns, contradictions, and emerging trends in the literature. In addition, industry reports and case studies from reputable organizations such as McKinsey, Cisco, and NIST were incorporated to complement academic findings with practical insights. This triangulation of sources enhances the validity and contextual richness of the analysis. Given the conceptual nature of the study, no primary data collection (e.g., surveys or interviews) was conducted. Instead, the research emphasizes a critical interpretative framework to examine the interrelationships among technological developments, consumer concerns, and ethical governance in IoT markets. The methodology ensures a holistic understanding of the current landscape and lays the groundwork for future empirical investigations.

Findings of the Study

The empirical and theoretical exploration of consumer trust, security, and ethical concerns in the Internet of Things (IoT) markets reveals significant insights across five thematic dimensions: trust determinants, security and privacy concerns, ethical data handling, regulatory awareness, and organizational strategies to rebuild and maintain trust. These findings stem from comprehensive literature reviews, case study analyses, and synthesis of global regulatory impacts.

1. Trust Determinants in IoT Adoption

Consumer trust is a cornerstone for successful IoT adoption. Trust in IoT ecosystems is influenced by perceived risk, transparency in communication, technical competence of IoT providers, and perceived benefits (Miltgen & Smith, 2015; Lee & Lee, 2015). Research consistently shows that consumers are more likely to adopt IoT technologies when they believe providers manage data responsibly and communicate transparently about data use and storage (Shin, 2010). A study by Deloitte (2021) highlights that over 70% of users consider trust in brand integrity and data management practices before adopting IoT-enabled products. Furthermore, users exhibit higher trust levels in companies that proactively communicate data practices and offer visible control over data usage (PwC, 2022). Companies like Apple and Samsung, for example, have implemented privacy-centric messaging to reassure customers and distinguish their brands from competitors (Accenture, 2020). Notably, the consumer perception of control significantly influences trust. If consumers feel they have control over how their data is collected, used, and stored, their trust increases (Cavoukian, 2012). IoT ecosystems that empower users with customizable privacy settings enhance trustworthiness.

2. Security and Privacy Challenges

One of the most prevalent findings across academic and industry reports is the heightened concern about IoT-related security breaches. The inherent interconnectedness of IoT devices expands the attack surface for cybercriminals. High-profile incidents, such as the Mirai botnet attack in 2016, which weaponized thousands of IoT devices, underscore the vulnerabilities in existing infrastructures (Antonakakis et al., 2017). The 2022 Norton Cyber Safety Insights Report showed that 78% of consumers worry about IoT devices compromising personal privacy. The top concerns include unauthorized data access, eavesdropping, device hijacking, and location tracking. Consumers also express concern over secondary uses of their data—particularly when data is shared with third-party vendors without explicit consent (Zeng et al., 2017). Research by Roman et al. (2013) identified that most consumer-grade IoT devices lack fundamental encryption protocols and regular firmware updates, making them susceptible to exploitation. Moreover, many users do not change default passwords or update devices regularly, further compounding vulnerabilities. While consumer awareness of security issues is increasing, studies suggest a significant knowledge gap about how to secure IoT devices. Thus, educational initiatives and simple security guidelines are needed to enhance digital hygiene and protect end-users (Weber, 2010.

3. Ethical Concerns in IoT Data Practices

The ethical implications of IoT are multifaceted and concern the entire data lifecycle—collection, processing, storage, and sharing. Data is continuously harvested by smart home devices, fitness trackers, voice assistants, and wearables, often without fully informed consent (Lupton, 2016). Such constant surveillance raises questions about autonomy, dignity, and freedom of choice. IoT-driven personalization, while valuable, often crosses ethical boundaries. For example, algorithmic profiling and predictive analytics used by retail and healthcare providers can lead to biased outcomes and discriminatory practices (Tufekci, 2015). An ethically troubling case emerged when Target's algorithm inferred a teenager's pregnancy and sent promotional materials—before her family was aware (Hill, 2012). Moreover, AI integration in IoT raises ethical concerns about decision-making transparency and algorithmic bias. When smart devices make automated decisions—like denying insurance based on behavioral data—the absence of human oversight becomes ethically questionable (Floridi et al., 2018). Researchers urge developers and companies to embrace "Ethics by Design" approaches, embedding ethical principles in IoT architecture (Van den Hoven et al., 2012). Consumers express anxiety over how much information is gathered without their explicit consent. A study by KPMG (2021) found that 86% of respondents want more control over their data, and 78% are willing to share less if companies do not clearly explain data use practices.

4. Regulatory Impacts and Consumer Expectation

The GDPR mandates that companies obtain explicit consent before collecting and processing personal data and allows individuals to access, rectify, or delete their data (Voigt & Von dem Bussche, 2017). For IoT businesses, this requires redesigning data practices to meet privacy-by-design and default principles. Studies show that companies that comply with GDPR not only avoid legal repercussions but also earn higher consumer trust (Binns, 2018). Similarly, the CCPA enhances transparency by requiring disclosures about the categories of data collected and shared. Consumers in California now possess the right to opt out of data sales, reinforcing individual autonomy and privacy expectations (Greenleaf, 2020). Despite these advancements, enforcement and compliance remain inconsistent. A Cisco (2021) consumer privacy survey reported that 81% of consumers believe organizations must exceed regulatory compliance to be trusted. Consumers are increasingly expecting proactive and voluntary transparency efforts from companies, not just minimum legal adherence. The emergence of global regulations has also created operational complexities for multinational IoT firms. For example, the China Personal Information Protection Law (PIPL) introduces strict data localization rules and requires government approval for cross-border transfers, impacting global IoT deployment (Chander & Lê, 2021). Companies must navigate diverse legal landscapes while maintaining ethical consistency across markets. An additional expectation revolves around corporate responses to breaches. Research by Ponemon Institute (2022) indicates that when companies act swiftly, communicate openly, and offer remedies (like credit monitoring), trust loss from a breach is significantly mitigated. This finding underscores the importance of breach responsiveness and recovery strategies as part of trust-building.

5. Corporate Initiatives to Rebuild and Maintain Trust

In response to consumer concerns and regulatory pressure, many companies have launched robust initiatives aimed at securing IoT ecosystems and rebuilding trust. These initiatives span across technical upgrades, policy reforms, and consumer empowerment strategies. Technical safeguards, such as end-to-end encryption, regular security updates, and secure boot mechanisms, are being increasingly adopted. Google Nest and Amazon Ring have recently enhanced security protocols, including multi-factor authentication and alert systems for suspicious activity (Amazon, 2023). These changes address the rising threat landscape and align with consumer demand for secure products. A notable trend is the adoption of Zero Trust Architecture (ZTA), a model that assumes no device or user is automatically trusted and requires continuous verification (Kindervag, 2010). ZTA is gaining traction in enterprise IoT as a strategy to prevent lateral movement of threats across connected systems. In terms of policy reforms, companies are updating privacy policies to be more readable, concise, and accessible. Microsoft, for instance, redesigned its privacy dashboard, allowing users to control data preferences in real-time. Similarly, Apple's "App Tracking Transparency" feature empowers users to prevent apps from tracking their activity across other companies' apps and websites (Apple, 2021). From a consumer engagement standpoint, organizations are investing in digital literacy initiatives. IBM and Cisco, for example, offer educational campaigns on IoT security best practices, targeting not only IT professionals but also general consumers (Cisco, 2021). Corporate digital responsibility is also extending into internal governance. The creation of Data Ethics Boards, Responsible AI Committees, and Chief Trust Officers reflects a growing recognition of ethical leadership in managing IoT risks (Raji et al., 2020). These roles ensure that decisions about data collection, usage, and sharing align with societal values and consumer expectations. Several case studies underscore the business benefits of trust-centric practices. For example, after implementing transparent IoT practices, Philips Hue Smart Lighting saw a 22% increase in consumer retention and a 30% boost in referrals, illustrating that trust drives not only compliance but also brand loyalty and market growth (Philips Annual Report, 2021).

6. The Role of Transparency in Trust Building

Transparency is increasingly recognized as a cornerstone in fostering consumer trust in IoT ecosystems. Transparent practices not only demystify the data lifecycle but also empower consumers to make informed decisions about their data and connected devices (Martin, 2018). One major aspect of transparency is clear and concise communication. Complex legal jargon in privacy policies and user agreements erodes trust and leads to informed consent challenges. Research by Milne and Culnan (2004) shows that simplified privacy statements improve consumer comprehension and foster greater trust in data practices. Companies like Mozilla and DuckDuckGo have been commended for offering user-friendly, readable privacy policies—leading to higher levels of trust among tech-savvy users. Another vital component is algorithmic transparency, particularly relevant in AI-powered IoT devices. Consumers are increasingly concerned about opaque algorithmic decisions—especially when such systems influence behavior or purchasing decisions. The concept of explainable AI (XAI), where decisions made by machine learning models can be interpreted and understood by humans, is emerging as a solution to demystify automated IoT processes (Gunning, 2017). For instance, smart thermostats or voice assistants that offer insight into why certain adjustments are made (e.g., energy-saving mode or advertising suggestions) tend to enjoy higher user satisfaction and trust (Shin, 2021). According to a 2022 Accenture report, 74% of IoT users want to understand how their data is being used and why specific actions are taken by connected devices. Real-time visibility into device activity is another factor. Dashboards that allow users to see data logs, control permissions, and revoke access enhance consumer agency. Fitbit, for example, offers an interactive dashboard that enables users to manage data-sharing settings with third parties—boosting perceptions of fairness and trust (Fitbit, 2023). Transparency is also linked to ethical corporate behavior. When companies disclose not just what data is collected but why it is needed—and the risks involved—they are more likely to be perceived as trustworthy (Culnan & Bies, 2003). Full-disclosure practices during a breach (including cause, scope, and mitigation steps) are key to maintaining or regaining trust post-incident.

7. Emerging Trends and the Future of IoT

Trust Looking ahead, several trends are shaping the future of consumer trust in IoT, influenced by both technological evolution and shifting societal expectations.

a) Blockchain for IoT Security and Transparency

Blockchain, a decentralized and immutable ledger system, offers a promising solution to enhance trust by ensuring data integrity, provenance, and traceability. In IoT, blockchain can be used to authenticate device identity, verify firmware updates, and track data usage (Christidis & Devetsikiotis, 2016). Startups like Filament and IOTA are using blockchain to secure device-to-device communication. These systems enable secure micropayments, decentralized identity, and auditable logs of device activity—all contributing to greater transparency and consumer assurance (Dorri et al., 2017).

b) Zero Trust Architecture (ZTA)

ZTA is gaining rapid adoption across IoT ecosystems, especially in industrial and smart city applications. Unlike perimeter-based security models, ZTA continuously authenticates users, devices, and actions—minimizing trust by default (Rose et al., 2020). In IoT, where multiple devices from various vendors interact, ZTA helps prevent lateral attacks and unauthorized access. Companies like Cisco and Palo Alto Networks are offering ZTA frameworks tailored for IoT. The adoption of these architectures not only strengthens security but aligns with consumer expectations for stringent protective measures.

c) Ethical AI and Human-Centered Design

The call for ethical AI in IoT devices is intensifying. Issues such as algorithmic bias, surveillance, and discrimination have raised concerns about fairness and accountability. Initiatives like Google's AI Principles and IBM's AI Fairness 360 toolkit exemplify industry efforts to design AI systems that are transparent, equitable, and privacy-preserving (Raji et al., 2020). Moreover, human-centered IoT design is becoming mainstream. This design philosophy prioritizes user autonomy, accessibility, and emotional engagement. Wearables designed for elderly care, for example, now integrate features that are not only functional but also psychologically comforting—such as voice companions that simulate human empathy (Shin & Park, 2019).

d) Data Sovereignty and Local Storage

Another key trend is the movement toward data sovereignty—storing data within the country of origin. This shift is driven by national regulations and consumer demand for localized control. For instance, India's proposed Data Protection Bill mandates local data storage for sensitive personal data, directly influencing IoT data infrastructures (Chander & Lê, 2021).

e) AI Audits and Accountability Mechanisms

The future of IoT trust will also rely heavily on institutional mechanisms that audit algorithms and data usage. These include external oversight bodies, internal audit teams, and certification systems for ethical IoT products. The concept of trust labels, similar to nutritional labels, is being explored by researchers as a way to convey security and privacy features of IoT devices to consumers at point of purchase (Luger & Rodden, 2013).

f) Socio-Technical Collaboration

Finally, a multi-stakeholder approach that integrates technical innovation with social responsibility will define the future of trust in IoT. Governments, businesses, researchers, and civil society must collaborate to establish norms, standards, and accountability systems that protect consumer rights while fostering innovation (Mann, 2020).

Implications of the Study

The findings of this study have wide-ranging implications for stakeholders involved in the Internet of Things (IoT) ecosystem, including technology developers, policymakers, businesses, and end-users. As IoT continues to evolve into a fundamental component of Industry 5.0, understanding how trust, ethical considerations, and data security intersect becomes essential for building resilient and consumer-friendly systems. These implications span across technological design, regulatory frameworks, business strategy, consumer education, and broader socio-economic considerations.

1. Implications for Technology Developers

The study reveals that consumer trust is deeply rooted in transparent, secure, and privacy-respecting technology design. For developers and manufacturers of IoT devices, this translates into a pressing need to embed privacy and ethical considerations during the design phase—a principle aligned with the concept of "privacy by design" (Cavoukian, 2011).

Developers must go beyond functional features and prioritize:

- End-to-end encryption for data transmission
- Minimal data collection aligned with purpose limitation
- User control features like data access dashboards and permission toggles
- Explainable AI (XAI) models that clarify how decisions are made by devices

These technical choices directly influence user perceptions of fairness and security. For instance, a smart home camera that explains how motion detection algorithms function and allows users to control storage settings will be more trusted than opaque alternatives (Gunning, 2017). In addition, device interoperability standards should also ensure secure device-to-device communication, a known vulnerability in many IoT applications (Roman et al., 2013). Developers can consider integrating blockchain or decentralized identity protocols for enhanced trustworthiness and authentication in peer interactions.

2. Implications for Policymakers and Regulators

The study reinforces the growing demand for strong regulatory frameworks to protect consumer data and ensure ethical practices in IoT deployments. Laws such as the EU's General Data Protection Regulation (GDPR) and the California Consumer Privacy Act (CCPA) are pioneering this direction, but continuous updates are needed to keep up with the pace of IoT evolution (Voigt & Von dem Bussche, 2017).

Policymakers should focus on:

- Creating sector-specific guidelines for IoT devices (e.g., medical wearables, smart toys)
- Mandating data breach disclosures and response protocols
- Enforcing algorithmic transparency requirements for AI-enabled IoT systems
- Promoting certification schemes and trust labels for consumer IoT products

Moreover, global cooperation on IoT standards is vital. Given that IoT supply chains and data flows cross borders, international bodies like ISO, IEEE, and ITU should collaborate to harmonize frameworks, reduce regulatory fragmentation, and enhance consumer trust globally (Tawalbeh et al., 2020).

3. Implications for Businesses and Marketers

For businesses leveraging IoT data to personalize services, the findings suggest that ethical data stewardship is no longer optional but a competitive advantage. Organizations must recognize that consumer trust is closely tied to their reputation for ethical behavior. Transparent data policies, regular communication about data practices, and quick, honest responses to security incidents are essential. Companies like Apple and Mozilla have seen trust gains through visible pro-privacy stances and user-centric innovations (Apple, 2021). Additionally, marketers must consider privacy-aware personalization strategies. Consumers appreciate personalized experiences but are increasingly uncomfortable with opaque data collection. Thus, businesses should pursue a "data value exchange" model, where consumers understand and agree to how their data will be used in exchange for tangible benefits (Martin & Murphy, 2017). Loyalty programs, discounts, or enhanced services in exchange for data sharing—if communicated transparently—can foster both engagement and trust.

4. Implications for Consumers and Digital Literacy

The study also highlights the need for enhanced consumer education and digital literacy. A large portion of consumers remain unaware of how IoT devices collect and use data, what risks are involved, or how to manage privacy settings effectively (Shin, 2021). Governments, educational institutions, and civil society should design awareness campaigns and user guides for IoT users—particularly for vulnerable populations like elderly users, children, or rural communities entering the digital ecosystem.

Informed consumers are more likely to:

- Recognize trustworthy brands
- Use device settings to limit unnecessary data collection
- Demand transparency and accountability from companies

Such proactive behavior can, over time, push companies toward more ethical and user-focused design.

5. Ethical and Societal Implications

From an ethical standpoint, the study raises concerns about digital surveillance, data commodification, and algorithmic bias in IoT ecosystems. If unchecked, IoT can deepen social inequalities, perpetuate discriminatory outcomes, and lead to loss of autonomy for users (Zuboff, 2019). For instance, smart insurance devices that track driving or health behavior may unfairly penalize certain demographics. Facial recognition in smart cities may disproportionately target minority groups. Therefore, the ethical governance of IoT must be multidisciplinary, involving ethicists, technologists, social scientists, and human rights advocates. Companies must implement AI fairness tools, regular algorithm audits, and inclusive datasets. Meanwhile, policymakers should ensure non-discrimination clauses in IoT-related legislation and provide grievance redressal mechanisms for affected users.

6. Implications for Future Research and Innovation

The study provides a fertile ground for future academic exploration and innovation in IoT ethics, trust models, and human-technology interaction. Scholars can explore:

- **The role of cultural differences in trust perceptions toward IoT**
- **Comparative effectiveness of different regulatory models**
- **The impact of AI explanations on user behavior and engagement**
- **Longitudinal studies on trust erosion and recovery post-breach**

Startups and universities can collaborate on human-centered IoT designs that prioritize ethics, usability, and emotional well-being. Government grants and incubators should support such socially responsible innovations.

CONCLUSION

The Internet of Things (IoT) has emerged as a transformative force, altering the fabric of daily life, business models, and societal interaction. From smart homes and wearable health trackers to industrial automation and connected cities, IoT technologies are reshaping the way humans interact with the world. However, as this digital revolution unfolds, it brings forth not only tremendous opportunities but also significant concerns surrounding consumer trust, data security, and ethical implications.

This chapter has explored these dimensions in depth, shedding light on the critical intersections between technological innovation and responsible governance. It is evident from the study that consumer trust acts as a cornerstone in the adoption and continued use of IoT technologies. Trust, in this context, is multifaceted—encompassing the belief that devices are secure, that personal data will be handled ethically, and that systems will act in the best interest of the user.

The Centrality of Trust in IoT Ecosystems

Trust is not automatically granted in IoT ecosystems—it must be earned through consistent, transparent, and ethical practices (Shin, 2010). The findings affirm that consumers tend to engage more with IoT devices and services when they perceive those platforms as secure, privacy-preserving, and aligned with their values (McKnight et al., 2002). Therefore, the challenge for IoT providers lies not only in delivering functional benefits but also in designing trust-enhancing experiences. Furthermore, as IoT ecosystems become more complex—featuring interconnected devices, AI-based decision-making, and automated responses—the opacity of operations can erode consumer confidence. This issue reinforces the need for explainable, user-centric technologies that reduce information asymmetry and foster informed consent (Gunning, 2017). Device manufacturers and platform providers must embrace principles such as "privacy by design," "ethics by design," and "transparency by design" to ensure trust is woven into the fabric of IoT systems (Cavoukian, 2011).

Ethical Considerations in a Hyperconnected World

The rapid integration of IoT into public and private life also raises pressing ethical questions. Issues such as data commodification, algorithmic bias, digital surveillance, consent fatigue, and information manipulation have emerged as critical concerns in the era of ubiquitous computing (Zuboff, 2019). IoT-enabled surveillance technologies, while beneficial in security and law enforcement contexts, can be abused to infringe upon personal freedoms and human rights. One of the core ethical dilemmas explored is the balance between personalization and privacy. While consumers value customized services, they are also increasingly aware of how much personal data is being harvested—often without explicit understanding or meaningful control (Martin & Murphy, 2017). The consent mechanisms embedded in many IoT devices are insufficient and often exploit user ignorance or habituation. Additionally, as artificial intelligence becomes embedded in IoT systems, concerns about algorithmic discrimination and lack of accountability are growing. For example, a smart recruitment tool could unintentionally exhibit bias in hiring decisions if trained on flawed data. Similarly, smart policing systems may target minority communities disproportionately. Addressing these ethical issues requires proactive governance, multistakeholder collaboration, and ethical auditing of algorithms to ensure fairness and equity.

Data Security as a Trust Enabler

Data security is arguably the most tangible and immediate concern for consumers when adopting IoT devices. The study highlights that security breaches significantly damage consumer trust, often leading to user attrition, reputational loss for businesses, and even legal consequences (Roman et al., 2013). The fragmented security practices in the current IoT landscape—such as weak authentication, unpatched firmware, and lack of data encryption—create vulnerabilities that malicious actors can exploit. To address these risks, businesses must move beyond reactive cybersecurity postures and adopt security-by-design frameworks, including device-level hardening, secure software updates, and real-time threat detection. Moreover, zero-trust architectures, where no device or system is inherently trusted, can be valuable in mitigating insider and lateral threats (Kindervag, 2010). In parallel, regulatory mechanisms must be strengthened to mandate minimum security requirements, enforce timely reporting of breaches, and hold manufacturers accountable for negligent practices. Legislation such as the EU's GDPR and California's IoT Security Law represent important steps in that direction, yet there remains a need for global harmonization of security standards (Voigt & Von dem Bussche, 2017).

Role of Policy, Business, and Society

Building a secure and ethical IoT ecosystem is not the responsibility of any single actor; it requires coordinated action from policymakers, businesses, civil society, and consumers. Governments must establish legal frameworks that safeguard individual rights, incentivize responsible innovation, and penalize unethical behavior. At the same time, businesses must recognize that trust and ethics are not constraints but strategic assets that differentiate brands in a competitive marketplace (Belanger & Crossler, 2011). From a societal perspective, there is a pressing need to improve digital literacy, especially around data rights, device settings, and risk awareness. Only when consumers are empowered with knowledge and tools can they participate meaningfully in shaping the digital world. Civil society organizations, educators, and tech advocates play a pivotal role in bridging this information gap.

Looking Ahead: A Human-Centric IoT Future

As we stand at the cusp of Industry 5.0, characterized by human-machine collaboration, personalized systems, and resilient ecosystems, it is imperative to ensure that the evolution of IoT aligns with human values. The future of IoT must be not only smart but also ethical, inclusive, and trustworthy (European Commission, 2021). Designing such a future involves embedding ethical foresight into innovation processes, conducting impact assessments, and co-creating policies with affected communities. Emerging technologies such as privacy-preserving machine learning, federated analytics, and decentralized identity systems offer new paradigms for balancing personalization and privacy (Dwork, 2006; Tawalbeh et al., 2020). Additionally, further research is needed to explore contextual trust models, cross-cultural perspectives on IoT ethics, and socio-technical resilience frameworks. Multidisciplinary inquiry—drawing from computer science, sociology, law, psychology, and ethics—will be essential to navigate the complex challenges ahead.

Suggestions for Future Studies

Future research on consumer trust in the Internet of Things (IoT) should adopt a multidimensional approach that integrates technological, behavioral, and regulatory perspectives. One promising direction is to explore context-specific trust formation, examining how trust varies across different IoT domains such as healthcare, smart homes, autonomous vehicles, and industrial applications. Each context presents unique privacy sensitivities and risk perceptions, which future studies could investigate using comparative frameworks. Additionally, longitudinal research designs could provide insights into how trust evolves over time as consumers gain experience with

IoT devices and as regulations, security standards, and technological capabilities advance. There is also a pressing need for cross-cultural and demographic studies to understand how cultural values, socioeconomic factors, and digital literacy influence trust and adoption behaviors. Such research could help identify global patterns and local nuances in IoT acceptance, offering valuable input for policymakers and developers seeking to create inclusive and equitable IoT ecosystems. Furthermore, experimental and simulation-based studies can test the impact of specific trust-enhancing mechanisms—such as blockchain-based transparency tools, explainable AI systems, or privacy-by-design interfaces—on user confidence and continued engagement.

In addition to consumer-focused investigations, future work should delve into organizational and ethical dimensions, exploring how companies can operationalize trust through corporate governance, ethical AI integration, and transparent data practices. Researchers may also examine how emerging technologies, such as edge computing and federated learning, can mitigate privacy risks and enhance user autonomy. Finally, policy-oriented studies could evaluate the effectiveness of existing data protection frameworks and propose adaptive governance models that balance innovation with accountability. By bridging these interdisciplinary gaps, future research can contribute to building a more secure, transparent, and trustworthy IoT environment that fosters both technological progress and consumer confidence.

Limitations

While this chapter provides a comprehensive analysis of the interplay between consumer trust, data security, and ethical implications in the Internet of Things (IoT) landscape, it is important to acknowledge several limitations that frame the scope and depth of the study. First, the study is largely conceptual and exploratory in nature, relying on existing literature, secondary data, and theoretical insights rather than empirical fieldwork or primary data collection. As a result, while the findings offer critical perspectives and highlight key challenges and trends, they may not fully capture the dynamic and contextual nuances of real-world IoT adoption across different geographies, industries, and consumer segments. Second, the rapidly evolving nature of IoT technologies presents a challenge in terms of relevance and timeliness. With new devices, platforms, and protocols emerging frequently, any analysis risks becoming quickly outdated. For instance, newer developments in edge computing, decentralized identity systems, or privacy-preserving AI may not have been fully explored due to publication timelines and evolving research trends. Third, the study assumes a degree of technological uniformity in IoT systems, yet in reality, the IoT ecosystem is highly fragmented. Devices vary in terms of capabilities, manufacturers, standards, and integration protocols. This heterogeneity makes it difficult to generalize findings or offer one-size-fits-all recommendations. The complexities of device interoperability, cross-vendor security compliance, and context-specific ethical concerns remain underexplored in this chapter. Fourth, consumer trust and ethical perceptions are deeply influenced by cultural, legal, and socioeconomic factors, which may not be fully represented in this study. The majority of existing research cited in this chapter stems from Western contexts—such as the U.S. and the European Union—where regulatory frameworks like GDPR have shaped public discourse around privacy and ethics. However, perspectives from the Global South, where legal protections and digital literacy may be limited, require further investigation to ensure inclusivity and cross-cultural applicability of findings. Fifth, the ethical assessment of IoT applications tends to be normative and subjective. Concepts such as fairness, transparency, and accountability can be interpreted differently by various stakeholders. While this chapter advocates for principles such as "ethics by design" and "privacy by design," it acknowledges that implementing these ideals in complex socio-technical systems is neither straightforward nor universally agreed upon. Additionally, the security analysis primarily focuses on consumer-facing IoT applications, such as smart home devices and wearables, with limited attention to industrial IoT (IIoT), critical infrastructure, or military-grade applications. Each of these sectors poses unique ethical and security challenges that merit independent, in-depth exploration. Lastly, the chapter does not include quantitative validation of trust metrics, risk assessments, or ethical outcomes. Future research can address this by using mixed methods—such as surveys, experimental designs, and machine learning models—to empirically test and validate the relationships among trust, security practices, ethical design, and consumer behavior in the IoT context.

In summary, while this chapter contributes valuable insights into the ethical and trust-related dimensions of IoT, its limitations underscore the need for continued, interdisciplinary, and empirical research that keeps pace with technological evolution and societal expectations.

REFERENCES

Accenture. (2020). *Technology Vision 2020: We, the post-digital people*. Accenture.

Alrawais, A., Alhothaily, A., Hu, C., & Cheng, X. (2017). Fog computing for the Internet of Things: Security and privacy issues. *IEEE Internet Computing*, *21*(2), 34–42. DOI: 10.1109/MIC.2017.37

Antonakakis, M., April, T., & Bailey, M.. (2017). Understanding the Mirai botnet. In *USENIX Security Symposium*.

Atzori, L., Iera, A., & Morabito, G. (2010). The Internet of Things: A survey. *Computer Networks*, *54*(15), 2787–2805. DOI: 10.1016/j.comnet.2010.05.010

Belanger, F., & Crossler, R. E. (2011). Privacy in the digital age: A review of information privacy research in information systems. *Management Information Systems Quarterly*, *35*(4), 1017–1041. DOI: 10.2307/41409971

Beldad, A., de Jong, M., & Steehouder, M. (2010). How shall I trust the faceless and the intangible? *Computers in Human Behavior*, *26*(5), 857–869. DOI: 10.1016/j.chb.2010.03.013

Brinkley, J. (2020). Designing inclusive IoT devices. *Journal of Information Technology & Politics*, *17*(2), 112–128.

Cavoukian, A. (2011). *Privacy by design: The 7 foundational principles*. Information and Privacy Commissioner of Ontario.

Cavoukian, A. (2012). Privacy by design: Origins, meaning, and prospects. In *Privacy protection measures and technologies in business organizations* (pp. 170–208). IGI Global. DOI: 10.4018/978-1-61350-501-4.ch007

Choe, E. K., Jung, J., Lee, B., & Fisher, K. (2018). The role of privacy and personalization in IoT. [TOCHI]. *ACM Transactions on Computer-Human Interaction*, *25*(1), 1–29.

Christidis, K., & Devetsikiotis, M. (2016). Blockchains and smart contracts for the Internet of Things. *IEEE Access : Practical Innovations, Open Solutions*, *4*, 2292–2303. DOI: 10.1109/ACCESS.2016.2566339

Conti, M., Dehghantanha, A., Franke, K., & Watson, S. (2018). Internet of Things security and forensics: Challenges and opportunities. *Future Generation Computer Systems*, *78*, 544–546. DOI: 10.1016/j.future.2017.07.060

Dorri, A., Kanhere, S. S., Jurdak, R., & Gauravaram, P. (2017, March). *Blockchain for IoT security and privacy: The case study of a smart home. In 2017 IEEE international conference on pervasive computing and communications workshops (PerCom workshops)*. IEEE.

Dwork, C. (2006). Differential privacy. *International Colloquium on Automata, Languages, and Programming*, 1–12.

European Commission. (2021). *Industry 5.0: Towards a sustainable, human-centric and resilient European industry*. Publications Office of the European Union.

Floridi, L., Cowls, J., Beltrametti, M., Chatila, R., Chazerand, P., Dignum, V., & Schafer, B. (2018). AI4People—An ethical framework for a good AI society: Opportunities, risks, principles, and recommendations. *Minds and Machines*, *28*(4), 689–707. DOI: 10.1007/s11023-018-9482-5

Gartner. (2021). *Consumer perceptions of IoT and privacy*.

Gefen, D. (2000). E-commerce: The role of familiarity and trust. *Omega*, *28*(6), 725–737. DOI: 10.1016/S0305-0483(00)00021-9

Gefen, D., Karahanna, E., & Straub, D. W. (2003). Trust and TAM in online shopping. *Management Information Systems Quarterly*, *27*(1), 51–90. DOI: 10.2307/30036519

Greenleaf, G. (2020). California's CCPA 2.0: Does the US Finally Have a Data Privacy Act?.

Gubbi, J., Buyya, R., Marusic, S., & Palaniswami, M. (2013). Internet of Things (IoT): A vision, architectural elements, and future directions. *Future Generation Computer Systems*, *29*(7), 1645–1660. DOI: 10.1016/j.future.2013.01.010

Gunning, D. (2017). *Explainable artificial intelligence (XAI)*. Defense Advanced Research Projects Agency (DARPA).

Hill, K. (2012, February 16). How Target figured out a teen girl was pregnant before her father did. Forbes. Available at: https://www.forbes.com/sites/kashmirhill/2012/02/16/how-target-figured-out-a-teen-girl-was-pregnant-before-her-father-did/

Kindervag, J. (2010). *No more chewy centers: Introducing the zero trust model of information security*. Forrester Research.

Kolias, C., Kambourakis, G., Stavrou, A., & Voas, J. (2017). DDoS in the IoT: Mirai and other botnets. *Computer*, *50*(7), 80–84. DOI: 10.1109/MC.2017.201

Lau, J., Zimmerman, B., & Schaub, F. (2018). Alexa, are you listening? Privacy perceptions, concerns and privacy-seeking behaviors with smart speakers. *Proceedings of the ACM on Human-Computer Interaction, 2*(CSCW), 1–31.

Lee, I., & Lee, K. (2015). The Internet of Things (IoT): Applications, investments, and challenges for enterprises. *Business Horizons, 58*(4), 431–440. DOI: 10.1016/j.bushor.2015.03.008

Lee, M. L., & Kobsa, A. (2016). Understanding user privacy in IoT. *IEEE Security and Privacy, 14*(2), 36–44.

Lupton, D. (2016). *The quantified self.* John Wiley & Sons.

Martin, K., & Murphy, P. E. (2017). The role of data privacy in marketing. *Journal of the Academy of Marketing Science, 45*(2), 135–155. DOI: 10.1007/s11747-016-0495-4

Mayer, R. C., Davis, J. H., & Schoorman, F. D. (1995). An integrative model of organizational trust. *Academy of Management Review, 20*(3), 709–734. DOI: 10.2307/258792

McKnight, D. H., & Chervany, N. L. (2002). What trust means in e-commerce customer relationships. *International Journal of Electronic Commerce, 6*(2), 35–59. DOI: 10.1080/10864415.2001.11044235

McKnight, D. H., Choudhury, V., & Kacmar, C. (2002). Developing and validating trust measures for e-commerce: An integrative typology. *Information Systems Research, 13*(3), 334–359. DOI: 10.1287/isre.13.3.334.81

Miltgen, C. L., & Smith, H. J. (2015). Exploring information privacy regulation, risks, trust, and behavior. *Information & Management, 52*(6), 741–759. DOI: 10.1016/j.im.2015.06.006

Mittelstadt, B. D., Allo, P., Taddeo, M., Wachter, S., & Floridi, L. (2016). The ethics of algorithms: Mapping the debate. *Big Data & Society, 3*(2), 1–21. DOI: 10.1177/2053951716679679

NIST. (2020). *Considerations for managing Internet of Things (IoT) cybersecurity and privacy risks (NISTIR 8228).* National Institute of Standards and Technology.

Park, E., Chung, K., & Lee, S. (2021). Understanding the acceptance of IoT in households. *Technological Forecasting and Social Change, 173*, 121108.

Park, S., Chung, K., & Jayaraman, P. P. (2017). Trust in IoT: Understanding trustworthiness of IoT systems. *IEEE Access : Practical Innovations, Open Solutions, 5*, 23416–23425.

PwC. (2022). 2022 Global Digital Trust Insights. Available at: https://www.pwc.com/gx/en/issues/cybersecurity/digital-trust-insights.html

Raji, I. D., Smart, A., White, R. N., Mitchell, M., Gebru, T., Hutchinson, B., & Barnes, P. (2020, January). Closing the AI accountability gap: Defining an end-to-end framework for internal algorithmic auditing. In *Proceedings of the 2020 conference on fairness, accountability, and transparency* (pp. 33-44). DOI: 10.1145/3351095.3372873

Roman, R., Zhou, J., & Lopez, J. (2013). On the features and challenges of security and privacy in distributed Internet of Things. *Computer Networks*, *57*(10), 2266–2279. DOI: 10.1016/j.comnet.2012.12.018

Shi, W., Cao, J., Zhang, Q., Li, Y., & Xu, L. (2016). Edge computing: Vision and challenges. *IEEE Internet of Things Journal*, *3*(5), 637–646. DOI: 10.1109/JIOT.2016.2579198

Shin, D. (2010). The effects of trust, security and privacy in social networking: A security-based approach to understand the pattern of adoption. *Interacting with Computers*, *22*(5), 428–438. DOI: 10.1016/j.intcom.2010.05.001

Shin, D., & Park, Y. J. (2019). Role of fairness, accountability, and transparency in algorithmic affordance. *Computers in Human Behavior*, *98*, 277–284. DOI: 10.1016/j.chb.2019.04.019

Sicari, S., Rizzardi, A., Grieco, L. A., & Coen-Porisini, A. (2015). Security, privacy and trust in Internet of Things: The road ahead. *Computer Networks*, *76*, 146–164. DOI: 10.1016/j.comnet.2014.11.008

Statista. (2023). *Internet of Things (IoT) connected devices installed base worldwide from 2015 to 2030*. Retrieved from https://www.statista.com/

Tawalbeh, L. A., Muheidat, F., Tawalbeh, M., & Quwaider, M. (2020). IoT privacy and security: Challenges and solutions. *Applied Sciences (Basel, Switzerland)*, *10*(12), 4102. DOI: 10.3390/app10124102

Tufekci, Z. (2015). Algorithmic harms beyond Facebook and Google: Privacy, big data and the internet of things. *Colorado Technology Law Journal*, 13(2).

Van Zoonen, L. (2016). Privacy concerns in smart cities. *Government Information Quarterly*, *33*(3), 472–480. DOI: 10.1016/j.giq.2016.06.004

Voigt, P., & Von dem Bussche, A. (2017). *The EU General Data Protection Regulation (GDPR): A practical guide*. Springer International Publishing. DOI: 10.1007/978-3-319-57959-7

Weber, R. H. (2010). Internet of Things – New security and privacy challenges. *Computer Law & Security Review*, *26*(1), 23–30. DOI: 10.1016/j.clsr.2009.11.008

Zeng, E., Mare, S., & Roesner, F. (2017). End user security and privacy concerns with smart homes. In *Thirteenth Symposium on Usable Privacy and Security (SOUPS 2017)* (pp. 65–80).

Zuboff, S. (2019). *The age of surveillance capitalism: The fight for a human future at the new frontier of power*. PublicAffairs.

KEY TERMS AND DEFINITIONS

Algorithmic Bias: Algorithmic bias occurs when IoT systems or AI algorithms make decisions that unfairly favor certain groups over others due to biased data or flawed design. This can lead to discrimination or errors in smart devices. Addressing bias is essential for ensuring fairness and equality in IoT applications.

Blockchain Technology: Blockchain is a decentralized and tamper-resistant ledger system that records transactions securely and transparently. In IoT networks, blockchain helps verify data authenticity, prevent tampering, and build trust between devices and users through transparent and immutable records.

Consumer Trust: Consumer trust represents the belief and confidence that users place in IoT technologies and providers to act securely, reliably, and ethically. It encompasses confidence in privacy, reliability, and integrity of IoT services. High trust encourages users to adopt IoT solutions, whereas mistrust leads to hesitation and resistance toward new technologies.

Cybersecurity: Cybersecurity in IoT refers to the methods and technologies designed to protect devices and networks from unauthorised access, data theft, and cyberattacks. Effective security measures such as encryption, firewalls, and regular updates safeguard data integrity and prevent breaches that can erode consumer trust.

Data Breach: A data breach occurs when unauthorized parties gain access to confidential or sensitive data from IoT systems. Such incidents expose personal or financial information and can severely damage both consumer confidence and company reputation. Events like the Mirai botnet attack underscore the vulnerabilities present in IoT ecosystems.

Data Governance: Data governance refers to the policies, processes, and standards that ensure data collected through IoT systems is managed ethically, securely, and lawfully. Strong governance structures clarify responsibilities, enforce compliance, and maintain accountability in data handling.

Data Privacy: Data privacy involves protecting personal and sensitive information gathered through IoT devices. It ensures users have control over how their data is collected, processed, shared, and stored. Since IoT devices often function continuously, privacy becomes a key concern for maintaining consumer confidence.

Digital Literacy: Digital literacy is the ability of individuals to understand, use, and manage digital technologies effectively. In the IoT context, it includes awareness of device functions, privacy controls, and potential risks. Higher digital literacy empowers consumers to make informed choices and engage safely with IoT technologies.

Edge Computing: Edge computing is a distributed data processing approach where computation occurs near the data source—such as in IoT devices or local gateways—rather than at a centralized cloud server. It enhances performance, reduces latency, and strengthens data privacy by minimizing data transmission risks.

Ethical Data Use: Ethical data use means handling consumer data responsibly and morally, ensuring it is used only for legitimate and fair purposes. It prevents exploitation, manipulation, or unauthorized sharing of user data. Companies that prioritize ethical data practices enhance their credibility and foster long-term consumer loyalty.

Internet of Things (IoT): The Internet of Things refers to a vast network of interconnected physical devices such as sensors, appliances, vehicles, and wearable gadgets that communicate and exchange data over the internet. These devices operate autonomously or semi-autonomously to monitor environments, collect information, and make decisions that enhance efficiency, comfort, and convenience. IoT systems are transforming industries like healthcare, agriculture, and manufacturing through automation and real-time data sharing.

Privacy by Design: Privacy by Design is an approach that integrates privacy and data protection principles into IoT device development from the beginning. It ensures privacy is embedded into system architecture through features like encryption, anonymization, and minimal data collection, promoting both compliance and user trust.

Regulatory Compliance: Regulatory compliance means adhering to legal standards and data protection laws such as the GDPR or India's Personal Data Protection Bill. Compliance ensures IoT providers follow ethical guidelines for data handling, user consent, and transparency, enhancing credibility and consumer trust.

Transparency: Transparency refers to the openness with which IoT providers disclose their data collection, sharing, and usage practices. It allows users to understand how their data is handled and builds confidence through honesty, accountability, and clear communication about potential risks.

User Consent: User consent is the explicit agreement provided by consumers for IoT devices to collect and use their data. Consent must be informed, voluntary, and revocable. Ensuring genuine consent reinforces transparency and respects individual autonomy, which is central to maintaining user trust.

Chapter 4

Digital Readiness and Organizational Transformation for IoT Adoption in African Enterprises

Johanna Pangeiko Nautwima
http://orcid.org/0009-0004-6153-5014
Namibia University of Science and Technology, Namibia

Asa Romeo Asa
Namibia University of Science and Technology, Namibia

ABSTRACT

The Internet of Things (IoT) is transforming business innovation and competitiveness, yet adoption across Africa remains uneven due to a deep digital divide. This review of 44 peer-reviewed studies (2015–2025) examined how digital readiness and organizational transformation shape IoT uptake. Results show that limited broadband, unstable electricity, and weak cloud systems constrain readiness, while skill shortages and poor digital leadership further slow progress. Many enterprises lack the technical capacity, managerial support, and flexibility required for IoT integration. External obstacles include fragmented regulation and scarce finance, though initiatives such as AfCFTA, the Smart Africa Alliance, and fintech programs offer new opportunities. Effective adoption depends not only on access to technology but also on firms' ability to sense, seize, and reconfigure resources. Building agility,

DOI: 10.4018/979-8-3373-3441-7.ch004

leadership, innovation culture, and robust infrastructure, underpinned by coherent policy and academia-industry collaboration, is crucial for sustainable IoT-driven growth in Africa.

1. INTRODUCTION

The Internet of Things (IoT) is widely regarded as a game changer for businesses worldwide, and African enterprises are eager to leverage its potential. IoT involves networks of smart devices that communicate and share data to optimize processes across various sectors (Kuaban et al., 2024). From agriculture and utilities to retail and mining, IoT solutions can help African businesses overcome traditional challenges by improving their efficiency and enabling new services. For example, telecommunications initiatives, such as the MTN's dedicated IoT network (spanning 23 countries), aim to equip African entrepreneurs with tools to solve age-old problems in innovative ways (Ndubuaku & Okereafor, 2015). Such technologies promise benefits in critical development areas, such as water management, electricity supply, transportation, and agriculture. However, despite this promise, the adoption of digital technologies like IoT among African firms remains uneven between countries and even within them (Cruz, 2024), meaning that many businesses may not yet be reaping IoT's full benefits. Key barriers, such as high costs and limited infrastructure, persist. Indeed, the costs of hardware, software, and connectivity in Africa are significantly higher than those in other regions, creating hurdles for widespread IoT implementation (Cruz, 2024). This underscores the importance of digital readiness and organizational change for a successful IoT uptake in Africa.

However, achieving value from IoT is not as simple as purchasing sensors or gadgets. It requires enterprises to be digitally ready and undergo internal transformation. In this context, digital readiness refers to the preparedness of an organization (or country) to adopt and absorb new technologies. It encompasses a robust ICT infrastructure, affordable Internet, digitally skilled workforce, supportive policies, and cybersecurity frameworks (Mphale et al., 2024). For instance, a recent review in Botswana examined factors such as e-commerce legislation, ICT education, infrastructure investment, and cybersecurity as components of technological readiness for IoT (Mphale et al., 2024). These foundational elements determine whether IoT innovations can be deployed effectively. Similarly, organizational transformation, often referred to as digital transformation, plays a critical role. The introduction of IoT may require companies to reinvent their business processes, update their skill sets, and foster an innovation-friendly culture (Kuaban et al., 2024). Scholars emphasize that understanding the steps and background needed for such transformation is crucial in an ICT-dependent world, and companies must be adequately prepared internally for digital initiatives to succeed (Lorenz & Buchwald, 2023; Michelotto & Joia, 2024). In other words, an enterprise with a clear digital strategy, strong leadership support, and a culture open to change is far more likely to implement IoT successfully than an enterprise that lacks these attributes. Digital transformation concerns people and processes as much as technology. This represents a cultural shift in which employees collectively embrace and learn new technologies (Wessel et al., 2021). Thus, an organization's digital readiness and willingness to transform are central to unlocking the benefits of IoT.

When examining IoT adoption in Africa, one finds gaps in the existing scholarship, especially from a local perspective. While IoT has been studied globally and some research has emerged in Africa, many of these studies have focused on specific countries or sectors. For example, IoT in the South African agricultural sector (Moeti et al., 2024) and IoT implementation challenges in Nigeria (Iwayemi, 2018) have not been extended to a broader continental view. These targeted studies provide valuable insights (such as identifying inadequate infrastructure, skill shortages, high costs, and cybersecurity concerns as barriers (Iwayemi, 2018). However, their narrow scope makes it difficult to generalize their findings across Africa's diverse business environments (Dosumu et al., 2023). The African context varies widely in terms of the economy, culture, and technological ecosystems (Iwayemi, 2018; Kuaban et al., 2024; Moeti et al., 2024). Therefore, insights from one region may not directly apply to another. Moreover, much of the mainstream IoT literature and frameworks originate outside Africa, often in high-income countries. International organizations, such as the World Bank and ITU, have highlighted the common challenges facing IoT adoption in developing regions (e.g., insufficient infrastructure, skill gaps, and regulatory hurdles) (Kuaban et al., 2024). However, these global reports do not always capture local nuances such as socioeconomic realities, political factors, and cultural considerations that influence how African enterprises adopt new technologies.

In short, there is a recognized need for more Africa-centric research that addresses local conditions and voices the experiences of African enterprises. This review seeks to fill this gap by synthesizing insights pertinent to Africa and identifying what may be distinct or overlooked in this context. In light of the above, this literature review aims to explore how digital readiness and organizational transformation affect IoT adoption in African enterprises and identify strategies that can facilitate successful implementation. This review was guided by several key questions.

1. What is the current state of IoT adoption among African enterprises and what potential does it hold for enterprise development across the continent?

2. How prepared (in terms of digital readiness) are African organizations for IoT, and what forms of organizational change or capacity building are necessary to support successful IoT integration?
3. What gaps exist in the existing literature on IoT adoption in Africa, and how can addressing these gaps help stakeholders (business leaders, policymakers, and researchers) overcome the challenges unique to the African context?

This review seeks to provide a holistic understanding of the interplay between IoT technologies and the organizational readiness of African enterprises. In so doing, we draw on peer-reviewed literature from 2015 to 2025, a period that captures the rapid evolution of IoT and digital transformation efforts over the last decade. The focus is on studies relevant to Africa and comparable emerging markets, ensuring that the insights are grounded in contexts similar to those of African enterprises. Most sources were drawn from Scopus-indexed journals to ensure that the evidence was both rigorous and accessible. Finally, surveying recent scholarship in this manner sets the stage for a comprehensive discussion on what it takes for African businesses to successfully embrace the IoT, from the groundwork of digital readiness to the journey of organizational transformation, and ultimately, to the innovative applications that drive enterprise development on the continent.

2. CONCEPTUAL AND THEORETICAL BACKGROUND

The digital transformation of enterprises through the Internet of Things (IoT) is not simply a matter of adopting new technologies, but navigating complex organizational, infrastructural, and environmental dynamics. Understanding how firms, particularly in Africa, prepare for and implement the IoT requires a clear conceptual foundation and theoretical framework. This section unpacks the key concepts underpinning enterprise IoT readiness, including IoT and digital readiness, organizational enablers of transformation, and theoretical frameworks that help explain how and why firms pursue IoT adoption. The discussion draws from the technology–organization–environment (TOE) framework, Dynamic Capabilities Theory (DCT), and Institutional Theory to provide a comprehensive lens through which to interpret both internal capabilities and external constraints shaping IoT transformations across African enterprises.

2.1. Internet of Things (IoT) and Enterprise Innovation

The Internet of Things (IoT) refers to a network of connected physical objects or smart devices equipped with sensors, software, and network connectivity, enabling these objects to collect and exchange data over the Internet (Hsu & Yeh, 2017). In business contexts, the IoT concept has evolved from early ideas, such as Kevin Ashton's 1999 RFID-based vision, to widespread adoption with the rise of Industry 4.0, around 2011 (Ahmetoglu et al., 2023). IoT technologies have become a transformative force in enterprise innovation and digital strategies. Embedding IoT sensors and connectivity in operations enables companies to gather real-time data across manufacturing lines, supply chains, and products, leading to smarter decision-making and automation (Lorenz & Buchwald, 2023; Savoury & Burchell, 2021). This connectivity enhances operational performance and efficiency, improves output, reduces downtime and costs, and increases productivity and profit. Thus, enterprises that leverage IoT gain new competitive advantages by using data-driven insights to optimize processes, innovate services, and better meet customer needs (Satar et al., 2018). IoT plays a pivotal role in modern digital transformation strategies, with firms that adopt IoT poised to outperform their rivals in the long run by unlocking greater value and innovation.

2.2. Digital Readiness

Digital readiness is the state of an organization's preparedness to successfully implement digital technologies and transformative initiatives, such as IoT (Gfrerer et al., 2021). In practice, this denotes an enterprise's capability and willingness to leverage digital tools and processes to achieve business objectives and improvements (Pingali et al., 2023). This concept has gained prominence because companies must be adequately ready for digital transformation (DT) initiatives to be successful (Michelotto & Joia, 2024). This implies that without sufficient digital readiness in terms of technology, skills, and organizational enablement, even promising IoT adoption efforts are likely to falter. This is highly relevant in African economies, where enterprises often operate amid infrastructure and resource constraints (Pingali et al., 2023). Many African firms face a rudimentary digital infrastructure, limited connectivity, and skill gaps, exacerbating the digital divide and hindering the uptake of advanced technologies (Omol et al., 2024). Hence, building digital readiness is a critical prerequisite for African enterprises striving to capitalize on the IoT and related Industry 4.0 innovations.

Research on digital transformation readiness highlights several core dimensions that organizations must develop to be ready for IoT adoption and similar initiatives to support digital change (Michelotto & Joia, 2024). One of the key dimensions is digital infrastructure. This refers to the technological resources and connectivity available to the enterprise, such as reliable Internet access, networks, hardware, and IoT-supporting infrastructure (Sheth, 2011). Robust digital infrastructure is the foundation of IoT readiness, ensuring that sensors, devices, and data streams can operate effectively. In many African contexts, inadequate infrastructure (e.g., limited broadband coverage and power reliability) remains a major barrier to digital readiness. Therefore, improving infrastructure investment and access is paramount for enterprises to embark on IoT projects.

Another dimension is human capital (skills and training), which refers to the workforce's digital skills, knowledge, and preparedness that are central to digital readiness (Pingali et al., 2023). Employees and managers need the right technical competencies (e.g., in IoT systems, data analytics, and cybersecurity) and a mindset of continuous learning to adapt to new technologies. Many African enterprises currently face a shortage of adequately skilled human resources, which undermines their readiness for IoT adoption (Ojubanire et al., 2025). Investing in training and education is crucial for staff to effectively implement and use IoT solutions. A higher level of digital literacy and expertise across an organization increases its capacity to absorb and benefit from emerging technologies.

Leadership and culture are also crucial dimensions, and top management support and organizational culture play decisive roles in transformation readiness. Effective digital transformation requires visionary leadership that articulates a clear digital strategy and commits to necessary resources (Michelotto & Joia, 2024). Cultivating an innovative and change-embracing culture among employees is equally important. Enterprises with leaders who champion digital initiatives and a culture open to experimentation are far more ready to implement IoT than those with resistant mindsets. Indeed, the literature identifies management capabilities and corporate culture as prominent factors in organizational digital readiness (Michelotto & Joia, 2024; Ojubanire et al., 2025). Conversely, a lack of leadership will or buy-in has been shown to significantly impede IoT and Industry 4.0 projects in African firms (Ojubanire et al., 2025). Therefore, building a pro-digital culture that encourages agility, collaboration, and data-driven decision-making is a core dimension of readiness.

The last dimension is the maturity of the IT system. This dimension reflects the maturity of an organization's existing IT systems and processes, including its ability to integrate new digital tools (Issa et al., 2018). High IT system maturity implies that the enterprise has well-developed and flexible information systems, data management practices, and cybersecurity measures. Such maturity enables the easier incorporation of IoT platforms and handling of large data flows from connected devices. Prior studies often link this to process maturity, which focuses on how optimized and digitized a firm's business processes are, and together with technology infrastructure, determines readiness for more advanced digital solutions (Issa et al., 2018; Mphale et al., 2024). In essence, organizations need a certain level of digital maturity in their internal systems (ERP, cloud platforms, etc.) to effectively scale the IoT. African enterprises with legacy or patchy IT systems may need to upgrade and integrate their systems to improve their digital readiness.

2.3. Organisational Transformation for IoT

Organizational transformation in the IoT context refers to the fundamental changes an enterprise undergoes in its structure, processes, and culture to effectively integrate IoT technologies. IoT adoption can catalyze digital transformation by fundamentally altering work practices and employees' perceptions of their roles (Westergren et al., 2024). That is, successfully leveraging IoT often demands reinventing how an organization operates, rather than just adding new gadgets. This is predominantly true for African enterprises aiming to harness IoT for development; the transformation must align technology with people and processes. Leadership is a key enabler of this journey. Studies have shown that proactive committed leadership is crucial for successful IoT initiatives (Hartl & Hess, 2017; McCarthy et al., 2022). Leaders need to set a clear vision for the IoT, communicate its value, and guide their teams through change. Strong executive sponsorship can help overcome resistance and resource constraints, ensuring that IoT projects receive support. For example, Rajabzadeh and Fatorachian (2023) noted that management support, essentially strong leadership, is vital to communicate the value and benefits of IoT and drive necessary changes. Such digital leadership directly influences IoT-driven transformation while cultivating organizational agility.

Organizational agility, which is the ability to rapidly sense and respond to change, is another enabler of IoT adoption. Agile enterprises can quickly adapt their business processes to exploit IoT insights and new market opportunities. Research on digital transformation has found that organizational agility positively impacts transformation outcomes (AlNuaimi et al., 2022). This means that African firms with agile structures can pilot IoT solutions more swiftly and scale their work. Notably, effective leadership and clear digital strategies tend to enhance agility, creating a virtuous cycle of innovation. Finally, an innovation-oriented culture underpins IoT readiness. An organizational culture that encourages experimentation, continuous learning, and calculated risk-taking supports IoT adoption. This type of digital culture, which integrates new values and behaviors around technology, is increasingly seen as a critical driver of successful digital transformation (Mashinini & Sethibe, 2025). Fostering such a culture means that the staff is empowered to explore IoT applications and is not afraid of change. Managers are advised to cultivate a culture of innovation and technological readiness to ensure that IoT solutions are smoothly assimilated into daily operations (Rajabzadeh & Fatorachian, 2023). In the African business context, building an innovation culture can help surmount external challenges (such as infrastructure gaps or skill shortages) by unlocking employees' creativity and adaptability, thus enabling enterprises to find home-grown solutions for IoT implementation.

2.4. Technology–Organisation–Environment (TOE) Framework

The TOE framework provides a holistic lens for understanding enterprise technology adoption by examining three contexts: technology, organization, and environment (Díaz-Arancibia et al., 2024). This model posits that innovation adoption is driven by technological factors, organizational readiness, and external environmental forces (Nautwima et al., 2025). Technological context refers to the availability, quality, and relevance of technologies (both existing IT infrastructure and new IoT innovations) that influence adoption decisions (Rahayu & Day, 2015). The IoT involves factors such as network connectivity, data security, and device compatibility. Organizational context refers to the internal attributes of a firm, such as size, structure, resources, and top management support that determine digital readiness. This encompasses an enterprise's IT expertise, workforce digital skills, and changing culture, all of which affect its capacity to implement IoT solutions (Nautwima et al., 2022). The environmental context refers to external pressures and opportunities, including industry competition, supply chain demands, and government regulations (Qalati et al., 2022). The policy and market environment, such as regulatory standards for data and incentives for innovation, are precisely relevant to IoT. Applied to IoT adoption, TOE suggests that African enterprises embrace IoT when the technology is perceived as beneficial and accessible, the organization is prepared (financially and skill-wise), and the broader environment supports its adoption.

Studies in developing regions have shown that inadequate ICT infrastructure or cybersecurity concerns can impede technological readiness for IoT (Garrity, 2015; Kuaban et al., 2024). Similarly, many African firms face organizational hurdles, such as scarce digital talent and low awareness of IoT's business value. The environmental context is equally critical, as competitive pressure to modernize and government e-transformation initiatives can push firms toward IoT, whereas weak policy frameworks or high costs hinder them (Kuaban et al., 2024). By accounting for all three dimensions, the TOE framework underscores that successful IoT adoption in Africa requires not only new gadgets but also aligned internal capabilities and an enabling external ecosystem. This comprehensive view helps identify where interventions (e.g., improving Internet infrastructure or offering training and policy support) can elevate digital readiness and drive organizational transformation for IoT in African enterprises.

2.5. Dynamic Capabilities Theory (DCT)

Dynamic Capabilities Theory (DCT) focuses on an organization's ability to continuously adapt and innovate in the face of rapid technological change. It defines dynamic capabilities as a firm's capacity to integrate, build, and reconfigure internal and external competencies to address rapidly changing environments (Alrub & Sánchez-Cañizares, 2025). In essence, DCT extends the resource-based view by emphasizing how companies renew their resources and skills over time to sustain their competitive advantage amid disruption. Core dynamic capabilities are divided into three categories. The first category is sensing, which includes monitoring and identifying new opportunities or threats to technologies and markets. For IoT, this means early recognition of emerging digital trends and customer needs (Al-Moaid & Almarhdi, 2024). Enterprises with strong sensing capabilities can foresee IoT use cases (e.g., smart logistics and predictive maintenance) and understand the value of these innovations. Another category is seizing, which includes mobilizing resources to capture opportunities through new products, processes, or business models (Ellström et al., 2022). In the IoT context, this involves investing in IoT solutions and restructuring operations to implement data-driven services when an opportunity is sensed. Effective seizing may include forming IoT pilot teams, training staff, and partnering with technology providers. The last category is reconfiguring (transforming), which refers to the continuous renewal and realignment of the organization's assets and structures to maintain a fit with the changing environment (Y. Wang & Wang, 2017). This could entail recalibrating workflows, redefining roles, or upskilling employees to ensure that IoT integration is sustained and scalable as conditions evolve. Research confirms that organizations with higher dynamic capabilities tend to have more successful digital transformation outcomes (Al-Moaid & Almarhdi, 2024; Marx et al., 2021; Valdez-de-Leon, 2016). Thus, dynamic capabilities are highly pertinent to digital transformation and IoT adoption. Cultivating these adaptive capabilities can be a game changer for IoT readiness in African enterprises.

Many firms in emerging markets operate in volatile environments with resource constraints. Thus, they must be agile and innovative to overcome challenges (such as limited funding or infrastructure gaps) and leverage new technologies (Marx et al., 2021; Telukdarie et al., 2022). For example, a business that can sense shifting consumer preferences toward connected services, seize the moment by deploying an IoT-based solution, and reconfigure its processes to support that solution will outpace its less agile competitors. Such capabilities help firms adopt IoT and derive value from it by aligning IoT initiatives with strategic goals and local market needs (Alkhamery et al., 2020). Overall, DCT provides a human-centered and strategic perspective on IoT adoption. This highlights that beyond acquiring technology, African enterprises need to learn, innovate, and adopt flexible management practices to truly transform through the IoT. Building dynamic capabilities, like organizational learning, innovation routines, and change management, enables continuous digital readiness rather than one-off adoption, ensuring that IoT and other emerging technologies can be absorbed and exploited for sustained development

2.6. Institutional Theory (for Africa's Policy and Regulatory Context)

Institutional theory examines how the broader institutional environment, rules, norms, and belief systems in society shape organizational behavior. This posits that firms conform to institutional pressure to gain legitimacy and support. In the context of technology adoption, this means that companies are influenced by government mandates, industry norms, and cultural expectations when deciding whether to implement innovation. Three central types of isomorphic pressure exist. These include coercive, normative, and mimetic pressures (Dubey et al., 2019). Coercive pressure refers to formal regulations and policies that compel or incentivize adoption. In Africa, government initiatives and ICT policies (e.g., national digital strategies and data protection laws) act as coercive forces, pushing organizations toward digital transformation. For instance, public sector requirements for e-procurement or smart city projects can compel suppliers and partners to adopt IoT-based solutions. Conversely, a lack of clear regulations can create uncertainty, which hinders adoption. Normative pressures include professional standards, values, and education that encourage specific practices. Industry associations and standard-setting bodies often promote best practices for IoT (security standards and interoperability protocols), creating normative expectations for firms to follow (Oredo et al., 2019). In Africa's developing markets, international norms (such as ISO standards or global corporate policies on technology use) can strongly influence local enterprises to modernize their processes in line with their global peers. Mimetic pressure refers to the tendency to imitate successful organizations in the face of uncertainty. When early IoT adopters in an industry show performance gains, other firms feel pressured to mimic that adoption to remain competitive. These mimetic forces can be especially potent when firms look to regional "tech champions" or foreign investors as models for innovation. For example, if a leading African telecom or bank rolls out IoT-enabled services, smaller firms may follow suit simply because "everyone is doing it," seeking legitimacy through this similarity. Hence, institutional factors are profoundly relevant to IoT adoption in Africa's policy and regulatory contexts.

Governments play a dual role: they can enable adoption by providing supportive infrastructure, subsidies, or legal frameworks, or hinder it through restrictive regulations or bureaucratic inertia. A positive example is the push for harmonized ICT policies across Africa, such as data-sharing regulations and spectrum policies, which create a stable environment for IoT investment (Kuaban et al., 2024). Analysts have noted that IoT uptake in regions such as Central Africa will thrive only if supportive regulatory frameworks (addressing data privacy, cybersecurity, and interoperability) are in place (Kuaban et al., 2024). Likewise, normative social factors, such as the technological culture of a city or the digital skills prevalent in the workforce, can significantly impact readiness. In some African countries, strong informal networks and community innovation hubs generate normative pressure by spreading awareness of IoT solutions (e.g., for agriculture or health), thereby encouraging peer adoption. In summary, this theory highlights that institutional voids, such as gaps in formal institutions common in developing markets, can slow digital transformation. Many African enterprises operate amid unreliable regulations or weak enforcement; consequently, they may hesitate to commit to IoT without clear legal guidance on issues such as data ownership or IoT device standards. Therefore, it is crucial to address these institutional gaps by reforming policies and strengthening industry networks to ensure that African regulators and stakeholders create an environment in which enterprises feel both pressure and support.

3. METHODOLOGY

This study employs a traditional narrative literature review approach to examine how African enterprises are preparing for and responding to the digital transformation imperative, with a particular focus on Internet of Things (IoT) readiness. The objective was to synthesize conceptual perspectives and empirical findings across a diverse set of peer-reviewed journal articles to identify recurring themes, enabling and constraining factors, and context-specific insights shaping enterprise digitalization across the African continent. Unlike systematic reviews, which rely on strict protocols, keyword-based screening, and replicable search strategies, narrative reviews offer greater interpretive flexibility. This is valuable when addressing complex and multidisciplinary issues, such as digital infrastructure, institutional reform, enterprise management, and technological innovation in developing economies. As noted by Snyder (2019), narrative reviews are well suited for generating integrative insights in which scholarly work intersects multiple academic domains and practical contexts. Paré and Kitsiou (2016) similarly argue that this approach enables critical engagement with theory, empirical patterns, and broader contextual dynamics without the limitations imposed by narrow inclusion criteria.

This review examined 44 peer-reviewed journal articles published between 2015 and 2025, all sourced from reputable Scopus-indexed journals. Articles were selected based on their conceptual contribution, methodological rigor, African geographic relevance, and direct alignment with digital transformation discourse in enterprise settings. The synthesis was structured around four core thematic dimensions of enterprise IoT readiness.

a) digital infrastructure and ecosystem readiness,
b) human capital and digital skills gaps,

c) organisational agility, change management, and leadership, and
d) regulatory, institutional, and financing factors.

Each article was reviewed in full to enable a comparative analysis across thematic clusters and geographic settings, in line with Torraco's (2005) guidance, which emphasizes analytical consistency in narrative reviews. As recommended by Greenhalgh et al. (2018), this approach balances breadth and depth by enabling both theoretical reflection and empirical contextualization. The purpose of this review was not merely to summarize existing work but also to produce an integrated understanding that informs future research, policy, and enterprise strategy on digital transformation in Africa.

4. THEMATIC SYNTHESIS OF LITERATURE

This section provides a structured synthesis of the existing literature on multidimensional enablers and constraints that shape IoT readiness in African enterprises. Drawing from peer-reviewed Scopus-indexed studies, this synthesis identifies and clusters key thematic areas that recur in scholarly discussions, policy analyses, and case-based evaluations. This study aims to illuminate how African firms respond to or are hindered by contextual factors at both the macro and micro levels. These themes span digital infrastructure and ecosystems, human capital and skill development, internal organizational capabilities, and the broader regulatory and financing landscape. Together, they provide an integrated perspective on the practical realities and strategic imperatives of IoT adoption across continents. This synthesis highlights commonalities across sectors and regions and draws attention to the variability in readiness levels, which reflects Africa's diverse digital economy. This section lays the empirical foundation for identifying best practices, key gaps, and areas that require targeted policy and organizational intervention.

4.1. Digital Infrastructure and Ecosystem Readiness in Africa

African enterprises' IoT readiness is fundamentally shaped by the continent's digital infrastructure. Overall connectivity levels in Africa remain low relative to global standards, with most countries still reporting Internet penetration below 10% of their population (Park et al., 2020). Only a handful of nations (e.g., South Africa and Mauritius) approach the global average in terms of online access, whereas most others lag far behind, with over a dozen African countries having fewer than one in ten people online (ITU Publication Africa, 2021). Mobile broadband networks have significantly expanded coverage; however, gaps persist between rural and underserved areas. Crucially, a reliable electricity supply, which is indispensable for powering IoT devices and networks, is often lacking, and the average per capita electricity access remains under 30% in many African countries (Park et al., 2020). These core infrastructure deficits in Internet connectivity, power, and network coverage create a fragile foundation for IoT adoption, as illustrated in Figure 4.1.

Figure 1. Digital infrastructure deficit in Africa

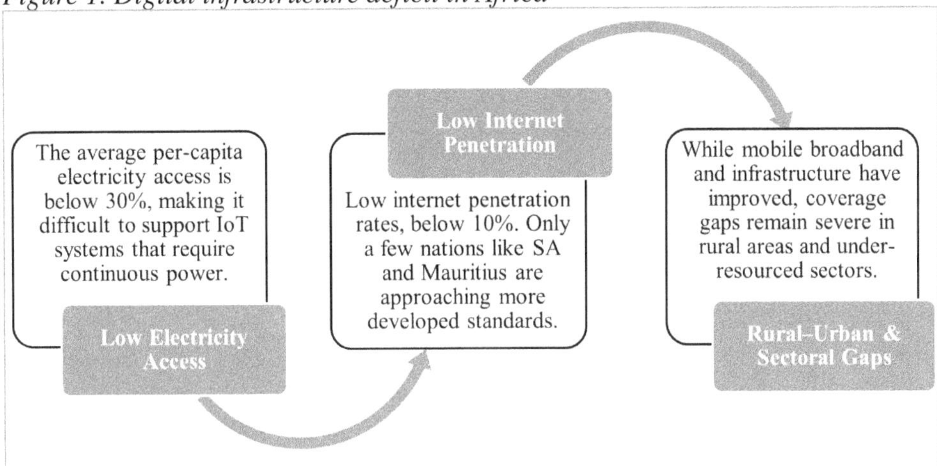

Source: Authors' construction (2025)

Nonetheless, recent years have seen concerted efforts to bolster Africa's digital ecosystem. Pan-African initiatives, such as the Smart Africa Alliance (aiming to establish a single digital market by 2030) and numerous national digital transformation strategies, signal a strong policy commitment to improving ICT infrastructure. Private sector investments are also accelerating. Submarine broadband cables and terrestrial fiber backbones are extending the Internet reach, while global cloud providers have begun establishing data centers on the continent. For instance, Africa's data center capacity is growing at over 12% annually, spurred by partnerships with hyperscale cloud firms such as Amazon Web Services, which opened its first African region in Cape Town, South Africa, and Microsoft Azure launched facilities in South Africa, with expansions to Nigeria, Kenya, and beyond (Abiodun, 2025). Similarly, telecom operators are rolling out 4G and piloting 5G networks in key markets to enhance mobile IoT connectivity (Israr et al., 2021). As depicted in Figure 4.2, these developments serve as critical enablers of IoT readiness across the region, as they improve bandwidth, nascent cloud computing infrastructure, and expanding mobile networks.

Figure 2. Emerging enablers of IoT readiness

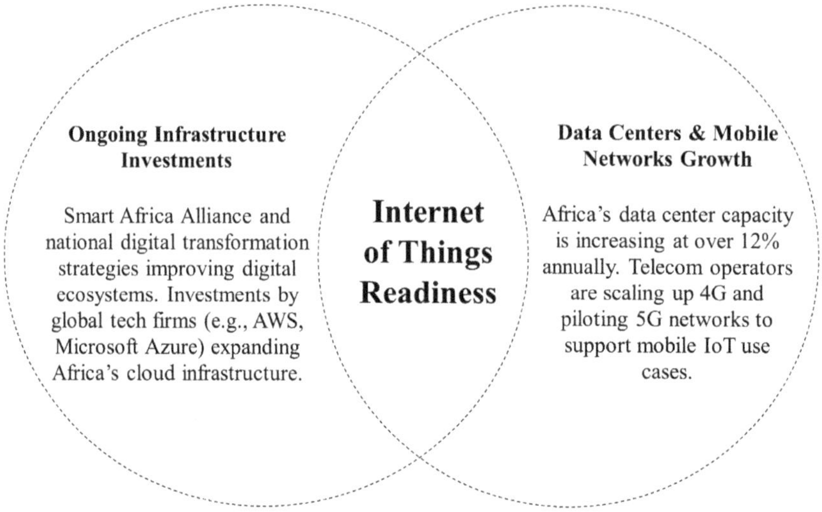

Source: Authors' construction (2025)

Despite this progress, persistent infrastructure gaps continue to hinder the deployment of IoT. Previous studies have consistently identified poor Internet connectivity and unreliable power supplies as common barriers to IoT uptake in sub-Saharan Africa (Dosumu et al., 2023; Iwayemi, 2018; Kuaban et al., 2024). The severity of these challenges varies across and within regions. Urban tech hubs may enjoy relatively better connectivity, whereas remote areas may face acute deficits (Kuaban et al., 2024). Sectoral differences are also evident in the results. For example, inadequate electricity and network infrastructure have been flagged as major impediments to IoT implementation in Nigeria's education sector (Iwayemi 2018). Similarly, a study of Rwanda's construction industry found that low awareness and poor Internet connectivity were the primary challenges in adopting IoT technologies at worksites (Dosumu et al., 2023). Such cases underscore that beyond national averages, IoT readiness differs widely by sector and locality. In summary, although Africa's digital infrastructure is gradually improving through strategic initiatives and investments, substantial constraints on connectivity, cloud access, and power reliability remain. These limitations must be addressed to unlock the full potential of IoT-driven transformation in African enterprises.

4.2. Human Capital and Digital Skills Gaps in Enterprise IoT Readiness

A critical determinant of IoT readiness in African enterprises is the availability of human capital with adequate digital literacy and technical competence. However, many African businesses face a pronounced digital skills gap that hampers their ability to adopt and leverage IoT. The literature documents a lack of digital skills as a significant barrier to technology adoption in the African context (Daramola & Etim, 2022). Limited digital literacy and a shortage of specialized IoT expertise within organizations can slow down digital transformation efforts. This skill deficit extends from frontline employees to management, where low awareness and understanding of new technologies can impede strategic adoption decisions and implementation. For instance, a study of SMEs in Zimbabwe found that 4IR technologies (including IoT) were adopted at low rates, partly because of ignorance or insufficient ICT knowledge among owners and managers (Munongo & Pooe, 2022). These findings underscore that even the best IoT strategies may falter without a workforce comfortable with digital tools and concepts.

The challenge for African enterprises is twofold: acquiring new talent with the requisite IoT skillsets and upskilling or reskilling the existing workforce. Skilled IoT professionals are in short supply, making talent acquisition highly competitive and expensive. Moreover, retaining such talent is difficult as global demand creates opportunities abroad, contributing to a "brain drain" of technology experts (Ebrahim & van den Berg, 2024). Consequently, companies must invest in continuous learning programs to develop their internal capabilities. Existing employees often need to be upgraded and reskilled to keep pace with evolving IoT roles and technologies (Gartoumi & Tekouabou, 2024). This entails not only technical training (e.g., in IoT systems, data analytics, and cybersecurity) but also fostering a culture of lifelong learning and adaptability. Proactively closes the digital skills gap through staff development enables enterprises to improve their IoT readiness and resilience.

Bridging the skill gap also requires collaborative approaches beyond individual firms. Effective talent development strategies frequently involve partnerships between educational institutions and training providers. The scarcity of IoT-skilled professionals has made industry–academia collaboration essential. Recent work emphasizes that partnering with universities and technical training programs is crucial for cultivating a competent IoT workforce and bridging the skill gap (Peter et al., 2022; Shan & Wang, 2024; Tondro et al., 2025). African enterprises are increasingly engaging in initiatives such as internship programs, curriculum co-design, and research collaborations with universities to ensure a pipeline of graduates equipped with relevant digital skills. These partnerships, often supported by public–private initiatives, help align academic output with industry needs and facilitate knowledge transfer. Therefore, African organizations can strengthen their human capital base for IoT adoption by leveraging external expertise and nurturing local talent. Overall, addressing human capital challenges through skill development, talent retention efforts, and educational partnerships, as displayed in Table 4.1, is pivotal for African enterprises to achieve digital readiness and drive successful IoT-enabled transformation.

Table 1. Human capital challenges and strategic response to IoT adoption

Human capital challenges	Strategic responses
Widespread Digital Skills Gap Many African enterprises struggle with low digital literacy and lack of specialized IoT expertise across all staff levels, from frontline workers to senior management.	**Industry–Academia Collaboration** Partnerships with universities and training institutes help bridge the skills gap through internships, curriculum co-design, and research programs suited to industry needs.
Talent Acquisition and Retention Issues The pool of skilled IoT professionals is limited, making hiring expensive and retention difficult due to brain drain and global competition for talent.	**Reskilling and Upskilling Existing Staff** Enterprises must invest in internal training for both technical (e.g. data analytics, cybersecurity) and soft skills to adapt to evolving IoT demands.

Source: Authors' construction (2025)

4.3. Organisational Agility, Change Management, and Leadership

Implementing IoT-driven transformations requires significant organizational agility and internal reconfiguration. Companies should often restructure their processes and organizational setups to fully leverage IoT. Research on digital transformation finds that firms need to overhaul traditional processes and structures, moving toward more agile operations and management practices (Zhang et al., 2025). Organizational agility, which is the ability to rapidly adapt and reconfigure resources, processes, and strategies, enables companies to replace legacy routines and redesign their structures to meet new technological demands (Ashrafi et al., 2019). Thus, businesses are better equipped to integrate IoT systems into their workflows and respond swiftly to emerging opportunities and disruptions by embracing agility. However, such changes are challenging. Organizational change management is crucial because resistance to change can undermine IoT initiatives.

Established firms that have long relied on successful legacy practices often exhibit greater reluctance to change and lower receptiveness to digital solutions. Rigid hierarchies and bureaucratic inertia in large organizations can further slow innovation (Zhang et al., 2025). Leadership plays a pivotal role in this regard. Visionary leaders with a clear digital transformation roadmap can align IoT projects with the company's strategic goals and culture. The literature indicates that leaders who are forward-looking and embrace change while focusing on customer and stakeholder needs are the most effective drivers of successful digitalization (Tagscherer & Carbon, 2023). As such, leadership can build organizational consensus, mitigate fear of change, and foster a culture that is open to IoT-driven innovation.

Table 2. Change management challenges and leadership to IoT adoption

Change Management challenges	Leadership as a transformation driver
Resistance to change Employees and managers accustomed to legacy systems may resist the introduction of IoT, especially in long-established firms with entrenched practices.	**Visionary leadership** Leaders who set a clear digital roadmap, communicate its benefits, and align transformation with strategic objectives are more likely to succeed.
Bureaucracy Slows Innovation Rigid organizational hierarchies often inhibit the rapid decision-making and experimentation needed for digital innovation.	**Culture of Innovation and Adaptability** Leaders must create a supportive environment that reduces fear of change and encourages learning, collaboration, and openness to technological experimentation.

Source: Authors' construction (2025)

Real-world IoT transformation journeys underscore the interplay between agility, change management, and leadership by articulating compelling visions and ensuring strategic alignment. For example, the Chinese appliance manufacturer Haier succeeded in its IoT-era digital transformation by continually adjusting its internal structure and management models to support new IoT-based strategies (Liu, 2023). This constant optimization, guided by strong leadership commitment, has allowed Haier to become more innovative and responsive to market needs. Such cases illustrate that, when firms cultivate agility, proactively manage change resistance, and have a bold vision of leadership, IoT transformations can deliver substantial competitive benefits.

4.4. Regulatory, Institutional, and Financing Factors in Africa

African enterprises adopting IoT face a complex external environment shaped by regulatory frameworks, institutional dynamics, and financing constraints. On the regulatory front, many countries are still developing clear policies regarding data governance, cybersecurity, and IoT-specific standards (Quaye et al., 2024). Although some progress has been made (for instance, South Africa's Protection of Personal Information Act provides robust data protection), other aspects of IoT regulations remain fragmented and underdeveloped. Many countries contend with complex and inconsistent regulations, where weak institutional frameworks, pervasive corruption, and bureaucratic red tape continue to hinder the ease of doing business (Ahsan et al., 2021; Asongu et al., 2018). Consequently, several African economies still rank low on ease-of-doing-business indices owing to cumbersome rules and ineffective governance structures (Luiz et al., 2017). These institutional fragilities, often manifested as political instability and inadequate law enforcement, create uncertainty for enterprises and investors (Adomako et al., 2024; Wang et al., 2020). In particular, poorly protected property rights and contract enforcement elevate the risk of disputes or expropriations, underscoring the need for stronger legal institutions (M. Wang et al., 2024). On a positive note, initiatives such as the African Continental Free Trade Area (AfCFTA) aim to streamline regulations and reduce trade barriers, offering a continent-wide framework to boost intra-African commerce and investment (Adomako et al., 2024). Such reforms at the macro-policy level are gradually creating a conducive business climate.

Access to finance remains a decisive factor in enterprise growth, and African firms have historically faced acute financing constraints in this regard. Studies have identified a lack of affordable credit as a predominant and persistent barrier to establishing and scaling businesses across the continent (Quartey et al., 2017). In practice, many small and medium-sized enterprises (SMEs) struggle to secure bank loans (Nautwima & Asa, 2021). For example, approximately 90% of small firms' loan applications are rejected by formal lenders, often due to insufficient collateral or information, and approximately 95% of African SMEs rely on personal savings or informal funding networks (Hamukwaya & Nautwima, 2019; Quartey et al., 2017). These financing gaps, driven by shallow financial systems and cautious banks, have direct consequences for firm performance and growth. However, recent trends have yielded promising results. The rise of fintech and alternative financing is revolutionizing financial inclusion, where mobile money transactions in Africa surpassed $1 trillion in 2022 and venture capital investment in African startups has rapidly grown (over $4 billion in 2022) to support new enterprises (African Development Bank, 2023). Combined with government and development initiatives to strengthen credit infrastructure, these emerging financing avenues help alleviate constraints. However, ensuring that such financial innovations and policies reach a broader base for SMEs remains crucial for fostering inclusive growth.

Table 3. Change management challenges and leadership to IoT adoption

Institutional and financial challenges	Responsive strategies
Weak Institutions and Bureaucracy Many African enterprises operate in environments marked by institutional weaknesses, such as inconsistent regulations, low contract enforcement, and bureaucratic inefficiencies, which increase operational uncertainty and risks.	**Progressive Policy Reforms at Regional Level** The African Continental Free Trade Area (AfCFTA) and other macro-level policy initiatives are gradually improving the regulatory climate by harmonizing standards and reducing trade barriers.
Access to Finance Barrier A significant proportion of African SMEs are excluded from formal credit markets. Roughly 90% of loan applications are rejected, and 95% of small firms rely on personal or informal funding due to lack of collateral or credit history.	**Fintech and Alternative Financing Offers** Rapid growth in mobile money and venture capital, such as over $1 trillion in mobile transactions and $4 billion in startup funding in 2022, signals a shift toward greater financial inclusion and support for tech-enabled enterprises.

Source: Authors' construction (2025)

5. DISCUSSION

The adoption of Internet of Things (IoT) technologies among African enterprises remains uneven and shaped by varying degrees of infrastructure readiness, digital skills, and institutional support. While progress has been made in terms of mobile network expansion, data center investments, and policy initiatives, such as the Smart Africa Alliance, the overall uptake of IoT solutions remains limited in many parts of the continent. Studies indicate that Internet penetration is still below 10 percent in most African countries, and electricity access remains unreliable, especially in rural and underserved areas. These infrastructure deficits create significant bottlenecks for widespread IoT deployment and limit innovation at the enterprise level (Park et al., 2020; ITU Publication Africa, 2021). Despite these challenges, IoT's potential for African enterprise development is substantial. Emerging use cases in sectors such as construction, manufacturing, and education demonstrate how sensor-enabled systems can improve productivity, reduce costs, and support real-time decision-making (Dosumu et al., 2023; Iwayemi, 2018). The expansion of mobile money, cloud infrastructure, and 5G pilots signals a growing digital ecosystem that can support smarter enterprise operations. Moreover, successful cases, such as Haier's IoT-enabled transformation, show how firms that embrace agility and leadership vision can leverage IoT to enhance competitiveness (Liu, 2023). As foundational barriers are gradually being addressed, IoT adoption is expected to play a transformative role in driving inclusive and technology-enabled enterprise development across Africa.

African organizations remain at varying levels of preparedness for Internet of Things (IoT) integration, with digital readiness constrained by infrastructure, human capital, and organizational limitations. While there have been notable improvements, such as expanding mobile broadband, increasing cloud infrastructure through partnerships with firms such as Amazon Web Services and Microsoft Azure, and national digital transformation strategies, widespread readiness remains limited. Internet penetration is still below 10 percent in most countries, and per-capita electricity access remains under 30 percent, particularly in rural and underserved regions (Park et al., 2020; ITU Publication Africa, 2021). These persistent infrastructure gaps reduce the capacity of organizations to deploy IoT systems reliably across operational environments. Internal digital capability is a critical determinant of connectivity and power. Many African enterprises face digital skill shortages at all levels, from frontline staff to executive leadership (Daramola & Etim, 2022). Limited ICT literacy and poor awareness among managers hinder informed decision-making regarding Internet of Things (IoT) investments (Munongo & Pooe, 2022). Moreover, organizational structures often lack the agility required to support innovation. Hierarchical and bureaucratic setups, which are common in large firms, may resist necessary internal reforms (Zhang et al., 2025). Therefore, effective IoT adoption requires more than just a technological upgrade. Enterprises must invest in upskilling their current staff, nurturing a culture of learning, and fostering partnerships with universities and training institutions to build a pipeline of IoT-competent professionals (Peter et al., 2022; Gartoumi & Tekouabou, 2024). Leadership commitment to organizational change, strategic alignment, and flexible restructuring are essential to support long-term IoT integration and enterprise transformation.

The existing literature on IoT adoption in Africa reveals important empirical and conceptual gaps that limit stakeholders' ability to fully understand and address the continent's unique challenges. Much of the research remains concentrated on infrastructural deficits, such as unreliable Internet connectivity and insufficient electricity access, particularly in rural and underserved areas (Dosumu et al., 2020; Dosumu et al., 2023; Kuaban et al., 2024). While these studies highlight significant barriers, they often do not explore how infrastructural limitations intersect with the sectoral or organizational dynamics of the healthcare system. For example, although some sectors, such as education and construction, have been examined (Iwayemi, 2018; Dosumu et al., 2023), other critical industries, such as manufacturing and healthcare, have received relatively less empirical attention despite their central role in economic development.

Moreover, the literature tends to focus on describing problems rather than proposing actionable strategies for enterprise-level changes. Longitudinal or comparative case studies tracing successful IoT transformation journeys across African firms are scarce. Real-world examples, such as Haier's experience in reconfiguring its structure for IoT integration (Liu, 2023), remain rare in the African context. This gap limits business leaders' ability to draw inspiration or identify best practices suited to local conditions. In addition, while the importance of organizational agility and leadership vision has been emphasized (Zhang et al., 2025; Tagscherer & Carbon, 2023), studies seldom provide concrete frameworks to guide leaders in fostering readiness for change. Research has also underrepresented the role of institutional and regulatory reforms in enabling IoT ecosystems. Although initiatives such as the African Continental Free Trade Area have been noted for their potential (Adomako et al., 2024), the practical implications of enterprise-level digital transformation remain underexplored. Furthermore, despite the growing interest in digital financing and fintech solutions, there has been limited assessment of how such tools directly support IoT investments among small and medium enterprises (Hamukwaya & Nautwima, 2019; African Development Bank, 2023). Addressing these gaps would enable researchers to generate more context-specific evidence, guide policymakers in reforming regulatory frameworks, and support business leaders in implementing scalable and sustainable IoT strategies that align with Africa's development priorities.

6. CONCLUSION

This study explored the dynamics of IoT adoption among African enterprises through a structured narrative literature review, highlighting both the promise and persistent challenges of digital transformation on the continent. Drawing from peer-reviewed articles published between 2015 and 2025, the review was organized into four thematic pillars: digital infrastructure and ecosystem readiness in Africa; gaps in human capital and digital skills in enterprise IoT readiness; organizational agility, change management, and leadership; and regulatory, institutional, and financing factors in Africa. Collectively, the findings reveal that while IoT holds substantial transformative potential for business innovation, productivity, and competitiveness, its deployment remains constrained by infrastructural limitations, digital skill shortages, leadership inertia, regulatory uncertainty, and financing gaps.

6.1. Policy Recommendations

Policymakers and development partners must prioritize investments in digital infrastructure, particularly broadband connectivity, power reliability, and cloud computing, to ensure foundational readiness for IoT deployment. This includes extending 4G and 5G coverage to rural and underserved areas and reinforcing initiatives such as the Smart Africa Alliance and AfCFTA to create a more integrated digital market. Enterprise leaders should foster organizational agility by reconfiguring internal structures, adopting change management strategies, and cultivating visionary leadership that aligns IoT projects with long-term strategic goals. To close the digital skills gap, businesses must invest in upskilling and reskilling initiatives supported by collaborative partnerships with academic institutions and technical training providers. On the financial front, stakeholders should expand access to alternative financing mechanisms, such as mobile money, venture capital, and blended finance instruments, to support IoT adoption, particularly among SMEs. Regulatory agencies must accelerate the formulation and enforcement of clear IoT-related policies, including data protection, cybersecurity, and technology standards, to create a stable and enabling environment.

6.2. Suggestions for Future Research

Future studies should address underexplored sectors, such as healthcare, agriculture, and manufacturing, to provide comparative case analyses of successful IoT implementation in African firms. Longitudinal research is also needed to track the evolution of IoT integration over time and evaluate its tangible impact on firm performance and resilience. Further investigation is warranted on how fintech solutions and digital financial services facilitate enterprise-level investments in IoT technologies. Researchers should also examine the intersection between gender, informality, and digital adoption to ensure that inclusive digital transformation strategies benefit all segments of African societies. Future research should generate context-rich, actionable insights that bridge the policy, enterprise, and technological dimensions of Africa's evolving digital ecosystem.

REFERENCES

Abiodun, K. (2025). Digital infrastructure & sustainable data centers investment in Africa: Role of Tier III & Tier IV. *International Journal of Multidisciplinary Research and Growth Evaluation*, *6*(1), 1878–1888. DOI: 10.54660/.IJMRGE.2025.6.1-1878-1888

Adomako, S., Shenkar, O., Liu, X., Amankwah-Amoah, J., & Ahsan, M. (2024). Editorial on doing business in Africa: Navigating opportunities and challenges in Africa's emerging markets. *Journal of International Management*, *30*(101189), 1–20. DOI: 10.1016/j.intman.2024.101189

African Development Bank. (2023). *African economic outlook 2023: Mobilizing private sector financing for climate and green growth in Africa*. African Development Bank Group. https://www.afdb.org/en/documents/african-economic-outlook-2023

Ahmetoglu, S., Che Cob, Z., & Ali, N. (2023). Internet of Things adoption in the manufacturing sector: A conceptual model from a multi-theoretical perspective. *Applied Sciences (Basel, Switzerland)*, *13*(3856), 1–21. DOI: 10.3390/app13063856

Ahsan, M., Adomako, S., & Mole, K. F. (2021). Perceived institutional support and small venture performance: The mediating role of entrepreneurial persistence. *International Small Business Journal*, *39*(1), 18–39. DOI: 10.1177/0266242620943194

Al-Moaid, N. A. A., & Almarhdi, S. G. (2024). Developing dynamic capabilities for successful digital transformation projects: The mediating role of change management. *Journal of Innovation and Entrepreneurship*, *13*(85), 1–26. DOI: 10.1186/s13731-024-00446-9

Alkhamery, N., Zainol, F. A., & Al-Nashmi, M. (2020). Conceptualizing the role of organizational capabilities in enhancing firms readiness for digital business transformation. *International Journal of Management*, *11*(12), 785–797. DOI: 10.34218/IJM.11.12.2020.072

AlNuaimi, B. K., Kumar Singh, S., Ren, S., Budhwar, P., & Vorobyev, D. (2022). Mastering digital transformation: The nexus between leadership, agility, and digital strategy. *Journal of Business Research*, *145*, 636–648. DOI: 10.1016/j.jbusres.2022.03.038

Alrub, Y. A., & Sánchez-Cañizares, S. M. (2025). Dynamic capabilities and digital transformation: Toward strategic planning in the digital age—Evidence from Palestine. *Administrative Sciences*, *15*(1), 21. Advance online publication. DOI: 10.3390/admsci15010021

Ashrafi, A., Zareravasan, A., Trkman, P., & Afshari, S. (2019). The role of business analytics capabilities in bolstering firms' agility and performance. *International Journal of Information Management, 47*, 1–15. DOI: 10.1016/j.ijinfomgt.2018.12.005

Asongu, S. A., Nwachukwu, J. C., & Orim, S.-M. I. (2018). Mobile phones, institutional quality and entrepreneurship in Sub-Saharan Africa. *Technological Forecasting and Social Change, 131*, 183–203. DOI: 10.1016/j.techfore.2017.08.007

Cruz, M. (Ed.). (2024). International Finance Corporation Research Series *Digital opportunities in African businesses*. World Bank Publications.

Daramola, O., & Etim, E. (2022). Affordances of digital platforms in sub-Saharan Africa: An analytical review. *The Electronic Journal on Information Systems in Developing Countries, 88*(4), 1–21. DOI: 10.1002/isd2.12213

Díaz-Arancibia, J., Hochstetter-Diez, J., Bustamante-Mora, A., Sepúlveda-Cuevas, S., Albayay, I., & Arango-López, J. (2024). Navigating digital transformation and technology adoption: A literature review from small and medium-sized enterprises in developing countries. *Sustainability (Basel), 16*(5946), 5946. Advance online publication. DOI: 10.3390/su16145946

Dosumu, O. S., Mahame, C., Niyitegeka, S., & Hahiirwuwambaza, J. A. (2023). Applications and challenges of adopting the Internet of Things (IoT) in the Rwandan construction industry. *Journal of Construction in Developing Countries, 28*(2), 81–100. DOI: 10.21315/jcdc-05-22-0098

Dubey, R., Gunasekaran, A., Childe, S. J., Blome, C., & Papadopoulos, T. (2019). Big data and predictive analytics and manufacturing performance: Integrating institutional theory, resource-based view and big data culture. *British Journal of Management, 30*(2), 341–361. DOI: 10.1111/1467-8551.12355

Ebrahim, A. Q., & van den Berg, C. L. (2024). The barriers to technology adoption among businesses in the informal economy in Cape Town. *South African Journal of Information Management, 26*(1), 1–13. DOI: 10.4102/sajim.v26i1.1872

Ellström, D., Holtström, J., Berg, E., & Josefsson, C. (2022). Dynamic capabilities for digital transformation. *Journal of Strategy and Management, 15*(2), 272–286. DOI: 10.1108/JSMA-04-2021-0089

Garrity, J. (2015). Harnessing the Internet of Things for global development. In SSRN *Electronic Journal* (pp. 1–61). DOI: 10.2139/ssrn.2588129

Gartoumi, K. I., & Tekouabou, S. C. K. (2024). Exploring African skills 4.0 required for 4IR industry: A systematic literature review. *Data & Policy, 6*(36), e36. Advance online publication. DOI: 10.1017/dap.2024.28

Gfrerer, A., Hutter, K., & Ströhle, T. (2021). Ready or not: Managers' and employees' different perceptions of digital readiness. *California Management Review, 63*(2), 94–117. DOI: 10.1177/0008125620977487

Greenhalgh, T., Thorne, S., & Malterud, K. (2018). Time to challenge the spurious hierarchy of systematic over narrative reviews? *European Journal of Clinical Investigation, 48*(6), 1–13. DOI: 10.1111/eci.12931

Hamukwaya, P. S., & Nautwima, J. P. (2019). Does microfinance really eradicate poverty in Africa? *Africa Growth Agenda, 16*(2).

Hartl, E., & Hess, T. (2017). The role of cultural values for digital transformation: Insights from a delphi study. *Twenty-Third Americas Conference on Information Systems, 23*, 1–10.

Hsu, C. W., & Yeh, C. C. (2017). Understanding the factors affecting the adoption of the Internet of Things. *Technology Analysis and Strategic Management, 29*(9), 1089–1102. DOI: 10.1080/09537325.2016.1269160

Israr, A., Yang, Q., Li, W., & Zomaya, A. Y. (2021). Renewable energy powered sustainable 5G network infrastructure: Opportunities, challenges and perspectives. *Journal of Network and Computer Applications, 175*(102910), 1–24. DOI: 10.1016/j.jnca.2020.102910

Issa, A., Hatiboglu, B., Bildstein, A., & Bauernhansl, T. (2018). Industrie 4.0 roadmap: Framework for digital transformation based on the concepts of capability maturity and alignment. *Procedia CIRP, 72*, 973–978. DOI: 10.1016/j.procir.2018.03.151

ITU Publication Africa. (2021). Digital trends in Africa 2021: Information and communication technology trends and developments in the Africa region 2017-2020. In *International Telecommunication Union Publication* (Vols. 2017–2020). https://elibrary.acbfpact.org/acbf/collect/acbf/index/assoc/HASH0146/faa3ee36/f864265c/9547.dir/Digital trends in Africa 2021.pdf

Iwayemi, A. (2018). Internet of Things: Implementation challenges in Nigeria. *American Journal of Engineering Research (AJER, 7*(12), 105–115. www.ajer.org

Kuaban, G. S., Nkemeni, V., Nwobodo, O. J., Czekalski, P., & Mieyeville, F. (2024). Internet of Things adoption in technology ecosystems within the Central African Region: The case of Silicon Mountain. *Future Internet, 16*(10), 376. Advance online publication. DOI: 10.3390/fi16100376

Liu, S. (2023). Digital transformation of enterprises in the mode of IoT - A case study of Haier. *Proceedings of the 2nd International Conference on Financial Technology and Business Analysis, 2*(1), 52–61. DOI: 10.54254/2754-1169/64/20231488

Lorenz, F., & Buchwald, A. (2023). Chief digital officers' social construction of and coping with digital transformation. *Academy of Management Proceedings, 2023*(1). DOI: 10.5465/AMPROC.2023.11220abstract

Luiz, J., Stringfellow, D., & Jefthas, A. (2017). Institutional complementarity and substitution as an internationalization strategy: The emergence of an African multinational giant. *Global Strategy Journal*, *7*(1), 83–103. DOI: 10.1002/gsj.1143

Marx, C., de Paula, D., & Uebernickel, F. (2021). Dynamic capabilities & digital transformation: A quantitative study on how to gain a competitive advantage in the digital age. *European Conference on Information Systems (ECIS)*. https://aisel.aisnet.org/ecis2021_rp/58

Mashinini, T., & Sethibe, T. (2025). A model of the interplay between leadership styles, culture and digital transformation. *South African Journal of Information Management*, *27*(1), 1–9. DOI: 10.4102/sajim.v27i1.1959

McCarthy, P., Sammon, D., & Alhassan, I. (2022). Digital transformation leadership characteristics: A literature analysis. *Journal of Decision Systems*, *32*(1), 79–109. DOI: 10.1080/12460125.2021.1908934

Michelotto, F., & Joia, L. A. (2024). Organizational digital transformation readiness: An exploratory investigation. *Journal of Theoretical and Applied Electronic Commerce Research*, *19*(4), 3283–3304. DOI: 10.3390/jtaer19040159

Moeti, M. N., Mokwena, S. N., & Selape, M. (2024). Factors influencing the adoption of Internet of Things in the agricultural sector in Limpopo province. *South African Journal of Information Management*, *26*(1), 1–8. DOI: 10.4102/sajim.v26i1.1669

Mphale, O., Gorejena, K. N., & Nojila, O. H. (2024). IoT adoption in Botswana's SMEs: Technological readiness and government initiatives. *Journal of Information Systems and Informatics*, *6*(4), 2419–2446. DOI: 10.51519/journalisi.v6i4.885

Munongo, S., & Pooe, D. (2022). Small and medium enterprises' adoption of 4IR technologies for supply chain resilience during the COVID-19 pandemic. *Journal of Transport and Supply Chain Management*, *16*(1), 1–11. DOI: 10.4102/jtscm.v16i0.747

Nautwima, J. P., & Asa, A. R. (2021). The impact of microfinance support on the development of manufacturing SMEs operating in Windhoek, Namibia. *Archives of Business Research*, *9*(12), 250–272. DOI: 10.14738/abr.912.11417

Nautwima, J. P., Asa, A. R., & Nendongo, V. P. (2022). Integrating gamification into middle school Mathematics curriculum : Game-based learning approach in Namibia. *International Journal of Operations Management*, *2*(4), 7–19. DOI: 10.18775/ijom.2757-0509.2020.24.4001

Nautwima, J. P., Obrenovic, B., Asa, A. R., Johannes, H. N., & Abueva, N. (2025). Determinants of technology adoption in small and medium-sized enterprises. *Sustainable Futures : An Applied Journal of Technology, Environment and Society*, *10*(100919), 100919. DOI: 10.1016/j.sftr.2025.100919

Ndubuaku, M., & Okereafor, D. (2015). Internet of things for Africa: Challenges and opportunities. *2015 International Conference on Cyberspace Governance - CyberAbuja2015, 9*, 23–31. DOI: 10.1007/978-3-319-04223-7_1

Ojubanire, O. A., Kolapo, A. G., Berbain, S., & Sebti, H. (2025). Awareness and perceived readiness of Industry4.0 in Africa: A case study of SMMEs in Nigeria. *Supply Chain Forum, 26*(2), 165–179. DOI: 10.1080/16258312.2024.2418794

Omol, E., Mburu, L., & Abuonji, P. (2024). Pioneering digital transformation in African: The path to maturity amidst unique challenges and opportunities. *Canadian Journal of Business and Information Studies*, *6*(2), 35–48. DOI: 10.34104/cjbis.024.035048

Oredo, J., Njihia, J., & Iraki, X. N. (2019). Institutional pressures and cloud computing adoption: The moderating effect of organizational mindfulness. *2019 IST-Africa Week Conference. IST-Africa, 2019*, 1–9. DOI: 10.23919/ISTAFRICA.2019.8764832

Paré, G., & Kitsiou, S. (2016). Methods for literature reviews. In Lau, F., & Kuziemsky, C. (Eds.), *Handbook of eHealth evaluation: An evidence-based approach* (pp. 157–179). University of Victoria., DOI: 10.1515/9781503604513-004

Park, M., Kayuni, M., Manda, T., & Kim, H. (2020). Modeling secure home area network based on IoT for resource constraints environment. *Journal of Computer and Communications*, *8*(1), 45–70. DOI: 10.4236/jcc.2020.81004

Peter, O., Pradhan, A., & Mbohwa, C. (2022). Industrial internet of things (IIoT): Opportunities, challenges, and requirements in manufacturing businesses in emerging economies. *Procedia Computer Science*, *217*, 856–865. DOI: 10.1016/j.procs.2022.12.282

Pingali, S. R., Singha, S., Arunachalam, S., & Pedada, K. (2023). Digital readiness of small and medium enterprises in emerging markets: The construct, propositions, measurement, and implications. *Journal of Business Research*, *164*(1139), 113973. DOI: 10.1016/j.jbusres.2023.113973

Qalati, S. A., Ostic, D., Sulaiman, M. A. B. A., Gopang, A. A., & Khan, A. (2022). Social media and SMEs' performance in developing countries: Effects of Technological-Organizational-Environmental factors on the adoption of social media. *SAGE Open*, *12*(2), 1–13. DOI: 10.1177/21582440221094594

Quartey, P., Turkson, E., Abor, J. Y., & Iddrisu, A. M. (2017). Financing the growth of SMEs in Africa: What are the contraints to SME financing within ECOWAS? *Review of Development Finance*, *7*(1), 18–28. DOI: 10.1016/j.rdf.2017.03.001

Quaye, W., Akon-Yamga, G., Akuffobea-Essilfie, M., & Onumah, J. A. (2024). Technology adoption, competitiveness and new market access among SMEs in Ghana: What are the limiting factors? *African Journal of Science, Technology, Innovation and Development*, *16*(7), 1023–1037. DOI: 10.1080/20421338.2024.2414949

Rahayu, R., & Day, J. (2015). Determinant factors of E-commerce adoption by SMEs in developing country: Evidence from Indonesia. *Procedia: Social and Behavioral Sciences*, *195*, 142–150. DOI: 10.1016/j.sbspro.2015.06.423

Rajabzadeh, M., & Fatorachian, H. (2023). Modelling factors influencing IoT adoption: With a focus on agricultural logistics operations. *Smart Cities*, *6*(6), 3266–3296. DOI: 10.3390/smartcities6060145

Satar, S. B. A., Hussin, A. R. C., & Ali, Y. S. (2018). Drivers of internet of things adoption in oil and gas industry. *Advanced Science Letters*, *24*(10), 7364–7370. DOI: 10.1166/asl.2018.12943

Savoury, R. D., & Burchell, J. M. (2021). Exploring the influential determinants of IoT adoption in the U.S. manufacturing sector. *International Journal of Applied Management and Technology*, *20*(1), 183–193. DOI: 10.5590/IJAMT.2021.20.1.10

Shan, Z., & Wang, Y. (2024). Strategic talent development in the knowledge economy: A comparative analysis of global practices. *Journal of the Knowledge Economy*, *15*(4), 19570–19596. DOI: 10.1007/s13132-024-01933-w

Sheth, J. N. (2011). Impact of emerging markets on marketing: Rethinking existing perspectives and practices. *Journal of Marketing*, *75*(4), 166–182. DOI: 10.1509/jmkg.75.4.166

Snyder, H. (2019). Literature review as a research methodology: An overview and guidelines. *Journal of Business Research*, *104*, 333–339. DOI: 10.1016/j.jbusres.2019.07.039

Tagscherer, F., & Carbon, C. C. (2023). Leadership for successful digitalization: A literature review on companies' internal and external aspects of digitalization. *Sustainable Technology and Entrepreneurship*, *2*(100039), 1–15. DOI: 10.1016/j.stae.2023.100039

Telukdarie, A., Dube, T., Matjuta, P., & Philbin, S. (2022). The opportunities and challenges of digitalization for SME's. *Procedia Computer Science*, *217*, 689–698. DOI: 10.1016/j.procs.2022.12.265

Tondro, M., Jahanbakht, M., & Ozay, D. (2025). Enhancing IoT technology acquisition in emerging economies: Insights and recommendations using analytical case study review of IoT startups. *Businesses*, *5*(20), 1–25. DOI: 10.3390/businesses5020020

Torraco, R. J. (2005). Writing integrative literature reviews: Guidelines and examples. *Human Resource Development Review*, *4*(3), 356–367. DOI: 10.1177/1534484305278283

Valdez-de-Leon, O. (2016). A Digital maturity model for telecommunications service providers. *Technology Innovation Management Review*, *6*(8), 19–32. DOI: 10.22215/timreview/1008

Wang, M., Wei, Y., Azumah, G., & Wang, C. L. (2024). African returnees in international knowledge transfer: A social capital perspective. *Journal of International Management*, *30*(101118), 1–26. DOI: 10.1016/j.intman.2023.101118

Wang, Y., & Wang, K. Y. (2017). How do firms tackle strategic change? A theoretical model of the choice between dynamic capability-based and ad hoc problem-solving approaches. *Journal of Organizational Change Management*, *30*(5), 725–743. DOI: 10.1108/JOCM-03-2016-0045

Wessel, L., Baiyere, A., Ologeanu-Taddei, R., Cha, J., & Jensen, T. B. (2021). Unpacking the difference between digital transformation and it-enabled organizational transformation. *Journal of the Association for Information Systems*, *22*(1), 102–129. DOI: 10.17705/1jais.00655

Westergren, U. H., Mähler, V., & Jadaan, T. (2024). Enabling digital transformation: Organizational implementation of the internet of things. *Information & Management*, *61*(103996), 103996. Advance online publication. DOI: 10.1016/j.im.2024.103996

Zhang, J., Zhang, S., Tan, X., & Zhao, H. (2025). The impact of digitalization on organizational agility: Evidence from the enterprise survey for innovation and entrepreneurship in China. [OPEN]. *Humanities & Social Sciences Communications*, *12*(917), 1–15. DOI: 10.1057/s41599-025-05256-2

Chapter 5
Enhancing Business Transformation Through Cybersecurity Frameworks in IoT Ecosystems:
Strategies for Risk Mitigation and Consumer Trust

Mercy Nyasha Magoso
http://orcid.org/0009-0007-9461-5098
Great Zimbabwe University, Zimbabwe

Clainos Chidoko
http://orcid.org/0000-0003-4530-7500
Great Zimbabwe University, Zimbabwe

Inos Chibidi
http://orcid.org/0009-0009-4201-1625
Great Zimbabwe University, Zimbabwe

Njodzi Ranganai
http://orcid.org/0000-0003-0451-1417
Great Zimbabwe University, Zimbabwe

ABSTRACT

The rapid growth of the Internet of Things (IoT) brings both opportunities and cybersecurity challenges for businesses. This chapter examines the integration of

DOI: 10.4018/979-8-3373-3441-7.ch005

cybersecurity frameworks within IoT ecosystems, highlighting their role in mitigating risks. It discusses frameworks like the NIST Cybersecurity Framework and ISO/IEC 27001 as essential tools for addressing vulnerabilities. Through qualitative analysis of case studies, the chapter assesses how organizations utilize these frameworks to identify risks, develop management strategies, and enhance security awareness. Findings reveal that adopting cybersecurity frameworks improves risk management and boosts consumer trust, enhancing operational resilience. The chapter concludes with recommendations for tailored frameworks, employee training, transparent consumer communication, and regular vulnerability assessments.

INTRODUCTION

The Internet of Things (IoT) has transitioned from a technological frontier to a foundational pillar of global business transformation. By weaving a digital fabric of sensors, actuators, and data analytics into the physical world, IoT ecosystems are unlocking unprecedented efficiencies, creating novel business models, and reshaping the interface between corporations and consumers. However, this hyper-connectivity introduces a commensurate expansion of the cyber-attack surface, making robust security not merely a technical requirement but a strategic imperative for sustainable growth and market acceptance. This chapter explores how the adoption of structured cybersecurity frameworks can mitigate these risks, enabling organizations to harness the full transformative potential of IoT while building and maintaining essential consumer trust.

The scale of IoT's integration into the global economy is staggering. By 2025, Gartner projects the total IoT market, encompassing hardware, software, and services, will reach US $821 billion, driven by a 16% compound annual growth rate from 2020 (Jinxuan et. al, 2020). This ecosystem will include over 2.6 billion enterprise-grade IoT machines in service, a 31% increase from 2020 levels (Jinxuan et. al, 2020). From a value-creation perspective, the McKinsey Global Institute estimates that IoT could generate up to US $11.1 trillion in annual economic impact by 2025, revolutionizing sectors from manufacturing and healthcare to urban infrastructure (Patel et al., 2017). Cellular connectivity, a key enabler, is also accelerating, with IDC forecasting 3.6 billion cellular-connected IoT lines by 2025, spurred by innovations like 5G and eSIM technology that expand the reach and viability of connected solutions (Shafique et al., 2020).

Despite this immense potential, the journey of digital transformation is fraught with peril. Cybersecurity risk has emerged as the single greatest inhibitor to scaling IoT initiatives. A 2022 McKinsey survey of 208 executives revealed that 54% of companies now cite cyber-risk as the primary barrier to broader IoT adoption, a significant increase from 40% in 2020 (Caso et al., 2023). The financial consequences of failing to manage this risk are severe. The global economic toll of all forms of cyber-crime is projected to hit US $10.5 trillion by 2025, a figure that has led the World Economic Forum (WEF) to classify large-scale cyber-physical attacks as a systemic threat on par with extreme weather events (Joshi et al., 2025). Breaches involving IoT and operational technology are disproportionately costly, while representing a smaller fraction of total enterprise endpoints, they are implicated in 34% of high-cost incidents, reflecting the potential for significant operational downtime and physical safety hazards (Dhirani et al., 2021).

In this context, IoT security transcends its traditional role as an IT back-office function and becomes a critical enabler of the broader digital-transformation agenda. As articulated in the WEF's "Global Cybersecurity Outlook 2025", the increasing integration of IoT in critical infrastructure means that the societal cost of a breach extends far beyond direct financial loss (Joshi et al., 2025). The report highlights that 84% of surveyed cyber-leaders anticipate that geopolitical instability will trigger a major cyber-physical event within the next two years (Joshi et al., 2025). This reality positions robust IoT security as a prerequisite for achieving strategic business objectives. McKinsey's research powerfully illustrates this link: buyers indicate a willingness to increase their spending on IoT solutions by 20-40% if their cybersecurity concerns were fully managed (Caso et al., 2023). This held-back demand represents a potential market uplift of $60-120 billion for suppliers by 2025, a clear incentive for embedding security into the core of product design and business strategy (Caso et al., 2023).

This chapter, therefore, argues that a systematic, structured framework to IoT cybersecurity is essential for mitigating risk, unlocking revenue, and building durable consumer trust. This section examines real-world case studies from diverse sectors and regions, compares leading international frameworks, and analyzes the economic and policy dimensions shaping the landscape. Finally, we will look toward future trends and provide actionable, managerial guidance for organizations of all sizes, from SADC-based SMEs to global multinationals, seeking to navigate this complex but rewarding domain.

LITERATURE REVIEW

The body of knowledge concerning the Internet of Things (IoT) and cybersecurity emphasizes the potential benefits offered by IoT technologies alongside the considerable risks they pose. This review amalgamates findings from both SADC nations and global sources to deliver a thorough insight into the challenges and strategies associated with cybersecurity in IoT settings.

The Dual Nature of IoT in SADC and Beyond

The Internet of Things (IoT) is a transformative force across various sectors, especially within the Southern African Development Community (SADC) (Echegu et al., 2024). This region, comprising 16 member states, has made significant technological advancements, positioning IoT as a catalyst for innovation in agriculture, healthcare, and manufacturing. Research by Suhandi et al. (2025) indicates that IoT enhances productivity and operational efficiency, evidenced by Mavhunga et al. (2021), who detail how IoT solutions have improved agricultural productivity in Zimbabwe through precision farming techniques. Farmers can monitor soil conditions and optimize resource allocation, leading to increased yields and improved food security.

In healthcare, IoT devices revolutionize patient care by facilitating remote monitoring and data collection (Nasir & Sultani, 2024). These devices enable real-time tracking of vital signs, improving response times and interventions, which is crucial in SADC countries with limited access to healthcare facilities (Liang et al., 2025).

The manufacturing sector also benefits from IoT integration (Ngepah et al., 2024). Intelligent technologies enhance automation, minimize downtime, and improve supply chain management, allowing organizations to monitor equipment performance and anticipate maintenance needs, thus boosting competitiveness.

However, the widespread adoption of IoT devices in SADC introduces vulnerabilities. Rukanda et al. (2020) highlight that many devices lack essential security features, making them susceptible to cyber threats. Cyberattacks can disrupt operations, compromise sensitive information, and threaten public safety, especially as IoT devices become integral to critical services. Weber (2017) emphasizes that expanding connectivity increases the potential for cybercriminal exploitation, underscoring the need for strong cybersecurity protocols to protect IoT ecosystems. A breach in one area can trigger a domino effect across multiple sectors (Atetedaye, 2024).

Addressing the dual nature of IoT its potential for innovation and inherent vulnerabilities is critical. Policymakers and industry leaders must prioritize comprehensive security frameworks. This includes establishing regulations that enforce security standards, promoting awareness of cybersecurity best practices, and fostering collaboration between public and private sectors. Investing in research and development is vital for enhancing IoT security, focusing on creating secure architectures from the outset (Xu et al., 2014). Additionally, educational programs that equip the workforce with skills to manage and secure IoT technologies will be essential as the digital landscape evolves (Omoseebi et al., 2025).

In summary, while IoT serves as a powerful driver of innovation, it also exposes users to significant security risks. A proactive strategy that balances the advantages of IoT with robust security measures is necessary to fully leverage this technology while mitigating associated risks. Ongoing research, collaboration, and strategic investments in cybersecurity will be crucial for navigating the complexities of IoT implementation and security in the SADC region and beyond.

Cybersecurity Frameworks

According to Alshar'e (2023), globally recognized cybersecurity frameworks like the NIST Cybersecurity Framework and ISO/IEC 27001 enhance organizational security by providing guidelines for managing cybersecurity risks. However, Vassilakos and Martin (2023) note that adoption in SADC countries is nascent, presenting challenges and opportunities for local businesses. Moyo et al. (2024) highlight uneven adoption, with larger South African enterprises integrating the NIST framework more readily, while smaller organizations face barriers like limited resources and inadequate infrastructure (Kortjan & Solms, 2014). This discrepancy underscores the need for tailored support for smaller enterprises, crucial to the region's economy.

Internationally, the NIST framework is valued for its flexibility, allowing organizations to customize their cybersecurity strategies (Lokare et al., 2025). Research by Alhassan & Islam (2021) shows that organizations using these frameworks significantly improve their risk management and operational resilience. The growing awareness of structured cybersecurity strategies in the SADC region is evident, but challenges for smaller organizations require collaborative efforts from both government and private sectors to provide necessary resources and training (Waiganjo et al., 2025). Embracing these frameworks is essential for enhancing organizational security and regional economic resilience against cyber threats.

Identifying Vulnerabilities in IoT

Recognizing vulnerabilities in Internet of Things (IoT) systems is essential for effective risk management in SADC nations. Chikandiwa et al. (2022) highlight insufficient authentication mechanisms in IoT devices, a concern echoed by Bertino & Islam (2017) on a global scale. Resource limitations in SADC exacerbate these issues, as organizations often overlook cybersecurity due to lack of awareness and financial constraints (Shaukat et al., 2021). This highlights the need for customized cybersecurity strategies that address the unique socio-economic contexts of SADC countries Vassilakos & Martin (2023). Comprehensive initiatives are vital for enhancing security and promoting awareness, enabling safer IoT technology implementation.

Risk Management Strategies

Effective risk management strategies are essential for reducing cybersecurity risks linked to Internet of Things (IoT) implementations. A comparative analysis by Nkosi et al. (2022) demonstrates that organizations in Botswana that proactively incorporated cybersecurity measures throughout their IoT lifecycle saw a notable decrease in security incidents. This observation is consistent with the suggestions of Kumar & Mallipeddi 2022, who highlight the necessity of integrating cybersecurity considerations from the initial design stage to the final deployment of IoT systems. Such a strategy guarantees that security is not merely an afterthought but a core component of the IoT framework, thus improving the resilience of these systems against potential threats. Moreover, the role of organizational culture in promoting cybersecurity awareness is of utmost importance. Research conducted by Shameli-Sendi et al. (2016) shows that organizations that emphasize investment in training and awareness initiatives experience lower instances of security breaches. This relationship highlights the imperative for organizations to develop a culture of security awareness, where employees are not only educated about possible threats but are also trained with the skills necessary to respond effectively. In the context of the SADC, fostering such a culture is particularly vital given the existing skills gaps in cybersecurity. Numerous organizations in the region encounter difficulties stemming from inadequate knowledge and resources, which can heighten vulnerabilities. By prioritizing cybersecurity education and nurturing an environment that promotes proactive engagement with security practices, organizations in SADC can significantly improve their overall cybersecurity stance (Abrahams et al., 2024). This comprehensive approach to risk management, which includes both technical strategies and organizational culture, is crucial for protecting IoT deployments against the ever-evolving landscape of cyber threats.

Consumer Trust and Behavioural Economics

Consumer trust plays a vital role in the effective adoption of Internet of Things (IoT) solutions. A study by Mbewe et al. (2021) in Zambia revealed that the application of robust cybersecurity measures significantly boosts consumer confidence in the security and dependability of IoT devices. This conclusion is supported by global research from Khan et al. (2020), which highlights the necessity of clear communication about data protection practices as a key factor in building trust between consumers and IoT service providers. The realm of data privacy and consumer protection is undergoing transformation, especially with the introduction of regulatory frameworks like the General Data Protection Regulation (GDPR) in Europe. This regulation has led organizations around the globe to acknowledge the importance of adhering to data privacy standards, thus enhancing consumer trust in the digital environment. Within the SADC, there is an increasing movement towards the implementation of comparable regulatory initiatives aimed at improving consumer protection. (Brey, 2016) A prominent instance is the Data Protection Bill in South Africa, which aims to create comprehensive guidelines for data management and privacy, as noted by Moyo (2024). The synchronization of local regulations with international standards not only aids in safeguarding consumer data but also strengthens the overall trust in IoT technologies across the SADC region. By establishing strong data protection protocols and ensuring open communication about these practices, organizations can greatly alleviate consumer concerns regarding the security of IoT devices (Iwuanyanwu et al., 2023). Consequently, this can foster a greater willingness among consumers to embrace IoT solutions, thereby propelling the expansion of the IoT market in these areas.

In conclusion, the interaction among robust cybersecurity practices, clear communication, and adherence to regulations is crucial for fostering consumer confidence. It is imperative for organizations to emphasize these factors to promote the uptake of IoT technologies, thereby leading to a more secure and reliable digital landscape.

The Power of Certification Labels and Third-Party Audits

The internal security architecture of IoT devices is often unclear to consumers, making certification labels and third-party audits vital for signaling quality and safety. Research shows that security labels significantly influence consumer choices; for example, a study with over 2,000 UK consumers found that a security label doubled the likelihood of selecting a secure device (Johnson et al., 2020). Buyers are willing to pay 20-40% more for devices with clear security labels, particularly those with de-identified cloud storage (Emami-Naeini et al., 2023). Additionally, security labels increased the mean willingness-to-pay by about £12 across various devices (Blythe et al., 2020). Labels certified by trusted entities can command a premium of around 30% (Garg & Kuehn, 2021). Consumer feedback emphasizes the need for ongoing audits and simpler label designs, such as binary or graded systems, while maintaining transparency about data practices (Caven et al., 2024; Chen et al., 2024). A multi-layer approach is optimal for conveying security information effectively.

Transparency Nudges and Choice Architecture

Beyond the point of sale, behavioral nudges can enhance secure behavior throughout a device's lifecycle. Systematic reviews show that transparency-oriented interventions, like dashboards visualizing data flows, increase users' sense of autonomy and trust (Amin et al., 2024). When users understand what data is collected, their intent to adopt the device and willingness to pay (WTP) rise. Choice architecture principles can facilitate security by defaulting to the most secure settings, significantly boosting adoption rates. Social proof nudges, such as indicating "80% of users have enabled automatic updates," further encourage compliance (Mirsch et al., 2017). However, these nudges must be transparent and reversible to avoid manipulation.

For managers, the takeaway is clear: investing in robust security is only part of the solution. Building consumer trust requires clear signals, transparent processes, third-party certification, and user experiences that promote safer practices.

Understanding the IoT Ecosystem and Its Unique Security Challenges

The Internet of Things (IoT) represents a paradigm shift in how businesses interact with the physical world, seamlessly integrating countless devices into a vast, interconnected network. This ubiquitous connectivity, while offering unprecedented convenience and innovation, simultaneously introduces a complex web of security challenges that demand careful consideration. This section delves into the fundamental components of the IoT ecosystem and dissects the unique vulnerabilities that make it a particularly attractive target for malicious actors.

The Anatomy of an IoT Ecosystem

According to Ansari et al., 2019 the heart of an IoT ecosystem is a synergistic convergence of diverse technologies working in concert to collect, transmit, process, and act upon data from the physical environment. Understanding the constituent parts of IoT is crucial to appreciating the multifaceted nature of its security landscape (see table 1).

Table 1. Anatomy of IoT Ecosystem

Component	Description	Key Features	Examples
Things (Devices)	Physical devices that collect and transmit data, equipped with sensors, actuators, and processors.	Vary in form factors, processing power, and connectivity options, contributing to security complexity.	Smart thermostats, medical implants, autonomous vehicle sensors, industrial control systems.
Networks	The communication backbone enabling data exchange between devices, cloud platforms, and applications.	Includes Wi-Fi, Bluetooth, 4G LTE, 5G, LPWANs (LoRaWAN, NB-IoT), and wired connections (Ethernet).	Smart cities, connected vehicles.
Cloud platforms	Central hubs that provide infrastructure for data ingestion, storage, processing, analysis, and management.	Device management, secure data collection, real-time analytics, and APIs for application development.	AWS IoT, Microsoft Azure IoT, Google Cloud IoT.
Applications	Software interfaces that provide users with insights, control capabilities, and automation based on processed data.	User-facing interfaces with a focus on security to protect data and device functionality.	Mobile apps for smart home control, industrial dashboards for factory performance.

Case Studies and Empirical Evidence

Atetedaye (2024) emphasizes that case studies are essential for extracting practical insights on the application and effectiveness of cybersecurity frameworks in Internet of Things (IoT) environments. For instance, a study of smart city projects in Cape Town demonstrated the significant impact of implementing the NIST cybersecurity framework, leading to reduced cybersecurity incidents and increased public confidence in the city's digital infrastructure (Ahmad et al., 2024). By addressing vulnerabilities, Cape Town created a safer environment, encouraging greater engagement with smart technologies (Sendjaja et al., 2024).

Similarly, healthcare institutions in Kenya that adopted ISO/IEC 27001 reported improved data protection practices, fostering trust among patients regarding their sensitive information (Muinga et al., 2020). Internationally, Singapore's smart transportation systems showcase the efficacy of structured cybersecurity protocols, which have enhanced operational efficiency and resilience against cyber threats (Ikpe & Ohwoekevwo, 2024: Oon Ling et al., 2019).

Overall, these case studies highlight the importance of structured cybersecurity frameworks in managing risks and building stakeholder trust. They underscore the necessity for ongoing research to adapt to evolving IoT and cybersecurity challenges, ensuring effective strategies for diverse organizations.

Real Life Case Studies of IoT Breaches

The consequences of IoT security failures extend far beyond data loss or financial fraud, impacting public safety, critical infrastructure, and even national security. The interconnectedness of IoT means that a vulnerability in one seemingly isolated device can have cascading effects across an entire system or even a city.

OT-Centric Example: Colonial Pipeline Ransomware Attack

The Colonial Pipeline incident serves as a stark reminder of the interconnectedness of operational technology (OT) and IT systems CISA, (2021). A ransomware attack disrupted the largest fuel pipeline in the U.S., causing widespread fuel shortages and panic, highlighting the vulnerability of industrial control systems and the cascading effects of breaches in interconnected environments.

Consumer-Device Example: Mirai Botnet

The Mirai Botnet attack demonstrated the power of compromised IoT devices, utilizing malware to scan for devices with default credentials, primarily DVRs and IP cameras (Krebs (2016). This botnet launched unprecedented DDoS attacks against high-profile targets, significantly disrupting internet access for millions and underscoring the need for secure device manufacturing and user responsibility in changing default passwords.

- **Jeep Cherokee Hack**: Researchers remotely hacked a Jeep Cherokee, gaining control of its steering and brakes through vulnerabilities in the Uconnect infotainment system, leading to a recall of 1.4 million vehicles Greenberg (2015).
- **Medical Device Vulnerabilities**: Vulnerabilities in internet-connected medical devices, such as pacemakers and insulin pumps, could lead to life-threatening consequences, including altered medication dosages and compromised patient privacy Medical Device Cybersecurity (2019).

Economic and Policy Dimensions of IoT Security

The decision to invest in IoT security is no longer solely a technical one; it is now heavily influenced by a complex interplay of economic incentives and a rapidly evolving regulatory landscape. Understanding these dimensions is crucial for any leader responsible for a digital transformation strategy.

Quantifying the Cost of a Breach

The financial impact of a cybersecurity incident can be catastrophic, especially in IoT-rich environments where digital failures can lead to physical disruptions. While global averages serve as a useful benchmark, regional data offers a more nuanced perspective for businesses in different markets. The global economic toll of cyber-crime is projected to reach US $10.5 trillion annually by 2025 (Joshi et al., 2025). In the SADC, the financial consequences are particularly severe. According to IBM's 2024 "Cost of a Data Breach" report, the average cost of a cybersecurity incident for a South African company is R53.1 million (approximately US $2.8 million) (Wang et al., 2025). Across the SADC bloc, cyber-crime is estimated to drain nearly US $1.9 billion from the economy each year (Vassilakos and Martin (2023). For many small and medium-sized enterprises (SMEs) in the region, a single major breach can be catastrophic, potentially exceeding their entire annual IT budget and posing an existential threat.

Key Regulatory Developments

Governments worldwide are responding to cybersecurity threats by enacting legislation that shifts the responsibility for security from the end-user to manufacturers and service providers. Key regulations impacting IoT deployments include the EU General Data Protection Regulation (GDPR), which, while not specific to IoT, mandates principles like privacy by design and by default, requiring organizations to conduct Data Protection Impact Assessments (DPIAs) for high-risk processing, obtain explicit consent, and notify authorities of data breaches within 72 hours (Wachter, 2018). Organizations often use standards like ISO 27001 or ETSI EN 303 645 to demonstrate compliance with the GDPR's requirements for appropriate technical and organizational measures. The African Union's Malabo Convention, officially the "AU Convention on Cyber Security and Personal Data Protection," aims to create a harmonized legal framework across the continent, obliging member states to adopt national laws that require technical and organizational security measures for electronic communications and data processing. As more SADC nations ratify this convention, it will establish a mandatory compliance baseline for IoT security in the region (Nimigan, 2019). The U.S. IoT Cybersecurity Improvement Act of 2020 leverages the federal government's purchasing power to enforce minimum-security standards by mandating compliance with NIST guidelines for all federally procured IoT devices, thereby incentivizing manufacturers globally to adopt these standards (Möller, 2023). Finally, Australia's 2023-2030 Cybersecurity Strategy aims to impose mandatory minimum cybersecurity standards on all network-connectable products sold in the country, effectively transferring the security burden to manufacturers and importers, who will need to provide statements of compliance (Harkin et al., 2022).

Supply-Chain Security and Downstream Financial Exposure

An organization's security is only as strong as its weakest link, and in the realm of IoT, that weak link is often found in the supply chain. Attacks targeting software dependencies, third-party components, and firmware update mechanisms are increasingly common, with the global cost of software supply-chain attacks projected to rise from $46 billion in 2023 to $60 billion by 2025 (Kumar & Mallipeddi, 2022). On average, a single supply-chain incident can cost an organization about $4.35 million, while critical infrastructure events may lead to hundreds of millions in indirect losses (Pandey et al., 2020). In response to this escalating threat, cybersecurity frameworks are evolving; for instance, the new NIST Cybersecurity Framework (CSF) 2.0 includes a dedicated "Govern" function that emphasizes Cybersecurity Supply Chain Risk Management (SCRM). Similarly, Australia's national strategy prioritizes SCRM for critical infrastructure (Harkin et al., 2022). Compliance requirements are also tightening; in the U.S., federal suppliers must attest to NIST's SCRM guidance (SP 800-161), and the EU's forthcoming Cyber Resilience Act (CRA) is expected to mandate the use of a Software Bill of Materials (SBOM) and formal vulnerability handling processes for IoT vendors. Consequently, for organizations, vetting suppliers, demanding transparency via SBOMs, and embedding security requirements into contracts are evolving from optional best practices to essential compliance activities. Cost-benefit analyses indicate that dedicating at least 1.5% of an IT budget to a SCRM program can yield a positive Net Present Value (NPV) within three years if the probability of a breach exceeds 8% (Mayeke, 2025).

Case-Study Matrix: IoT Security in Practice

To ground the discussion in practical reality, this section presents a matrix of five case studies from diverse sectors across Africa and Asia. These examples illustrate how different organizations have adopted cybersecurity frameworks to achieve measurable operational benefits and enhance stakeholder trust.

Table 2. IoT security case-study matrix

Case	Sector	Cybersecurity framework used	Measurable outcomes	Relevance to consumer trust
Cape Town, South Africa	Smart City / Utilities	NIST IoT-Enabled Smart-City Framework (Karie et al., 2021)	26% reduction in non-revenue water in pilot precincts within 12 months of smart meter rollout (Gyrard et al., 2018). Security Operations Center incident resolution time reduced from 48 hours to 14 hours after NIST playbook alignment (Mhangara et al., 2016).	It demonstrates competent and efficient municipal governance, building citizen trust that public funds and resources are managed effectively and securely.
Kenya	Public Healthcare	Hybrid model mapping NIST CSF and ISO/IEC 27001 controls to Ministry of Health eHealth standards (Hautamäki & Kokkonen, 2020).	22% mean revenue growth in four public hospitals due to closing billing leakages with digital systems. 31% faster patient-scheduling cycles. Average vulnerability findings per connected medical device fell from 7.4 to 2.1 in six months (Muinga et al., 2020).	Improved financial health and operational efficiency of hospitals directly translates to better and more reliable patient care, enhancing public confidence in the healthcare system's digital transformation.
Singapore	Land Transport	IMDA "IoT Cyber-Security Guide" (extending NIST CSF) and CSA Cybersecurity Labelling Scheme (CLS-IoT) (Ferro-Escobar et al., 2022).	37% year-on-year decrease in transport-sector IoT security incidents following enforcement of the CLS. 4.8% improvement in mean bus-fleet availability through secure predictive maintenance analytics.	Visible security labels (CLS) on public infrastructure and a quantifiable reduction in incidents provide commuters with tangible assurance of the system's safety and reliability.

continued on following page

Table 2. Continued

Case	Sector	Cybersecurity framework used	Measurable outcomes	Relevance to consumer trust
Zimbabwe	Agriculture	ISO/IEC 27001 Annex A controls and FAO "Digital Village" cyber-safety checklist (aligned with NIST SP 800-183) (Zengeya et al., 2021).	Pilot project showed 18% increase in maize output and 12% reduction in water usage. Reported cyber-incidents dropped to zero after implementing a key-rotation policy.	Securing farm data and control systems protects farmers' livelihoods and ensures food supply chain integrity, building trust among agricultural cooperatives and downstream buyers.
Botswana	Discrete Manufacturing	ISO/IEC 27001:2022, encouraged by the Botswana Bureau of Standards (Mphale, et al. 2024).	Downtime from cyber-related PLC outages fell from 9.2 hours/quarter to 2.3 hours/quarter. External audit confirmed a 96% control-implementation score, up from an 84% baseline before certification.	ISO 27001 certification acts as a trusted, internationally recognized signal to B2B customers that the manufacturer's production lines are resilient and secure, protecting against supply chain disruptions.

Comparative Analysis of Key Cybersecurity Frameworks

Choosing the right cybersecurity framework is a critical strategic decision. While many frameworks exist, they differ in scope, prescriptiveness, and applicability to IoT-specific challenges. Below we compare four IoT-relevant frameworks on philosophy, mechanism and IoT control depth (see table 3).

Table 3. Key Cybersecurity Frameworks

Dimension	NIST Cybersecurity Framework (CSF) 2.0 + SP 800-213	ISO/IEC 27001:2022 + 27400	Australian Cybersecurity Strategy (2023-2030)	U.S. IoT Cybersecurity Improvement Act (2020)
Core Philosophy	An outcome-based, voluntary framework (Identify, Protect, Detect, Respond, Recover, Govern) to manage enterprise-wide cyber risk.	A certifiable standard for an Information Security Management System (ISMS), focusing on risk assessment and the implementation of a broad set of controls.	A national policy initiative to make Australia a world leader in cybersecurity by 2030, mandating baseline standards for critical infrastructure and connected products.	A federal law mandating minimum security standards for IoT devices procured by the U.S. government.
IoT-Specific Controls	Explicit and Granular. NIST SP 800-213A provides a detailed catalog of 17 baseline device capabilities (e.g., secure boot, authenticated updates, asset ID) that are explicitly mapped to the CSF functions (Fagan et al., 2021).	Implicit and Guideline-Based. The core standard is technology-agnostic. IoT specifics are provided in a separate guideline, ISO/IEC 27400, which details controls for device lifecycle, constrained cryptography, and onboarding processes (Malatji, 2023).	Mandatory and Standards-Aligned. The strategy mandates "minimum cybersecurity standards for all network-connectable products." It explicitly references alignment with international standards like ISO 27001 and IEC 62443 for IoT/OT environments (Harkin et al., 2022).	Mandatory and NIST-Aligned. The Act legally requires federal agencies to only purchase IoT devices that comply with NIST's guidance. This effectively makes NIST SP 800-213/213A the mandatory baseline for the vast U.S. federal market (Möller, 2023).
Mechanism	Guidance and best practices. Adoption is voluntary for the private sector but often used as a de facto standard.	Third-party accredited certification. The ISO 27001 certificate is a globally recognized market signal of security maturity.	National legislation (Cyber Security Act 2024) and regulatory enforcement. Requires manufacturers to issue compliance statements (Harkin et al., 2022).	Federal procurement law. Compliance is a prerequisite for selling IoT devices to U.S. government agencies.
Best for...	Organizations seeking a flexible, risk-based language to communicate with stakeholders and a detailed technical baseline for IoT device capabilities.	Organizations seeking a globally recognized certification to demonstrate security diligence to customers and partners, particularly in international markets.	Manufacturers and service providers operating in or selling to the Australian market, especially in critical infrastructure sectors.	Any IoT device manufacturer targeting the U.S. federal government, with significant downstream influence on the broader commercial market.

METHODOLOGY

This chapter employs qualitative research methodology to investigate the integration of cybersecurity frameworks within Internet of Things (IoT) ecosystems, focusing on data collection and case study analysis. A literature review identified key themes and gaps in existing research (Lawami and Ilegbedion, 2024), guiding the selection of relevant case studies from organizations in SADC countries and beyond. Thematic analysis, including coding, revealed significant themes related to the research objectives (McLeod, 2024). A cross-comparative analysis was conducted to contextualize findings across different cases, enhancing understanding of how organizations mitigate IoT-related cybersecurity risks. To ensure reliability, a member-checking process engaged participants to confirm data interpretations. While the qualitative approach offers deep insights, its specificity may limit generalizability (Ugwu & Eze, 2023). Future research could adopt a mixed-methods strategy to expand findings across diverse IoT contexts (Ahmed et al., 2024). Ultimately, this methodology aims to assist organizations in developing effective cybersecurity strategies within IoT frameworks.

RESULTS

The results of the chapter yield critical insights into the integration of cybersecurity frameworks within Internet of Things (IoT) ecosystems. Analyzing case studies and existing literature provides a comprehensive understanding of how organizations can effectively manage cybersecurity risks associated with IoT deployment. The results are organized into several key themes: enhanced risk management, vulnerabilities present in IoT systems, the importance of cybersecurity frameworks, and their impact on consumer trust.

Improved Risk Management

Organizations that have effectively adopted cybersecurity frameworks have noted considerable enhancements in their risk management strategies. Case studies from South Africa and Zimbabwe demonstrated that the implementation of the NIST Cybersecurity Framework allowed these organizations to systematically recognize and prioritize risks associated with their IoT devices. For example, a smart manufacturing firm in South Africa employed the framework to perform regular vulnerability assessments, resulting in a 30% decrease in security incidents over the course of a year. This proactive strategy enabled prompt reactions to potential threats and fostered a culture of ongoing monitoring and enhancement.

Vulnerabilities in IoT Systems

The investigation uncovered prevalent vulnerabilities in IoT systems across various sectors. Numerous organizations reported challenges related to weak authentication methods and inadequate encryption protocols, rendering their devices vulnerable to unauthorized access. A case study centered on agricultural IoT applications in Zimbabwe revealed that several devices were devoid of critical security features, raising concerns regarding data integrity and privacy. This observation is consistent with international literature, which highlights that many IoT devices entering the market fail to meet sufficient security standards, thereby heightening the risk of cyberattacks.

The Importance of Cybersecurity Frameworks

The study highlighted the essential function of cybersecurity frameworks in assisting organizations to manage the intricacies of IoT security. The NIST Cybersecurity Framework and ISO/IEC 27001 were often referenced as valuable instruments for developing strong cybersecurity practices. Organizations that embraced these frameworks saw improved communication and collaboration among stakeholders, resulting in more thorough security strategies. For example, a healthcare provider in Kenya that adopted ISO/IEC 27001 reported enhancements in data management processes, which not only protected patient information but also ensured adherence to new data protection regulations.

Effect on Consumer Trust

A key finding was the positive relationship between strong cybersecurity practices and consumer trust. Organizations that emphasized cybersecurity and openly communicated their data protection initiatives experienced heightened levels of consumer confidence. For instance, a smart home technology firm in Botswana found that effective security measures and transparent communication regarding data management resulted in a 25% rise in customer satisfaction ratings. This observation aligns with international research indicating that consumers are more inclined to engage with IoT solutions when they believe their data is secure.

Challenges Encountered

Despite the favorable results associated with the implementation of cybersecurity frameworks, organizations encountered numerous challenges. Resource limitations, particularly within small and medium enterprises (SMEs), obstructed the execution of comprehensive cybersecurity strategies. A significant number of organizations indicated difficulties in allocating financial resources and personnel towards cybersecurity initiatives, resulting in an inconsistent application of security measures. Furthermore, the scarcity of cybersecurity expertise in the region presented substantial obstacles to the effective implementation and upkeep of security protocols.

In conclusion, the findings underscore the necessity of adopting structured cybersecurity frameworks to mitigate risks associated with the deployment of IoT. Organizations that successfully implement these frameworks can improve their risk management strategies, address vulnerabilities inherent in IoT systems, and foster consumer trust. Nevertheless, challenges such as constrained resources and the imperative for enhanced cybersecurity skills must be addressed to fully capitalize on the advantages of these frameworks and ensure the secure integration of IoT technologies. These insights provide crucial guidance for organizations aiming to navigate the complexities of cybersecurity in an increasingly interconnected environment.

Importance of Enhanced Risk Management

The results indicate that organizations that adopt structured cybersecurity frameworks, such as the NIST Cybersecurity Framework, significantly enhance their risk management capabilities. This is particularly important in the context of IoT, where the rapid growth of interconnected devices introduces intricate security challenges. By systematically identifying and prioritizing risks, organizations can allocate resources more effectively, ensuring that critical vulnerabilities are addressed promptly. The proactive approach to risk management illustrated in the case studies shows that organizations are beginning to regard cybersecurity as a strategic priority rather than merely a compliance requirement. This shift is essential for fostering resilience in an environment where cyber threats are becoming increasingly sophisticated. As organizations embrace this viewpoint, they not only protect their assets but also position themselves to take advantage of the competitive advantages offered by IoT technologies.

Addressing Vulnerabilities in IoT Systems

The identification of widespread vulnerabilities in IoT systems underscores the urgent need for improved security standards and practices. Various organizations have encountered difficulties related to weak authentication and inadequate data encryption, which serve as significant points of exploitation for cybercriminals. These observations align with global research indicating that numerous IoT devices are launched with insufficient security measures, often due to the pressures of rapid market entry. To mitigate these vulnerabilities, organizations must emphasize the implementation of strong security protocols during the development phase of IoT devices. This includes the incorporation of security features such as rigorous password policies, encryption, and regular software updates. Furthermore, collaboration among stakeholders including manufacturers, regulators, and consumers is crucial to establish industry-wide standards that enhance the security of IoT ecosystems.

Effectiveness of Cybersecurity Frameworks

The study highlights the effectiveness of established cybersecurity frameworks in helping organizations navigate the intricacies of IoT security. The NIST Cybersecurity Framework and ISO/IEC 27001 are acknowledged as essential tools that provide structured approaches for managing security risks. These frameworks not only facilitate compliance with regulatory requirements but also foster a culture of security awareness within organizations. The positive results associated with these frameworks suggest that organizations should prioritize training and capacity-building initiatives to empower employees across all levels. By cultivating a security-conscious culture, organizations can significantly reduce the likelihood of human errors, which often play a major role in cybersecurity breaches. Moreover, as organizations experience the advantages of these frameworks, they may advocate for their broader adoption within their industries, thereby contributing to a more secure IoT ecosystem.

Impact on Consumer Trust

This study emphasizes the essential link between robust cybersecurity measures and consumer trust. Organizations that openly share their data protection policies and exhibit a dedication to cybersecurity are more inclined to gain consumer confidence, particularly in the Internet of Things (IoT) domain, where privacy issues are significant. Case studies indicate that focusing on cybersecurity not only safeguards data but also improves reputation and cultivates customer loyalty. Clear communication regarding data management and security is vital. As regulatory frameworks develop, organizations that proactively tackle these challenges are likely to achieve a competitive advantage in drawing in and keeping customers.

Challenges and Future Directions

The study underscores the considerable challenges that organizations encounter when attempting to implement effective cybersecurity measures, especially within small and medium enterprises (SMEs) that frequently lack adequate resources. Financial and human resource limitations impede the development of strong security protocols, resulting in an inconsistent application of best practices. To address these challenges, enhanced collaboration among stakeholders such as government bodies, industry associations, and educational institutions is crucial. Programs that provide training and support for SMEs can assist in closing the cybersecurity skills gap. Policymakers should also explore incentives to promote investments in cybersecurity, thereby improving the security of the IoT landscape. Incorporating cybersecurity frameworks into IoT strategies is essential for reducing risks and fostering consumer trust. By implementing systematic cybersecurity measures, organizations can more effectively protect themselves against threats while leveraging the transformative capabilities of IoT. Tackling resource constraints and promoting industry collaboration will be essential for optimizing the advantages of these frameworks as the IoT landscape continues to develop.

CONCLUSION

This chapter has explored the critical intersection of the Internet of Things (IoT) and cybersecurity, highlighting the challenges and opportunities that arise from their integration. The findings stress the importance of established cybersecurity frameworks, such as the NIST Cybersecurity Framework and ISO/IEC 27001, which provide structured approaches for identifying and mitigating cybersecurity risks in interconnected IoT environments. Implementing these frameworks enhances organizations' risk management capabilities and fosters resilience against emerging threats.

The research identifies widespread vulnerabilities, particularly related to weak authentication and inadequate data encryption, underscoring the need for robust security protocols and comprehensive industry standards. Additionally, effective cybersecurity practices correlate strongly with consumer trust, as organizations that prioritize transparent data protection strategies are more likely to build confidence among users.

Challenges persist, especially for small and medium enterprises (SMEs) that often lack resources and expertise. Collaboration among stakeholders is vital to enhance cybersecurity awareness and skills. Continuous research is necessary to adapt to evolving threats and integrate innovative solutions into existing frameworks, ensuring that cybersecurity measures are essential for managing risks and fostering trust in an increasingly interconnected world.

RECOMMENDATIONS

In light of the findings presented in this chapter, a series of essential recommendations are proposed to enhance the integration of cybersecurity frameworks within

Internet of Things (IoT) ecosystems. These recommendations aim to improve risk management practices, address vulnerabilities, foster consumer trust, and support organizations, particularly small and medium enterprises (SMEs), in navigating the complex landscape of IoT security.

Adoption of Structured Cybersecurity Frameworks

Organizations should prioritize the adoption of established cybersecurity frameworks, such as the NIST Cybersecurity Framework and ISO/IEC 27001. These frameworks provide comprehensive methodologies for identifying, assessing, and mitigating cybersecurity risks. It is vital for organizations to invest in training programs that ensure employees at all levels are familiar with these frameworks and understand their importance in managing IoT security. Regular audits and assessments should be conducted to evaluate the effectiveness of these frameworks and implement necessary adjustments.

Strengthening Security Protocols in IoT Devices

To address the vulnerabilities identified in various IoT systems, organizations must focus on establishing robust security measures during the design and development phases of IoT devices. This includes Enhancing Authentication Mechanisms: The implementation of strong authentication protocols, such as multi-factor authentication, is crucial to prevent unauthorized access to devices. Data Encryption: It is essential to ensure that data transmitted between IoT devices and servers is encrypted to protect against interception and tampering. Regular Software Updates: Organizations should create processes for timely updates and patches to resolve known vulnerabilities and enhance device security.

Industry Collaboration for Standardization

Collaboration among diverse stakeholders including manufacturers, industry associations, regulatory bodies, and consumers is essential for the creation of comprehensive security standards applicable to IoT devices. Organizations should participate in initiatives that promote the formulation of these standards, ensuring that security considerations are embedded in IoT devices from the outset. This collective endeavor can also facilitate the sharing of best practices and resources, thus enhancing the overall security of the IoT ecosystem.

Promoting Cybersecurity Awareness and Training

Organizations ought to dedicate resources to cybersecurity awareness initiatives that educate employees on the importance of cybersecurity and their roles in maintaining it. Regular training sessions should cover subjects such as recognizing phishing attempts, safe data handling techniques, and incident reporting procedures. Cultivating a culture of security awareness will help reduce the likelihood of human errors, which often play a significant role in the success of cyberattacks.

Supporting Small and Medium Enterprises (SMEs)

Given the resource constraints faced by SMEs, targeted support programs are crucial to help them implement effective cybersecurity strategies. Governments and industry organizations should consider launching initiatives that provide: Financial Assistance: Grants or subsidies to enable SMEs to invest in cybersecurity infrastructure and training. Access to Resources: Offering SMEs access to cybersecurity tools, resources, and expertise, including partnerships with cybersecurity firms or educational institutions. Simplified Compliance Guidelines: Developing clear and user-friendly guidelines that assist SMEs in comprehending and complying with cybersecurity regulations and best practices.

Enhancing Consumer Communication

Organizations must prioritize transparent communication with consumers regarding their data protection practices. This includes Clear Privacy Policies: Providing privacy policies that are straightforward and outline how consumer data is collected, used, and protected. Incident Response Communication: Establishing protocols for timely communication with consumers in the event of a data breach, ensuring they are informed and aware of potential risks. Feedback Mechanisms: Creating avenues through which consumers can voice their concerns and offer feedback on data security practices, thereby fostering trust and engagement.

Encouraging Ongoing Research and Development

Ultimately, there should be a concerted effort to promote continuous research and development in the field of IoT security. This entails funding research initiatives that explore innovative security solutions, the development of new technologies, and the identification of emerging threats. Collaboration among academia, industry, and government can drive advancements in cybersecurity practices that keep pace with the rapidly evolving IoT landscape. By implementing these recommendations, organizations can significantly enhance their cybersecurity posture in the context of IoT, effectively manage risks, and cultivate consumer trust. The proactive adoption of structured frameworks, collaboration among stakeholders, and a dedication to continuous improvement will be essential for securing the future of interconnected technologies. As the IoT landscape continues to progress, these strategies will aid organizations in navigating the complexities of cybersecurity and leveraging the full potential of IoT innovations.

Forward-Looking Trends in IoT Security

The IoT landscape is in a constant state of flux, with emerging technologies creating both new opportunities and new vectors for attack. Staying ahead of the curve requires anticipating these trends and understanding their implications for security frameworks (see table 4).

Table 4. Trends in IoT security

Emerging trend	Description and opportunity	Probable risk profile and required framework updates
5G, Edge and Fog Computing	The rollout of 5G Standalone (SA) networks enables ultra-reliable low-latency communication (URLLC) and massive machine-type communication (mMTC). This allows processing to move from the cloud to the network edge (MEC) or even to the device itself (fog), reducing latency for applications like autonomous vehicles and remote surgery.	**Risk:** "Slice-pivot" attacks, where an attacker moves laterally from a low-security network slice to a high-security one. Misconfigured orchestration APIs can also lead to data leakage or DDoS amplification (Narciandi-Rodriguez et al., 2025). **Framework Update:** 3GPP standards need to evolve to include a "Zero-Trust Edge" profile, mandating mutual attestation between network functions and MEC applications. NIST CSF should incorporate guidance on "Dynamic Slice Posture Management" (Dutta, et al., 2020).
AI/ML-based threat detection	Artificial Intelligence (AI) and Machine Learning (ML) models are being deployed at the edge to perform real-time anomaly detection. Federated learning allows multiple devices to collaboratively train a model without sharing their raw, sensitive data, enhancing both privacy and detection speed (Bukhari, et al., 2024).	**Risk:** AI model poisoning, where an attacker injects malicious data to corrupt the learning process. Adversarial attacks can trick models into misclassifying threats. **Framework Update:** NIST CSF 2.0's new focus on SCRM must be extended to the "ML Supply Chain." Frameworks need controls for model validation, adversarial robustness testing, and explainability to ensure that AI-driven decisions can be trusted and audited (Dutta, et al., 2020).
Blockchain for device integrity	Lightweight distributed ledgers are being used to create an immutable record of a device's lifecycle. This includes registering firmware hashes, security patch updates, and data provenance, making it possible to cryptographically verify device and data integrity from the factory to the field (Radanliev, 2024).	**Risk:** 51% of attacks on smaller, private blockchains can rewrite history. Private keys stored on insecure devices can be compromised, allowing an attacker to impersonate a legitimate device on the ledger. **Framework Update:** ISO/IEC 27001 needs a new control annex for "Distributed Ledger Technology Security," covering node hardening, consensus mechanism security, and smart contract auditing. Best practices should mandate pairing on-chain hashes with off-chain, hardware-based secure elements (Radanliev, 2024).
Metaverse-linked IoT scenarios	The convergence of IoT with augmented and virtual reality (AR/VR) is creating the "Spatial IoT." Digital twins of factories are controlled by operators in a virtual environment, and haptic feedback suits respond to real-world sensor data. This blurs the line between the physical and digital realms.	**Risk:** "Reality privilege escalation," where a virtual exploit has physical consequences (e.g., hacking an avatar to crash a real-world drone). Biometric data (gait, iris scans) used for avatar control creates massive privacy risks not covered by current policies (Radanliev, 2024). **Framework Update:** NIST SP 800-53 needs a new control family for "Extended Reality (XR) Identity Management," addressing the secure binding of biometric data to digital avatars and mandating spatial-anchored data minimization principles (Radanliev, 2024).

To prepare for this future, organizations must adopt a posture of continuous adaptation. Security architecture must be built on Zero-Trust principles, assuming no part of the network is inherently secure. Privacy Impact Assessments must be extended to cover new data types like biometric and immersive sensor streams. And leaders must begin mapping their current controls to emerging standards drafts to avoid future compliance gaps.

Managerial and Practical Implications

While the strategic importance of IoT security is clear, implementation can be daunting, especially for resource-constrained organizations. This section provides practical guidance for two key audiences: large multinational corporations and Small and Medium-sized Enterprises (SMEs) in regions like SADC. To secure executive buy-in and budget allocation, security leaders must frame their proposals in financial terms. A clear cost-benefit analysis (CBA) moves the conversation from technical jargon to business value (see table 5).

Table 5. A Cost-Benefit Outline for Justifying Investment

Financial metric	Key components for IoT security	How to quantify for a Business Case
Capital Expenditure (CAPEX)	**Hardware:** Secure-by-design gateways, sensors with built-in secure elements, network segmentation hardware. **Software:** Initial licenses for IoT device management platforms, security information and event management (SIEM) systems. **One-Time Services:** Initial security architecture design, penetration testing, and framework implementation consulting (Tedeschi et al., 2018).	Amortize hardware and one-time costs over the expected asset lifecycle to present a realistic annual cost. Use vendor quotes and consulting proposals for firm figures.
Operational Expenditure (OPEX)	**Managed Services:** Subscriptions for Managed Detection and Response (MDR), threat intelligence feeds. **Personnel:** Salaries for security analysts, cost of ongoing training and certification. **Recurring Costs:** Cloud hosting for IoT data, patch management services, annual certification/audit fees (Tedeschi et al., 2018).	Tag each OPEX line item to a specific risk it mitigates. Use subscription pricing and headcount costs. A good rule of thumb is to budget 60% of total security spend for OPEX and 40% for CAPEX (Joshi et al., 2025).
Return on Investment (ROI)	**ROI = (Benefits - Annual OPEX) / Total CAPEX** Benefits = **(Breach Cost Avoidance + Operational Efficiency Gains + Revenue Enablement)**	**Breach Cost Avoidance:** Use regional data multiplied by the percentage reduction in breach likelihood your program aims to achieve. **Operational Gains:** Quantify the value of increased uptime and resource savings **Revenue Enablement:** Factor in the 20-40% potential revenue uplift from "held-back demand" identified by McKinsey (Caso et al., 2023).

Guidance for large Multinationals

Large organizations face challenges in IoT security, including scale, consistency, and supply chain management. Establishing a centralized IoT security office is vital, using a hybrid framework that combines ISO 27001 and NIST SP 800-213. This ensures uniformity across units. Organizations should also enforce secure supply chain practices, requiring suppliers to provide a Software Bill of Materials (SBOM) and comply with security standards.

For resource-constrained firms, especially SMEs, the focus should be on risk reduction with minimal investment. Initially, they can use free tools to identify security gaps and prioritize low-cost controls. Adopting a "secure-by-design" approach for new projects will further enhance their security posture.

DIRECTIONS FOR FUTURE RESEARCH

Future investigations within the domain of the Internet of Things (IoT) and cybersecurity should prioritize several pivotal areas to tackle emerging challenges and improve security protocols. Initially, it is crucial to develop and enhance cybersecurity frameworks specifically designed for IoT environments, as current frameworks may not adequately address the unique challenges presented by various device types and dynamic networks. In-depth research on vulnerability assessment and threat modeling tailored to IoT devices is also necessary to pinpoint common vulnerabilities and create adaptive threat models that progress alongside technological advancements. Furthermore, examining the influence of emerging technologies such as artificial intelligence, machine learning, and block chain on IoT security could yield significant insights into improving threat detection and ensuring data integrity. Grasping the human factors that contribute to cybersecurity risks is essential for formulating effective training and awareness initiatives, as is the evaluation of policy and regulatory frameworks to guarantee compliance while upholding strong security measures. Documenting case studies that highlight successful implementations of cybersecurity frameworks in IoT settings will aid in disseminating best practices, while research on collaboration among stakeholders can promote the sharing of threat intelligence and resources. By concentrating on these areas, future research can greatly enhance the establishment of a more secure IoT ecosystem, ultimately nurturing a culture of security awareness that is crucial for the widespread adoption and trust in IoT technologies.

REFERENCES

Abrahams, T., Farayola, O., Kaggwa, S., Uwaoma, P., Hassan, A., & Dawodu, S. (2024). Cybersecurity Awareness and Education Programs: A Review of Employee Engagement and Accountability. Computer Science and IT Research Journal. Vol 5. page (100-119).

Ahmad, I., Anyanwu, A., Onwusinkwue, S., Dawodu, S., Akagha, O., & Ejairu, E. (2024). Cybersecurity Challenges in Smart Cities: A Case Review of African Metropolises. *Computer Science and IT Research Journal.*, *5*(2), 254–269. DOI: 10.51594/csitrj.v5i2.756

Alhassan, I., & Islam, K. A. (2021). Credit management strategies and financial performance of industrial goods sector in Nigeria. *Indian Journal of Finance and Banking*, *8*(1), 59–74.

Alshar'e, M. (2023). Cyber Security Framework Selection: Comparision of NIST and ISO27001. Applied computing Journal, Volume 3, Issue 1, (pp. 245-255).

Amin, M. S., Kim, S., Rishat, M. A. S. A., Tang, Z., & Ahn, H. (2024). A Systematic Literature Review of Privacy Information Disclosure in AI-Integrated Internet of Things (IoT) Technologies. *Sustainability (Basel)*, *17*(1), 8. DOI: 10.3390/su17010008

. Ansari, M., Ali, S., & Alam, M. (2019). A Synergistic Approach for Internet of Things and Cloud Integration: Current Research and Future Direction.

Atetedaye, J. (2024). *Cybersecurity in the Internet of Things (IoT)*. Challenges and Solutions.

Bertino, E., & Islam, N. (2017). Botnets and internet of things security. *Computer*, *50*(2), 76–79. DOI: 10.1109/MC.2017.62

Blythe, J. M., Johnson, S. D., & Manning, M. (2020). What is security worth to consumers? Investigating willingness to pay for secure Internet of Things devices. *Crime Science*, *9*(1), 1. DOI: 10.1186/s40163-019-0110-3

. Brey, Z., Chisadza, S., Ludin, A., & Stern, M. (2016). Consumer Protection in SADC.

Bukhari, S. M. S., Zafar, M. H., Abou Houran, M., Qadir, Z., Moosavi, S. K. R., & Sanfilippo, F. (2024). Enhancing cybersecurity in Edge IIoT networks: An asynchronous federated learning approach with a deep hybrid detection model. *Internet of Things : Engineering Cyber Physical Human Systems*, *27*, 101252. DOI: 10.1016/j.iot.2024.101252

Caso, J., Cole, Z., Patel, M., & Zhu, W. (2023). Cybersecurity for the IoT: How trust can unlock value. *McKinsey & Company, 7.*

Caven, P., Zhang, Z., Abbott, J., Ma, X., & Camp, L. (2024, May). Comparing the Use and Usefulness of Four IoT Security Labels. In *Proceedings of the 2024 CHI Conference on Human Factors in Computing Systems* (pp. 1-31). DOI: 10.1145/3613904.3642951

Chen, C. C., Shu, D., Ravishankar, H., Li, X., Agarwal, Y., & Cranor, L. F. (2024, May). Is a Trustmark and QR code enough? The effect of IoT security and privacy label information complexity on consumer comprehension and behavior. In *Proceedings of the 2024 CHI Conference on Human Factors in Computing Systems* (pp. 1-32). DOI: 10.1145/3613904.3642011

. Chikandiwa, C. T., Zviyita, I., & Mapudzi, H. (2022). Social Media and the COVID-19 Disinfodemic in the Digital Space: Disempowering the Public and Threatening Public Health. *Acta Universitatis Danubius. Communicatio, 16*(2).

CISA. (2021, May 27). Advisory: Colonial Pipeline Incident. Cybersecurity and Infrastructure Security Agency. https://www.cisa.gov/news-events/cybersecurity-advisories/aa21-147a

Dhirani, L. L., Armstrong, E., & Newe, T. (2021). Industrial IoT, cyber threats, and standards landscape: Evaluation and roadmap. *Sensors (Basel), 21*(11), 3901. DOI: 10.3390/s21113901 PMID: 34198727

Dutta, A., & Hammad, E. (2020, September). 5G security challenges and opportunities: A system approach. In *2020 IEEE 3rd 5G world forum (5GWF)* (pp. 109-114). IEEE.

. Echegu, A., & Agwu, C. University VII, Kampala International. (2024). Introduction to the Transformative Potential of the Internet of Things (IoT) in East Africa. INOSR Scientific Research. 11. (page 8-16).

Emami-Naeini, P., Dheenadhayalan, J., Agarwal, Y., & Cranor, L. F. (2023). Are Consumers Willing to Pay for Security and Privacy of {IoT} Devices. In *32nd USENIX Security Symposium (USENIX Security 23)* (pp. 1505-1522).

Fagan, M., Marron, J., Brady, K. G.Jr, Cuthill, B. B., Megas, K. N., Herold, R., & Hoehn, B. (2021). Iot device cybersecurity guidance for the federal government. *NIST Special Publication, 800*, 213.

Ferro-Escobar, R., Vacca-González, H., & Gómez-Castillo, H. (2022). Smart and sustainable cities in collaboration with IoT: the Singapore success case. In *Machine learning for smart environments/cities: An IoT approach* (pp. 213–243). Springer International Publishing. DOI: 10.1007/978-3-030-97516-6_12

. Garg, A. V., & Kuehn, A. (2021). Squeezing the Cybersecurity Lemons–A Labeling Regime for IoT Products.

Greenberg, A. (2015, July 21). Hackers Remotely Kill a Jeep on the Highway—With Me in It. Wired. https://www.wired.com/2015/07/hackers-remotely-kill-jeep-highway/

Gyrard, A., Zimmermann, A., & Sheth, A. (2018). Building IoT-based applications for smart cities: How can ontology catalogs help. *IEEE Internet of Things Journal*, *5*(5), 3978–3990. DOI: 10.1109/JIOT.2018.2854278 PMID: 34734100

Harkin, D., Mann, M., & Warren, I. (2022). Consumer IoT and its under-regulation: Findings from an Australian study. *Policy and Internet*, *14*(1), 96–113. DOI: 10.1002/poi3.285

Hautamäki, J., & Kokkonen, T. (2020, June). Model for cyber security information sharing in healthcare sector. In *2020 International Conference on Electrical, Communication, and Computer Engineering (ICECCE)* (pp. 1-5). IEEE. DOI: 10.1109/ICECCE49384.2020.9179175

Ikpe, A. & Ohwoekevwo, J. (2024). Intelligent Transportation Systems as a Pivotal Instrument in the Development of Smart Cities in the 21st Century.

Jinxuan, T., Tianjun, M., & Qianwen, L. (2020). Trends Prediction of Big Data: A Case Study based on Fusion Data, Procedia Computer Science, Volume 174, Pages 181-190, ISSN 1877-0509, https://doi.org/DOI: 10.1016/j.procs.2020.06.073

Johnson, S. D., Blythe, J. M., Manning, M., & Wong, G. T. (2020). The impact of IoT security labelling on consumer product choice and willingness to pay. *PLoS One*, *15*(1), e0227800. DOI: 10.1371/journal.pone.0227800 PMID: 31978096

Joshi, A., Moschetta, G., & Winslow, E. (2025). Global cybersecurity outlook 2025. In *World Economic Forum (WEF), Geneva, Switzerland, Tech. Rep* (Vol. 1).

Karie, N. M., Sahri, N. M., Yang, W., Valli, C., & Kebande, V. R. (2021). A review of security standards and frameworks for IoT-based smart environments. *IEEE Access : Practical Innovations, Open Solutions*, *9*, 121975–121995. DOI: 10.1109/ACCESS.2021.3109886

Khan, S., Parkinson, S., Grant, L., Liu, N., & Mcguire, S. (2020). Biometric systems utilising health data from wearable devices: Applications and future challenges in computer security. *ACM Computing Surveys*, *53*(4), 1–29. DOI: 10.1145/3400030

Kortjan, N., & Solms, R. (2014). A conceptual framework for cyber security awareness and education in SA. *South African Computer Journal = Suid-Afrikaanse Rekenaartydskrif, 52*(52), 29–41. DOI: 10.18489/sacj.v52i0.201

Krebs, B. (2016). Who makes the IoT Things Attacking https://www.google.com/search?q=BrianKrebs.com? KrebsOnSecurity. https://krebsonsecurity.com/2016/10/who-makes-the-iot-things-attacking-briankrebs-com/

Kumar, S., & Mallipeddi, R. R. (2022). Impact of cybersecurity on operations and supply chain management: Emerging trends and future research directions. *Production and Operations Management, 31*(12), 4488–4500. DOI: 10.1111/poms.13859

Liang, W., Rajuroy, A., Chaudhary, P., Cai, M., & Johnson Mary, B. (2025). IoT and Cultural Knowledge in Transforming Healthcare Operations.

Lokare, A., Bankar, S., & Mhaske, P. (2025). Integrating Cybersecurity Frameworks into IT Security: A Comprehensive Analysis of Threat Mitigation Strategies and Adaptive Technologies.

Malatji, M. (2023, January). Management of enterprise cyber security: A review of ISO/IEC 27001: 2022. In *2023 International conference on cyber management and engineering (CyMaEn)* (pp. 117-122). IEEE. DOI: 10.1109/CyMaEn57228.2023.10051114

Mayeke, N. R. (2025). *Evaluating the Cost-Benefit Dynamics of Cybersecurity Compliance Investments: A Multi-Sectoral Analysis Across Financial*. Educational, and Ecommerce Industries.

Mbewe, E. S., & Chavula, J. (2021, December). Security mental models and personal security practices of Internet users in Africa. In *International Conference on e-Infrastructure and e-Services for Developing Countries* (pp. 47-68). Cham: Springer International Publishing.

Medical Device Cybersecurity. (2019). *FDA's Role and Public Health Mission*. U.S. Food and Drug Administration.

Mhangara, P., Mudau, N., Mboup, G., & Mwaniki, D. (2016). Transforming the City of Cape Town from an Apartheid City to an Inclusive Smart City: The Long March to a Sustainable, Inclusive and Prosperous City. In *Smart Economy in Smart Cities: International Collaborative Research: Ottawa, St. Louis, Stuttgart, Bologna, Cape Town, Nairobi, Dakar, Lagos, New Delhi, Varanasi, Vijayawada, Kozhikode, Hong Kong* (pp. 951–983). Springer Singapore.

Mirsch, T., Lehrer, C., & Jung, R. (2017). *Digital nudging: Altering user behavior in digital environments. Proceedings der 13.* Internationalen Tagung Wirtschafts-informatik.

Möller, D. P. (2023). NIST cybersecurity framework and MITRE cybersecurity criteria. In *Guide to Cybersecurity in Digital Transformation: Trends, Methods, Technologies, Applications and Best Practices* (pp. 231–271). Springer Nature Switzerland. DOI: 10.1007/978-3-031-26845-8_5

Moyo, A., Makota, J., & Kabote, F. (2024). Changes in the Data and Information Systems in Zimbabwe: Lessons from Legislation and Policy Post 2018. *Lighthouse: The Zimbabwe Ezekiel Guti University Journal of Law, Economics and Public Policy*, 1-15.

Mphale, O., Gorejena, K. N., & Nojila, O. H. (2024). IoT Adoption in Botswana's SMEs: Technological Readiness and Government Initiatives. *Journal of Information Systems and Informatics*, *6*(4), 2419–2446. DOI: 10.51519/journalisi.v6i4.885

Muinga, N., Magare, S., Monda, J., English, M., Fraser, H., Powell, J., & Paton, C. (2020). Digital health Systems in Kenyan Public Hospitals: A mixed-methods survey. *BMC Medical Informatics and Decision Making*, *20*(1), 2. DOI: 10.1186/s12911-019-1005-7 PMID: 31906932

Narciandi-Rodriguez, D., Aveleira-Mata, J., Garcia-Ordas, M. T., Alfonso-Cendon, J., Benavides, C., & Alaiz-Moreton, H. (2025). A cybersecurity review in IoT 5G networks. *Internet of Things : Engineering Cyber Physical Human Systems*, *30*, 101478. DOI: 10.1016/j.iot.2024.101478

Nasir, F., & Sultani, H. (n.d.). IoT in Healthcare: Advanced Remote Monitoring and Telemedicine Solutions. *International Journal of Advanced Engineering Technologies and Innovations*, *10*(2), 604048.

Ngepah, N., Saba, C., & Kajewole, D. (2024). The impact of industry 4.0 on South Africa's manufacturing sector. *Journal of Open Innovation*, *10*(1), 1–23. DOI: 10.1016/j.joitmc.2024.100226

Nimigan, S. (2019). The Malabo Protocol, the ICC, and the idea of 'regional complementarity'. *Journal of International Criminal Justice*, *17*(5), 1005–1029. DOI: 10.1093/jicj/mqz040

Omoseebi, A., Jayson, A., and Winston, W. (2025). Skill Development: Training Programs to Equip Employees with Digital Skills.

Oon Ling, L., Tay, R., Too, S., & Gorod, A. (2019). A Smart City Transportation System of Systems Governance Framework: A Case Study of Singapore. page 37-42.

Pandey, S., Singh, R. K., Gunasekaran, A., & Kaushik, A. (2020). Cyber security risks in globalized supply chains: Conceptual framework. *Journal of Global Operations and Strategic Sourcing*, *13*(1), 103–128. DOI: 10.1108/JGOSS-05-2019-0042

Patel, M., Shangkuan, J., & Thomas, C. (2017). What's new with the Internet of Things. *McKinsey & Company*, 1-8.

Radanliev, P. (2024). Integrated cybersecurity for metaverse systems operating with artificial intelligence, blockchains, and cloud computing. *Frontiers in Blockchain*, *7*, 1359130. DOI: 10.3389/fbloc.2024.1359130

Sendjaja, T., Prastiawan, E., Suryani, Y., & Fatmawati, E. (2024). Cybersecurity In the Digital Age: Developing Robust Strategies to Protect Against Evolving Global Digital Threats and Cyber Attacks. *The International Journal of Science in Society*, *6*(1), 1008–1019. DOI: 10.54783/ijsoc.v6i1.1098

Shafique, K., Khawaja, B. A., Sabir, F., Qazi, S., & Mustaqim, M. (2020). Internet of things (IoT) for next-generation smart systems: A review of current challenges, future trends and prospects for emerging 5G-IoT scenarios. *IEEE Access : Practical Innovations, Open Solutions*, *8*, 23022–23040. DOI: 10.1109/ACCESS.2020.2970118

Shameli-Sendi, A., Aghababaei-Barzegar, R., & Cheriet, M. (2016). Taxonomy of information security risk assessment (ISRA). *Computers & Security*, *57*, 14–30. DOI: 10.1016/j.cose.2015.11.001

Shaukat, K., Alam, T. M., Hameed, I. A., Khan, W. A., Abbas, N., & Luo, S. (2021, September). A review on security challenges in internet of things (IoT). In 2021 26th international conference on automation and computing (ICAC) (pp. 1-6). IEEE.

. Suhandi, P.S., Ahsanitaqwim, R., & Nurm, S. (2025). The Role of Automation and IoT in Enhancing Operational Efficiency: Evidence from PLS-SEM Analysis. APTISI Transactions on Management (ATM). 9(1). 72-81.

Tedeschi, S., Rodrigues, D., Emmanouilidis, C., Erkoyuncu, J., Roy, R., & Starr, A. (2018). A cost estimation approach for IoT modular architectures implementation in legacy systems. *Procedia Manufacturing*, *19*, 103–110. DOI: 10.1016/j.promfg.2018.01.015

Vassilakos, A., & Martin, R. (2023). Understanding the Challenge of Cybersecurity in Africa: A Holistic Analysis of Southern African Development Community (SADC) and Foundation for Future Research. HOLISTICA - Journal of Business and Public Administration. Volume 14, Issue 1, 162-172.

Wachter, S. (2018). The GDPR and the Internet of Things: A three-step transparency model. *Law, Innovation and Technology*, *10*(2), 266–294. DOI: 10.1080/17579961.2018.1527479

Waiganjo, I., Osakwe, J., & Azeta, A. (2025). Cybersecurity in Namibia: Challenges, strategies and prospects. *Global Journal of Engineering and Technology Advances.*, *22*(3), 1–008. DOI: 10.30574/gjeta.2025.22.3.0048

Wang, Q., Peng, C. H., Jin, Y., & Jiang, S. (2025). Impact of Data Breach on IT Investment: Embracing Both Failure Learning and Threat Rigidity. *Production and Operations Management*, *34*(6), 1256–1275. DOI: 10.1177/10591478241277455

Weber, S. (2017). Coercion in cybersecurity: What public health models reveal. *Journal of Cybersecurity*, *3*(3), 173–183. DOI: 10.1093/cybsec/tyx005

Xu, T., Wendt, J., & Potkonjak, M. (2014). Security of IoT Systems: *Design Challenges and Opportunities. IEEE/ACM International Conference on Computer-Aided Design (ICCAD)*. 417-423.

Zengeya, T., Sambo, P., & Mabika, N. (2021). The adoption of the internet of things for smart agriculture In Zimbabwe. *Computer Science and Information Technology*, *2021*, 99–106.

KEY TERMS AND DEFINITIONS

Cyber Threats: are possible harmful assaults intended to undermine the confidentiality, integrity, or availability of information systems and data. These threats can manifest in many ways, such as malware, phishing, ransomware, and denial-of-service attacks, and may focus on individuals, organizations, or infrastructure.

Data Privacy: means safeguarding of personal and sensitive information against unauthorized access, usage, or disclosure. It is regulated by laws and regulations designed to protect individual rights.

ISO/IEC 27001: is a globally recognized standard for information security management systems (ISMS). It offers a structured approach for organizations to systematically and securely handle sensitive information, thereby ensuring the confidentiality, integrity, and availability of data through the implementation of risk management processes and security controls.

NIST Cybersecurity Framework: is a voluntary guideline created by the National Institute of Standards and Technology (NIST) to assist organizations in managing and mitigating cybersecurity risks.

Operational Resilience: Operational resilience means an organization's capability to foresee, prepare for, react to, and recover from disruptive incidents while preserving critical functions and services. It includes the ability to adjust to alterations and challenges, whether they stem from cyberattacks, natural calamities, supply chain interruptions, or other unexpected situations.

Risk Management: Risk management represent a systematic approach to identifying, evaluating, and prioritizing risks, followed by the coordinated deployment of resources aimed at minimizing, monitoring, and controlling the likelihood and consequences of unexpected events. The main aim is to protect an organization's assets, ensure adherence to regulations, and enhance decision-making through a structured methodology for managing uncertainty.

Southern African Development Community (SADC): is an intergovernmental organization that consists of 16 member states located in southern Africa. It was established to foster regional integration and socio-economic development. SADC prioritizes several sectors, such as trade, security, and sustainable development, with the goal of improving the quality of life for the inhabitants of the region.

Smart Manufacturing: means the application of cutting-edge technologies, including the Internet of Things (IoT), Artificial Intelligence (AI), and big data analytics, to enhance manufacturing processes.

Vulnerabilities: Vulnerabilities refer to the weaknesses present in a system, network, application, or process that can be targeted by threats to undermine security, integrity, or functionality. When these vulnerabilities are exploited, they can result in unauthorized access, data breaches, service interruptions, and various other harmful outcomes.

Chapter 6
From Connectivity to Competitive Edge:
IoT as a Catalyst for Business Innovation and Market Adoption

Suman Lata
http://orcid.org/0000-0002-9862-0739
Amity University, Noida, India

Krishma Rana
http://orcid.org/0000-0003-0747-4260
Independent Researcher, India

ABSTRACT

The Internet of Things (IoT) has emerged as a transformative force, reshaping industries by enabling smarter operations, data-driven decision-making, and enhanced consumer experiences. As businesses increasingly adopt IoT technologies, they face both opportunities and challenges in leveraging connected ecosystems for business transformation and consumer adoption. This paper explores the strategic management of IoT to drive organizational growth, operational efficiency, and market competitiveness while addressing barriers to widespread consumer acceptance. Key factors in successful IoT implementation include robust data security, seamless integration with existing systems, and scalable infrastructure. Businesses must navigate challenges such as interoperability, privacy concerns, and high deployment costs to fully capitalize on IoT's potential. Additionally, fostering consumer trust through transparent data practices and user-friendly interfaces is critical for mass adoption.

DOI: 10.4018/979-8-3373-3441-7.ch006

1. INTRODUCTION

In the era of rapid digital transformation, the Internet of Things (IoT) has emerged as a powerful technological force revolutionizing the way organizations operate, innovate, and compete. IoT, characterized by the interconnection of devices, sensors, and systems, enables real-time data exchange and automation across diverse domains such as manufacturing, healthcare, logistics, retail, and smart cities (Judijanto et al., 2024). Its potential to generate actionable insights, streamline operations, and enhance customer experiences is driving an unprecedented wave of digital disruption across industries. Organizations are increasingly viewing IoT not merely as a tool for technological upgrade but as a strategic asset to achieve sustainable growth, improve operational efficiency, and gain a competitive edge in an ever-evolving marketplace. The strategic integration of IoT into business models is no longer optional but imperative for firms aiming to thrive in a data-driven economy (Munara et al., 2025). Successful adoption of IoT can lead to cost optimization, predictive maintenance, supply chain transparency, improved product and service innovation, and enhanced customer engagement. Companies such as Amazon, GE, and Siemens have demonstrated how IoT can be embedded into core operations to transform service delivery and achieve substantial performance gains (Vishwakarma et al., 2025). However, while the benefits are well-documented in isolated case studies, there remains a significant disparity in how organizations approach IoT adoption and management, particularly in aligning it with long-term strategic objectives.

Despite the proliferation of IoT technologies, many organizations struggle to transition from pilot programs to scalable, integrated IoT ecosystems (Khan, 2025). This gap underscores the need for a comprehensive understanding of the strategic management of IoT—how firms can plan, implement, and govern IoT initiatives effectively to maximize value. Most existing literature tends to focus on the technical or operational aspects of IoT, such as architecture, connectivity, or cybersecurity (Kioufi & Chen, 2023). While these are crucial, they often overlook the broader managerial perspective that encompasses strategy formulation, stakeholder alignment, performance measurement, and change management. Moreover, as the IoT landscape becomes more complex, businesses face multiple challenges including data privacy concerns, lack of interoperability, high implementation costs, and workforce readiness. These barriers hinder widespread consumer acceptance and pose risks to long-term investment returns (Nachanuya & Itabitha-Patience, 2025). Therefore, the need arises for a strategic framework that not only highlights the drivers of successful IoT implementation but also addresses the enablers and inhibitors from an organizational and consumer-centric perspective.

While a growing body of research acknowledges the transformative role of IoT in the digital economy, several gaps persist that limit our holistic understanding of its strategic management. Firstly, there is limited empirical evidence on how organizations align IoT initiatives with broader strategic goals such as innovation, customer value, and market expansion. Most studies remain fragmented, offering sector-specific insights without providing a cross-industry perspective that can inform generalizable best practices (Purnima et al., 2024). There are literature lacks in an integrative approach that connects internal organizational capabilities with external market dynamics in the context of IoT. Factors such as leadership commitment, cross-functional collaboration, and organizational culture have not been sufficiently explored in relation to IoT strategy formulation and execution (Sturm et al., 2023). Additionally, few studies adequately examine how consumer-related concerns—such as data security, trust, usability, and perceived value—influence the success of IoT solutions, thereby limiting the ability of organizations to drive adoption at scale. Further, there is a paucity of research that critically evaluates the long-term impact of IoT on competitive advantage and business sustainability. While technological advancements are often discussed, less attention is paid to how IoT contributes to strategic differentiation or redefines business models in highly dynamic environments (Mukherjee et al., 2024).

2. LITERATURE REVIEW

2.1 Smart Technology

Smart technology refers to the integration of advanced digital systems, automation, artificial intelligence (AI), and the Internet of Things (IoT) to enhance the functionality, responsiveness, and efficiency of devices, environments, and services (Putra et al., 2024). Unlike traditional technologies that function in isolation or require manual control, smart technologies operate through interconnected networks, enabling them to collect data, learn from patterns, and make autonomous decisions. From smart homes and wearable devices to intelligent transportation systems and industrial automation, smart technologies are transforming the way individuals live, work, and interact with their environment (Perera et al., 2015).

At the core of smart technology lies the ability to sense, process, and act upon data in real-time. Devices embedded with sensors and connected to cloud computing systems can continuously monitor conditions, communicate with other devices, and respond adaptively to changing inputs (Mineraud et al., 2015). This not only enhances user experience but also leads to optimized resource utilization, improved energy efficiency, predictive maintenance, and proactive problem-solving. For example, smart thermostats learn user preferences and adjust room temperatures accordingly, while smart cities use interconnected infrastructure to manage traffic flow, waste management, and energy consumption more effectively.

In the corporate and industrial spheres, smart technology plays a crucial role in achieving operational excellence. It enables automation of repetitive tasks, enhances supply chain visibility, supports data-driven decision-making, and facilitates innovation in products and services (Rehman et al., 2019). The rise of Industry 4.0, characterized by smart manufacturing and cyber-physical systems, highlights the growing reliance on intelligent technologies for competitiveness and agility. Organizations leveraging smart technologies are better positioned to anticipate market demands, personalize customer experiences, and adapt to disruptions with greater resilience.

Moreover, smart technology contributes significantly to sustainability goals by reducing waste, conserving energy, and promoting responsible consumption. For instance, smart grids allow better energy distribution and load management, while smart agriculture uses data analytics to optimize irrigation, fertilizer use, and crop yields (Brouns et al., 2018). However, the widespread deployment of smart technologies also brings challenges, including data privacy concerns, cybersecurity risks, and the need for regulatory frameworks that balance innovation with ethical considerations. Smart technology represents a paradigm shift in how technology is conceived and utilized (Barney, 1986). It empowers users and organizations to move from reactive to proactive approaches, offering enhanced control, efficiency, and intelligence in virtually every aspect of modern life. As these technologies continue to evolve, they hold the potential to reshape economies, societies, and daily human experiences in profound and lasting ways.

2.2 Role of IoT in Business Innovation

The Internet of Things (IoT) plays a pivotal role in driving business innovation by enabling organizations to collect, analyze, and act upon real-time data across a vast network of interconnected devices. As a transformative digital technology, IoT facilitates smarter decision-making, enhances operational efficiency, and creates new avenues for product and service innovation (Porter & Heppelmann, 2014). By connecting physical assets with digital intelligence, IoT allows businesses to transition from reactive models to proactive and predictive operations, ultimately reshaping how value is created and delivered. The essence of IoT lies in its ability to generate data from devices embedded with sensors and transmit that data through cloud-based platforms for analysis. This stream of information empowers businesses with insights into customer behavior, asset performance, and environmental conditions, which can be used to innovate processes, improve customer experience, and design intelligent products (Atzori et al., 2010).

One of the most significant contributions of IoT to business innovation is in optimizing internal processes. In manufacturing, for instance, IoT-driven smart factories utilize real-time monitoring systems and predictive maintenance tools to minimize downtime and maximize productivity. Machines equipped with sensors can alert managers before failures occur, reducing repair costs and improving operational continuity (Ding et al., 2021). In logistics and supply chain management, IoT devices provide visibility into inventory levels, vehicle tracking, and delivery routes, enabling more efficient resource allocation and timely responses to disruptions. Such innovations allow businesses to reduce waste, lower operational costs, and enhance agility in rapidly changing environments. Moreover, IoT enables automation at scale, allowing organizations to reallocate human capital to higher-value tasks and accelerate digital transformation (Teece, 2007).

Beyond operational gains, IoT is fostering innovation in customer engagement and service delivery. Businesses are using IoT to offer personalized experiences by understanding individual usage patterns and preferences (Cozzolino et al., 2018). For example, wearable devices in healthcare can monitor patient vitals and transmit data to medical professionals in real time, allowing for timely interventions and customized care plans. In the retail sector, smart shelves and beacons track consumer movement and product interaction, helping retailers personalize marketing strategies and enhance the shopping experience. These innovations not only strengthen customer relationships but also provide new monetization models through subscription-based services, data-driven upselling, and value-added offerings (Volberda et al., 2021).

Furthermore, IoT is opening up entirely new business models and revenue streams. The concept of "product-as-a-service" has gained momentum, where businesses offer usage-based models rather than one-time sales. For instance, companies in industrial sectors are deploying IoT-enabled machinery that customers can pay for based on usage or performance, supported by continuous monitoring and remote diagnostics (Westerman et al., 2014). This model not only creates recurring revenue but also deepens the relationship between providers and customers through ongoing service engagement. Additionally, IoT facilitates co-creation and collaborative innovation by integrating customer feedback loops into product development cycles, allowing companies to iterate and evolve their offerings in alignment with real-world usage data.

Despite its immense potential, IoT-driven innovation does not come without challenges. Data privacy and security concerns are paramount, as the proliferation of connected devices increases the risk of cyberattacks and data breaches (Snyder, 2019). Businesses must invest in robust cybersecurity infrastructure and adopt ethical data governance practices to ensure trust and compliance. Interoperability across devices, scalability of platforms, and integration with legacy systems are also key concerns that need strategic planning and investment. Furthermore, organizations must cultivate a culture of innovation and digital readiness, equipping their workforce with the necessary skills to harness the benefits of IoT (Vecchiato, 2012).

2.3 Case Studies

2.3.1 Case Study of Estonia

Estonia, a small Baltic nation, has emerged as a global leader in leveraging technology for business innovation and public service delivery. Often referred to as the world's most advanced digital society, Estonia has successfully transformed its economy through the strategic integration of digital technologies across all sectors. Following its independence in the early 1990s, Estonia prioritized digital infrastructure as a cornerstone of national development, launching the e-Estonia initiative to build a robust digital ecosystem. At the heart of Estonia's success is its e-Government platform, which provides over 99% of public services online, including business registration, tax filing, licensing, and procurement. Entrepreneurs can register a company in under 20 minutes, allowing for rapid business setup and reduced bureaucratic overhead. This seamless integration of technology has significantly improved ease of doing business, attracting startups and foreign investors alike. Moreover, Estonia introduced the world's first e-Residency program in 2014, enabling global entrepreneurs to establish and manage a location-independent EU-based business entirely online. This innovation has empowered thousands of digital nomads and small business owners to access European markets without physical relocation. Estonia also fosters a strong startup ecosystem supported by government initiatives, digital infrastructure, and widespread digital literacy. Companies like TransferWise (now Wise) and Bolt originated in Estonia and have achieved global success, showcasing the country's commitment to innovation-driven entrepreneurship. Cybersecurity, digital identity (via secure ID cards), and blockchain-backed services further enhance trust and efficiency in digital transactions. Estonia's model demonstrates how purposeful investment in digital tools and transparent governance can create a thriving environment for business growth.

2.3.2 Case Study of Singapore

Singapore stands out as a leading example of how a nation can harness technology to foster business innovation, economic growth, and global competitiveness. Known for its pro-business environment, Singapore has systematically integrated digital technologies into its national development strategy through initiatives such as the Smart Nation program launched in 2014. This ambitious vision seeks to transform

Singapore into a hyper-connected country where technology enhances everyday life, business efficiency, and public services. One of the most significant areas of impact has been in the digitalization of small and medium enterprises (SMEs). Through programs like SMEs Go Digital, the government provides funding, training, and digital toolkits to help businesses adopt technologies such as cloud computing, data analytics, e-commerce platforms, and cybersecurity solutions. This has enabled even traditional sectors like retail, food services, and logistics to innovate, streamline operations, and improve customer engagement. Singapore has also positioned itself as a global hub for fintech, attracting companies with its regulatory sandbox, favorable tax policies, and robust IT infrastructure. The Monetary Authority of Singapore (MAS) actively promotes innovation in financial services by collaborating with startups and established firms to develop digital banking, blockchain applications, and AI-driven solutions. This has led to the emergence of numerous fintech firms and the adoption of cutting-edge solutions across banking and finance. Additionally, Singapore's investment in research and development through institutions like A*STAR and partnerships with global tech companies has led to advancements in areas such as smart manufacturing, healthcare technology, and urban mobility. The government's emphasis on digital literacy and skills upgrading ensures that the workforce remains future-ready.

2.3.3 Case Study of India

India, one of the fastest-growing major economies in the world, has embraced digital technology as a core driver of business transformation and inclusive economic development. With a population exceeding 1.4 billion and a burgeoning startup ecosystem, India's digital strategy has focused on fostering innovation, enhancing connectivity, and empowering both enterprises and citizens. A cornerstone of India's digital journey is the Digital India initiative, launched in 2015. This ambitious program aims to transform the country into a digitally empowered society and knowledge economy. It promotes the adoption of digital infrastructure, e-governance, and internet connectivity, particularly in rural and underserved areas. Through this initiative, services such as digital payments, online business registration, and e-marketplaces have become widely accessible, reducing bureaucratic barriers and improving ease of doing business. One of the most impactful innovations has been the development of India Stack, a set of APIs that includes Aadhaar (biometric ID), UPI (Unified Payments Interface), and e-KYC. These platforms have enabled millions of individuals and businesses to participate in the digital economy. For instance, UPI revolutionized the financial sector by facilitating real-time, low-cost, cashless transactions, helping small businesses, startups, and consumers transact seamlessly. India has also become a global startup hub, home to numerous unicorns in sectors such as fintech, health tech, edtech, and e-commerce. Initiatives like Startup India and government-supported incubators have created a conducive environment for innovation and entrepreneurship. Furthermore, sectors like agriculture, manufacturing, and logistics are increasingly integrating technologies like IoT, AI, and blockchain to improve efficiency and scalability. Despite infrastructure and digital literacy challenges in some regions, India's technology-driven approach has democratized access to opportunities and reshaped the business landscape. The country's model highlights how digital innovation, when aligned with policy and inclusion goals, can stimulate growth and transform the economy at scale.

3. RESEARCH METHODOLOGY

This study adopts a conceptual research methodology aimed at systematically analyzing and synthesizing existing literature, theories, and frameworks to explore the strategic management of the Internet of Things (IoT) in driving organizational growth, operational efficiency, and market competitiveness, while identifying barriers to widespread consumer acceptance. A conceptual approach is well-suited for this research as it facilitates the development of a theoretical foundation that integrates diverse viewpoints, empirical findings, and strategic models into a cohesive understanding of IoT's role in business innovation. The methodology focuses on reviewing relevant academic literature, industry reports, white papers, and case studies across multiple sectors where IoT has been effectively deployed. By identifying patterns, common themes, and gaps within the existing body of knowledge, this research aims to construct a structured conceptual framework that organizations can utilize in aligning IoT with their strategic objectives.

The study begins with an extensive literature review covering areas such as IoT adoption strategies, digital transformation, business model innovation, consumer behavior, and technology acceptance models. Sources are selected from peer-reviewed journals, authoritative databases, and industry publications to ensure reliability and depth. Key concepts such as strategic alignment, value co-creation, data-driven decision-making, and customer-centric innovation are analyzed within the context of IoT deployment. The review also considers challenges such as data privacy, security, cost, and interoperability to understand the inhibitors of IoT adoption and acceptance.

Through thematic analysis, the study categorizes findings into core dimensions including organizational readiness, technology integration, user trust, and policy frameworks. These dimensions are then synthesized into a conceptual model that illustrates how organizations can strategically manage IoT to maximize business outcomes. The conceptual framework also reflects on how consumer perceptions and ecosystem-level factors (such as regulations and standards) impact the scalability and effectiveness of IoT initiatives. This methodology does not involve primary data collection but offers a rigorous qualitative synthesis aimed at advancing theoretical insight and managerial understanding. The outcome is a conceptual guide that contributes to both academic discourse and practical application, helping decision-makers navigate the complexities of IoT integration in the dynamic business environment.

4. FINDINGS

a) Strategic Alignment is Crucial for IoT Success

Strategic alignment is fundamental for the successful implementation of the Internet of Things (IoT) in any organization. Companies that align IoT initiatives with their long-term business objectives are better positioned to derive measurable benefits. Rather than viewing IoT as an isolated technology project, it should be integrated into the broader strategic framework that drives growth, competitiveness, and innovation. When IoT initiatives are synchronized with business goals, organizations can leverage connected systems to enhance operational efficiency, develop new products or services, and improve customer engagement. This alignment ensures that IoT investments are purpose-driven, yield sustainable value, and contribute to the overall mission of the company. Furthermore, it enables cross-departmental collaboration, data-driven decision-making, and resource optimization, ensuring that every IoT deployment supports the company's strategic priorities and delivers tangible business outcomes rather than remaining a mere technological experiment.

b) Operational Efficiency is a Major Driver of Adoption

One of the primary motivations behind the adoption of IoT technologies is the pursuit of operational efficiency. Organizations across various industries, including manufacturing, logistics, agriculture, and retail, are leveraging IoT to streamline operations and reduce costs. Connected devices and sensors provide real-time data that enable predictive maintenance, preventing costly downtime and equipment failures. Similarly, IoT systems facilitate inventory optimization, energy management, and process automation, which enhance productivity and reduce waste. In logistics and supply chain management, IoT offers precise tracking and monitoring of goods, improving transparency and reliability. By using real-time analytics, businesses can identify inefficiencies and respond proactively to operational challenges. This continuous flow of actionable data empowers companies to make smarter decisions, minimize human error, and boost overall productivity. Ultimately, IoT adoption transforms traditional business processes into intelligent, data-driven ecosystems that foster efficiency and long-term sustainability.

c) Consumer Trust and Data Privacy Concerns Hinder Acceptance

Despite rapid technological progress, widespread consumer acceptance of IoT remains constrained by concerns over data privacy, security, and surveillance. Many users fear that their personal information collected by smart devices could be misused, sold, or exposed through cyberattacks. These apprehensions are heightened by incidents of data breaches and lack of transparency in how organizations handle sensitive information. To overcome these barriers, companies must prioritize ethical data practices, implement robust security measures, and maintain open communication about data usage policies. Establishing trust requires clear consent mechanisms, encryption protocols, and compliance with privacy regulations such as GDPR. Moreover, organizations should adopt transparent governance models and ethical frameworks that place consumer rights at the center of IoT innovation. When consumers feel confident that their data is handled responsibly, their willingness to engage with IoT technologies increases, enabling broader adoption and fostering a secure, trustworthy digital ecosystem.

d) Organizational Readiness Influences Implementation Success

The success of IoT implementation depends significantly on an organization's internal readiness and adaptability. Factors such as leadership commitment, cross-departmental collaboration, employee digital literacy, and change management play critical roles in ensuring smooth integration. Without strong executive support and a clear strategic vision, IoT projects risk becoming fragmented or unsustainable. Organizations must foster a culture of innovation that encourages employees to embrace digital transformation and develop the necessary technical skills. Cross-functional teamwork ensures that IoT initiatives align with broader organizational objectives rather than being confined to specific departments. Additionally, effective change management strategies help overcome resistance and facilitate the adoption of new technologies. Companies that invest in workforce training, infrastructure modernization, and data governance frameworks are better equipped to realize the full potential of IoT. Thus, organizational readiness serves as the foundation upon which technological capabilities translate into tangible business value.

e) Regulatory Support and Ecosystem Collaboration are Enablers

A supportive regulatory environment and collaborative ecosystem are essential for scalable and sustainable IoT development. Government policies that encourage digital innovation, ensure cybersecurity, and promote data interoperability provide a stable foundation for IoT growth. Standardization efforts across industries help prevent fragmentation, allowing devices and platforms from different vendors to work seamlessly together. Collaboration among key stakeholders—technology providers, policymakers, businesses, and consumers—drives knowledge sharing, co-creation, and innovation. Public-private partnerships can also accelerate infrastructure development and promote the use of IoT in public services such as healthcare, transportation, and smart cities. Moreover, clear regulatory frameworks addressing privacy, liability, and ethical concerns enhance trust and accountability within the IoT ecosystem. By fostering open collaboration and well-defined standards, the IoT landscape becomes more cohesive, inclusive, and future-ready, enabling organizations to deploy connected solutions efficiently and responsibly on a global scale.

5. DISCUSSION

a) The Evolving Role of IoT in Business Strategy

The Internet of Things (IoT) has evolved from being a purely operational enabler to a central element in shaping modern business strategies. Organizations increasingly recognize IoT not just as a technology for automation or data collection but as a transformative driver of innovation, market expansion, and customer-centric business models. According to Zahra (2006), strategic entrepreneurship requires leveraging emerging technologies to create new opportunities and sustain competitive advantage. IoT facilitates this by enabling predictive insights, enhancing customer engagement, and supporting agile decision-making. Businesses that strategically embed IoT within their long-term vision can identify new value propositions, improve responsiveness to market dynamics, and enhance service personalization. This evolution demands strategic foresight, investment in digital infrastructure, and continuous alignment of IoT initiatives with organizational objectives. Ultimately, IoT's role extends beyond efficiency—it empowers organizations to innovate, differentiate, and lead in an increasingly connected global economy.

(b) Balancing Innovation with Consumer Privacy

While IoT presents immense potential for innovation, it simultaneously introduces significant ethical, privacy, and data protection challenges. The constant data exchange between devices and systems raises concerns about surveillance, unauthorized data use, and loss of consumer autonomy. As Faraj and Leonardi (2022) emphasize, organizations must establish responsible data governance practices that prioritize transparency and accountability. This includes implementing clear consent mechanisms, anonymization protocols, and adherence to data protection regulations such as the GDPR. Achieving this balance requires companies to embed ethical considerations into every phase of IoT development—from design to deployment. Trust becomes a strategic asset when consumers are assured that their data is managed securely and ethically. Therefore, organizations must ensure that innovation does not come at the cost of individual rights. A robust ethical framework that balances technological advancement with privacy safeguards is essential to fostering sustainable IoT adoption and long-term consumer confidence.

(c) Cross-Industry Learning and Best Practices

The adoption and implementation of IoT vary across industries, creating opportunities for shared learning and collaboration. Each sector—whether manufacturing, healthcare, logistics, or retail—develops unique insights into integrating IoT for operational and strategic gains. For instance, lessons from smart manufacturing—where IoT drives predictive maintenance and efficiency—can inform similar applications in healthcare for patient monitoring or in retail for inventory management. Etemad (2023) highlights the importance of cross-sector knowledge exchange as a mechanism to accelerate innovation and reduce the likelihood of costly implementation failures. Collaborative platforms, industry consortiums, and research partnerships can serve as valuable avenues for sharing best practices and developing interoperable standards. By learning from other sectors' experiences, organizations can avoid duplication of mistakes, shorten adoption curves, and optimize the return on IoT investments. Ultimately, cross-industry collaboration fosters a more mature IoT ecosystem, enabling collective advancement toward smarter and more resilient business environments.

(d) Integration Challenges in Legacy Systems

Integrating IoT solutions within existing legacy infrastructures remains one of the most significant barriers to digital transformation. Many organizations operate on outdated IT systems that are incompatible with modern IoT frameworks, leading to data silos, inefficiencies, and cybersecurity vulnerabilities. As Munara et al. (2025) note, addressing this challenge requires a phased and strategic approach that prioritizes interoperability and system modernization. Businesses must invest in middleware platforms, cloud-based integration tools, and modular architectures that allow seamless communication between old and new technologies. Additionally, revisiting enterprise IT strategies to accommodate scalability and future innovation is critical. Failure to modernize legacy systems can limit the full potential of IoT adoption, resulting in fragmented operations and missed opportunities. Therefore, organizations should treat integration not as a technical afterthought but as a strategic priority, ensuring that technological upgrades align with long-term digital transformation goals and business continuity needs.

(e) The Need for a Skilled and Adaptable Workforce

The successful adoption of IoT technologies hinges on the availability of a skilled and adaptable workforce capable of navigating complex digital environments. As Vishwakarma et al. (2020) emphasize, employees must develop competencies in data analytics, cybersecurity, programming, and systems integration to manage IoT-driven operations effectively. Beyond technical expertise, adaptability, problem-solving, and continuous learning are equally vital as IoT environments evolve rapidly. Organizations must therefore invest in structured training programs, reskilling initiatives, and digital literacy development across all levels. Cultivating a culture that embraces technological change and innovation helps reduce resistance and encourages collaboration. Moreover, fostering interdisciplinary teams that combine technical, managerial, and strategic insights ensures that IoT adoption delivers holistic business value. By prioritizing talent development and continuous learning, companies can not only keep pace with technological advancement but also sustain a competitive edge in the increasingly digitized global marketplace.

6. PRACTICAL IMPLICATIONS

The findings of this study offer several practical implications for business leaders, policymakers, and technology managers seeking to integrate IoT into their organizational strategy. First and foremost, businesses must treat IoT as a strategic investment rather than a purely technological upgrade. For IoT adoption to yield tangible outcomes such as improved productivity, innovation, and competitive advantage, organizations must align IoT initiatives with their core business objectives. This involves cross-functional collaboration between IT, operations, marketing, and leadership teams to ensure strategic fit, resource allocation, and long-term planning.

Second, the study underscores the importance of building organizational readiness. Successful IoT implementation requires more than just deploying smart devices—it necessitates a supportive culture, digitally skilled employees, and agile processes. Companies must invest in training programs to upskill their workforce, promote digital literacy, and foster openness to change. Moreover, creating internal governance structures to oversee data usage, security, and ethical compliance ensures smoother transitions and sustained performance.

Another practical implication lies in addressing consumer trust and data privacy concerns. As IoT devices increasingly collect and share sensitive data, businesses must implement robust cybersecurity protocols and transparent data handling practices. This includes providing users with control over their data, adhering to legal frameworks such as GDPR, and being proactive in communicating privacy safeguards. Trust is a key determinant of consumer adoption; hence, businesses that prioritize security and transparency will be better positioned to scale their IoT initiatives. Furthermore, policymakers and regulators play a critical role in shaping the IoT ecosystem. Governments should promote the development of open standards, interoperability frameworks, and innovation-friendly regulations that support IoT adoption across sectors. Public-private partnerships can also help in funding pilot programs, particularly for small and medium-sized enterprises (SMEs) that face resource constraints. Also, the study highlights the value of ecosystem collaboration. Businesses should actively engage with technology providers, research institutions, startups, and customers to co-create IoT solutions that are scalable, inclusive, and user-centric. Open innovation models and feedback loops can enhance the design and functionality of IoT offerings while accelerating their adoption. Organizations that approach IoT strategically—with strong internal capabilities, consumer trust, and ecosystem alignment—can unlock new growth opportunities and future-proof their business in a rapidly evolving digital economy.

7. CONCLUSION

The Internet of Things (IoT) has emerged as a transformative force in the digital economy, offering organizations unprecedented opportunities to innovate, streamline operations, and enhance competitiveness. This study has examined the strategic management of IoT, emphasizing its role in driving organizational growth, operational efficiency, and customer-centric value creation (Nachanuya & Itabitha-Patience, 2025). It also addressed the critical barriers to widespread consumer acceptance, such as data privacy, security concerns, and organizational readiness. This study reveal that IoT can no longer be viewed as a standalone technological initiative. Instead, it must be strategically embedded within the broader organizational framework to align with long-term goals and value propositions. Businesses that integrate IoT into their strategic planning processes are better positioned to harness real-time data, automate decision-making, and create intelligent ecosystems that respond dynamically to market demands. However, the success of IoT adoption is heavily dependent on an organization's internal capabilities, leadership commitment, and adaptability to change.

Equally important is the need to address consumer trust and ethical considerations in data usage. As IoT devices collect vast amounts of personal and behavioral data, building transparent and secure systems is essential for fostering public confidence and encouraging user adoption. Organizations must balance innovation with accountability, ensuring that data privacy and ethical governance are prioritized alongside technological advancement. Moreover, the study underscores the importance of collaboration among stakeholders—businesses, governments, technology providers, and consumers—to create an enabling environment for IoT growth. Policymakers must support the development of standardized protocols, regulatory frameworks, and funding mechanisms to encourage adoption, particularly among SMEs. Businesses, on the other hand, must invest in workforce development and cross-sector learning to maximize the potential of IoT.

In conclusion, the strategic management of IoT offers a pathway for sustainable growth, operational transformation, and digital innovation. By adopting a holistic, consumer-aware, and future-ready approach, organizations can overcome current barriers and fully realize the transformative potential of IoT. As the technology continues to evolve, those who act strategically and responsibly will lead the next wave of digital disruption and define the future of smart, connected enterprises.

REFERENCES

Atzori, L., Iera, A., & Morabito, G. (2010). The Internet of things: A survey. *Computer Networks*, *54*(15), 2787–2805. DOI: 10.1016/j.comnet.2010.05.010

Barney, J. B. (1986). Organizational culture: Can it be a source of sustained competitive advantage? *Academy of Management Review*, *11*(3), 656–665. DOI: 10.2307/258317

Brouns, N., Tata, S., Ludwig, H., Asensio, E. S., & Grefen, P. (2018). Modeling IoT-aware business processes - A state of the art report. *arXiv*. https://arxiv.org/abs/1811.00652

Cozzolino, A., Verona, G., & Rothaermel, F. T. (2018). Unpacking the disruption process: New technology, business models, and incumbent adaptation. *Journal of Management Studies*, *55*(7), 1166–1202. DOI: 10.1111/joms.12352

Ding, Y., Jin, M., Li, S., & Feng, D. (2021). Smart logistics based on the Internet of Things technology: An overview. *International Journal of Logistics*, *24*(4), 323–345. DOI: 10.1080/13675567.2020.1757053

Etemad, H. (2023). The need for strategic redirection and business model change: The impact of evolving influential forces of change on international entrepreneurship environment. *Journal of International Entrepreneurship*, *21*(4), 441–463. DOI: 10.1007/s10843-024-00348-7

Faraj, S., & Leonardi, P. M. (2022). Strategic organization in the digital age: Rethinking the concept of technology. *Strategic Organization*, *20*(4), 771–785. DOI: 10.1177/14761270221130253

Judijanto, L., Triwiyatno, A., & Sofyan, S. (2024). The influence of Internet of Things (IoT) on operational efficiency and competitive advantage in the information technology industry in Indonesia. *The Eastasouth Journal of Information System and Computer Science, 1*(3), 155–166. arXiv+1BW Journal+1DOI: 10.58812/esiscs.v1i03.240

Khan, W. U.Waseem Ullah Khan. (2025). The business value of IoT and big data analytics. *Journal of Business and Management Studies*, *7*(1), 279–283. DOI: 10.32996/jbms.2025.7.1.23

Kioufi, N., & Chen, W. (2023). Exploring IoT adoption and operational efficiency within the international chilled beverages industry. *Journal of Industrial and Production Engineering*, *41*(2), 158–181. DOI: 10.1080/21681015.2023.2270994

Mineraud, J., Mazhelis, O., Su, X., & Tarkoma, S. (2015). A gap analysis of Internet-of-Things platforms. *arXiv*. https://arxiv.org/abs/1502.01181

Mukherjee, S., Baral, M. M., Chittipaka, V., Nagariya, R., & Patel, B. S. (2024). Achieving organizational performance by integrating industrial Internet of things in SMEs: A developing country perspective. *The TQM Journal*, *36*(1), 265–287. DOI: 10.1108/TQM-07-2022-0221

Munara, K. J., Kamil, U. S. A., Rizki, M., Pahala, I., & Handaru, A. W. (2025). Strategic technology adaptation framework: AI, IoT, and the shift in strategic paradigms. *JEMSI (Jurnal Ekonomi, Manajemen, dan Akuntansi, 11*(3), 1575–1582. DOI: 10.35870/jemsi.v11i3.4154

Nachanuya, S., & Itabitha-Patience, J. (2025). IoT as a managerial tool for effective business management. *BW Academic Journal*. Retrieved from https://bwjournal.org/index.php/bsjournal/article/view/2626

Perera, C., Liu, C. H., Jayawardena, S., & Chen, M. (2015). Context-aware computing in the Internet of Things: A survey on IoT from industrial market perspective. *International Journal of Distributed Sensor Networks*. Advance online publication. DOI: 10.1155/2015/967415

Porter, M. E., & Heppelmann, J. E. (2014). How smart, connected products are transforming competition. *Harvard Business Review*, *92*(11), 64–88.

Purnima, F. H., Mosaddek, N., Chanchal, M. A. U., & Khan, B. (2024). Integration of IoT in strategic management: A review of current trends, future possibilities, and challenges. *International Journal of Science and Research Archive*, *12*(2), 2634–2645. DOI: 10.30574/ijsra.2024.12.2.1565

Putra, R. H., Sutjipto, M. R., Widodo, A., & Kuntadi, S. (2024). Business ecosystem architecture development: A case study of IoT business in the transportation industry. *Journal of Asian Multicultural Research for Economy and Management Study*, *5*(3), 25–41. DOI: 10.47616/jamrems.v5i3.536

Rehman, M. H. ur., Yaqoob, I., Salah, K., Imran, M., Jayaraman, P. P., & Perera, C. (2019). The role of big data analytics in industrial Internet of Things. *arXiv*. https://arxiv.org/abs/1904.05556

Snyder, H. (2019). Literature review as a research methodology: An overview and guidelines. *Journal of Business Research*, *104*, 333–339. DOI: 10.1016/j.jbusres.2019.07.039

Sturm, M., Weking, J., Böhm, M., & Krcmar, H. (2023). How two leading partners learn to tango: The case of IoT-based business model co-innovation between a retailer and an electronics supplier. *Electronic Markets*, *33*(1), 34. DOI: 10.1007/s12525-023-00645-4

Teece, D. J. (2007). Explicating dynamic capabilities: The nature and microfoundations of (sustainable) enterprise performance. *Strategic Management Journal*, *28*(13), 1319–1350. DOI: 10.1002/smj.640

Vecchiato, R. (2012). Environmental uncertainty, foresight and strategic decision making: An integrated study. *Technological Forecasting and Social Change*, *79*(3), 436–447. DOI: 10.1016/j.techfore.2011.07.010

Vishwakarma, N. K., Singh, R. K., & Sharma, R. R. K. (2020). Internet of things architectures: Do organizational strategies matter? *Business Process Management Journal*, *26*(1), 102–131. DOI: 10.1108/BPMJ-03-2018-0092

Volberda, H. W., Khanagha, S., Baden-Fuller, C., Mihalache, O. R., & Birkinshaw, J. (2021). Strategizing in a digital world: Overcoming cognitive barriers, reconfiguring routines and introducing new organizational forms. *Long Range Planning*, *54*(5), 102110. DOI: 10.1016/j.lrp.2021.102110

Westerman, G., Bonnet, D., & McAfee, A. (2014). *Leading digital: Turning technology into business transformation*. Harvard Business Press.

Zahra, S. A., Sapienza, H. J., & Davidsson, P. (2006). Entrepreneurship and dynamic capabilities: A review, model and research agenda. *Journal of Management Studies*, *43*(4), 917–955. DOI: 10.1111/j.1467-6486.2006.00616.x

Chapter 7
Harnessing IoT for Scalable Transformation:
Bridging Enterprises and End Users

N. Sathyanarayana
http://orcid.org/0000-0002-4185-7751
Jain University, India

G. Srividhya
http://orcid.org/0000-0002-5216-546X
Jain University, India

Usha Prabhu
http://orcid.org/0000-0001-6219-5358
Jain University, India

Varanasi Rahul
http://orcid.org/0000-0003-2407-7654
Jain University, India

Madireddi S. S. V. Sri Kumar
http://orcid.org/0000-0003-1190-1552
Global Business School, Koneru Lakshmaiah Education Foundation, India

ABSTRACT

This chapter explores the transformative role of the Internet of Things (IoT) in driving scalable digital transformation across enterprises and end-user domains. It investigates the foundational technologies, architecture, and real-time analytics that underpin IoT systems, emphasising their application in smart industries, health-

DOI: 10.4018/979-8-3373-3441-7.ch007

care, agriculture, and urban infrastructure. The discussion extends to the strategic alignment of IoT with business goals, data governance, and the empowerment of non-technical users through end-user development frameworks. Case studies highlight successful IoT integration in sectors like manufacturing, retail, and telecom. The chapter concludes with critical insights into scalability challenges, ethical considerations, and future prospects, including AI, 5G, and digital twins, positioning IoT as a catalyst for equitable, intelligent, and sustainable innovation.

1 INTRODUCTION

The Internet of things (IoT) has emerged as a digital transformation pillar which can network objects, data and humanity with the capacity to attain action and real-time discernment. IoT today is an enabler of digital excellence (or capability to achieve scalability, inclusiveness, and ethical innovation) in both enterprise and consumer domains in addition to its technical pillars of sensors, connectivity, and analytics. Within the context of organisations, IoT gives data-driven predictive analytics, process automation, and decision-making that were previously in the manufacturing sector, but currently in the healthcare sector. Nevertheless, it can be achieved to the fullest by involving businesses and consumers in shared digital ecosystems. The IoT allows the consumer to become a partner in the value creation process based on adaptive design and feedback loop, which also helps to establish the building of a two-way bridge between business efficiency and personalised experience. When scaling IoT, however, governance, privacy and interoperability are a challenge. Strong data governance, sensible design, and inclusive models between innovation and responsibility should be inculcated by the businesses as one of the approaches to the sustainable change. In the chapter, it is discussed that the enterprises and consumers can be leveraged in strategic means through the IoT to transform them at scale. It combines the technical analysis, management paradigms and case-studies of real-life situations to demonstrate the new position as an IoT catalyst of intelligent, ethical and equitable digital innovation.

2 COMPONENTS OF IOT

The Internet of Things (IoT) is a system that functions based on an organized network of elements which bring about automatization, connectivity, and real-time data intelligence. According to Table 1, the IoT ecosystem consists of 7 connected components sensors and devices, connectivity, edge devices, cloud infrastructure, data analytics, user interfaces, and security and governance layers. These elements are combined to process raw environmental and operational data into actionable insights to both enterprises and end-users (Gubbi et al., 2013; Sadeeq et al., 2021).

Table 1. Core Components of the Internet of Things (IoT)

Component	Function	Example Application	Managerial Relevance
Sensors & Devices	Capture physical or environmental data such as temperature, motion, or pressure.	Smart homes, wearable trackers, agricultural sensors (Gubbi et al., 2013).	Enable real-time visibility and predictive maintenance.
Connectivity	Facilitate data transmission through wireless networks and protocols.	Wi-Fi, Bluetooth, Zigbee, 5G in vehicles and cities (Osseiran et al., 2014; Çeken, 2024).	Determines scalability, latency, and reliability of operations.
Edge Devices / Gateways	Process data locally before cloud transfer, reducing latency.	Smart gateways in connected vehicles or healthcare systems.	Enhances responsiveness and operational efficiency.
Cloud Infrastructure	Stores and integrates vast data streams for analysis.	AWS IoT, Azure IoT, and Google Cloud IoT used in logistics and manufacturing.	Enables scalability and enterprise-wide data visibility.
Data Analytics & Intelligence	Convert raw data into insights using AI and ML algorithms.	Predictive maintenance, health tracking dashboards (Yadav et al., 2024).	Supports informed decision-making and innovation.
User Interface (UI) & Applications	Provide platforms for interaction and data visualization.	Mobile apps for smart homes, industrial dashboards (Sanctorum & Lujan, 2024).	Improves user engagement and accessibility.
Security & Governance Layer	Safeguard data privacy, integrity, and compliance.	Encryption frameworks, GDPR-aligned policies (Sicari et al., 2015; Weber, 2015).	Builds user trust and ensures sustainable adoption.

Source: Authors contribution's

In real-world uses, the IoT transforms various industries by integrating these elements into ecosystems-specific environments. Smart homes present the possibility of controlling appliances, lighting, security, and so on remotely via mobile or voice-assisted mediums through sensor-impeded connectivity layers, enhancing convenience and reducing energy consumption. Connected cars adopt edge and cloud computing to enhance analytical procedures of real-time traffic congestion, remote diagnostics, and autonomous driving to improve safety and driving experience. Wearable technology uses the data analytics layer of IoT to track health indicators, which provide personalised feedback to encourage wellness and preventive health (Richard Bevis, 2023). Sensors and edge analytics have been used in agriculture to monitor soil conditions and weather patterns to assist in precision farming and optimisation of resources. Retail and logistics systems utilise inventory tracking and customer personalisation through cloud-based analytics, while smart city networks employ IoT sensors to manage traffic, waste, and urban environmental conditions, promoting sustainable urban living. On the same note, IoT can be used in health-care applications to monitor patients remotely and use their data to treat them and in smart manufacturing, IoT architectures can be used to prevent downtime due to predictive maintenance and increase productivity. Smart grids also rely on sensors and control systems that are powered by IoT to balance the energy distribution, track the consumption, and maintain the stability of the grid (Osseiran et al., 2014; Çeken, 2024).

All these illustrate how the elements of the IoT architecture when used correctly enable scalability, efficiency, and innovation in industries that eventually enable the bridging of enterprises and end-users in an effort to achieve digital excellence.

3 THE ENTERPRISE VIEW: IOT STRATEGIC INTEGRATION

The fast development of the Internet of Things (IoT) is changing the nature in which businesses are functioning by allowing real-time decision making, predictive analytics, as well as enhanced operational efficiency. The IoT has ceased to be a technical upgrade when it comes to strategic integration into enterprise systems; it is a business requirement of organisations that want to gain competitive edge and digital transformation (Attah et al.,2024). IoT enables physical devices to gather and share information, providing them with novel information about the performance of assets, supply chains, and customer engagements (Seetharaman, 2021). IoT can drive innovation in manufacturing, logistics, retail, and energy when well positioned with the enterprise objectives (Egbuhuzor et al.,2024).

3.1 Operational Advantages of IOT Integration

The impact of IoT on enterprises is one of the greatest, and predictive maintenance is not an exception. Through the use of sensors attached to equipment, businesses can know the state of equipment and forecast failures before they can happen thus reducing downtime and reducing the life cycle of equipment. This is an objective-based method of lowering the maintenance cost and supports continuity of operations. Indicatively, IoT-based predictive maintenance systems in the manufacturing industry have been demonstrated to enhance uptime and decrease the number of unplanned failures by a significant margin (Agarwal et al., 2024). Another major result of the use of IoT is supply chain optimisation. Immediacy in tracking of the goods and resources by means of IoT-based logistics systems make the companies to handle inventory accurately and dynamically react to changes in demand. The IoT has enhanced resilience in the supply chain of the energy sector, providing predictions and real-time insights on possible disruptions (Cui et al.,2022). The IoT sensors assist in ensuring the optimum inventory level and identify the inefficiency early enough, minimizing the wastage and enhancing the sustainability of the logistical operations (Sallam et al.,2023). Moreover, IoT integration provides an opportunity to make decisions in real-time. The sensor data can be used by the enterprises to make immediate modifications in operations, assign resources, and react to the changes in the market. This real-time responsiveness is essential in industries like automotive production and oil and gas whereby the situation evolves quickly, and responsiveness is indispensable (Yadav et al., 2024).

3.2 Aligning on Digital Transformation

The integration of IoT should be planned in a way that is linked to wider objectives of digital transformation in order to achieve the maximum possibility of the IoT. It will imply the integration of IoT into the enterprise architecture and aligning it with the key business processes, leadership vision, and performance indicators. A cross-sector study design will ensure the alignment of digital technologies such as IoT with business strategies, which positively influence the customer experience, streamlined operations, and long-term sustainability (Attah et al.,2024). Smart factories are applied in manufacturing to combine robotics and real-time monitoring and predictive repairs to boost productivity. With regards to retail, IoT boosts customer experience by means of connected shelves and customised services. IoT is applied to fleet management, route optimisation, and warehouse automation by logistics companies, which makes these applications consistent with business objectives, including cost reduction and speed of delivery (Mu X & Antwi-Afari, M.F.,2024). Another aspect of strategic implementation is to overcome the organisational resistance and develop a digital-first culture. The organisations that are committed to the concept of IoT, investing in digital literacy, well structured IT governance, and change management are likely to be successful in their digital transformation (Yadav et al., 2024).

3.3 Intelligent Insights and Data Utilisation

The real strength of IoT is the ability to produce enormous amounts of data that can be converted into practical information. Businesses are becoming more intertwined with IoT and artificial intelligence (AI), machine learning, and cloud computing to derive patterns, identify anomalies, and have automated responses. The insights do not only assist in the day-to-day operations, but also in long-term strategic planning. Digital twins, virtual models that run on IoT data, can be used in the energy industry, such as to simulate the behaviour of assets in different conditions and react proactively to risks (Erhueh et al., 2024). In another case, IoT systems that are SAP-integrated allow predictive analytics and real-time resource of the whole procurement and logistics operation, thereby optimising supply chains (Seetharaman, 2021). This fact-based strategy is not restricted to the operations but empowers the executive-level decision-making. Dashboards and analytics platforms enabling leaders to visualise the most important indicators of the IoT can be used to set goals dynamically, budget and monitor performance across business units (Malik, 2024).

4 EMPOWERING END-USERS THROUGH IOT

The Internet of Things (IoT) has transformed how we interact with technology through increasingly personalised interpretation of user needs and reactions. Smart consumer applications, e.g., fitness trackers, voice-controlled assistants, and smart thermostats, learn the user's behaviour and preferences to build an adaptive environment to improve comfort, convenience, and health monitoring. Such personalised feature-rich services are made possible by interlinked sensors and analytics devices that collect and process real-time data to support services based on personalised needs (Sarker et al., 2024). One of the great strengths of IoT is building in feedback loops, where observed user data is pumped back into the system over time, and the quality of service and behaviour of the product can be improved. Such loops support incremental customisation and adaptive learning, which means that devices and platforms can grow with the user. For instance, smart homes rely on sensor data to automatically control the lighting/temperature, and fitness trackers adjust goals based on activity trends (Elmalaki, 2021). Feedback systems are equally important in health care, wherein an IoT-based artificial pancreas system employs continuous glucose monitoring (CGM) and adaptive insulin therapy to sustain glycaemic control among diabetic patients (Chakrabarty et al., 2019). Besides customisation, IoT also have a transformative value in digital inclusiveness. IoT can assist marginalised populations by enabling telehealth, smart agriculture and education to reach more people with little or no physical or geographical access. Under the umbrella of smart agriculture, IoT tech is tracking soil health, irrigation, and crop conditions as never before, giving small farmers the tools they need to maintain high productivity while treading lightly on the land. (Bhor et al., 2024). IoT also makes inclusive education for persons with disabilities possible. For instance, digital twin-based interactive learning, which enables students with mobility impairments to interact with virtual instances of laboratory tools, addresses physical obstacles and personalises their learning experiences. This increases access to education and skills development and develops a higher level of engagement. (Kumar et al.2024).

4.1 IOT Application End User Generation Model

4.1.1 Concept of End User Generation in IoT

End-user generation in IoT refers to offering means to end-users to create IoT solutions through intuitive interfaces and automation. Such systems rely heavily on End-User Development (EUD), which provides a framework for the users to customise the behaviour of the devices through visual or logic-based tools. Many such tools use trigger-action rules (e.g., if motion is detected, then switch on light), allowing users to create basic IoT behaviours without coding (Sanctorum, A., & Lujan, B. O., 2024).

4.1.2 *Frameworks Supporting End User Development*

Several tools have been developed to help end users develop their own IOT applications. One such example is AutoIoT, a tool that leverages a technique called Model-Driven Engineering (MDE). Essentially, users using AutoIoT only have to describe how they would like it to behave as a system in a simple JSON file. The system then auto-generates that file into a real working IoT application, so users do not need to monkey around with ugly code. In one test, 54 developers tried it, and 80% said they found it easy to use and would be using the tool somehow. For example, consider a user who desires a smart system for her greenhouse. They want it to switch on a water pump when the soil is dry and alert their phone. The device then reads this file and instantiates the code, and there we have a ready-to-run IoT application code which connects the soil sensor, the water pump and the phone notification service (Nepomuceno et al., 2020).

4.1.3 Model Architecture for End User IoT Generation

An IoT end-user generation model with layers for non-technical users to develop smart applications easily is designed to classify the system into three plain layers. The top layer is the user-centric interface, which provides Shelling peanuts-type tools, such as drag-and-drop builders or visual flowcharts. These tools allow people to build automation rules without writing any code. Users can, say, create a rule like "if motion occurs, turn on the light," simply by connecting blocks on a screen. The second is the abstraction and logic layer, which translates the user's rule into machine-readable commands. If the user specifies "after sunset", for example, the system will decode this to a real time based on local sunset information and issue the relevant instructions. The third component is the device management layer, which talks directly to your IoT devices, performs the actions and verifies whether things like a light turns on, or a notification is sent. Some applications, such as EUPont, are even smarter, since they use semantic models. This is to say, the system/application knows the command's meaning and has device adaptability. For instance, if the rule a user sets is "cool the room if it gets too hot," the system may decide whether to turn on a fan or an air-conditioning system, depending on what is available. The combined work of these three layers enables any user to develop and manage, at any scale, an IoT system customised to meet their needs (Roffarello, A. M. 2018).

4.1.4 Personalisation and UI Generation in IoT

Personalisation and UI generation are key to making IoT solutions more reachable and fun, especially to non-technical users. Personalisation enables IoT systems to follow user personal preferences. For instance, a smart home system can learn that a user likes his/her rooms cooler at night and set thermostats at the appropriate levels. Likewise, intelligent lighting systems can recognise user habits such as turning on certain lights at night and take over for the user. (Sanctorum, A., & Lujan, B. O., 2024). UI generation aims to build user-friendly screens to match the requirements of each user. Instead of displaying a messy interface with everything the system can do, show what the user needs to do. For instance, the elderly prefer large, high contrast buttons, while the younger, technology-savvy users are comfortable with small, tight layouts. In recent times, there has been research where deep learning models have been used to generate personalised UI layouts on-the-fly, from a mix of user data and visual design principles. A hybrid AI model with good personalised accuracy and fast responses in 2024 provided ROI regarding user satisfaction (Zhan et.al.,2024).

4.2 Managerial Insights: IoT Integration in Enterprises

- **Align Technology with Strategy:** IoT adoption must be driven by business goals, not technology enthusiasm. Aligning IoT initiatives with the organisation's strategic objectives ensures measurable outcomes such as improved efficiency and customer engagement (Attah et al., 2024).
- **Invest in Digital Readiness:** Employee upskilling, change management, and leadership commitment are as critical as infrastructure upgrades. A digital-first culture accelerates adoption and innovation (Yadav et al., 2024).
- **Leverage Data as an Asset:** Real-time analytics and predictive insights from IoT data empower proactive decision-making and long-term planning (Malik, 2024).

- **Governance Enables Trust:** Integrate data governance and security frameworks early to ensure compliance, transparency, and system reliability (Sicari et al., 2015).

Strategic integration of IoT transforms isolated digital projects into enterprise-wide capabilities that drive resilience, agility, and sustainable performance.

5 SCALABILITY: BUILDING FOR GROWTH

Scalability is one of the major factors towards creating the current digital systems capable of scaling with the surge of users, cumulative sums of data or service requirements. To be scalable, we have two basic concepts; horizontal and vertical scaling. Horizontal scaling is a method that is used to link several computers or cloud instances to operate as one Wi-Fi system to boost their performance and capacity of operating a large number of tasks at a time. This method is even more effective when there are a number of servers involved and distribute the loads of the tasks equally, which offers improved fault tolerance and system strength. (Roy et al.2018). Conversely, a vertical scale enhances the capacity of the existing servers (substituting the CPU and the memory). This method is best applied to low-latency and real-time-type solutions, though it can be resource-limiting and prone to more failure since it includes a single system (Rai et al., 2021). A hybrid design can implement both scaling techniques, providing responsiveness and wide scaling benefits. Systems such as HoloScale and HyScale are good examples showing how an intelligent control algorithm can exploit the speed of up by dealing with large-scale workloads in a horizontal scale-out fashion (Millnert & Eker, 2020).

It is a revolution of scalable system design via edge and cloud computing collaboration. With an explosion of connected devices and generated data, it is not efficient and cost-effective to shuttle all generated data to centralised cloud servers. To address this issue, the edge computing paradigm analyses the data closer to where it originates to lower latency, save on bandwidth, and enhance responsiveness in real-time. Meanwhile, the cloud provides high computational and data storage capabilities and long-term analytics. The inter-supplementation of edge and cloud resources facilitates more effective sharing of tasks in paying attention to the difference among them (particularly, those tasks communicated between edge-computing and cloud), where low-latency or security-critical operations are processed in the edge. In contrast, high-power processing and archival operations are delegated to the cloud (Sadeeq et al., 2021). The adoption of Internet of Things (IoT) sensing devices is skyrocketing due to their ability to provide real-time services. However, it is constrained by limited data storage and processing power. It offloads its massive data stream to edge devices and the cloud for adequate storage and processing. Optimised orchestration strategies applying good judgment over this handing over can considerably shrink the task completion times, particularly for low-complexity executable processes spread in many cloud centres (Edje et al., 2023). An Intelligent Defect Detection System leveraging cloud-edge synergy technology enhances industrial inspection accuracy and response time. Edge devices can handle data at the point of entry to detect defects in real-time, lessening the time delay and making sure that decisions are made quicker. At the same time, the cloud supports sophisticated analytics, model training, and long-term database to sustain improvement of the system. Such a hybrid architecture allows effectively allocating resources, scalability, and easily integrating manufacturing lines. Consequently, industries are able to attain increased quality of the products, less downtimes, and agile operations (Zhang et al., 2024).

5.1 Managerial Insight: Scalable IoT Systems Construction

- **Design to Be Flexible:** Both horizontal and vertical scalability must be designed early on using modular designs that allow scalability (Roy et al., 2018; Rai et al., 2021).
- **Balance Edge and Cloud Resources:** Local edge processing and cloud computing are a powerful combination, which optimises performance, minimizes latency, and allows scaling at a reasonable cost (Sadeequ et al., 2021).
- **Secure Each Layer:** With the increase in system size, vulnerabilities are increased. Defend with the use of security by design and ongoing monitoring of strong resilience (Dhirani et al., 2021).
- **Measure Performance in Real Time:** Have KPIs in place to track the uptime, latency and data accuracy of the system in order to keep it efficient as user demand increases.

IoT ecosystems do not just exist as a result of technical capacity but rather through adaptability, governance and proactive resource management.

6 CASE STUDIES: SUCCESSFUL IOT TRANSFORMATION

6.1 Case: Sustainable Excellence in Paper Making: IoT takes the Technology age to another in Paper Production.

6.1.1 Introduction

One of the companies that were producing machinery papers mid-sized lacked productivity of the machineries resulting in operational inefficiencies. The root of the problem was the inability of the company to use the emerging Internet of Things (IoT) technology in its manufacturing. By using the right digital tune through the digital transformation promoted by IoT, the company improved its output in production by a maximum of 20 as well as minimized the operation expenses by 15. A combination of digital technologies and long-term strategic direction only created such a change, showing how IoT would allow achieving sustainable operational excellence in the older traditional industries, including the paper industry.

6.1.2 Strategic Analysis

The revolution in the paper industry is no exception and a heavy trend toward sustainability and digital advancement is being realized. The competitive environment is being affected by a number of forces. The level of competition amongst the internal players is high due to the presence of many well established competitors that have low product differentiation and thus companies need to differentiate themselves based on efficiency and innovation. Moderate supplier power: It fluctuates depending on the availability of the raw material and limitations involved in sourcing of eco-pulp. Buyers power is high when giant customers (such as publishers and package companies) possess good bargaining power. The risk of new entrants is minimal because of a large amount of capital requirements and comparatively high environmental standards. In the meantime, its threat of substitution is medium particularly with its digital substitutes and packaging materials. The Trends that Determine the Current Development of the Industry The industry is rapidly developing, and the gradually growing focus on green production, the rise of automation, the development of digital technologies, and severe sustainability rules drive its changes.

Although such developments bring risks, including added costs and compliance challenges, they also bring the opportunity for innovation, efficiency, and competitive advantage. To successfully navigate these dynamics, a strategy that targets IoT and automation must be implemented and simultaneously address investment and workforce transformation.

6.1.3 Integration Frameworks and Change Management

The McKinsey 7S Framework was used in the implementation of the IoT to align the strategy, structure, systems, shared values, skills, staff, and style. The company also changed its organisational structure, and improved data capture and analysis systems and also trained engineers to become IoT experts. The leadership programs created an innovation and flexibility culture, which guaranteed the integration of the IoT was not local but applied throughout the company, not just by the engineering departments. The ADKAR Model- emphasizing on Awareness, Desire, Knowledge, Ability and Reinforcement was also conducive to change. Knowledge and ability were developed through communication campaigns developing awareness, incentive programs developing desire and the development of structure through training. The culture of continuous recognition and reinforcement was used to internalise the new culture to reduce any form of resistance to change.

6.1.4 Results and Conclusion

Combining strategic planning with strong change management and well-established frameworks such as McKinsey 7S and ADKAR, the company was able to shift to IoT-driven operations smoothly. The results were tangible and transformational: a 15% decrease in opex and a 20% increase in production in the first year of deployment. In addition to the financial benefits, the company witnessed increased employee engagement and a larger market share for sustainable products while reinforcing its competitive positioning. This case highlights the importance of matching technology to organisational readiness and strategy. Also, it demonstrates how digital transformation, when implemented comprehensively, can lead to sustained excellence and sustainability in traditional manufacturing.

6.2 Case: IoT Orchestration for A Large Retail Chain Across the World

6.2.1 Introduction

A global multinational retail company is expanding rapidly worldwide. However, handling the large amounts of data generated by the proliferating network of IOT devices is challenging as the company increases its global reach. Despite its promise for insights, efficiencies, and customer service, many organisations struggle without a coherent IoT strategy. Data management hurdles, insufficient infrastructure, and skill gaps are adding to the difficulty in realising the true potential of IoT in the organisation.

6.2.2 A Framework of Six Phases for IoT Strategy Execution

A structured six-stage approach is suggested to tackle the organisation's problems. The first stage is "Define Objectives," which requires the enterprise to establish unique business objectives for IoT deployment, such as better inventory management, greater customer personalisation, or decreased operational expenses. The second phase, data review, checks the nature of the current IoT data and its amount and movement to perceive its nature and use. The third phase is technology assessment, since existing infrastructures are evaluated concerning scalability and compatibility needed for a successful deployment of the IoT. The fourth phase, Strategy Formulation, requires the development of a custom IoT road-map in the context of the organisation's objectives. The fifth phase is implementation, which runs operations with system integration of IoT in all business functions and ongoing performance monitoring. The sixth step, post-implementation evaluation, ensures that the outcomes are consistent with the starting goals and looks for opportunities for iteration or scaling.

6.2.3 IoT and Business and Technology Integration

Aligning the IoT efforts with the general company strategy was one of the essential success factors. The company also changed its perception of IoT as an independent technical project to that of a strategic key to its growth. As an example, in case customer experience was among the strategic priorities, IoT-enabled applications like customised offers, live updates of stocks, and smart queue management were created to contribute to satisfaction and loyalty. Technologically the firm was also interested in developing a strong digital backbone that would be able to carry huge data streams. This encompassed high-performance cloud infrastructure, edge computing, and real-time insights AI-based engines. The issue of cybersecurity came into focus. The company also enhanced adhesion to endpoint security, data encryption, and access management regulations after Bain and Company reported that cybersecurity issues are the paramount obstacle to the success of the IoT. This proactive attitude provided compliance with regulations, continuity of business, and confidence among customers in a marketplace that was becoming more conscious of data. The coordination of business strategy and technology meant that all the IoT investments provided quantifiable strategic pay-off - operational efficiencies or increased customer interaction.

6.2.4 Data Governance, Workforce and Change Management

The company realised the fact that without human change, there would be no technological change. In this way, it initiated a sequence of human resource development projects aimed at the creation of IoT-centric expertise such as data analytics, device management, cloud security, and predictive modeling. The philosophy of learn-and-grow made the employees embrace new tools without any hesitation and reduced the risk of job displacement. The change of culture was supported with the help of regular change management which was based on the ADKAR Model (Awareness, Desire, Knowledge, Ability, and Reinforcement). Role-based training, communication campaigns and incentive mechanisms assisted the employees to seamlessly enter into the digital era. Simultaneously, data governance became one of the pillars. As the IoT ecosystem produces petabytes of sensitive operational and customer data, governance mechanisms were necessary to achieve compliance, accuracy and ethical usage. The company established the position of data stewardship, implemented policies of management of data lifecycle, and made governance structure compliant with international laws, such as GDPR. Sound governance, in addition to alleviating risk, also helped Project Free TV to be viewed as a reliable digital brand, which increased customer loyalty and positive investor sentiment.

6.2.5 Aligning IoT With Business Strategy

One of the most significant factors in determining the success of IoT projects is the integration of IoT initiatives with the overall corporate strategy. When thoughtfully harnessed within the business, IoT becomes a growth and innovation accelerator, not a technology experiment with a lack of business impact. For example, suppose customer experience is a high priority on the strategic agenda. In that case, IoT applications that deliver tailored in-store promotions, real-time inventory updates, and innovative shelf applications can be delivered to move the needle on customer satisfaction in tangible ways. PwC adds that firms that articulate business objectives around IoT are 1.6 times more likely to see a strong return on investment, underscoring the need for strategic planning from the beginning.

6.2.6 Key Results and Strategic Impact

After enabling an expansive IoT solution, the company saw a 15% improvement in productivity thanks to augmented workflows and the elimination of overlap. Restructuring the hosting infrastructure to facilitate the high-volume data processing resulted in a 20% decrease in the scheduled downtime period. Improving practices around data governance led to a 10% rise in customer trust, pivotal at a time when concerns over data privacy grip the computing universe. By focusing on targeted change management programs, employees' abilities around IoT device management were considerably accelerated. Inventory accuracy increased 25%, driven by real-time data integration and predictive analytics.

6.2.7 Evaluation and Strategic Recommendations

Although good numbers are being achieved, there can be further strategic actions for a better long-term advantage. Investigating potential partnerships with top IoT vendors or tech companies may help combat the innovation stagnation that pervades small- and medium-sized organisations and expedite time-to-value for new solutions. Iterative technology upgrades could offer a nimbler response to shifts in market needs rather than a significant, infrequently necessary overhaul. Furthermore, spending more on developing and educating the workforce would guarantee prolonged capacity expansion and innovation readiness. Finally, you should plan periodic technology assessments/benchmarks to ensure the organisation's IoT capabilities remain current and future-proof.

6.3 Case: IoT Integration Strategy for Telecom Industry Competitive Landscape

6.3.1 Introduction and Business Context

In a fiercely competitive telecommunications market in the world, innovation, agility, and efficiency are the distinguishing factors. The IoT revolution has placed telecom operators at the center of the revolution because self-driving cars, drones, and other connected devices rely on the communication networks that they run. Nonetheless, a telecom company experienced acute problems of stability, security, and efficiency of the network which compromised its competitiveness and efficiency.

Although dealing with large data volumes of endpoints of the IoT, the company did not have a well-thought-out plan of integrating IoT and strong digital infrastructure. Lack of cohesiveness in approach resulted in divided operations, increased operation expenses, repetitive service interruptions, and lack of uniform customer experiences. These issues required an extensive IoT integration roadmap - the one that could streamline the performance, increase customer confidence, and position the organisation as a digitally developed market leader.

6.3.2 IoT Deployment Strategic Roadmap

The company developed a phased approach of implementing an IoT strategy based on the best practice of consulting and aligned to the reality of the telecom industry.

Diagnostic Assessment: The first phase was an in-depth analysis of the current IoT ecosystem and network infrastructure. Connections and data flow pathways between devices were found to experience bottlenecks, performance problems, and security vulnerabilities. This diagnosis was useful in identifying inefficiency and working out strong infrastructure upgrades.

Strategy Development: A revised vision of IoT was developed, which was according to the core strategy of the organisation, that is, enhancing the customer experience, network reliability, and cost-effectiveness. The firm focused on investing in scalable technology, robust cyber security systems, and mature analytics. The resultant multi-year investment roadmap meant that it defined orderly funding and accountability principles.

Process Optimisation: The re-engineering of the operational processes was done to remove redundancies and enhance governance. They adopted the best practices in the area of device bootstrapping, encryption, authentication, and maintenance to be efficient and compliant.

Implementation and Scaling: Pilot programs using IoT were undertaken to test the programs. To create in-house skills, training programs were introduced, and employee buy-in and cultural alignment were encouraged through the use of leadership workshops. The stages-based implementation plan minimized risks and interruptions, as well as promoted constant learning.

Performance Management: The organisation created a performance analytics dashboard to view the performance in real time based on the main performance indicators such as network uptime, customer satisfaction, and operational efficiency. This data-driven service enhanced the process of improvement through the iterative approach and agile decision-making that made sure that the IoT was to be in line with the short-term objectives and the long-term strategy.

6.3.3 Key Outcomes and Business Transformation

The IoT integration initiative produced measurable, enterprise-wide benefits that demonstrated the power of aligning digital transformation with strategic intent:

- **15% reduction in network outages and service interruptions**, achieved through improved infrastructure design and process control.
- **20% decrease in security incidents**, thanks to standardised security frameworks and employee upskilling.

- **25% increase in actionable insights** from data analytics and visualisation tools, enabling faster and more informed decision-making.
- **30% reduction in operational costs**, achieved through process automation, redundancy elimination, and efficiency gains.
- Improved **cross-functional collaboration**, breaking down organisational silos and fostering innovation across teams.

These outcomes validated the effectiveness of the **phased IoT integration strategy**, showing that careful planning, stakeholder engagement, and iterative learning can transform technological potential into tangible business value.

6.3.4 Challenges of Implementation and Foundations of Governance

Although the integration of IoT was successful, there were a number of challenges encountered in its implementation that demanded concerted efforts. The most acute problem was a constraint of old infrastructure that was not as scalable and with processing power to further support the intensifying IoT traffic. To solve this, there was a need to upgrade and re-engineer. There was also the issue of cultural resistance because the employees were reluctant to use new technologies. To address this, structured ADKAR based change management program was adopted by the company, which involved awareness creation, training and reinforcement, which made the adoption smoother and enhanced employee engagement.

The volume of data generated by IoT was another burning issue that led to data governance. The company has reacted to this by setting up a strong governance system that specifies the ownership and privacy level of data and access control such that it does not violate international rules such as GDPR. In a bid to maintain the change, a list of Key Performance Indicators (KPIs) such as network uptime, time to respond to an incident, customer satisfaction, operational cost savings, and IoT-inspired increase in revenue were established. These KPIs established a continuous feedback system to track progress, enhance decision-making, and stay strategic.

6.3.5 Strategic insights, scalability and future suggestions

The IoT project showcased the most important learning which informed the long-term digital approach of the company. The organisational silos that used to exist were eliminated which promoted cross-functional working that enhanced productivity and speed of innovation. The strengthening of a customer-focused strategy also meant that any investments made in IoT directly improved the level of customer satisfaction, which aligns with Gartner in the sense that experience-driven companies win brand loyalty over their competitors.

Scalability and flexibility were made strategic priorities. Embracing modular and cloud-native systems and collaborating with technology providers helped the company make the innovation process much faster and adapt to the changing business requirements simpler. Improved analytics and machine learning opportunities transformed IoT data into actionable intelligence, which made it possible to conduct predictive maintenance, demand forecasting, and personalised services. Data security and privacy such as encryption and authentication ensured security and enhanced customer confidence.

To achieve success in the long-term, the company ought to keep modernising legacy infrastructure, investing in data governance and workforce development and building ecosystem partnerships in order to maintain innovation. A culture of agility and continuous improvement will assist the organisation to stay afloat and competitive in the fast-moving telecommunication environment.

6.3.6 Conclusion and Recommendations

The IoT integration approach significantly improved network reliability, data protection, operational efficiency, and business innovation, making it a successful digital transformation project for the telco company. However, long-term sustainability and competitiveness require more. Further investment in advanced analytics and strong data governance is needed to unlock IoT data's power and help ensure better decision-making. Also critical is the reinforcement of change management programs that promote cultural alignment and secure employee buy-in as the business matures. Updating legacy infrastructure is still one of the top priorities since it can accommodate growing device connectivity and the associated volume of data, while offering scalability and future-proofing. "Furthermore, driving innovation through strategic relationships in the technology ecosystem will enable the company to continue to be nimble, working closely with industry partners and quickly adapting to market change." By internalising these behaviours in its operational and strategic DNA, the firm will be able to lead in a fast-evolving digital and connected telecom world.

6.4 Lessons Learned from all three IoT case studies

Table 2. Cross-Case Insights: Comparative Lessons from IoT Transformation Initiatives

Dimension	Case 1: Paper Manufacturing	Case 2: Global Retail Chain	Case 3: Telecom Industry	Cross-Case Insight
Strategic Alignment	IoT integrated with sustainability and efficiency goals through McKinsey's 7S framework.	IoT linked directly to core business objectives—inventory accuracy, customer experience, cost efficiency.	IoT aligned with corporate priorities—network reliability, innovation, and customer-centric growth.	Alignment of IoT initiatives with overall business strategy is a universal driver of transformation success.
Change Management	ADKAR model reduced resistance and built digital skills.	Structured training and communication ensured cultural readiness.	Leadership-led collaboration dismantled silos and encouraged innovation.	Effective change management and employee engagement are critical enablers of IoT adoption.
Performance Measurement (KPIs)	KPIs tracked operational cost, productivity, and sustainability outcomes.	KPI dashboard measured productivity, customer satisfaction, and system uptime.	Real-time analytics and KPIs guided continuous improvement and innovation.	Data-driven KPI frameworks sustain accountability and strategic focus during digital transformation.
Data Governance & Security	Data management embedded within operational frameworks for reliability.	Strong data governance enhanced trust and compliance across regions.	Cybersecurity and compliance reinforced customer confidence.	Governance and security are foundational pillars of scalable and trustworthy IoT ecosystems.
Scalability & Technology Integration	Hybrid IoT architecture enabled process automation and predictive maintenance.	Six-phase framework supported scalable deployment across global stores.	Modular, cloud-native infrastructure enabled future 5G and AI integration.	Scalable design and modular architectures ensure agility and future readiness.
Sustainability & Value Creation	Demonstrated that digital innovation and sustainability can coexist profitably.	Balanced operational efficiency with customer personalization.	Strengthened competitive positioning while improving energy efficiency.	Sustainable digital excellence integrates economic, environmental, and social value.
Human Capital & Partnerships	Upskilling initiatives built long-term capability.	Collaboration with technology vendors accelerated implementation.	Ecosystem partnerships fostered continuous innovation.	Investing in people and partnerships amplifies IoT-driven transformation impact.

Source: Authors contributions

The comparison of the three cases of IoT transformations in Paper Manufacturing, Global Retail Chain, and Telecom Industry demonstrates the same tendency of strategic, operational, and cultural enablers that enable successful digital transformation. As concluded in Table 2, strategic alignment between the IoT initiatives and the organisational goals proved to be the most important factor in attaining quantifiable business value. Both organisations proved that IoT as part of the corporate strategy has guaranteed that the investments in technology have been translated into sustainable performance benefits. The decisive role was also played by change management and human capital development models, which included ADKAR and leadership-driven engagement that withdrew the resistance and led to digital fluency development. The availability of clear Key Performance Indicators (KPIs) also allowed companies to monitor efficiency and productivity of operations, as well as customer satisfaction, and continuously improve. Also, effective data governance and security systems played a crucial role in creating trust, ensuring compliance, and enhancing the scalability of the systems. Modular architecture, sustainability goals, and ecosystem alliances as part of dynamic environment flexibility and creativity were present in both instances. Combined with these observations, the transformation of the IoT is broader than the implementation of the technology: it is an organisational capacity rooted in strategy, culture, governance, cooperation and based on long-term digital excellence and resilience across industries.

7 FINDINGS

The importance of privacy and ethical consideration lies in the fact that the amount of personal and behavioural information that is gathered will be huge in the case of IoT applications. Trust is obligatory respecting the consent of users and privacy of sensitive data. Practical privacy frameworks may not exist and therefore, end-users may be tracked or abused. Ethical data governance is also related to transparency and accountability in case end-users of products use data to build smart homes, healthcare, or wearables (Weber, 2015). Companies should follow the laws and regulations of data usage and privacy in order to ensure that the rights of users are not violated and to avoid law violations. Data laws like the European Union General Data Protection Regulation (GDPR) have stringent stipulations regarding the collection, storage and processing of such personal data. Adherence to such legislations ensures protection of users and creation of trust and reliability towards the use of IoT systems. This may result in serious financial fines and bad publicity in case of failure. This means that regulatory compliance becomes an essential component of any mitigation planning of IoT no matter the fly-by-wire type of operations, in both the initial stages and throughout the activities (Sicari et al.,

2015). There are considerable barriers in cost and infrastructure especially to the SMEs and in certain regions. The investment in IOT solutions typically involves a large initial expense of hardware, connectivity and data management. It is possible that the high price of SME will deter their adoption and innovative growth (Whitmore et al., 2015). Moreover, a good proportion of these digitally underserved areas already has compromised digital infrastructure, bad internet connectivity, bad power supply and bad technical literacy. The bridging of this divide is a government role, along with the partnership of the state and the private with scalable and low-cost IOT systems (Ray, 2018). Problems also include standardisation and interoperability. Universal and non-interoperable systems have created siloed ecosystems that do not allow devices and platforms of different manufacturers to effectively exchange data. Such fragmentation not only results in an added complexity in the implementation, but also exposes security vulnerabilities and magnifies the scaling (Borgia, 2014).

The industry should collaborate to reach the open standards and make sure that the difference in devices and networks can still be available. The right direction is taken by such projects like the IETF (Internet Engineering Task Force) and OCF (Open Connectivity Foundation). Nevertheless, they need something more harmonious on an international level. Overcoming these obstacles is a big milestone towards the realisation of the potential of IoT as a disruptive element. Companies have a long way to go in regard to privacy by design introduction, infrastructure advancement, and standardisation cooperation. The other point of view is to incorporate the voices of the users in the design and governance of IoT. The responsible innovation enables the businesses to overcome the digital divide, achieve the trust of users and use the potential of IoT to spur value throughout the system (Dhirani et.al 2021).

8 ETHICAL AND GOVERNANCE CONSIDERATIONS

The increasing Internet of Things (IoT) is associated with pressing ethical and governance concerns regarding privacy, accountability, inclusiveness and security. As billions of devices collect and distribute information, the problem of data ownership, permission, and monitoring is gaining relevance. Uncontrolled, and massive, personal and behavioural data can be misused, or exploited (Weber, 2015; Sicari et al., 2015). Thereafter, effective data governance systems should be in place to prevent privacy rule breaches such as the GDPR without creating transparency and user trust. Accountability is also challenging due to decentralisation and heterogeneity of networks of IoT, and thus it requires particular stewardship and interoperable standards (Ray, 2018; Borgia, 2014). Moreover, the relationship between AI-based analytics and the IoT is also rooted in the ethical concerns of prejudice, algorithmic equitability, and clarity (Ullah et al., 2024). Digital inclusiveness as the concept of low-cost connectivity and equitable access has been a priority in preventing the rising digital divide (Bhor et al., 2024). Finally, strong encryption, authentication and the resilience-by-design concepts are policies that make it possible to protect against systemic vulnerabilities (Dhirani et al., 2021). Incorporating ethics and governance into the entire cycle of designing and setting up is a certain assurance that IoT systems would encourage responsible, open, and equitable digital transformation besides aligning innovation with societal well-being.

9 FUTURE IMPLICATIONS

The age of connection infiltrates the age of the Internet of Things (IoT), and taking everything into consideration, to the future of a more connected and smarter world, which is driven by disruptive powers such as 5G, Artificial Intelligence (AI) and digital twins. All those efforts converge to change the manner in which devices communicate, the manner in which information is captured and processed, as well as how a user interacts with virtual worlds (Goyal et al., 2021). These services require only 5G connectivity to ensure that they fulfil ultra-fast, ultra-reliable, low-latency, high-density devices, and real-time connectivity among other conditions. This is the new network design that is central to applications in autonomous cars, telemedicine, and robotics in the industrial world. Besides processing large volumes of data at once, 5G is capable of giving rise to high-quality and reliable communications of a huge scale (Osseiran et al., 2014). In the meantime, AI implementation on the level of the IoT ecosystem transforms raw input data into acted results. AI helps clarify the user behaviour to the devices to predict the results and self-enhance the processes. Such a change may transform IoT as a reactive to a source of proactive decision-making to increase the efficiency of operation and customer experience. One of the most well-established and potent themes of transformation in the digital world (Ullah et al.,2024) is the advent of digital twins which are dynamic and computer-based models of the physical objects, systems and even processes. Knowledgeable about the newest information coming out of sensorised IoT devices, the digital twins allow businesses to model scenarios, anticipate whatever will occur or how it will look in advance and fine tune and be efficient prior to altering the physical world. This approach enhances the control and risk management and supports well-informed data-driven decisions in challenging and quickly evolving situations (Fuller et al., 2020). As of today, the major obstacle to the development of the IoT is incompatible standards and disjointed platforms. It needs open standards, collaborative governance and competing sectoral practices to get flawless interchangeability between gadgets and platforms (Gubbi et al., 2013). User-centred design of next-generation IoT systems should be fostered through clear data practices, user privacy controls, and design accessibility. The next step of IoT should pay attention to ethical problems and solve the digital divide to make IoT affordable and invincible, especially in poor and underdeveloped areas (Weber et al., 2018).

10 CONCLUSION

The IoT is a revolutionary connection between the enterprise and its customers. Connected ecosystems are created and exchanged, based on real-time information, innovation, personalisation and operational efficiency. As IoT matures, enterprises are redefining the potential of the connected world to deliver value for businesses, changing how they operate and engage with customers, employees and partners. Health tracking systems, smart homes, smart logistics chains or urban mobility, you name it; from health to industry, from assets to people, IoT transforms how people interact across every industry by placing the user at the heart of the digital experience." (Din et al.,2018). However, as businesses invest in IoT, the requirement for inclusive, scalable, and ethical design becomes more important than ever. Inclusion means IoT solutions should be available to everyone, including disenfranchised groups such as small businesses and people in areas with poor connectivity. Without planned design decisions to cure the digital divide, social and economic disparities could increase further. For example, it is well known that some classes of small and medium-sized enterprises (SMEs) face costs and infrastructure issues that can constrain their participation within the IoT economy (Gubbi et al.,2013). Scalability is another essential pillar. When millions (or even billions) of devices connect to the internet, we must use agile, interoperable and dependable architectures to build IoT systems. 5G, edge computing and digital twins are significant in that these make scalable real-time operation possible and the rapid proliferation of device networks, irrespective of domain and geography (Hildebrandt et al.,2024). The power of the Internet of Things (IoT) can never be fully realised based on its new technologies, but in the new ways it must be used to improve people's lives in connected urban environments. In order to fulfil this promise, businesses need to react to IoT with an integrated approach from end to end –one that fuses digital transformation with social responsibility. This includes driving equitable access to IoT, investing in scalable and resilient infrastructure and embedding ethical governance throughout deployments. By embracing such principles, businesses can also prevent digital divides and ensure that IoT is for everyone, not just the 'IoT elite'. In this way, the IoT becomes a driver of connectivity and equity, which helps to form a brighter and fairer future (Weber, 2015).

REFERENCES

Agarwal, V., Purwar, S., & Agrawal, S. (2024, November). IoT-Driven Environmental Surveillance to Foster Sustainable Development. In *2024 3rd Edition of IEEE Delhi Section Flagship Conference (DELCON)* (pp. 1-6). IEEE. DOI: 10.1109/DELCON64804.2024.10866673

Attah, R. U., Garba, B. M. P., Gil-Ozoudeh, I., & Iwuanyanwu, O. (2024). Strategic frameworks for digital transformation across logistics and energy sectors: Bridging technology with business strategy. *Open Access Res J Sci Technol, 12*(02), 070-80.

Bhor, P. P., Mishra, J. R., Valvi, P. R., Thale, R. J., & Dodia, S. (2024, December). A systematic review on the application of IoT in agriculture. In *IET Conference Proceedings CP900* (Vol. 2024, No. 23, pp. 12-18). Stevenage, UK: The Institution of Engineering and Technology.

Borgia, E. (2014). Internet of Things vision: Key features, applications and open issues. *Computer Communications, 54*, 1–31. DOI: 10.1016/j.comcom.2014.09.008

Çeken, C. (2024). *Design and Implementation of a Scalable IoT-Based Real-Time Environmental Monitoring and Alarm System: An Experimental Study. Vestnik of M.* Kozybayev North Kazakhstan University. DOI: 10.54596/2958-0048-2024-3-155-164

Chakrabarty, A., Zavitsanou, S., Sowrirajan, T., Doyle, F. J., III, & Dassau, E. (2019). Getting IoT-ready: The face of next generation artificial pancreas systems. In *The Artificial Pancreas* (pp. 29-57). Academic Press.

Cui, L., Gao, M., Dai, J., & Mou, J. (2022). Improving supply chain collaboration through operational excellence approaches: An IoT perspective. *Industrial Management & Data Systems, 122*(3), 565–591. DOI: 10.1108/IMDS-01-2020-0016

Dhirani, L. L., Armstrong, E., & Newe, T. (2021). Industrial IoT, cyber threats, and standards landscape: Evaluation and roadmap. *Sensors (Basel), 21*(11), 3901. DOI: 10.3390/s21113901 PMID: 34198727

Din, I. U., Guizani, M., Hassan, S., Kim, B. S., Khan, M. K., Atiquzzaman, M., & Ahmed, S. H. (2018). The Internet of Things: A review of enabled technologies and future challenges. *IEEE Access : Practical Innovations, Open Solutions, 7*, 7606–7640. DOI: 10.1109/ACCESS.2018.2886601

Edje, A. E., Abd Latiff, M. S., & Chan, W. H. (2023). IoT data analytic algorithms on edge-cloud infrastructure: A review. *Digital Communications and Networks, 9*(6), 1486–1515. DOI: 10.1016/j.dcan.2023.10.002

Egbuhuzor, N. S., Ajayi, A. J., Akhigbe, E. E., & Agbede, O. O. (2024). Leveraging AI and cloud solutions for energy efficiency in large-scale manufacturing. *International Journal of Science and Research Archive, 13*(2), 4170–4192. DOI: 10.30574/ijsra.2024.13.2.2314

Elmalaki, S. (2021, May). Fair-IoT: Fairness-aware human-in-the-loop reinforcement learning for harnessing human variability in personalised IoT. In *Proceedings of the International Conference on Internet-of-Things Design and Implementation* (pp. 119-132). DOI: 10.1145/3450268.3453525

Erhueh, O. V., Elete, T., Akano, O. A., Nwakile, C., & Hanson, E. (2024). Application of Internet of Things (IoT) in energy infrastructure: Lessons for the future of operations and maintenance. *Comprehensive Research and Reviews in Science and Technology, 2*(2), 28–54. DOI: 10.57219/crrst.2024.2.2.0036

Fuller, A., Fan, Z., Day, C., & Barlow, C. (2020). Digital twin: Enabling technologies, challenges and open research. *IEEE Access : Practical Innovations, Open Solutions, 8*, 108952–108971. DOI: 10.1109/ACCESS.2020.2998358

Goyal, P., Sahoo, A. K., & Sharma, T. K. (2021). Internet of things: Architecture and enabling technologies. *Materials Today: Proceedings, 34*, 719–735. DOI: 10.1016/j.matpr.2020.04.678

Gubbi, J., Buyya, R., Marusic, S., & Palaniswami, M. (2013). Internet of Things (IoT): A vision, architectural elements, and future directions. *Future Generation Computer Systems, 29*(7), 1645–1660.

Hildebrandt, G., Dittler, D., Habiger, P., Drath, R., & Weyrich, M. (2024). Data integration for digital twins in industrial automation: A systematic literature review. *IEEE Access : Practical Innovations, Open Solutions, 12*, 139129–139153. DOI: 10.1109/ACCESS.2024.3465632

Kumar, A., Saudagar, A. K. J., & Khan, M. B. (2024). Enhanced medical education for physically disabled people through integration of IoT and digital twin technologies. *Systems, 12*(9), 325. DOI: 10.3390/systems12090325

Malik, S. (2024). Data-driven decision-making: Leveraging the IoT for real-time sustainability in organizational behavior. *Sustainability (Basel), 16*(15), 6302. DOI: 10.3390/su16156302

Millnert, V., & Eker, J. (2020, December). HoloScale: Horizontal and vertical scaling of cloud resources. In *2020 IEEE/ACM 13th International Conference on Utility and Cloud Computing (UCC)* (pp. 196-205). IEEE.

Mu, X., & Antwi-Afari, M. F. (2024). The applications of Internet of Things (IoT) in industrial management: A science mapping review. *International Journal of Production Research*, *62*(5), 1928–1952. DOI: 10.1080/00207543.2023.2290229

Nepomuceno, T., Carneiro, T., Maia, P. H., Adnan, M., Nepomuceno, T., & Martin, A. (2020, March). AutoIoT: A framework based on user-driven MDE for generating IoT applications. In *Proceedings of the 35th Annual ACM Symposium on Applied Computing* (pp. 719-728). DOI: 10.1145/3341105.3373873

Osseiran, A., Boccardi, F., Braun, V., Kusume, K., Marsch, P., Maternia, M., Queseth, O., Schellmann, M., Schotten, H., Taoka, H., Tullberg, H., Uusitalo, M. A., Timus, B., & Fallgren, M. (2014). Scenarios for 5G mobile and wireless communications: The vision of the METIS project. *IEEE Communications Magazine*, *52*(5), 26–35. DOI: 10.1109/MCOM.2014.6815890

Rai, K., Sahana, B., Pai, A. N., Gautham, S., & Dhanush, U. (2021, August). Vertical scaling of virtual machines in cloud environment. In *2021 International Conference on Recent Trends on Electronics, Information, Communication & Technology (RTE-ICT)* (pp. 458-462). IEEE. DOI: 10.1109/RTEICT52294.2021.9573715

Ray, P. P. (2018). A survey on Internet of Things architectures. *Journal of King Saud University. Computer and Information Sciences*, *30*(3), 291–319. DOI: 10.1016/j.jksuci.2016.10.003

Richard Bevis, R. B. (2023, April 19). *7 Examples of IoT in Everyday Life*.

Roffarello, A. M. (2018, June). End user development in the IoT: a semantic approach. In *2018, 14th International Conference on Intelligent Environments (IE)* (pp. 107-110). IEEE. DOI: 10.1109/IE.2018.00026

Roy, C., Pandey, M., & Rautaray, S. S. (2018). An approach for optimal horizontal scaling in big data scenario. In Advances in Data and Information Sciences: Proceedings of ICDIS-2017, Volume 1 (pp. 223-230). Springer Singapore

Sadeeq, M. M., Abdulkareem, N. M., Zeebaree, S. R., Ahmed, D. M., Sami, A. S., & Zebari, R. R. (2021). IoT and Cloud computing issues, challenges and opportunities: A review. *Qubahan Academic Journal*, *1*(2), 1–7. DOI: 10.48161/qaj.v1n2a36

Sallam, K., Mohamed, M., & Mohamed, A. W. (2023). Internet of Things (IoT) in supply chain management: Challenges, opportunities, and best practices. *Sustainable Machine Intelligence Journal*, *2*, 3–1. DOI: 10.61185/SMIJ.2023.22103

Sanctorum, A., & Lujan, B. O. (2024, June). Towards End-User-Driven Generation of IoT Applications. In *Companion Proceedings of the 16th ACM SIGCHI Symposium on Engineering Interactive Computing Systems* (pp. 66-73). DOI: 10.1145/3660515.3661332

Sarker, A., Jesser, A., & Speidel, M. (2024, April). Enhancing Decentralized Federated Learning with User Feedback Loops: A Novel Approach for Personalized and Adaptive Learning in IoT Environments. In *2024 IEEE 3rd International Conference on Computing and Machine Intelligence (ICMI)* (pp. 1-5). IEEE. DOI: 10.1109/ICMI60790.2024.10585926

Seetharaman, K. M. R.Karthika Murugandi Reddiar Seetharaman. (2021). Internet of Things (IoT) Applications in SAP: A Survey of Trends, Challenges, and Opportunities. *Int. J. Adv. Res. Sci. Commun. Technol*, *3*(2), 499–508. DOI: 10.48175/IJARSCT-6268B

Sicari, S., Rizzardi, A., Grieco, L. A., & Coen-Porisini, A. (2015). Security, privacy and trust in Internet of Things: The road ahead. *Computer Networks*, *76*, 146–164. DOI: 10.1016/j.comnet.2014.11.008

Ullah, R., Yahya, M., Mostarda, L., Alshammari, A., Alutaibi, A. I., Sarwar, N., Ullah, F., & Ullah, S. (2024). Intelligent decision making for energy efficient fog nodes selection and smart switching in the IOT: A machine learning approach. *PeerJ. Computer Science*, *10*, e1833. DOI: 10.7717/peerj-cs.1833 PMID: 38660213

Weber, R. H. (2015). Internet of things: A review of privacy concerns. *Computer Law & Security Review*, *31*(5), 618–627. DOI: 10.1016/j.clsr.2015.07.002

Whitmore, A., Agarwal, A., & Da Xu, L. (2015). The Internet of Things—A survey of topics and trends. *Information Systems Frontiers*, *17*(2), 261–274. DOI: 10.1007/s10796-014-9489-2

Yadav, N., Gupta, V., & Garg, A. (2024). Industrial Automation Through AI-Powered Intelligent Machines—Enabling Real-Time Decision-Making. In *Recent Trends in Artificial Intelligence Towards a Smart World: Applications in Industries and Sectors* (pp. 145–178). Springer Nature Singapore. DOI: 10.1007/978-981-97-6790-8_5

Zhan, X., Xu, Y., & Liu, Y. (2024). Personalized UI layout generation using deep learning: An adaptive interface design approach for enhanced user experience. *International Journal of Engineering and Management Research*, *14*(5), 134–147.

Zhang, H., Hou, L., Yang, H., Bai, Y., Lu, Z., & Liu, Y. (2024, May). Intelligent Defect Detection System Based on Cloud-edge Synergy Technology. In *2024 IEEE 9th International Conference on Smart Cloud (SmartCloud)* (pp. 103-108). IEEE Computer Society. DOI: 10.1109/SmartCloud62736.2024.00026

KEY TERMS AND DEFINITIONS

Artificial Intelligence (AI): This is the process of simulating human intelligence processes through machines, especially to analyze data, identify patterns, and make forecasts as a part of the IoT system.

Cloud Computing: Provision of computing services such as servers, storage and databases through internet thereby facilitating scalable infrastructure and data analytics of IoT systems.

Data Governance: The policies and practices that make sure that there is proper data management, quality, security and compliance of the data created and processed in the IoT systems.

Digital Transformation: The integration of digital technologies such as IoT, AI, and cloud computing into business operations to improve efficiency, innovation, and customer experience.

Digital Twin: A virtual replica of a physical asset or system that uses real-time IoT data to simulate, monitor, and optimize performance, enhancing predictive analytics and maintenance.

Edge Computing: A distributed computing architecture in which data processing is performed at the source (the edge of a network) as opposed to completely depending on centralized cloud servers, and further minimizing latency and bandwidth consumption.

End-User Development (EUD): A framework allowing non-technical users to create or customize IoT applications through intuitive interfaces and automation rules, such as "if-this-then-that" logic.

Internet of Things (IoT): A network of interconnected devices equipped with sensors, software, and connectivity that enables them to collect, exchange, and analyze data over the internet, fostering automation and intelligent decision-making across industries.

Predictive Maintenance: This is a type of data-based strategy that involves utilizing IoT sensors to detect equipment and anticipate failures in advance and minimize downtime and maintenance expenses.

Scalability: The capability of a system to handle increasing workloads: users, or devices without compromising performance or reliability, achieved through horizontal or vertical scaling.

Smart Systems: Integrated environments (e.g., smart homes, cities, or factories) that leverage IoT devices and analytics to automate and optimize operations based on real-time data.

Sustainability: The concept of utilizing IoT and other technologies to enhance the efficiency of resources, minimize waste, and encourage sustainable businesses in all industries.

Chapter 8
Marketing Strategies for IoT Consumer Adoption:
Understanding Consumer Psychology and Building Brand Trust

F. Sammy
SRM Institute of Science and Technology, India

A. Prema
Velammal Engineering College, India

M. Mohana
Vel Tech Multi Tech Dr. Rangarajan Dr. Sakunthala Engineering College, India

T. P. Anish
http://orcid.org/0000-0002-4308-9645
R.M.K. College of Engineering and Technology, India

G. Manisha
R.M.D. Engineering College, India

M. G. Dinesh
http://orcid.org/0009-0009-7643-5338
EASA College of Engineering and Technology, India

ABSTRACT

The rapid growth of Internet of Things (IoT) consumer products has transformed daily life, yet widespread adoption remains a challenge due to privacy concerns, perceived risks, and usability barriers. This chapter explores marketing strategies that enhance IoT consumer adoption by integrating insights from consumer psychology and trust-building practices. It explores key psychological factors influencing adoption, such as perceived usefulness, risk, and social influence, and highlights the importance of transparent communication and brand reputation. Strategies like education campaigns, personalized messaging, and influencer engagement are discussed as means to address consumer fears and motivations. The chapter also

DOI: 10.4018/979-8-3373-3441-7.ch008

identifies future directions including personalized marketing, gamification, and ethical considerations. By combining psychological understanding with targeted marketing and trust-building, IoT companies can better engage consumers and foster sustained adoption in a competitive and evolving market.

1. INTRODUCTION

1.1 Background

The Internet of Things (IoT) means that daily physical devices can be linked together over the internet to gather and share their data(Gokhale et al 2018). In the world of consumer products, IoT has moved from an unusual technology to one that changes the way people live, work and interact with their surroundings. Consumer IoT products cover many devices, including smart appliances for the home, devices that monitor health, connected automobiles and voice-controlled assistants(Kashyap, R. 2019). Because sensors are now more affordable, wireless connections are improving and smartphones are being used more widely, smart devices are being used more everywhere. Over the last few years, the number of IoT consumer products has increased a lot and experts expect worldwide markets to expand rapidly. Researchers expect that within the next decade, billions of devices will be connected in homes. The reason for this growth is the promise of easier service, better efficiency and more personal choices. Smart thermostats adjust themselves to fit how people live and fitness trackers let them see their health in real time. Though the market is moving strongly, people's willingness to use technology varies widely by region and product, suggesting that many different things affect its acceptance(Soumyalatha 2016).

1.2 Importance of Consumer Adoption in IoT

IoT technologies need consumers to use them for them to succeed and remain sustainable. While innovation drives the industry, the real factor in a product's success is how consumers choose to adopt these new devices(Gadre, M., & Deoskar, A. 2020). Adoption brings many different challenges. Many people are concerned about privacy and security because IoT devices regularly collect their data and remain connected to the internet. People are concerned about their data being stolen, watched without permission and being misused. Moreover, problems with how easy it is to use and connect devices made by different manufacturers stand in the way. People are more likely to buy and use IoT products if they trust the value and usefulness will be worth the money and the risks. There may not be a mass adoption of technology until the main problems are addressed. Marketing can significantly help to address these problems that prevent customers from adopting new products (Siva et al., 2022; Yamini et al., 2024). Brands can use communication to teach consumers the real benefits of IoT devices and ease their doubts. By marketing, companies can line up their products with what consumers value and do which makes the technology more appealing. At the same time, creating a brand people trust is important since people's trust in a company affects their willingness to use technology that takes privacy and security into account.

1.3 Objectives of the Chapter

The survey chapter goals are to bring together existing research on marketing tactics for IoT and to focus on the psychology influencing consumer behavior. The first step is to figure out and group the main ways companies promote IoT products. This means looking at both traditional and new digital and interactive marketing strategies that fit the IoT world. The chapter also looks at how consumer psychology shapes people's decisions to adopt new products. Marketers must know how consumers view usefulness, ease of use, risk and trust in IoT devices to make their marketing messages effective. By connecting TAM and Diffusion of Innovation with actual IoT marketing cases, this chapter will show how consumer attitudes can influence whether or not people adopt IoT products. The chapter also looks at how trust in a brand is a major factor in deciding to use IoT devices. The things that build trust a brand's competence, integrity and reliability are very important to people who are uncertain about data security and privacy. This chapter looks at how businesses gain trust, assist customers and provide consistent value to promote the use of IoT technologies by consumers.

1.4 Structure of the Chapter

The chapter is organized to explore the difficult topic of how consumers adopt IoT technologies. After the introduction, Section 2 explains the consumer IoT market, what kinds of products are available, the most recent trends and what makes it difficult for people to adopt. Section 3 talks about consumer psychology, setting out the main theories and things that affect consumer decisions about IoT products. Section 4 examines the strategies companies use to encourage more people to use IoT, including educational activities, types of messages, costs, channels and examples of social proof. The fifth section examines techniques and strategies for building trust in branding for the IoT market and their influence on how customers act. Section 6 shows how companies use ideas from consumer psychology and group customers by type to help plan their marketing strategies. In Section 7, the authors talk about new problems, possible future improvements and existing research gaps. The final section of the chapter summarizes the main points and suggests clear steps for marketers and IoT companies to encourage more consumers to use their products.

2. OVERVIEW OF IOT CONSUMER MARKET

The market for the consumer Internet of Things (IoT) is growing and changing very rapidly(Gubbi et al 2013). This area brings together many linked devices that seek to make life simpler, more secure and better for everyone by using smart technology that talks to each other over networks. This chapter examines the kinds of consumer IoT products, important trends in the market, the way consumers adopt them and the major obstacles and barriers that can influence both consumer actions and market growth. Knowing about these factors is necessary for all players, including manufacturers and service providers, hoping to benefit from the large possibilities of IoT in the consumer market(MAY et al., 2025).

2.1 Types of Consumers IoT Products

There are many different consumer IoT products on the market and this number is rising all the time. They are meant to support various daily tasks such as house automation, health monitoring, entertainment and using cars. Several categories have gained importance because so many people use them and because of their innovative developments. Smart home technology is a leading part of consumer IoT. In this category are devices such as smart thermostats, intelligent lighting, security cameras, smart locks and voice-activated digital assistants. Homeowners can use their devices to keep an eye on and manage their homes from anywhere, helping to save energy, boost security and make their homes more comfortable. Smart thermostats are able to sense a person's habits and control heating and cooling to use the least energy and smart lighting can be managed or set up remotely for easy use and increased safety. When security cameras and smart locks are used, users can check their homes remotely and receive immediate alerts. Wearable devices represent a major and quickly expanding area in consumer IoT(Jaffrin et al., 2025). Fitness trackers, smartwatches, health monitors and new smart clothing with biosensors are considered part of this. Health and wellness rely greatly on wearables because they always monitor heart rate, how well you sleep, how often you exercise and even your blood oxygen levels. Using these devices with their smartphones and the cloud gives users valuable information about their health, encouraging them to make healthier choices and find medical problems early. Apart from helping with fitness, wearables can also give notifications, allow you to communicate and let you make payments without touching a card. More and more smart or connected appliances are coming onto the market. More and more, newer refrigerators, washing machines, ovens and other appliances are using sensors and connectivity to support users. With these appliances, you can check their own performance, be alerted to any maintenance needs, have them work efficiently based on how you use them and often manage them from a distance. Thanks to a smart refrigerator, you can find out when your food will expire, get grocery suggestions and even order groceries online which helps you reduce wasting food and enjoy convenience. Furthermore, you can preheat your oven from a distance or put in recipes for it to cook accurately, cutting down on both your time and energy. Though mainly known in the automotive sector, connected vehicles are a key aspect of the consumer IoT world. Many modern cars come with features like live diagnostics, GPS, the ability to monitor your car from afar and smart home connectivity. Such features improve your drive and help make it safer and easier. As an example, a connected car can let the owner know when it needs servicing, allow them to remotely lock or unlock it and set the climate before getting in. In addition, self-driving and partially self-driving cars depend a lot on IoT technology and this could transform how people travel soon(Kumar et al 2020). Apart from the main categories, there are many new IoT products that meet the needs of a small group such as smart trackers for pets, connected toys, systems for home gardening and personal safety devices. They help grow the range of IoT applications and show that more people want integrated solutions with data to make their lives easier. All these groups demonstrate how IoT technologies are used in many different ways for consumers. Because IoT offers such a wide variety of products, it is now an essential part of making life more comfortable, secure, efficient and personal for people everywhere.

2.2 Market Trends and Adoption Rates

Different technological, economic and social factors have played a big role in the impressive changes seen in the consumer IoT market during the last decade. At present, billions of IoT devices bring consumers closer to their environments, with each one adding to an ever-expanding ecosystem that will deliver more innovation and integration shortly. Growing Faster Than Expected: The consumer IoT market has quickly expanded and grown at a great rate. Thanks to new sensor technology, improved wireless standards and lower device manufacturing costs, smart devices have become available to many more people. Forecasts in the industry show that connected consumer IoT devices will increase to tens of billions worldwide in the next five years, indicating that demand is strong and many are being deployed. Smart home ecosystems are helping to drive more consumers to use Internet of Things technology. Now, more and more individuals decide to use smart home systems where various devices talk to each other and are controlled by a single system. Amazon

Alexa, Google Home, Apple HomeKit and Samsung SmartThings are now at the heart of this method. Thanks to their intuitive design, voice features and automation, these platforms help to create unified and simple smart homes. This model makes it easier for users and also adds value to IoT products by showing how simple it is to control and automate everything at once. Consumer IoT devices are now being revolutionized by the addition of artificial intelligence (AI) and machine learning. Devices become smart by learning from users' actions, interests and the situation around them to automate jobs and improve tasks. Smart thermostats analyze patterns and outdoor weather to know when to turn on heat and cooling, while AI in security cameras helps it identify people it recognizes from those it doesn't. Being "smart" means there's less need for human help and users get more personalized experiences which helps attract customers. More people became interested in IoT health products because of the COVID-19 pandemic. When individuals started to pay more attention to their health and remote monitoring, many wanted wearables and health products including pulse oximeters, blood pressure monitors and smart scales. More people using telehealth and online consultations have made clear the part IoT plays in tracking health outside clinics all the time. The trend is likely to keep growing, as IoT helps with care before disease develops, managing chronic conditions and promoting wellness. Adoption of IoT varies a lot by both demographic groups and regions, even though there are good prospects for its growth. Usually, people who are both young and have a high income are the first to adopt IoT, as they are drawn to try out new devices by their curiosity. At the same time, older people and those with less money frequently find that cost, how easy it is to use and its value are obstacles. In general, adoption of financial services is highest in areas with advanced digital networks, high consumer trust in technology and well-established e-commerce systems including North America, Western Europe and certain parts of Asia-Pacific. In these markets, the slow growth of infrastructure and worries about privacy can block the use of IoT. More people are learning about the benefits and abilities of IoT. As a result of marketing by tech companies, more news stories and real-world experience with early items, people are getting to know IoT technology better. Because of this, people now expect devices to be easy to use, compatible with other devices, very secure and to provide useful information. The consumer IoT sector can only grow if these expectations are met. In short, the consumer IoT market is growing quickly thanks to new technology, the growth of its ecosystem and changing wants from consumers. Even so, the way markets develop is not the same, since some segments are more ready and open to change than others are.

2.3 Common Barriers to IoT Adoption

Although consumer IoT devices are popular and have many benefits, a number of major obstacles stop many from using them. Such problems involve technology, society, the economy and rules which show how difficult it is to encourage trust and interest among different buyers(Alenizi, A. S., & Al-Karawi, K. A. 2022). Privacy is likely the biggest reason why many people are hesitant to use consumer IoT. A lot of consumers realize that IoT gadgets gather a large amount of personal and behavioral information, making them worried about its storage, use and sharing. People are always worried about unapproved monitoring, data breaches and the exposure of sensitive data. What's more, many manufacturers do not clearly explain their data handling practices which makes people feel less confident in them. Many people are holding back from using IoT devices because of famous data leaks and worries about how their data will be used(Al-Rawashdeh et al 2022). A big problem for many is how complicated IoT devices and their systems seem. Many of today's smart devices must be installed in a complicated way, require several apps to run and can be difficult to manage when it comes to working with other devices. It is often frustrating for users to combine products from various brands or platforms, because the experience can differ greatly. Since these products are complicated, not everyone feels confident to continue after their first try. Making things straightforward and simple to use is important for getting more people to accept cryptocurrency. Costing is a significant part of choosing consumer IoT devices (Sathya et al., 2024). The price to buy many IoT products is beyond what some people can afford. In addition to the first purchase, users may have to pay for cloud subscriptions, special features or updates(Kumar et al 2023). People should decide if what they are getting makes the expenses worthwhile. When the expected value is not well understood or hardly important, the use of the technology can slow. In emerging markets and among those with lower incomes, people show a strong focus on costs. Security matters increase privacy risks and directly threaten users. Because of poor security measures, default passwords and unaddressed weaknesses, IoT devices are frequently the target of cyber attackers. Attacks that succeed can expose your data, interrupt the function of your devices or in the case of smart locks, surveillance cameras or medical devices, put you at risk. Hacking incidents being reported reduce consumer trust and prove that tougher security rules and accountability from manufacturers are needed. There is currently no standardized way for devices in the IoT to communicate and the platforms are divided. As a result of this, it is more difficult for devices to interact and for users to enjoy a seamless experience, since people have to work with several apps and accounts based on what their device supports(Ahmetoglu et al 2022). Because universal standards do not exist, expanding IoT use is hard and people's trust in the ecosystem is reduced. Regulatory aspects of IoT are not fully developed in many regions at this time. Because there are no clear rules for data privacy, security and consumer protection, both manufacturers and consumers have uncertainty. Problems related to owning data, granting consent and the possibility of being watched need to be handled with the right rules and corporate care. Consumers are becoming aware of IoT, yet a lot of them still do not understand what IoT can do or the dangers it brings. Not having this information can cause people to feel nervous and opposed. For more people to trust and use IoT, clear education and honest communication are important. In brief, the consumer IoT market offers a huge chance to change everyday life with smart, connected devices. Because IoT is used in homes, on our bodies and in vehicles, its many product categories highlight its wide use and popularity. Technological progress, the growth of the ecosystem and new consumer behaviors are what are causing the market to grow rapidly. Even so, to make the most of this potential, we need to overcome persistent difficulties with privacy, security, cost, complexity and uncertainty in regulations. In the coming years, building trust and growing the number of users will depend on strong security, simple user interfaces, clear messages and helpful policies.

3. CONSUMER PSYCHOLOGY IN IOT ADOPTION

3.1 Theories and Models Relevant to Technology Adoption

People's decisions to use or avoid IoT devices are best explained by studying consumer psychology. Many theories give useful structures for looking at how adoption happens. TAM is widely used because it suggests that a user's decision to use technology is shaped by how useful they think it is and how easy it is to operate. Perceived usefulness is how much a consumer thinks using a certain technology will improve their success or daily life. It refers to how easy a consumer thinks the technology is to use. They form our opinions on using the technology and the wish to adopt it.

TAM is the basis for UTAUT which brings together several models into a single framework. According to UTAUT, adopting new technology is mainly affected by performance expectancy, ease of use, social influences and helpful conditions. Since there is a lot of uncertainty with emerging technologies like IoT, social influence reminds us that consumers may be guided by what their peers, family or respected people think and do. Facilitating conditions include everything that helps consumers make good use of the technology.

Diffusion of Innovation Theory gives a larger sociological explanation for the adoption of technology. It breaks consumers into five categories innovators, early adopters, early majority, late majority and laggards depending on how soon they are willing to use new products. According to the theory, adoption happens when communication channels, social systems and the properties of the innovation such as its relative advantage, fit with the user's values and are not too complex or hard to try out, influence the process. Because of this framework, marketers can find the right target segments and design strategies to suit each consumer group's stage of readiness.

3.2 Psychological Factors Affecting Adoption

A number of psychological reasons based on these theories play a major role in decisions about IoT adoption. People are much more likely to use IoT gadgets if they can notice real value from them and if the devices are easy to understand and operate. A messy layout or slow response can greatly reduce the number of users. People's judgment about risk and trust have equal effects. Because IoT devices must be online and collect data all the time, they increase risks to privacy and security. People will only adopt a technology if they believe the brand and technology provider will protect their private information and keep them safe from cyber-attacks. If there is no trust, the risks often seem greater than the benefits, stopping people from adopting. You build trust by using technology and by open and regular communication, as well as by keeping the brand's behavior consistent. How ready and creative people are as consumers is also very important. Usually, those who try out new technologies early are more comfortable with uncertain situations and more eager to investigate new technologies. They are driven by wanting to know more, feeling important for leading the way and hoping to gain an advantage in their field or life. Alternatively, the majority of people adopt a new product only after they are convinced and have proof of its reliability. Knowing these psychological differences enables companies to divide their customers into groups and communicate differently.

3.3 Emotional and Cognitive Responses to IoT

Besides using reason, what people feel and think about IoT technologies greatly affects their use of them. A lot of people experience privacy and security anxiety. People may feel uncomfortable when their devices which collect data about them, are always watching and monitoring their actions. Because of this anxiety, consumers may be cautious or resist brands until these companies explain their privacy policies, make their systems secure and earn their trust. How much people believe they can manage their IoT devices matters in their decision to use them. If users believe they can change their settings, control who sees their data and interfere with automatic decisions, they are more pleased and certain. Because autonomy prevents people from feeling controlled by technology, it encourages them to have a better view of adopting it. Ultimately, what friends and peers say can affect both your feelings and thoughts. Many people trust words or recommendations from those they know or from well-regarded influencers, to make things clearer. Positive social proof helps people trust the product and feels safer trying it out. When news of security issues is shared, it can quickly damage consumer trust in a company. This research shows that adopting IoT depends on both the technology and the emotional, social and trust factors involved. Therefore, good marketing plans need to include these points to get the attention of consumers.

4. MARKETING STRATEGIES FOR ENHANCING IOT CONSUMER ADOPTION

4.1 Education and Awareness Campaigns

Marketing strategies to boost IoT consumer adoption are built around teaching and informing the public. Since the IoT is not well known to many people and can be confusing, it's important to share how the technology can be used and what it can do. Because of these campaigns, more people learn how IoT products can improve daily tasks, increase safety, reduce energy costs and raise the standard of living. For example, pointing out that smart thermostats can save money on electricity and connected security cameras let people know what's happening in their home in real time helps convince them of the benefits. Another important job of education campaigns is to correct misunderstandings and fears that prevent many people from adopting. Most consumers worry about privacy and security and marketing communications should make it clear what protections are available and how devices are secured. Describing the ways data is handled and giving clear rules for safe device use helps ease worries and increase confidence. Short tutorials, webinars and interesting information on common topics can help people feel prepared to use IoT devices.

4.2 Product Positioning and Messaging

Placing a product well and creating messages that fit various groups helps to stress the important strengths of IoT. Marketers put greater attention on convenience, safety and making life better, because these are what most people look for. As an example, smart home messaging could talk about easy voice control and security, while wearables could point out customized health information and help with fitness. By promoting the product as something that helps people connect better, the company can touch the consumer's emotions. It is just as important to modify messages for each group of people you want to reach. Those who buy new technology often like messages that highlight its advanced features, but people who make fewer purchases usually look for something that is easy to use and dependable. When we communicate differently based on the needs or wishes of groups such as busy professionals, families or senior users, our messages become more important and effective. Messaging in several languages and with cultural sensitivity can help a company sell to people all over the world.

4.3 Pricing and Incentives

How a product is priced has a big impact on whether consumers are willing to use IoT technologies. If you price your products at a level that customers consider value for their money and keep them affordable, it reduces the money required to start using them. When you have basic, standard and premium pricing, consumers can buy what they need at a price they can afford. In addition, when you purchase smart security cameras with home automation hubs, you save money and are more likely to choose more devices which helps adoption. Many data storage, device upgrade and security service providers now use subscription plans as their main pricing method. With these plans, companies get steady income and consumers keep getting benefits. Yet, it is important for marketers to explain what consumers will get and the terms of their subscriptions to prevent buyers from rejecting them due to concerns. Special discounts, the chance to trade in old devices and rewards for inviting friends encourage people to get involved at the start.

4.4 Distribution and Accessibility

For IoT use to grow, it needs to be accessible to many users easily. Using omni-channel marketing, customers can discover, buy and get help anywhere they please. A lot of people do research on IoT products online, yet they still want to see and experience them in real stores. For this reason, being available in big retailers, electronics shops and online stores helps your products be seen and bought easier.

Working together with known retailers and service providers helps IoT products gain trust from buyers. For instance, joining forces with major telecom or home security brands helps consumers feel more confident about the quality of your products and the help they will get after buying them. In addition, helping customers with installation, giving them clear user instructions and being available for customer service over accessible channels makes technology easier for consumers.

4.5 Use of Social Proof and Influencers

Both social proof and influencer marketing are now important ways to increase interest in IoT products among consumers. Real comments and experiences from users provide accurate information to help you decide and confirm what a product claims. Reading about others' positive encounters can help reluctant buyers to make a purchase. Sites that support rating, question and answer and detailed product talk help build a loyal and knowledgeable user group. Cooperating with well-known technology influencers, bloggers and YouTubers helps expand your marketing messages. With the help of influencers, people can understand the features of IoT devices, hear honest views about them and receive useful tutorials. Many younger or tech-savvy people put more trust in celebrity recommendations than in traditional ads. Working with influencers who tell real stories builds a connection with people and helps products be accepted more quickly.

5. BUILDING AND SUSTAINING BRAND TRUST IN IOT

5.1 Importance of Trust in IoT Context

Trust plays an essential role in deciding whether people will use IoT consumer products. Many traditional items do not, but IoT devices always require ongoing data gathering, sharing and processing. Because of this, people need to trust companies before they will accept new technologies. People depend on trust to judge how safe their information is and how stable and secure their devices are from cyber-attacks. Many privacy concerns arise in IoT because these devices work in close areas such as homes and healthcare settings, where people's sensitive information is generated. People expect businesses that manage their data to do so responsibly and honestly. Just as with other devices, the security issues found in IoT gadgets call for consumers to rely on brands to use strong safeguards. If people have no trust in them, some of the most creative or helpful IoT products may not succeed. As a result, keeping trust in the brand is vital for a company to succeed in the long run.

5.2 Trust-Building Strategies

Trust in the IoT is built by brands using a number of strategic tactics. Ensuring clear and open data privacy policies is most important. All firms should explain which data is collected, why it is used, how it will be stored and shared and what rights customers have concerned their details. Policies about privacy should be easy to find, free of confusing language and supported by real steps, like asking users for their consent and anonymizing their data. Being open and honest helps reduce people's concerns and proves the brand values user privacy.

Being certified with security standards is essential for winning the trust of customers. Such certifications for information security or regulation rules give outside confirmation of a company's security measures. They tell consumers that products have been tested for strict security standards. Advertising these achievements in your marketing materials helps to prove that you are serious and trustworthy. Strong customer support and after-sales service add a lot to a brand's trustworthiness. Since IoT devices might be tricky, providing users with helpful support for setup, troubleshooting and updates encourages them. Product integrity and consumer protection are demonstrated by brands that keep their software up to date and apply security patches. Good customer service creates feelings that keep people connected to a brand and convinced of its quality.

5.3 Role of Brand Reputation and Reliability

A brand's reputation is what supports trust in the IoT consumer market. Trust is built in consumers when brands are reliable and consistently ethical and good at what they do. If products perform well, privacy is respected and communication is open, a company's reputation improves with time. It is clear from several successful IoT brands that reputation helps determine how many users adopt their systems. Companies such as Nest and Fitbit are well known for offering top quality and safety in their smart home and wearable gadgets. Thanks to their commitment to new ideas and open user communication, customers continue to trust them despite issues in the industry. Experiences of these brands reveal that using new technology must go hand in hand with being reliable.

5.4 Communicating Trust Through Marketing Channels

Trust should be clearly communicated just like it is built. Marketing channels give brands a way to show they are trustworthy by displaying reliable endorsements and certifications. Companies should put badges, security audit results and awards about privacy and security on their websites and packaging. They play a role in how people see and decide about a product. Being honest and clear when you discuss how you handle data is just as important. Being clear about how consumers' data is kept safe, who can see it and what is done to avoid risks makes your company more transparent. Telling real-life tales of positive data management and protecting customers' privacy can help the brand feel more human. All in all, establishing and maintaining faith in a brand in the IoT world needs to include being open, having others confirm it, good customer care and constantly delivering as promised. Once trust is created, companies can separate themselves in the market and make consumers feel safe using IoT.

6. INTEGRATION OF CONSUMER PSYCHOLOGY AND MARKETING STRATEGIES

6.1 Tailoring Strategies to Psychological Insights

For marketing IoT, it is important to use consumer psychology. When marketers know what consumers are afraid of, want and think about IoT products, they can design messages that touch them more deeply. Many are concerned about privacy and security which prevents them from using IoT products. Messages that address user concerns about privacy and security and give clear answers to those concerns help build trust more effectively than general advertising.

Likewise, pointing out that IoT devices make life easier, better and more manageable can make their advantages more appealing. According to TAM and related psychological theories, making products user-friendly and easy to use helps consumers see their benefits which marketers can do by highlighting both aspects. If an ad focuses on empowerment, autonomy and security, it also meets consumers' cognitive needs and helps them get past any doubts. Matching strategies to these insights allows brands to lessen the feeling of risk and increase the chance that people will adopt the product.

6.2 Segmenting Consumer Groups Based on Adoption Readiness

It's important to understand that people are not the same in their willingness to use new technology when marketing IoT. The theory sorts consumers into groups innovators, early adopters, early majority, late majority and laggards and each type has its own way of responding to new innovations. When marketers use messages that fit each segment, they can better involve each group. People who are early to try new things and understand technology often react positively to messages that highlight what's new, standout features and special offers. They like to receive detailed technical data and value being early adopters. For these groups, marketers may use beta testing, early access and work with influencers. Unlike the innovators and early adopters, the early and late majority groups look for proof of reliability, simple use and value. Messages to these consumers should focus on the positive results, what users think and simple ways the technology fits into their everyday routines. Security for customers and fewer perceived risks are achieved through guarantees, warranties and easy access to customer service. Those who resist change the most usually start using new technology after it has become popular or necessary. For them, affordable prices, basic forms of the product and simple explanations may be important themes in marketing. Understanding the differences allows companies to make the most of their resources and help a broad group of consumers.

6.3 Feedback Loops and Continuous Improvement

Making marketing and product development reactive and flexible is vital because the IoT world changes quickly. Once feedback loops are in place, companies can find out what consumers think of their product and make needed improvements. Customer surveys, watching social media, reading user forums and direct help desk interactions give us useful information about what people like, dislike and are concerned about. Looking at what customers say helps marketers change their messages to deal with new worries, make the most of popular features and find areas to communicate better. If people say they find privacy settings confusing, marketing might create information that helps them better grasp this topic. In addition, product teams can use customer comments to improve how easy the product is to use, boost its security and add requested features which helps improve satisfaction and leads to more positive reviews. Ongoing changes based on what consumers say help the product match the market and increase trust in the brand. If customers notice their opinions make a difference, they trust the brand more and become more loyal. To keep adopting IoT successfully, companies must listen, learn and adapt over and over again.

7. CHALLENGES AND FUTURE DIRECTIONS

7.1 Emerging Challenges in IoT Marketing

With IoT technology moving forward so quickly, it's becoming harder for marketers to encourage people to use it. A key issue is that new technology evolves faster than many people can learn about and trust it. With each new feature added to IoT products, marketing tactics should help customers learn about them and set up their expectations. But, because IoT systems are so complex, users may become tired of adopting them or start to doubt their usefulness. At the same time as technology changes, people's expectations about products and services are changing fast. People now expect their devices to be useful, blend easily into their lives, offer great privacy and handle their data openly. Missing these goals can cause people to lose trust and be unwilling to use the technology. Now, consumers want marketing to be personalized for them which means marketers have to be even better. There are important problems related to regulations and ethics when it comes to IoT marketing. Marketers are responsible for figuring out these laws to comply and still run successful marketing campaigns. Issues about ethics also involve modifying data, using data too frequently to target people and exploiting those who are at risk. To keep trust, IoT marketers need to promote the technology strongly but still respect people's privacy and independence.

7.2 Opportunities for Enhanced Consumer Engagement

With these problems, IoT marketing offers businesses the potential to reach consumers more effectively with new technologies and new ideas. Using artificial intelligence (AI) and data analytics for personalizing marketing shows a lot of promise. With information about consumer habits, brands are better able to give users content and offers that truly appeal to them. Personalizing a website helps people engage more, reduces how interrupting the site seems and makes them more likely to make a purchase. Using gamification and experiential marketing helps companies engage their customers in the Internet of Things (IoT) world. Adding things like rewards, challenges and leaderboards into marketing or user experiences makes the experience more fun and encourages users to keep engaging. People can directly use IoT products during experiential marketing by taking part in virtual or augmented reality demos, attending pop-up events or trying them out themselves. They remove the mystery from IoT, build positive feelings for the brand and encourage customers to take part in what the brand does. Besides, IoT devices can also be used as a way for consumers to interact. Devices with useful notifications, personal advice or engaging features can hold a consumer's interest after they buy and motivate them to stay involved. Making marketing and device features go hand in hand means there are no disruptions as the consumer moves through their journey.

7.3 Research Gaps and Potential Studies

Many scholars are paying more attention to consumer psychology and IoT marketing, but several important gaps in our knowledge still exist. There is a need for extended research to study the process of developing consumer trust. Trust between a consumer and a company change as the consumer uses and interacts with their products. Such studies allow us to observe changes in trust over time which guides actions to protect trust in the future. There is another shortage in awareness of how cultural differences affect IoT adoption. People's opinions on privacy, technology and trust change widely depending on where they live. Comparing these variations can guide global firms in designing marketing strategies that match the needs of different markets. It can also show the differences between what drives adoption everywhere and in different cultures which improves both theories and practical use. More studies could be done to see how new technologies such as edge computing, 5G and blockchain, affect how people view marketing and how companies approach it. Tracking the reactions of consumers to new IoT security tools can help decide how to move forward and improve communication. In addition, understanding how using ethical marketing affects consumer trust and the use of IoT is an important but not thoroughly explored subject.

8. CONCLUSION

The results point out that consumer adoption in the IoT market is complex and requires companies to focus on people's minds and the trust they have in a brand. It is clear from the data that privacy, security and a perception of complexity are important factors in whether people are willing to use IoT technologies. Educating the public, sending targeted messages and making information clear can lower the barriers to adoption. Besides, dividing customers by their readiness to use and customizing their experiences leads to more engagement and faster adoption. Trust is important which is made possible by clear data policies, strong security certifications, helpful customer support and a reputation you can count on. These results show marketers and IoT firms that using psychological knowledge in marketing is crucial. A uniform solution is not enough in the face of today's wide range of customers. If you use strategies that address what your consumers are afraid of, want and expect, you will see better results. Being transparent and working hard to build trust should be key parts of creating products and communicating with customers, as trust is linked to customers sticking with your brand. AI and gamification are useful tools for companies to improve how customers feel and act towards their brand. To maintain a strong reputation for years, companies should pay attention to new rules and ethical ways of advertising. In short, helping consumers use IoT products requires a good idea of their minds and trustworthy marketing tactics. By dealing with the feelings and thoughts of consumers, IoT brands can form valuable links that surpass the simple benefits of their products. When you trust a brand, you can feel confident using its IoT devices. To succeed in the future, companies need to keep evolving their marketing, so it matches what consumers value and need which will make sure new products are really used and accepted.

REFERENCES

Ahmetoglu, S., Che Cob, Z., & Ali, N. A. (2022). A systematic review of Internet of Things adoption in organizations: Taxonomy, benefits, challenges and critical factors. *applied sciences, 12*(9), 4117.

Al-Rawashdeh, M., Keikhosrokiani, P., Belaton, B., Alawida, M., & Zwiri, A. (2022). IoT adoption and application for smart healthcare: A systematic review. *Sensors (Basel), 22*(14), 5377. DOI: 10.3390/s22145377 PMID: 35891056

Alenizi, A. S., & Al-Karawi, K. A. (2022, July). Internet of things (IoT) adoption: challenges and barriers. In *Proceedings of Seventh International Congress on Information and Communication Technology: ICICT 2022, London,* Volume 3 (pp. 217-229). Singapore: Springer Nature Singapore.

Gadre, M., & Deoskar, A. (2020). Industry 4.0–digital transformation, challenges and benefits. *International Journal of Future Generation Communication and Networking, 13*(2), 139–149.

Gokhale, P., Bhat, O., & Bhat, S. (2018). Introduction to IOT. *International Advanced Research Journal in Science. Engineering and Technology, 5*(1), 41–44.

Gubbi, J., Buyya, R., Marusic, S., & Palaniswami, M. (2013). Internet of Things (IoT): A vision, architectural elements, and future directions. *Future Generation Computer Systems, 29*(7), 1645–1660. DOI: 10.1016/j.future.2013.01.010

Jaffrin, L. C., Nithya, T., & Divya, J. (2025, April). IoT for Sustainable Development: Enhancing Environmental Efficiency and Resource Optimization. In *2025 5th International Conference on Trends in Material Science and Inventive Materials (ICTMIM)* (pp. 1224-1230). IEEE.

Kashyap, R. (2019). Machine Learning, data mining for IOT-based systems. In *Handbook of Research on Big Data and the IoT* (pp. 314–338). IGI Global. DOI: 10.4018/978-1-5225-7432-3.ch018

Kumar, A., Dhingra, S., & Falwadiya, H. (2023). Adoption of internet of things: A systematic literature review and future research agenda. *International Journal of Consumer Studies, 47*(6), 2553–2582. DOI: 10.1111/ijcs.12964

Kumar, K. V. R., Kumar, K. D., Poluru, R. K., Basha, S. M., & Reddy, M. P. K. (2020). Internet of things and fog computing applications in intelligent transportation systems. In *Architecture and security issues in fog computing applications* (pp. 131–150). IGI Global. DOI: 10.4018/978-1-7998-0194-8.ch008

MAY. P. M. A., Savitha, V., Gayathri, S., & Mahalakshmi, S. (2025, April). Exploring Sustainable Computing: IoT, Big Data, and Energy-Efficient Solutions. In *2025 5th International Conference on Trends in Material Science and Inventive Materials (ICTMIM)* (pp. 1218-1223). IEEE.

Sathya, U., Hashini, S., Lakshmipriya, C., Varun, C. M., & Nalini, M. (2024, December). Emerging Trends and Future Prospects in Internet of Things (IoT) Technology. In *2024 International Conference on Sustainable Communication Networks and Application (ICSCNA)* (pp. 79-85). IEEE.

Siva, S. R., Bushra, S. N., Maheswari, B., & Prabukumar, M. K. (2022, April). Performance Analysis of Different Machine Learning in Customer Prediction. In *2022 6th International Conference on Trends in Electronics and Informatics (ICOEI)* (pp. 1425-1430). IEEE. DOI: 10.1109/ICOEI53556.2022.9776714

Soumyalatha, S. G. H. (2016, May). Study of IoT: Understanding IoT architecture, applications, issues and challenges. In *1st International Conference on Innovations in Computing & Net-working (ICICN16), CSE, RRCE. International Journal of Advanced Networking & Applications*, *478*, 14.

Yamini, B., Ramana, K. V., Nalini, M., Devi, D. C., Maheswari, B., & Siva, S. R. (2024). Customer churn prediction model in enterprises using machine learning. *International Journal of Advanced Technology and Engineering Exploration*, *11*(110), 94.

Chapter 9
Navigating the Future: The Strategic Role of IoT in Business and Consumer Environments

Sharmin Jahan
http://orcid.org/0009-0005-8489-2636
Daffodil International University, Bangladesh

Md Mehedi Hasan Emon
http://orcid.org/0000-0002-6224-9552
American International University-Bangladesh, Bangladesh

Zerin Tasnim
http://orcid.org/0000-0002-5705-1648
North South University, Bangladesh

Md. Adnan Rahman
http://orcid.org/0000-0003-3378-0958
Uttara University, Bangladesh

Abid Aziz
http://orcid.org/0009-0002-1582-9113
Uttara University, Bangladesh

Nabid Aziz
http://orcid.org/0009-0004-2944-7321
Uttara University, Bangladesh

ABSTRACT

This chapter explores the transformative role of the Internet of Things (IoT) in shaping both business operations and consumer interactions. It examines how IoT technologies enable businesses to enhance operational efficiencies, create innovative consumer experiences, and develop new business models. Through strategic frameworks, IoT adoption is positioned as a key driver of digital transformation. The chapter further delves into the behavioral dimensions of consumer engagement with IoT, highlighting personalization and real-time data utilization. Additionally, it addresses the challenges of IoT integration, including technical barriers, data

DOI: 10.4018/979-8-3373-3441-7.ch009

privacy concerns, and regulatory compliance. Lastly, the future of IoT is considered, with a focus on its convergence with emerging technologies, and its potential for fostering sustainability, inclusivity, and societal well-being.

INTRODUCTION

The strategic importance of the Internet of Things (IoT) as a transformation that pushes its way through the day-to-day business environment and consumer constructs is what we are interested in learning in this chapter. The digital transformation in organizations has its requirements, and IoT is at the edge of- evolution that can bring unparalleled prospects of transforming internal operations, re-inventing customer interaction, and building robust data-driven business frameworks. The chapter is based on critical examination of the theories developed and the eventual empirical transformations that have been experienced with the view of equipping the reader with a multifaceted insight of how the IoT can be tactically integrated into the current organizational environment. The discussion introduction starts with the description of the historical development of-the IoT and its perceived technological maturity in the larger industrial and civil context. Based on informative case studies, we argue on the manner in-which the exemplary companies in the various industries have been utilizing the internet of things and how they have been putting the use of the technology to the- efforts of facilitating innovation, efficiency and competitive distance. Next in line comes the development of strategic frameworks which is necessary in deep integration of IoT where we discuss the necessity to align technological competences with organizational objectives as well as with market momentum .

The chapter aimed to realize how IoT alters the behavior of the consumers; it introduces the emphasis on the most significant features of personalization, usability, and trust regarding the condition of acceptance among the consumers. This part explores profoundly into psychological and behavioral motivation that generates the adoption of the IoT-enabled product and services and the ethical and regulatory aspect of data privacy and security. We also examine the role of IoT in driving new marketing strategy paradigm through real-time customer analytics to immersive experiential campaigns. Despite its opportunities, the application of the- Internet of Things is not without issues. The main obstacles that have been discussed in the chapter include interoperability, infrastructural expenses, lack of requisite skills, and change-in-judicial standards. It further examines the emerging interface of IoT with other edge technologies that can likely typify the next phase of the digital enterprise, that is, artificial intelligence, block chain, and edge computing. Lastly, the chapter examines the impact of the IoT on strategic foresight, innovation capabilities and sustainable growth. We hold that the fact that IoT opens a wide range of value creation opportunities, deploying IoT requires a meaningful approach supported by ethics and interdisciplinary. Thus, the chapter provides critical glimpses of information for the scholars, practitioners, policy makers and the discipline in the IoT integration landscape and the identification of strategic ways of future readiness.

THE EVOLUTION OF IOT IN BUSINESS AND CONSUMER SPACES

Historical Context and Current Trajectories

The history of the concept of Internet of Things (IoT) holds in its roots in the bigger picture of the history of automation and sensor-based technology and while the formalization of the concept found more credible expression towards the end of the 1990s and at the beginning of the 2000s. Living in Britain, one of the pioneers in technology, Kevin Ashton is credited with having coined the term "Internet of Things" in the year 1999 while at work for Procter & Gamble in which he imagined the possibility of linking radio-frequency identification (RFID) tags to the internet to improve the management of stocks (Reyes, 2023). Though theoretical Construct has emerged from logistical considerations, the technological basis for IoT, i.e., including sensors, communication protocols and embedded systems, was coming into existence under the influence of the advancements in microelectromechanical systems (MEMS), wireless communication and cloud computing. The first chapter of IoT was largely Industrial and infrastructural and it was in harmony with the philosophy of the industry 3.0 and it slowly transitioned into the larger digitalization of the industry 4.0 mandate. IIoT was primarily interested in assets tracking and diagnostics of equipment along with automation. In the manufacturing and logistics industries, respective companies like General Electrics and Bosch adopted the use of the IoT so as to enhance the visibility of processes therein and to eradicate downtime (Mubarik & Khan, 2024). These industrial deployments were mainly concerned with control systems, real time viewing, and in which the act of communication machine-to-machine (M2M) comprised most of the use cases for IoT (Khan et al., 2025).

At the time when the network of broadband was expanding, the bulk of mobile gadgets were exploding, and maturing cloud platforms –IoT began to emerge out of a niche industrial application towards the mass-scale consumer and enterprise technology. It gained pace in the 20.10's with the democratization of the sensor technology, with the falling cost of the hardware and development of low-power wide-area networks (LPWANs) (Allioui & Mourdi, 2023) such as NB-IoT and LoRaWAN, which supported long- At the moment, integration of IoT encompasses various aspects of a firm's operations and those of respective consumer experiences. In the business setup, IoT is a digital transformative enabler. It supports real time inventory, creates manufacturing processes with the use of predictive analytics and supports sustainability goals through the measurement of energy consumption (Khan et al., 2024; Ma et al., 2022). IoT is a significant player as a chief enabler of personalized treatments, convenience of lifestyle in the consumer world. Practical examples of the things of the IoT include the smart thermostats, for example, Nest, wearable health monitors like Fitbit, or home automation implementations that talk to the consumer's daily activities. The devices continuously harvest the data concerning behaviors and the environment surrounding people in order for companies to be in the position to change services and offer personalized solutions (Hassan et al., 2024; Javaid et al., 2021). With the ubiquity of IoT, the growth of ambient intelligence, where the digital environments are context-aware, and respond to the needs of the user, has accelerated. At the same time, the emerging IoT strategic potential is being re-defined as the result of convergence with other technologies, AI, edge computing, blockchain, and 5G. AI supports IoT as it develops methods of deriving useful information from the large sets of data-heterogeneous data generated from connected devices (Bzai et al., 2022).

CASE STUDIES OF SUCCESSFUL IOT IMPLEMENTATIONS

Ideal examples of the strategic application of IoT across industries are initiatives undertaken by organizations, where they have measurably changed the way organizations work, customer interactions, or opened new sources of revenue. Such success can be illustrated by the following examples:

Siemens' MindSphere Platform

The MindSphere by Siemens is a flagship in the industrial world; a cloud based open IoT operating system that enables physical infrastructure to be able to digitize in the digital world. MindSphere collects and analyses operation data of the connected machines and enables them to do predictive maintenance, remote diagnostics, and process fine-tuning. Siemens applies MindSphere to monitor the health of equipment in real-time in terms of manufacturing that cuts unplanned downtime by up to 45% and throughput (Crespo Márquez, 2022; Jamil et al., 2025). MindSphere integrates AI and digital twin technology to offer to its clients a holistic visualization of behaviors of machines as preemptive measures to increase efficiency and product quality. It should be noted that Siemens has also made it possible to allow third-party developers to build industry-specific applications on the MindSphere platform and therefore creating a wider ecosystem (Fortino et al., 2022).

Amazon Go

In the area of retail, Amazon Go is the definition of extreme restructuring of in-person purchase process through IoT. Amazon Go stores were launched in 2018, and thus, cashiers could be replaced with the help of the variety of IoT sensors, computer vision, etc. Customers walk into the store, log on with their app, pick some things and leave without waiting in a line up, or paying someone; The system will automatically take from their account what they take. The "Just Walk Out" technology employs devices for IoT that trace movements of consumers and choice of products which are connected to inventory management systems (Bentalha & Hmioui, 2022). Apart from enhancing customer convenience this easy transaction model provides Amazon with minute-level behavioral data which could be exploited in improving the in-store design, product inventory, and specific promotion to individual customers.

John Deere's Precision Agriculture Solutions

John Deere has revolutionized farming in agriculture with the use of precision agriculture through IoT. The connected tractors, planters and harvesters of the company are also packed full of GPS, soil sensors, and telematics that allow one to keep a close eye on the growth of crops, soil, and equipment in real time (Paul et al., 2022). And in John Deere Operations center, the farmers can access field level data thus, through which, appropriate measures of irrigation, fertilization and plantation can be employed. Recent sources indicate that by the rate of 15% increases have been attained in yields, while inputs cost and environmental impact have been also reduced (Bridhikitti et al., 2023). Moreover, the integration of AI can be used to do predictive approaches, which utilizes the weather patterns and the cycles of the crops thereby encouraging sustainable farming.

Philips' HealthSuite Digital Platform

In healthcare, Philips' HealthSuite has a cloud basis, which helps patients, clinicians and devices communicate with one another in an interoperable ecosystem environment with security. With the current modern wearables and home monitoring devices, the patient's information such as heart rate, glucose level, and sleeping pattern always get to the hands of health care providers. Such data leads to the early detection of the disease and remote consultations outside the office and individual regimes. Noteworthy is that HealthSuite adheres to globally defined security of data practice, which is a representation of how IoT can be safely implemented in a tender arena. Using AI in revealing abnormality improves the diagnosis accuracy and outcome of the patient (Hossen et al., 2024; Khalifa & Albadawy, 2024). Overall, such cases are indicative of the variety of functions and the revolution potential of IoT in the respective areas. If it enhances productivity in manufacture or reinvents the consumer experience in retail or empowers data-driven agriculture or perfects the patient care, the role of IoT is evident, strategically. Besides, the examples draw out the fact that, besides technological issues, successful application of the IoT is an organizational problem that requires clear governance structures and constant innovations.

CONSUMER ENGAGEMENT AND IOT

The outburst of IoT has unified the limits of the interferences of the consumers to an unparalleled scale. As the digital ecosystems are changing, modalities through which businesses and- consumers interact are dependent on smart and connected technology that does not merely automate but personalizes and contextualizes the experience of the people. It is the grasp of consumer behavior that is at the core of the transformation that is the adoption of and continued use of IoT-enabled devices taking place in the ever-evolving world of psychological factors, along with the technological and social factors (Kang & Hwang, 2022). From wearables, smart appliances, connected vehicles, and voice-activated assistants, IoT is more than just a form of technological evolution but a shift in consumer behavior on how they live, communicate, and interact with brands.

Behavioral Dimensions of IoT Adoption

For one to know about consumer engagement of IoT technologies, there is need to talk about the line behind the adoption and use of such technologies. Based on the TAM originally proposed by Davis et al., (1989), and later on to be developed by the subsequent extensions like the UTAUT by Venkatesh (2022), it was possible to elaborate the drivers of the user adoption of technology. These models claim that in the first iteration perceived usefulness and perceived ease of use are the key determinants of user acceptance; however, while in later iterations social influence, facilitating conditions and hedonic motivation are the additional factors. For the case of the IoT, perceived usefulness is often associated with automatization, convenience, and efficiency. Smart home devices, for example, are appealing to the consumers because they automate the usual functions such as lights switch off, appliances function on a cycle programmed, and surveillance is distant. Perceived ease of use as well is a strong influence on the resistance of technology. The IoT systems that do not imply significant configuration and offer the user a comfortable interface (UI) will be more demanded by non-tech-savviest users (Abbas et al., 2020; Maio et al., 2024). Furthermore, social influence could be noted from peer-usage, online reviews and community endorsement and plays an important position in the consumer attitude towards purchasing new IoT devices. Privacy concerns opposed to sustained adoption, a well-known phenomenon that is referred to as "privacy paradox" is one of the critical and paradoxical behavioral dimensions. Although when surveys are conducted, they find out that consumers are always very concerned with regards to their data security and personal privacy, in most instances, such concerns are not translated into restrictive behavior. Those are exchanged by the users with devices that track, record and analyze very personal data. A number of studies have also been conducted such as Zhou (2024), in which case when consumers think that convenience would be a benefit, they would exchange privacy within a short period of time, particularly when they think that a benefit would be immediate and tangible. This cognitive contradiction highlights the imperative to the companies to use a transparent policy of data, easier time of consent and customization of the privacy settings to the consumer to give them the feeling that they have reclaimed their control over the data.

Enhancing Experience Through Personalization

In the era of the-IoT, personalization became the characteristic feature of consumer interaction. The fact that the IoT devices can process, act, and analyze real-time data-streams is what changes the old school uniform, roundabout customer engagement in tailor-made customer interaction and responsiveness. The principle of this transformation is the context-awareness of the system to construct its actions depending on the information about the environment of the user, his/her desires and habits etc., even- physiological state. As an example, we can mention the smart thermostat Nest. It is required to know how the user behaves when locals are likely to wake up or leave the house/come back home to program the temperatures to make the occupants as comfortable as possible but not to use power unnecessarily. Not only this is good for user satisfaction but this also goes with the sustainability purposes thus making personalization experiential and functional (Khan & Emon, 2025b; Nair & Manohar, 2024). Wearable fitness devices, like the ones from Fitbit or Apple, take it a step further by giving data-based recommendations specific to an individual's health goals. Based on measurements of such metrics as heart rate, patterns of sleep, and physical activity these devices give users feedback and recommendations individualized to them, improving their sense of agency and motivation. Even health outcomes have been associated with such devices which indicates the possibility of transformation that personalized involvement through IoT carries with it (Bhatt & Chakraborty, 2023). Retail is another of the sectors that have adopted personalization by means of IoT rapidly. In store, beacons and sensors would be able to identify the place, browse history or buying potential of a customer and send the aimed promotion to their Smartphone. For example, a person who passes by a favorite part of clothes can receive a notification about sales or a product suggestion, according to the customer's purchases. Such a type of micro-targeting not only increases the likelihood of purchase but also increases the customer relation with the brand on relevance and timeliness basis (Chaudhary et al., 2022).

CHALLENGES IN IOT IMPLEMENTATION

The IoT implementation by the current business and consumer culture is quite promising. The implication of its potential is that it is about to transform those industries in which it will optimize the operational efficiencies, trigger the innovations, and, finally, individualize the community experiences. However, challenges have been unavoidable as well in even its strengths of transformation about embracing the use of IoT. Such problems manifest themselves at the organizational and at the technical level and they are also aggravated by several aspects related to data privacy, security, and regulatory aspects. This efficient handling of the same is a prerequisite in getting the best of IoT without sacrificing sustainability and security in deployments.

Organizational and Technical Barriers

Interoperability Issues

Some main technical impediments to the use of IoT include interoperability. IoT systems are systems of a heterogeneous nature in terms of different devices, platforms and communication protocols by design. This contradiction of architecture reveals gigantic issues to the organizations that are focused on using the IoT devices and implementing in the current architecture of the organizations. As it has been stated by the scholars Alabadi et al. (2022), that just having an enormous number of the multiplicity of the types of the devices starting from sensors and actuators up to rather sophisticated systems very often leads to the compatibility problems when various systems operated by different manufacturers fail to work coherently as a whole. These are not merely obstacles to the complications of operations but also costs to businesses that try to achieve consistent IOT ecosystems. For instance, one example of a smart city venture would be the one that would include the controlling of traffic, consumption of power and the protection systems, and for such a venture, there is a need for an integration of many IoT devices made by various vendors. Such devices are also not capable of relating well because of diverse protocols or data format, and the entire system could be inefficiently and split up into fragments. In order to address these interoperability problems, there are other options where the companies can spend their money on custom integration solutions or middleware platform integration, which is intended to eliminate gaps between communicating heterogeneous systems (Sadeghi et al., 2024).

High Initial Investment

The startup cost implicated with any implementation of the IoT is still a major barrier, especially for the SMEs. IoT solutions entail upfront costs in the form of devices, sensors and networking as far as storage and analytics systems are concerned. It has been found out from a study conducted by Edquist et al. (2021), that capital intensive nature of investments in IoT primarily deters small players from venturing in such technologies. Such costs can, however, pose very sharp problems, especially in SMEs with no indication whatsoever, as to whether there would be a return on investments (ROI) in the short term. For large organizations the initial integration costs of the IoT devices shall be less but high. A full-scale IoT system also has a network of sensors and devices, secure connections to communication, storage and processing facilities on cloud level and powerful data analysis facilities. The installation and maintenance of such systems, however, are only possible through the special employees and other machinery and as well adds more to the cost. Such a kind of financial burden is especially critical for the industries, which do not have much of a margin for profit, or which is not clear how to make money with the IoT incorporation. To overcome this barrier, it needs to do more than reduce the costs of hardware and services, but it must provide some ROI which is represented by improved operational efficiency and customer experience.

Skill Gaps

The deployment of IoT technologies implies so the special knowledge and skills, namely designing systems of IoT, processing data, and cybersecurity. However, there is a vast lack of professionals trained to implement, develop, and solve points concerning the IoT-solutions. According to Ahmad et al. (2022), indicate that Internet of things talent voices are horizontally highly unsatisfied in comparison with supply, but mostly due to the lack of experts in such spheres. the area of data science, embedded systems, and network security. Such a gap in talent represents one of the major obstacles to organizations keen on deploying and scaling the IoT projects. It is most acutely felt in the field of cybersecurity when the issue of the absence of viable professionals is concerned. Because there are several increments of the IoT systems not only but the connection between the systems also increased the chances of security attacks increase exponentially. The installation of IoT devices is dangerous if the due levels of security are not embraced as there are discrepancies that can easily be hijacked by unscrupulous people. The closing of this space will need a vast number of workforce development practices that include special training programs in the areas related to IoT, cooperation with academic representatives regarding the training of a new generation of IoT experts (Zikria et al., 2021). In addition, the organizations should not overlook the fact that they need to make their current workers capable of managing and operating the systems that are associated with IoT in a secure manner.

Data Privacy, Security, and Regulation

Cybersecurity Vulnerabilities

IoT systems constitute net-of-base vulnerability to the cyber threat because of the huge attack surface. Each of the IoT devices can become the opening for cyber threats, and there is a great number of such unprotected devices. An example of such vulnerability of the IoT devices is default password, unpatched firmware, no encryption, that most often leads to attack. According to a report published by Hammi et al. (2022), it has been revealed that there have been more than half of all the IoT devices which are in danger of attacks because they are full of diverse flaws starting from vulnerable defaults up to poor practices in data encryption. Such problems increase with the spread of the deployment of IoT. For example, there may be lots of pieces of equipment attached to smart home systems, and all possible access points. Compromised smart thermostats or security cameras could also be an entry point to use in compromising the network and compromising the people's data and actual existence. The growth of connected devices in industries like healthcare, manufacturing or transportation amplifies the risk even more as many of the IoT systems work with the sensitive data of a personal health record or with controlling systems. To combat these attacks to cybersecurity, then organizations will need to vigorously deploy propulsive measures of security along the continuum of life cycle of the devices in IoT from the development and implantation phase, straight to daily operations. In this case device authenticity, regular software maintenance, encryption on the data and real time monitoring on the connected systems is being applied (Khan & Hasan Emon, 2024; Raheja & Kumar Manocha, 2022). Furthermore, it is required creating the existing standards and practices with respect to using IQs to eliminate vulnerabilities and create trust in the consumer and the businesses.

Regulatory Compliance

As the IoT systems are generating an enormous volume of data, the growing concern of the businesses on their compliance with the regulations of data protection and privacy may be justified properly. The cases of law that govern the business entities with strict rules on the matters taking place with collection, storing and processing personal data include the cases such as The European Union's General Data Protection Regulation (GDPR). These regulations set high-level structures in data governance which companies should implement to institute transparency, accountability, and consent of the consumer. Breaches of such regulations may attract huge financial penalties and loss of reputation. Furthermore, there is also the emergence of forms of regulations that are to act as monitors to the accelerated growth recorded in the adoption of IoT technologies. It is exactly the field that governments from all corners of the world are seeking to stabilize in the equilibrium between the profit of an IoT innovation formulation and interests of consumers' protection. While, the integration of the IoT is increasingly becoming more participatorily in our daily life, the question of the ownership of the data, the consent of the data as well as the ethical implementation of the AI algorithms should be regulated both at the legal and organizational levels (Ahmad et al., 2022). Businesses need to ensure that they invest in broad policies data, get consent from the consumers to use their data and they should be able to make it possible to make transfer and erasure of data easy. Auditing services regularly and according to international standards can help to guarantee compliance and to establish confidence in IoT technologies among the consumers.

Ethical Implications

In addition, the ethical implications of putting in place IoT for deployment are also enormous. IoT systems have a propensity to collect massive data of people and their behavior, which raises the issue of surveillance, consent, and algorithmic bias. As an example, smart devices in homes or wearable health trackers can gather secretive information about one's habits, routine and health condition. However, with the absence of ethical standards, this data may be misused, and this would lead to invasions of privacy and discrimination. The problem of algorithmic bias is the next ethical dilemma. The IoT systems, particularly the ones that use artificial intelligence and machine learning, rely on data to make decisions. However, if the data, against which the algorithms are trained, are biased or do not represent the population, then these results can be used for reinforcing inequalities or some groups being excluded. For instance, an instance of a biased algorithm in the healthcare system can lead to negative health outcomes among the disadvantaged population.

Thus, it is important that the IoT systems should be developed keeping in mind the aspect of fairness, transparency and the accountability (Khan & Emon, 2025; Kuiler & McNeely, 2023).

INNOVATIVE MARKETING STRATEGIES POWERED BY IOT

Internet of things (IoT) is not only transforming the operational efficiencies and coining new experiences for consumers but also rewriting the horizon of marketing strategies. The propagation of connected devices and real time ability to collect massive data has brought new avenues through which businesses can be innovative and optimize marketing activities. The technologies of the IoT present the opportunity for the marketers to offer consumers more personalized and data- logical and immersive experiences (Khan et al., 2025). With the device interconnectivity, companies can engage with customers in a way that is totally impossible. This area is going to study several of the IoT-enabled revolutionary approaches to marketing like data-based marketing, live engagement, together with experiential marketing, approaches that are establishing new standards in the field of traditional marketing.

Data-Driven Marketing and Real-Time Engagement

It is one of the most useful outcomes of IoT in contemporary marketing that it offers the possibility to remold interaction between companies and consumers based on data-centered strategies. Previous marketing approaches were retrospective with regards to marketing data used for targeting wide, vaguely defined consumer groups. However, with IoT, companies can leverage real-time data and make better business decisions by changing from reactive to predictive and prescriptive marketing strategy. Based on the data gathered and processed from the connected devices, firms can deliver personalized experience to the consumers and target the consumers effectively depending on what they require and what message is suitable for them.

Monitoring Product Usage Patterns

The IoT enables businesses to also understand real time use of their products/ services by consumers as well. Such information helps companies to know the customers even more, including what they need and want and thus properly identifying the marketing initiatives. For example, wearable gadgets, such as fitness trackers (e.g., Fitbit, Apple Watch), are utilized to obtain information on users' activity, heart rates and patterns of their sleep. Companies will have data on which it will base personalized recommendations, promotions, or upgrades suitable to that person's health targets or behaviors. In the world of automobiles, Tesla is a good example whereby IoT monitoring on the use of the product as well as improving the product marketing strategies. Tesla, in getting hold of the driving data via connected vehicles, not only learns about vehicle performance, but what the consumers like and do. The information enables Tesla to deliver updates to software, based on car usage, for instance, enhancement of the navigation system or optimizing its driving. Using such IoT-enabled data, Tesla can deliver more focused marketing messages and product invention that will enhance its brand loyalty (Khalid et al., 2024).

Delivering Context-Aware Promotions

The IoT ecosystem is native to contexts as devices are becoming more and more aware of the real world of the consumers in. Such an awareness creates new possibilities to send broadly relevant but deep targeting, context-aware promotions in real time. For instance, IoT-based beacons can discover whether a consumer has been to a store and can direct personalized offers to his or her mobile phone with the help of his or her previous shopping record or tendencies. This kind of personality not only gives a better chance of a conversion but refines the shopping experience, making it more seamless and natural. The presence of context-aware promotion is one of the salient instances, and in that sense, the use of Starbucks' specific mobile device, which provides individual offers to the customer based on the location, history of purchases, even time of the day can be mentioned as one of the context-aware promotion forms. When the customer arrives at some Starbucks store, the application registers his/her presence and sends a personalized offer to buy something to drink or to eat, what he/she had bought before. Such a combination of real-time marketing with the data of the IoT provides Starbucks with opportunities to strengthen its relations with the customers and stimulate sales.

PREDICTING CONSUMER CHURN AND INTERVENING WITH TARGETED OFFERS

IoT data can be extremely crucial in predicting the churn behavior of the consumers if the consumers are ready to switch the brand or service they are using and offering them personalized deals or rewards to prevent them from switching. By always observing how customers behave and how they use products, companies can engineer pattern studies to identify churn possibilities, that's the decline of interest for the product or consistent complaints. IoT-based predictive analytics will then help initiate personalized marketing initiatives that will bring these customers back on the fold before they make up their minds. For instance, it can be able for the telecommunication companies to track the data usage habits of the customer's devices and know if a client can downgrade or cancel his/her subscription after experiencing dissatisfaction and lack of engagement services. Based on IoT insights, these companies could use individualized offers to their customers, i.e. discounts or individually tailored bundle offers to retain them and ensure the loyalty of their customers.

Experiential Marketing in the IoT Era

The IoT revolution is also transforming the way brands will be delivering immersive and interactive marketing experience. IoT technologies enable firms to engage with their customers physically and virtually on both sides since crossing the boundaries integrates both types of connections. Companies can apply connected devices to make experiences more meaningful and personalized to enhance brand perception thus forming long term relationships with the consumers emotionally.

Smart Packaging and Augmented Reality

The concept of using intelligent packaging as one of the most exciting of all the inventions that ever took place in the field of experiential marketing represents the interaction between the consumers and The AR (augmented reality). Intelligent packaging via the internet of objects offers the consumer a possibility to interact more with the product than a label and instructions. Through QR code or an application for a smartphone, the consumers can receive additional content like video presentation of the product, virtual try-ons, or 3D product presentation. This helps to make it more immersive and very engaging and as such give the brands a chance to stand out in a very competitive market. For example, Coca Cola has experimented with IOT enabled smart packaging to allow consumers to have access to exclusive content through their phones. Upon scanning a label of the product, the consumers can see personalized video content or get involved in social media challenges. This use of augmented reality and IoT enables Coca-Cola to interact with the consumers in a more entertaining and evoking manner which helps to establish loyalty to the brand in terms of enhancing customer experience on the whole (Gupta et al., 2020).

Interactive Billboards and Wearable Devices

Another example of experience marketing during the age of IoT is using interactive billboards that recognize wearable devices or mobile apps used by the consumer. Companies can update their advertisements according to people's choice and lifestyle using data from the wearable devices (smartwatch, etc.). Personalized messages, offers or promotions may be shown on these interactive billboards based on one's interests or location. For instance, in 2019, one of the British retailers has been using the billboards, which could be IoT-enabled and could be responding to the weather situation and peoples' moves, that is, advertising different products at different times of the day or even based on how close a person was. The billboards would be able to access smartphones' and wearables' data and offer more personalized information such as personal styling suggestions or special offers in accordance with the consumer's activity or location (Ferreira et al., 2021).

Voice-Activated Shopping via Smart Assistants

Voice-activated shopping that is enabled by the IoT-associated gadgets like Amazon Alexa or Google Assistant is another wise marketing trend transforming the form of retail. These smart assistants allow consumers to do shopping, re-order the products, and receive personalized recommendations on speaking commands, a hands-free shopping experience. Voice assistants correspond to IoT technologies assisting them to get consumer preferences' information and offering them personalized products based on the history of purchase/browsing history. More brands are increasingly using voice-activated shopping as one way of being close to the consumers in a more relaxed manner. For instance, Amazon's Alexa can offer products based on what the user says to it such that a user can discover new commodities and services through a natural process. As a way of utilizing the power of smart assistants, IoT-enabled, marketers too are bringing this technology into their marketing practices on their part giving consumers who use voice-activated devices to engage with their brand special discounts, personalized recommendations and even loyalty rewards (Vinoth & Srivastava, 2024).

IoT and Dynamic Pricing Strategies

One of the greatest uses of IoT is dynamic pricing. Dynamic pricing involves changing prices of a certain product or service depending on several factors which include demand, competition and the needs of the consumers. The data made available online using IoT can help businesses tune pricing strategies in real time in accordance with the customers' choice and prevailing market conditions, and the actions of their competitors. For example, airlines and Uber (ride sharing companies) use IoT (real time data) to know how to charge according to demand. To use the supply and demand at equilibrium and to maximize its revenue Uber uses dynamic pricing when demand is high to manipulate the rates. Similarly, hotels can also make use of the IoT-enabled systems that can be used to monitor the levels of occupancy and adjust the cost of the rooms based on the level of occupation (Emon & Chowdhury,

2025). The use of IoT Data to introduce dynamic pricing will assist businesses to achieve the highest amount of revenue and use dynamic pricing that is up to date with regards to conditions to enhance customer service.

Enhancing Customer Loyalty Programs With IoT

Customer loyalty programs form a crucial part of any marketing strategy and IoT will be able to dig deep and make such programs gush with tremendous amounts of personalization of rewards and strategy of engagement. Through IoT-enabled devices, businesses will be in a suitable position to monitor customer behaviors and preferences so that they will be able to establish loyalty programs that will fulfill the needs of the customers. For instance, in the sphere of retail, loyalty programs can track consumers' purchases with the help of IoT-based smart tags or mobile apps and provide clients with individual discounts or special offers based on their prior purchase records. This will make the experience- more attractive and satisfying to the customers, and it is also likely to lead to-the follow up purchases and brand loyalty. Besides this, using the information provided by-the IoT, the companies- can calculate how to- locate their most important customers, and provide them with special incentives, thereby instilling in them a strong sense of connection to the brand.

The Future of IoT in Marketing: Trends and Opportunities

IOT will introduce a new twist into the marketing strategies in the future as the amount of connected- devices will increase, 5G networks will become more widespread, and the IoT devices will become able to transfer the information more quickly and establish real-time interactions. Besides, AI and- machine learning will allow the business to operate with better analytics to predict the behavior of consumers, personalize the marketing content and adjust the degree of interaction with the customer. The more extensive the technologies will align with the Internet-of-the-things (IoT) the more the marketers will- resort to deploying them and will provide the omnichannel experience that will be seamlessly transferred between the digital and the real world. The brands which will be capable of surviving in the new reality of marketing will be the ones that will consider the opportunities of IoT in providing personalized, data-driven, and immersive experience.

FUTURE PERSPECTIVES ON IOT IN BUSINESS

Internet of Things (IoT) is a novel radical force in the business landscape, which provides new dimensions in the framework of efficient operations, interaction with clients, product innovation. From now on the direction of the IoT ecosystem will depend on its synthesis with other upcoming technologies, alignment of its development with sustainable and inclusive agenda, and contribution in developing the future models of governance. This part addresses the possibilities of the IoT in business where it has been converging with artificial intelligence (AI), edge computing, and blockchain paying attention to sustainability, inclusivity, and governance in shaping the future of IoT technologies. The potential of the IoT is boosted when it has the luck of intersecting with other rising technologies. As these technologies are being developed new opportunities arise for IoT to operate more efficiently, smartly and securely. The IoT Integration with artificial intelligence (AI), edge computing and block chain define the boundaries of imaginative opportunities as to how even more autonomous, scalable and trustworthy systems will transform business operations and customer experience.

Artificial Intelligence (AI) and IoT: Intelligent Automation and Decision-Making

IoT-artificial intelligence (AI) convergence happens to be one of the most promising ones. Even though IoT provides an infrastructure suitable for gathering huge sources of data through the connected devices through the internet, AI provides intelligent analysis of the data for extraction of valuable insights that could have an influence on decision making and automation. By the combination of IoT and AI, smart systems are architected to perform complex activities on their own, such as the predictive maintenance in manufacturing to personalized product suggestion in retail. In industrial settings, the AI-empowered IoT systems can monitor the performance of equipment; predict the failures and arrange the maintenance automatically; decrease downtime and operation efficiency. This combination of both AI and IOT does not only raise the value to be received from the data but also sparks mighty cost reduction and enhances the correctness of decisions. For instance in the retail industry AI-driven IoT systems enable tracking of certain customer experience, as they can have an access to the data from connected devices that contain wearable or smartphone to deliver tailor-made product offers, promotions, and services (Emon, 2025a; Manoharan et al., 2024). The future of the IoT in a business environment will include increased use of AI when it comes to automation of processes, optimization of supply chains, as well as enhanced customer experience.

Edge Computing: Reducing Latency and Enabling Time-Sensitive Applications

The second one is edge computing, which is another emerging technology that is very critical in the development of IoT. In the normal architectures for cloud computing, data generated from IoT devices are forwarded to central data centers for processing. This, however, could create latency particularly if time sensitive applications are used that require real time processing such as in use in cases of automated vehicles, industrial automation and health monitoring. This issue can be resolved with the use of the edge computing, which can process data at the "edge" of the network by the place where the data is generated, which minimizes latency, and hence forces faster decision-making. Edge computing decreases the overhead by executing computation and storing resources closer to data generation, which optimizes the performance of the Internet of Things systems and improves possibilities for it to respond immediately to real-time events (Ahmed & Ahmed, 2026). For example, in the case of automotive industry, the IoT sensors in autonomous vehicles can communicate to the edge computing nodes and use instant action like changing speed or navigate around an obstacle without requiring a cloud server (Arthurs et al., 2022; Emon, 2025b). In addition, edge computing is relevant to applications in industries such as healthcare, where there are continuous data streams in forms of information generated from such devices as wearable health trackers. In other words, if this data was processed by the healthcare providers on a local machine, it would be possible to monitor the patients in real-time and diagnose the abnormalities on them, and to interfere when there is a need for it. This ability impacts upon the care for patients favorably and lowers the response times and overall outcomes that is how the future of IoT-empowered services will further be shaped by edge computing.

Blockchain: Ensuring Data Integrity and Security

As the internet of things devices will gain steam, it would be wise to ensure that data generated is secure and is not amenable to change. Blockchain is one of the greatest blockchain technologies that maintain IoT transactions. Blockchain is a distributed ledger technology that encrypts the records of the transactions in such a safe and visible form that it can be used for the application in IoT networks where there is a data transfer of massive sizes in a confidential form through devices, systems, and users. Blockchain can be helpful in overcoming such significant issues of IoT security as data integrity, authentication, and tamper-resistance. Businesses can use blockchain to ensure that the data produced from the use of the IoT devices would become immutable and no one could change it without being noted. For example, blockchain technology is able to be applied in supply chain management to trace the origin of goods with the assurance that the sensor-captured information on IoT is true and impeccable (Khan et al., 2020).

Toward a Sustainable and Inclusive IoT Future

As the scope and complexity of IoT are expanding, it is critical to make sure that the expansion of IoT follows general objectives in society, including, but not limited, to sustainability, inclusivity, as well as responsible innovation. As for the IoT future directions, besides technical ones, the environment, social, and ethics issues of a massive IoT implementation are also necessary.

Green IoT Practices: Reducing Energy Consumption

Apart from other issues engulfing the subject of IoT, its effect on the environment and consumption of power are important points of consideration particularly in the latter aspect of consuming energy. The connected devices and sensors in the IoT ecosystems are massive in number and therefore lots of energy is required for them to operate, the more devices the more energy it calls for. This contributes to the fact that very serious questions can be asked regarding the sustainability of IoT technologies in the long run. To address these problems, the businesses practicing green IoT and the policymakers should address the green IoT practices that can assist the reduction of IoT devices' energy consumption and their Carbon footprint (Ahmed et al., 2026). This includes such actions as development of energy-efficient hardware and optimization of data transmission protocols for decreasing the energy costs and inclusion of renewable sources in the structures of the IoT networks. A good example is the development of low-power IoT devices that use energy efficient sensors and communication technology such as LoRaWAN (Long Range Wide Area Network) which is designed for low power and long-range communications. Furthermore, the IoT-based smart grids can present a perfect opportunity for increasing the efficiency of energy in cities and industries.

Inclusive Design: Accommodating Diverse User Needs

IoT technologies should be designed to have in mind inclusiveness in their capacity that they are available and can be of use to every stratum in society. This entails recognition of the need of disabled, the aged and forgotten communities in the development of products and services of Internet of Things. For example, those IoT-enabled healthcare devices that are remote monitoring systems or assistive technologies should be developed to address the variation in an individual's thinking ability and ability to act differently. Using smart home systems one can customize them providing increased accessibility to elder people or those who have some disability, such voice-activated appliances, automatic lights and remote monitoring of a person's health. With the introduction of the inclusive principles to IoT development, companies get a chance to create products and services that would target more users and therefore promise that the benefits of IoT's availability will be realized by all.

Human-Centric Governance Frameworks: Aligning Technology With Societal Well-Being

As we advance in developing IoT technologies, there should be an improved development of governance framework in which the well-being of people and society takes priority. Human centric governance is interested in how IoT technologies are being designed and rolled out to address privacy, ethics and societal value compliance. This entails the development of policies and regulations that will deal with the major issues such as data privacy, cyber security and ethical issues as far as usage of IoT applications are concerned. Recent data privacy laws such as General Data Protection Regulation (GDPR) in Europe have put stringent guidelines for the collection and use of personal data to safeguard consumer rights in the IoT environment. Moreover, the human-centric governance should address the rhythms of equity and fairness; the benefits arising from the utilization of IoT technologies need to be shared among the different social groups in a fair manner. This involves productive working relationships between governments, businesses and the aspects of civil society in a manner IoT development can benefit the populace and that its goal complements the larger picture of society.

IoT and the Evolution of Digital Business Models

IoT future will also result in the creation of business models due to the growth of the use of IoT technology in transformation and provision of new value offering in the organization. Data driven business models take an interest in the monetization of the large quantity of the data produced by- connected-devices and it will be manifested in the field of IoT in particular. The companies will shift towards service-oriented models to provide consumers with more flexible and customized solutions they are trying to offer. As an example, products and services on a subscription basis will be common to the IoT enabled products and services where firms would be allowed to enjoy the flow of data emanating constantly in relation to the connected devices. An example of the automobile industry, Tesla already provides subscription services in the form of software updates, not to mention the extra features via the assistance of the IoT connection. More so, the IoT will facilitate businesses to pursue more-timely, customer-driven business models concerned with time-based engagement, customized value propositions and- ongoing (time-based) value provision. This paradigm shift will cause the businesses to reconsider their value chain and exploit internet of things to its full potential by introducing new technologies to replace their use of other technologies, including AI, machine learning and blockchain, among others.

CONCLUSION

Internet of Things (IoT) strategic positioning in the business and consumer worlds is an incredibly profound transformation that is already changing businesses and societies. This chapter has explored how IoT, with its network of connected devices, not only leads to-the operational efficiency but it also assists in opening new opportunities in the field of innovation and increased customer-experience and business. The impact of IoT in terms of impacting strategic decision-making processes, nature of consumers' behaviors, as well as organizations' capabilities is also expected to increase with the continued development of IoT and thus enable its entrenchment as an underlying pillar of digital transformation. Establishment of combinations of upcoming technologies such as artificial intelligence, edge computing and blockchain is accelerating the possibility of IoT. Synergies of this kind enable more agile, responsive systems that would not only enable businesses to automate operations but continue extracting actionable insight from terabytes upon terabytes of real-time data. Equipped with capabilities for enhancing predictability and personalizing involvement of consumers, IoT is giving new alliance to the new era of data-driven marketing, operations enhancement, and service transformation. Although companies turn to IoT to address ever more digital and wired world's needs, they get more agile and adaptable, more-consumer driven, preparation for the complexities of the new market environment. Nevertheless, there are quite a few challenges with the opportunities provided by the IoT. The integration of the IoT in the prevailing business process has presented challenges at the organization level, at the technical level and at a regulatory level, which would have to be overcome with well-thinking out strategies and investments. Interoperability issues, data privacy and security as well as other issues still need to be addressed, particularly against the backdrop of more-and-more diverse IoT networks. Furthermore, there are ethical issues of IoT specifically with reference to surveillance, consent and use of the data, which will have to be considered to make the technological breakthrough compatible with society values and its rights. Now that businesses look ahead, it is important to note that they embrace IoT as an enabler of long-term value, and not just an improvement on technology. For organizations to take advantage of the potential of IoT, it is going to take a visionary approach, i.e. embedding the technology of IoT into its business model, relationship with consumers and pipeline of innovation. In the same way, regulatory bodies and the policy makers are also essential in defining the legal and ethical routes that will be built around IoT, such that the latter will be sustainable to the public good, and directed towards the greater sustainability, inclusivity and well-being of society.

REFERENCES

Abbas, T., Khan, V.-J., & Markopoulos, P. (2020). Investigating the Crowd's Creativity for Creating On-Demand IoT Scenarios. *International Journal of Human-Computer Interaction, 36*(11), 1022–1049. DOI: 10.1080/10447318.2019.1709331

Ahmad, K., Maabreh, M., Ghaly, M., Khan, K., Qadir, J., & Al-Fuqaha, A. (2022). Developing future human-centered smart cities: Critical analysis of smart city security, Data management, and Ethical challenges. *Computer Science Review, 43*, 100452. DOI: 10.1016/j.cosrev.2021.100452

Ahmad, T., Madonski, R., Zhang, D., Huang, C., & Mujeeb, A. (2022). Data-driven probabilistic machine learning in sustainable smart energy/smart energy systems: Key developments, challenges, and future research opportunities in the context of smart grid paradigm. *Renewable & Sustainable Energy Reviews, 160*, 112128. DOI: 10.1016/j.rser.2022.112128

Ahmed, M., & Ahmed, M. J. (2026). Sustainable Industrial Operations Through IoT-Generated Big Data Insights. In *Sustainable Operations in the Age of AI and Big Data* (pp. 37–82). DOI: 10.4018/979-8-2600-0216-2.ch002

Ahmed, M., Al Amareen, O. S., & Arafat, Y. (2026). Harnessing Big Data for Reverse Logistics and Waste Management: Pathways to Sustainable Supply Chains. In *Enhancing Sustainability in Global Supply Chains With Big Data Analytics* (pp. 175–210). IGI Global Scientific Publishing. DOI: 10.4018/979-8-3373-6896-2.ch006

Alabadi, M., Habbal, A., & Wei, X. (2022). Industrial Internet of Things: Requirements, Architecture, Challenges, and Future Research Directions. *IEEE Access : Practical Innovations, Open Solutions, 10*, 66374–66400. DOI: 10.1109/ACCESS.2022.3185049

Allioui, H., & Mourdi, Y. (2023). Exploring the Full Potentials of IoT for Better Financial Growth and Stability: A Comprehensive Survey. *Sensors (Basel), 23*(19), 8015. DOI: 10.3390/s23198015 PMID: 37836845

Arthurs, P., Gillam, L., Krause, P., Wang, N., Halder, K., & Mouzakitis, A. (2022). A Taxonomy and Survey of Edge Cloud Computing for Intelligent Transportation Systems and Connected Vehicles. *IEEE Transactions on Intelligent Transportation Systems, 23*(7), 6206–6221. DOI: 10.1109/TITS.2021.3084396

Bentalha, B., & Hmioui, A. (2022). *Smart Service Supply Chain and Just Walk Out Technology: A Netnographic Approach* (pp. 223–236). DOI: 10.1007/978-3-030-94191-8_18

Bhatt, V., & Chakraborty, S. (2023). Improving service engagement in healthcare through internet of things based healthcare systems. *Journal of Science and Technology Policy Management*, *14*(1), 53–73. DOI: 10.1108/JSTPM-03-2021-0040

Bridhikitti, A., Kaewsuk, J., Karaket, N., Friend, R., Sallach, B., Chong, J. P. J., & Redeker, K. R. (2023). Balancing Agriculture and Industry through Waste Utilization for Sugarcane Sustainability. *Sustainability (Basel)*, *15*(20), 14711. DOI: 10.3390/su152014711

Bzai, J., Alam, F., Dhafer, A., Bojović, M., Altowaijri, S. M., Niazi, I. K., & Mehmood, R. (2022). Machine Learning-Enabled Internet of Things (IoT): Data, Applications, and Industry Perspective. *Electronics (Basel)*, *11*(17), 2676. DOI: 10.3390/electronics11172676

Chaudhary, P., Kiran, P., Kate, N., & Pandey, S. (2022). Experiential tourism – role and application of micro-targeting in enhancing customer experience, engagement and loyalty. *Journal of Information and Optimization Sciences*, *43*(6), 1463–1473. DOI: 10.1080/02522667.2022.2139929

Crespo Márquez, A. (2022). *Digital Maintenance Management*. Springer International Publishing., DOI: 10.1007/978-3-030-97660-6

Davis, F. D., Bagozzi, R. P., & Warshaw, P. R. (1989). User acceptance of computer technology: A comparison of two theoretical models. *Management Science*, *35*(8), 982–1003. DOI: 10.1287/mnsc.35.8.982

Edquist, H., Goodridge, P., & Haskel, J. (2021). The Internet of Things and economic growth in a panel of countries. *Economics of Innovation and New Technology*, *30*(3), 262–283. DOI: 10.1080/10438599.2019.1695941

Emon, M. M. H. (2025a). Ethical Intelligence in Motion: Leveraging AI for Responsible Sourcing in Supply Chain and Logistics. In *Navigating Responsible Business Practices Through Ethical AI* (pp. 207–240). DOI: 10.4018/979-8-3373-3104-1.ch008

Emon, M. M. H. (2025b). Overcoming Hurdles: Navigating Challenges in the Adoption of Smart Logistics. In *Emerging Trends in Smart Logistics Technologies* (A. Hlali, pp. 197–228). IGI Global Scientific Publishing. DOI: 10.4018/979-8-3373-2434-0.ch007

Emon, M. M. H., & Chowdhury, M. S. A. (2025). AI and IoT-Powered Smart Logistics: Transforming Supply Chains for Efficiency and Sustainability. In *Emerging Trends in Smart Logistics Technologies* (A. Hlali, pp. 45–72). IGI Global Scientific Publishing. DOI: 10.4018/979-8-3373-2434-0.ch002

Ferreira, J. J., Fernandes, C. I., Rammal, H. G., & Veiga, P. M. (2021). Wearable technology and consumer interaction: A systematic review and research agenda. *Computers in Human Behavior, 118*, 106710. DOI: 10.1016/j.chb.2021.106710

Fortino, G., Guerrieri, A., Pace, P., Savaglio, C., & Spezzano, G. (2022). IoT Platforms and Security: An Analysis of the Leading Industrial/Commercial Solutions. *Sensors (Basel), 22*(6), 2196. DOI: 10.3390/s22062196 PMID: 35336368

Gupta, S., Leszkiewicz, A., Kumar, V., Bijmolt, T., & Potapov, D. (2020). Digital analytics: Modeling for insights and new methods. *Journal of Interactive Marketing, 51*(1), 26–43. DOI: 10.1016/j.intmar.2020.04.003

Hammi, B., Zeadally, S., Khatoun, R., & Nebhen, J. (2022). Survey on smart homes: Vulnerabilities, risks, and countermeasures. *Computers & Security, 117*, 102677. DOI: 10.1016/j.cose.2022.102677

Hassan, M. M., Fahim Abrar, M., Kakon, S., Hossen, A., & Arafat, Y. (2024). Improving Loan Approval Decisions: The Impact of Data Balancing on the Classifier's Performance in Predicting Borrower Reliability. *2024 27th International Conference on Computer and Information Technology (ICCIT)*, 1690–1695. DOI: 10.1109/ICCIT64611.2024.11022094

Hossen, A., Arafat, Y., Sarker, M. N., Jamil, M. H., Islam, M. A., & Hasan, R. (2024). A Predictive Framework for Financial Crashes Using Advanced Time Series Techniques. *2024 International Conference on Progressive Innovations in Intelligent Systems and Data Science (ICPIDS)*, 476–483. DOI: 10.1109/ICPIDS65698.2024.00080

Jamil, M. H., Hossen, A., Talukder, S. I., Arafat, Y., & Sozib, H. M. (2025). Big Data Analytics and Its Usage on Financial Fraud Detection in the USA. *Advances in Machine Learning IoT and Data Security, 1*, amlid25001. Advance online publication. DOI: 10.63471/amlid25001

Javaid, M., Haleem, A., Singh, R. P., Rab, S., & Suman, R. (2021). Internet of Behaviours (IoB) and its role in customer services. *Sensors International, 2*, 100122. DOI: 10.1016/j.sintl.2021.100122

Kang, M. J., & Hwang, Y. C. (2022). Exploring the Factors Affecting the Continued Usage Intention of IoT-Based Healthcare Wearable Devices Using the TAM Model. *Sustainability (Basel), 14*(19), 12492. DOI: 10.3390/su141912492

Khalid, H. G., Abbas, H. H., Hussein, M. J., Abu-AlShaeer, M. J., Mukhlif, S. K., & Khlaponin, D. (2024). Unveiling the Next Frontier: The Future of Connected Technologies. *2024 36th Conference of Open Innovations Association (FRUCT)*, 207–218. DOI: 10.23919/FRUCT64283.2024.10749851

Khalifa, M., & Albadawy, M. (2024). AI in diagnostic imaging: Revolutionising accuracy and efficiency. *Computer Methods and Programs in Biomedicine Update*, *5*, 100146. DOI: 10.1016/j.cmpbup.2024.100146

Khan, P. W., Byun, Y.-C., & Park, N. (2020). IoT-Blockchain Enabled Optimized Provenance System for Food Industry 4.0 Using Advanced Deep Learning. *Sensors (Basel)*, *20*(10), 2990. DOI: 10.3390/s20102990 PMID: 32466209

Khan, T., & Emon, M. M. H. (2025a). Preparing for the Next Disruption: Lessons Learned From Past Crises and Building a Playbook for Future Supply Chain Shocks. In *Supply Chain Disruptions and Impact on Global Inflation* (pp. 253–286). IGI Global Scientific Publishing. DOI: 10.4018/979-8-3373-1982-7.ch010

Khan, T., & Emon, M. M. H. (2025b). Resilient Supply Chains: Lessons From Past Crisis Strategies Companies Can Adopt to Create More Resilient Supply Chains. In *Mass Media and Impact of Fake News on Supply Chains* (pp. 285–318). IGI Global. DOI: 10.4018/979-8-3373-2175-2.ch011

Khan, T., Emon, M. M. H., Rahman, K. M., Nipa, M. N., & Fuad, M. N. (2025). The Role of AI in Driving Customer Engagement Through Technological, Organizational and Environmental Enablers in E-Commerce. *2025 International Conference on Quantum Photonics, Artificial Intelligence, and Networking (QPAIN)*, 1–6. DOI: 10.1109/QPAIN66474.2025.11171949

Khan, T., Emon, M. M. H., Rahman, M. A., Hamid, A. B. A., Yaakub, N. I., Abdul Hamid, A. B., & Ya'akub, N. I. B. (2024). Bridging the Gap: Realizing Green-Tech Potential. *AI and Green Technology Applications in Society*, 91–121. DOI: 10.4018/979-8-3693-9879-1.ch004

Khan, T., & Hasan Emon, M. M. (2024). Determinants of AI Image Generator Adoption Among Marketing Agencies: The Mediating Effects of Perceived Usefulness. *2024 IEEE 3rd International Conference on Robotics, Automation, Artificial-Intelligence and Internet-of-Things (RAAICON)*, 177–182. DOI: 10.1109/RAAICON64172.2024.10928548

Kuiler, E. W., & McNeely, C. L. (2023). Panopticon implications of ethical AI: equity, disparity, and inequality in healthcare. In *AI Assurance* (pp. 429–451). Elsevier., DOI: 10.1016/B978-0-32-391919-7.00026-3

Ma, S., Ding, W., Liu, Y., Ren, S., & Yang, H. (2022). Digital twin and big data-driven sustainable smart manufacturing based on information management systems for energy-intensive industries. *Applied Energy*, *326*, 119986. DOI: 10.1016/j.apenergy.2022.119986

Maio, R., Araújo, T., Marques, B., Santos, A., Ramalho, P., Almeida, D., Dias, P., & Santos, B. S. (2024). Pervasive Augmented Reality to support real-time data monitoring in industrial scenarios: Shop floor visualization evaluation and user study. *Computers & Graphics*, *118*, 11–22. DOI: 10.1016/j.cag.2023.10.025

Manoharan, G., Ashtikar, S. P., Nivedha, M., & Dutta, P. K. (2024). *Tailoring the Future—The Ascendancy of Artificial Intelligence in the Fashion Industry* (pp. 503–520). DOI: 10.1007/978-3-031-71052-0_20

Mubarik, M. S., & Khan, S. A. (2024). Digital Supply Chain and Industry 4.0 Technologies. In *The Theory, Methods and Application of Managing Digital Supply Chains* (pp. 121–132). Emerald Publishing Limited. DOI: 10.1108/978-1-80455-968-020241008

Nair, A. J., & Manohar, S. (2024). Green Service Consumption: Unlocking Customer Expectations on Technological Transformations Enhancing Purchase Experience in Retail Store. *International Journal of Information Management Data Insights*, *4*(2), 100277. DOI: 10.1016/j.jjimei.2024.100277

Paul, K., Chatterjee, S. S., Pai, P., Varshney, A., Juikar, S., Prasad, V., Bhadra, B., & Dasgupta, S. (2022). Viable smart sensors and their application in data driven agriculture. *Computers and Electronics in Agriculture*, *198*, 107096. DOI: 10.1016/j.compag.2022.107096

Raheja, N., & Kumar Manocha, A. (2022). IoT based ECG monitoring system with encryption and authentication in secure data transmission for clinical health care approach. *Biomedical Signal Processing and Control*, *74*, 103481. DOI: 10.1016/j.bspc.2022.103481

Reyes, P. M. (2023). Radio Frequency Identification (RFID) and Supply Chain Management. In *The Palgrave Handbook of Supply Chain Management* (pp. 1–35). Springer International Publishing. DOI: 10.1007/978-3-030-89822-9_109-1

Sadeghi, M., Carenini, A., Corcho, O., Rossi, M., Santoro, R., & Vogelsang, A. (2024). Interoperability of heterogeneous Systems of Systems: From requirements to a reference architecture. *The Journal of Supercomputing*, *80*(7), 8954–8987. DOI: 10.1007/s11227-023-05774-3

Venkatesh, V. (2022). Adoption and use of AI tools: A research agenda grounded in UTAUT. *Annals of Operations Research*, *308*(1–2), 641–652. DOI: 10.1007/s10479-020-03918-9

Vinoth, S., & Srivastava, N. (2024). Unveiling the Power of Omni-channel Retail Strategies. In *Augmenting Retail Reality, Part B: Blockchain, AR, VR, and AI* (pp. 85–112). Emerald Publishing Limited. DOI: 10.1108/978-1-83608-708-320241014

Zhou, Z. (2024). Data extraction in dockless bikeshare: An analysis from users' perspective. *Big Data & Society*, *11*(4), 20539517241299724. Advance online publication. DOI: 10.1177/20539517241299724

Zikria, Y., Ali, R., Afzal, M. K., & Kim, S. W. (2021). Next-Generation Internet of Things (IoT): Opportunities, Challenges, and Solutions. *Sensors (Basel)*, *21*(4), 1174. DOI: 10.3390/s21041174 PMID: 33562343

KEY TERMS AND DEFINITIONS

Consumer Engagement: The connection between consumers and brands through which consumers interact with brands with the intension of creating loyalty and providing the best customer experience facilitated by digital platforms.

Data Privacy: The right of the individuals to decide on how their personal data is gathered, utilized, and shared, especially in IoT ecologies.

Digital Transformation: The digitalization of businesses, which changes the way enterprises operate- and generate value to their clients.

Edge Computing: A computing paradigm that computes information where it is generated or at the sources eliminating the need to transfer information to a central location. This reduces response times and bandwidth utilization.

Internet of Things (IoT): It is a system of sensors that gather, transmit and-analyze data to make intelligent decisions and utilize automation, which is inter-connected with a network of devices.

Interoperability: The capability of the various kinds of IoT devices and systems to communicate with each other and work together on a single coherent digital landscape.

Real-Time Analytics: The process of measuring data as it is generated with a view to enabling businesses to make the instant data-based decisions.

Strategic Framework: An organized technique that is implemented by the organizations to bring technology adoption like IoT in line with their long-term goals and objectives.

Chapter 10
The Future of IoT in Business and Consumer Environments

Sucheta Kanchi
http://orcid.org/0000-0001-7489-8616
Bharati Vidyapeeth, Pune, India

T. C. Manjunath
http://orcid.org/0000-0003-2545-9160
Rajarajeswari College of Engineering, India

P. Selvakumar
http://orcid.org/0000-0002-3650-4548
Department of Science and Humanities, Nehru Institute of Technology, Coimbatore, India

Subramaniam Iyer
http://orcid.org/0000-0002-3843-9399
Datta Meghe Institute of Management Studies, India

Cyril Crasto
http://orcid.org/0000-0001-8703-2010
Sri Balaji University, Pune, India

Ruchika Paidalwar
Datta Meghe Institute of Management Studies, India

ABSTRACT

This paradigm is rapidly revolutionizing the way businesses operate, governments function, and consumers engage with their environments. consumer environments, emphasizing the wide-ranging impact of this technology. Defining the Internet of Things, from wearable fitness trackers to smart vehicles, and from agricultural sensors to connected healthcare devices. The key characteristics that define IoT include connectivity, automation, data exchange, and smart decision-making. to make decisions without human intervention. Over time, IoT systems learn from the data they collect, resulting in more intelligent and efficient operations. Thus, IoT is not just about connecting devices but also about enabling machines to make decisions and improve their functionality autonomously. Actuators: Actuators are

DOI: 10.4018/979-8-3373-3441-7.ch010

responsible for carrying out the actions based on the data and decisions made by the IoT system(Adolphs & Winkelmann, 2010). For example, an actuator might turn on a heating system in response to a drop in temperature detected by a sensor.

INTRODUCTION TO IOT: DEFINING THE TECHNOLOGY AND ITS APPLICATIONS

This paradigm is rapidly revolutionizing the way businesses operate, governments function, and consumers engage with their environments. consumer environments, emphasizing the wide-ranging impact of this technology. Defining the Internet of Things, from wearable fitness trackers to smart vehicles, and from agricultural sensors to connected healthcare devices. The key characteristics that define IoT include connectivity, automation, data exchange, and smart decision-making. to make decisions without human intervention. Over time, IoT systems learn from the data they collect, resulting in more intelligent and efficient operations. Thus, IoT is not just about connecting devices but also about enabling machines to make decisions and improve their functionality autonomously. Actuators: Actuators are responsible for carrying out the actions based on the data and decisions made by the IoT system(Adolphs & Winkelmann, 2010). For example, an actuator might turn on a heating system in response to a drop in temperature detected by a sensor.. User Interface: or voice assistants. User interfaces enable monitoring, control, and alerts related to IoT devices.(Allen et al., 2013)Asset management is another area where IoT is having a significant impact. Businesses can track and monitor the condition, location, and performance of assets such as machinery, vehicles, or even office equipment. This allows for better asset utilization, reduced maintenance costs, and improved compliance with regulations. For example, IoT sensors can be attached to vehicles in a fleet to monitor engine health, fuel consumption, and driving patterns, which helps fleet managers make data-driven decisions regarding maintenance and operations. and consumer experiences across the globe. From smart manufacturing to connected homes, IoT is enabling greater efficiency, improved decision-making, and enhanced convenience in various aspects of daily life. As IoT technology continues to evolve, its applications will only become more widespread, impacting everything from healthcare to transportation to environmental sustainability. By embracing IoT, businesses and consumers alike can unlock new possibilities for innovation, productivity, and a smarter future. The potential of IoT is immense, and its continued

THE CURRENT STATE OF IOT: ADOPTION RATES, TRENDS, AND CHALLENGES

Understanding these aspects is critical for stakeholders across industries as they navigate this fast-changing and highly disruptive domain. Adoption Rates of IoT Technologyadoption of rapid growth over the past decade. According to various industry connected devices worldwide has surged, and projections suggest that IoT will continue to expand significantly in the coming years. Statista estimates that by 2030, there will be over 30 billion around 26%.adoption has been more gradual. For example, in the business-to-business (B2B) space, IoT is being leveraged for industrial automation, supply chain optimization, and predictive maintenance. (Al-Obeidat et al., 2018) A significant proportion of large companies have already integrated IoT into their operations. According to a survey by McKinsey, 50% of organizations across various sectors had implemented IoT solutions by 2021, with industries like automotive, healthcare, and manufacturing leading the way., wearables, and connected vehicles has grown steadily but remains below its potential. While smart home devices, for instance, have seen increasing adoption, particularly in developed markets, IoT in the consumer market has yet to fully penetrate regions with lower technological infrastructure and limited access to high-speed internet. Despite the challenges associated with wide-scale adoption, IoT adoption rates are steadily increasing. Governments, enterprises, and consumers alike are realizing the potential of IoT in improving efficiency, productivity, and quality of life, which fuels further investment in the technology. Major industries and sectors are all moving towards incorporating IoT solutions into their daily operations, and the trend shows no sign of slowing down.The roll-out of 5G networks is another major trend that is accelerating the growth of IoT(Bærentsen & Trettvik, 2002). 5G technology offers vastly improved data speeds, lower latency, and greater capacity for connected devices, which will unlock new IoT applications that were previously impractical due to network limitations. With 5G, IoT devices can communicate in real time, with minimal delays, even in high-density environments.

THE FUTURE OF IOT: PREDICTIONS, OPPORTUNITIES, AND THREATS

The future of IoT holds immense potential for further innovation, with predictions indicating that IoT will touch virtually every aspect of human life, from how we work to how we interact with the environment. At the same time, the rise of IoT will present a variety of threats, including security vulnerabilities, privacy concerns, and the environmental impact of increased device proliferation. This article will explore the future of IoT, providing a look at potential predictions for its evolution, the opportunities it offers, and the threats that need to be mitigated.Predictions for the Future of IoT As IoT continues to mature, several key predictions suggest how it will evolve over the next decade and beyond. These predictions are based on current trends, technological advancements, and expert analysis across various industries.(Baethge et al., 2016) The future of IoT is expected to be shaped by the following developments: to include everyday objects like clothing, kitchen appliances, and wearable health monitors. The next decade will witness an explosion of IoT-enabled devices, making connectivity ubiquitous and an integral part of the physical environment.IoT will become seamlessly integrated into our daily lives, often functioning without our explicit awareness. From smart cities to personalized healthcare, IoT devices will operate in the background, continuously vast networks of devices infrastructure, making IoT systems more efficient and cost-effective.Artificial Intelligence (AI) and Machine Learning (ML) will increasingly without human intervention. equipment failures, optimize production schedules, and improve supply chain management. will enable real-time monitoring of critical infrastructure, such as roads, bridges, and utilities,(Barbosa, 2015) ensuring that problems are detected and addressed before they become costly or dangerous.As IoT technology becomes more pervasive, it will open up new business models, services, and markets. For example, businesses will be able to leverage IoT to offer subscription-based services, predictive maintenance, and data-driven insights. Industries like agriculture will benefit from precision farming, where In the consumer market, IoT will fuel the growth of smart home ecosystems, connected health devices, and wearables.

These new market opportunities will drive investment in IoT innovation and foster competition among technology companies to develop the next generation of IoT products and services.Additionally, IoT-, leading to improved decision-making and a more personalized customer experience.. Sustainability and Environmental Impact IoT will provide significant opportunities for sustainability by, powered by IoT, will enable better management of energy consumption, reducing waste IoT can also optimize water usage by detecting leaks and monitoring consumption in real-time, which will contribute to water conservation efforts.In agriculture, IoT will enable precision farming, reducing the managing emergency services more effectively. In the workplace, IoT sensors can monitor equipment health and safety conditions, reducing workplace accidents and improving employee well-being.To mitigate these concerns, clear data privacy policies and regulations must be established. Governments and industry bodies need to enforce stricter data protection measures to ensure that users' personal information is not exploited. Transparent consent processes and strong encryption standards will be essential for building trust with consumers.The increasing proliferation of IoT devices poses an environmental challenge. The production, disposal, and recycling of billions of connected devices can contribute to electronic waste and pollution. The demand for more connected devices will also strain energy resources, increasing the carbon footprint of IoT systems.To address these challenges, manufacturers must focus on creating sustainable IoT devices that are energy-efficient, durable, and recyclable. A more circular approach to the lifecycle of IoT devices, including better recycling programs and product longevity, will be essential for mitigating the environmental impact of IoT.

INDUSTRIAL IOT (IIOT): TRANSFORMING MANUFACTURING, LOGISTICS, AND SUPPLY CHAIN MANAGEMENT

IIoT is a critical component of this revolution, driving the digital transformation of industries through automation, data analytics, and machine-to-machine communication. In an IIoT-enabled environment, machines are equipped with sensors, software, and other intelligent devices that allow them to monitor their performance, detect issues in real-time, and communicate with one another to optimize processes. These devices generate vast amounts of data, which are collected, analyzed, and used to improve operations across the entire production chain.IIoT goes beyond traditional IoT by focusing specifically on industrial applications, using sensorand automation to facilitate improved control and management of manufacturing processes, supply chains, and logistics. adaptive logistical systems. (Chua et al., 2005)The adoption of IIoT is accelerating as industries realize the potential for cost savings, efficiency gains, and increased competitiveness in the market.Applications of IIoT in Manufacturing Manufacturing is one of the most prominent industries benefiting from IIoT. In a smart factory, machines and production lines are i The integration of IIoT into manufacturing has numerous applications that are transforming the way production systems operate.. These methods can result in unplanned downtime, costly repairs, and inefficient maintenance procedures. IIoT, on the other hand, allows manufacturers to implement predictive maintenance strategies. By equipping machines with sensors that monitor variables such as temperature, vibration,Real-time monitoring also facilitates the optimization of processes through continuous feedback loops. For instance, if production slows down or product quality drops below a certain threshold, the IIoT system can automatically adjust parameters such as machine speed or temperature, helping to maintain optimal conditions and reduce the likelihood of defects.facturing. Robotics and automated systems equipped with IoT sensors can perform repetitive and dangerous tasks, reducing the need for human intervention. In some factories, autonomous mobile robots (AMRs) are used to transport materials between workstations or assist in the assembly process.(Chunxia et al., 2010) These robots are connected to the IIoT system and can communicate with other machines to coordinate their movements, ensuring a smooth and efficient production flow.

The use of robots and automation also enhances safety, as dangerous tasks, such as welding or lifting heavy materials, are handled by machines rather than human workers.The ability to track shipments in real time improves customer satisfaction, as consumers can receive accurate delivery time estimates and notifications about their shipments. Furthermore, it helps logistics companies optimize routes and make quick adjustments in the event of disruptions, such as traffic congestion or weather-related delays.

IOT IN RETAIL: ENHANCING CUSTOMER EXPERIENCE, IMPROVING OPERATIONS, AND INCREASING SALES

IoT is enabling retailers to optimize various aspects of their business. Below are some of the key applications of IoT in the retail industry. track customers' behavior in real-time. When customers enter the store, they may be greeted by personalized offers, notifications, or promotions based on their shopping history or preferences. (Deloitte, 2016) For instance, if a customer is browsing a particular section of the store, an IoT-powered system could send a targeted discount or product recommendation directly to their smartphone.Furthermore, IoT-enabled beacons and sensors can guide customers through the store, helping them find specific products more easily. This type of technology is especially useful in large stores or malls, where customers may struggle to locate certain items. By providing tailored recommendations and assistance, IoT enhances the shopping experience, making it more efficient and enjoyable for customers. IoT-enabled mirrors, sensors, and interactive displays that allow customers to try on clothes virtually, request different sizes or colors, and access personalized product recommendations—all without leaving the fitting room. (Clarke, 2008)These mirrors can display digital images of the customer wearing different outfits, helping them visualize how clothing will look without physically trying it on. lines often lead to long wait times, which can frustrate customers and negatively impact their shopping experience. To address this issue, retailers are implementing IoT-powered checkout solutions, such as smart carts or cashier-less stores. These systems use sensors, cameras, and RFID technology to automatically detect items that customers have selected, allowing them to pay for their purchases without the need for a cashier. IoT also enables predictive analytics, allowing retailers to anticipate delays, optimize routes, and adjust inventory levels in real-time based on changing demand.sensitive products are transported under optimal conditions. energy-saving measures. By optimizing energy use and reducing waste, retailers can lower operational costs and reduce their carbon footprint, contributing to sustainability goals.By utilizing IoT to gather insights into customer preferences, shopping behavior, and purchasing patterns, retailers can improve product offerings and marketing strategies, leading to increased sales and revenue. Personalized recommendations and targeted promotions drive higher conversion rates, while real-time inventory tracking ensures that popular items are always available. Additionally, automated checkout systems make the purchasing process faster and more convenient, leading to a higher volume of transactions and reduced cart abandonment rates.which products are most popular, which promotions are most effective, and where improvements are needed in the store layout or product assortment. Similarly, real-time data from the supply chain enables retailers to make more accurate forecasts and optimize inventory management, reducing waste and improving profitability.(Evans, 2017) The sheer volume of data generated by IoT devices can overwhelm retailers if not properly managed. Retailers need to invest in data analytics tools and platforms to process, analyze, and derive actionable insights from this data. Additionally, retailers must ensure that they have the right talent and expertise to interpret the data and make data-driven decision, personalized recommendations, and supply chain optimization, IoT is helping retailers stay competitive.

SMART BUILDINGS AND CITIES: THE ROLE OF IOT IN CREATING SUSTAINABLE AND EFFICIENT INFRASTRUCTURE

The growing focus on environmental impact, energy conservation, and resource optimization has driven a shift toward IoT-based solutions in urban environments and buildings. In this analysis, we explore the key role of IoT in creating sustainable and efficient infrastructure in smart buildings and cities, examining its applications, benefits, challenges, and transformative impact on the built environment.(Fox et al., 2006)The Concept of Smart Buildings and Cities The goal is to increase efficiency, improve comfort, enhance safety, and reduce environmental impact. Similarly, smart cities integrate IoT into city-wide infrastructure, including transportation, waste management, utilities, and public services, to improve urban living conditions while promoting sustainability and resource efficiency. Both smart buildings and smart cities rely on i enable better management of resources, improved energy efficiency, reduced carbon emissions, and enhanced overall functionality.Smart buildings harness IoT buildings.. Energy Management and Efficiency One of the most significant benefits of IoT in smart buildings is its ability to monitor and optimize energy consumption. IoT-enabled smart meters, sensors, and energy management platforms collect data on energy usage across different building systems, such as HVAC, lighting, and appliances(Frambach et al., 2007). This data is then analyzed to identify inefficiencies, predict energy demand, and optimize the operation of building system . For example, in offices, smart lights can automatically adjust to the ambient light in a room or be programmed to turn off when no one is present, reducing energy consumption.detectors linked to smart lighting systems can trigger lights to turn on in response to movement, making it easier to navigate dark areas or alert security personnel of potential intruders. The ability to control lighting remotely through mobile apps or centralized systems offers added convenience for building managers and tenants entrances and exits, detect unauthorized access, and notify security personnel of potential threats. Automated access control systems can also grant or deny entry based on biometric data, on real-time data. Smart sensors placed on faucets, toilets, and water meters provide continuous feedback on water flow and consumption patterns.In the event of a leak or excessive water use, the system can automatically alert building managers or occupants, enabling quick intervention to prevent waste and damage.

Additionally, rainwater harvesting systems can be integrated into IoT networks to collect and reuse water for irrigation or cooling systems, contributing to overall sustainability efforts.Smart cities leverage IoT to monitor environmental factors such as air quality, water quality, noise pollution, and weather conditions. IoT sensors placed throughout the city collect data on these environmental variables, providing real-time insights into urban conditions. For example, air quality sensors can monitor pollution levels and send alerts when air quality falls below safe thresholds, enabling authorities to take action to protect public health.(Gaur et al., 2015)IoT systems can also be used to monitor the efficiency of green spaces, such as parks and urban forests. Sensors can track soil moisture levels, temperature, and plant health, allowing city planners to optimize irrigation and maintenance schedules. This ensures that green spaces remain sustainable and contribute to the overall well-being of city residents., and real-time health data collection. IoT-enabled devices, such as wearable health monitors and smart medical equipment, can transmit patient data to healthcare providers, enabling remote consultations and timely interventions. This reduces the strain on healthcare facilities and improves access to care, especially in underserved areas.Additionally, IoT can be used to monitor public health trends, such as disease outbreaks or air pollution-related health issues, allowing cities to take proactive measures to protect the well-being of residents., and waste management, IoT contributes to significant energy and resource savings. This is crucial for achieving sustainability goals and reducing operational costs.oT technologies help create more livable and comfortable spaces for individuals and communities. which lowers utility bills, while smart cities optimize traffic flow and waste collection, reducing operational costs for municipalities.

SMART HOMES AND IOT: ENHANCING CONVENIENCE, COMFORT, AND SECURITY

These devices communicate with each other and their users, making it easier to manage various aspects of a home, from security and energy usage to entertainment and daily routines. As IoT technologies continue to evolve, smart homes are becoming more integrated, intelligent, and efficient. . In this article, we will explore the applications, benefits, and challenges of IoT in smart homes, and examine how it is revolutionizing modern living.Applications of IoT in Smart HomesIoT technologies are embedded in numerous devices and systems within smart homes, which Below are the key applications of IoT in smart homes., smart lighting systems can be programmed to simulate presence in the home while the occupants are away, deterring potential intruders and improving home security. By optimizing energy usage and creating the ideal ambiance, smart lighting enhances both convenience and sustainability.These devices use machine learning to understand when the home is occupied or unoccupied, adjusting the temperature accordingly to minimize unnecessary energy use.Homeowners can control their thermostats remotely, set schedules, or adjust settings based on weather filters, preventing system inefficiency and extending the lifespan of the equipment.systems integrate a variety of IoT-enabled devices, such as cameras, doorbell cameras, motion detectors, smart locks, and alarms, to provide comprehensive home security. These devices work together to monitor the home's perimeter, alert homeowners of potential threats, and allow them to take action, all from their mobile phones or smart devices. Homeowners can also set up security routines, such as arming the alarm system when leaving the house or activating cameras when going to sleep, for added peace of mind.. Some advanced systems use facial recognition to grant access to authorized individuals, enhancing the security of the home.IoT has revolutionized everyday household appliances, making them smarter and more connected. (Hartson, 2003)For instance, a smart refrigerator can notify homeowners when food is about to expire, or when a grocery item is running low.

A smart oven can be preheated remotely, ensuring that dinner is ready as soon as you walk through the door. Washing machines can send alerts when a cycle is complete, and even start a wash remotely, providing added convenience for busy homeowners (Hasan & Kazlauskas, 2014). Some smart appliances can also learn user preferences over time and adjust their operations accordingly. A smart coffee maker may brew coffee at a specific time each morning based on your routine, or a washing machine may optimize the wash cycle based on the type of clothes being washed. These devices enhance convenience, efficiency, and reduce the amount of time spent on household chores. conservation and efficient management are critical components of a smart home. IoT-enabled water management systems can monitor water usage throughout the home, detecting leaks, reducing waste, and promoting sustainability. Smart water sensors can be placed under sinks, near appliances, or in water pipes to detect leaks and alert homeowners before they result in significant damage.Additionally, smart irrigation systems, such as Rachio, use weather data and soil moisture levels to automatically adjust watering schedules, ensuring that the lawn or garden is watered only when necessary. These systems help conserve water, reduce landscaping costs, and contribute to overall environmental sustainability.Additionally, IoT-based fitness equipment, such as smart treadmills or cycling machines, can provide users with workout data and integrate with health tracking apps to monitor progress. As the smart home ecosystem expands, health-focused IoT devices are becoming integral to providing a healthier living environment.

WEARABLES AND IOT: THE FUTURE OF HEALTH AND FITNESS TRACKING

The ability to collect and transmit real-time data has paved the way for more personalized health management, improved fitness outcomes, and greater convenience in tracking progress over time. However, despite their vast potential, wearables and IoT-based health solutions come with their own set of challenges. In this article, we will explore the applications, benefits, and challenges of wearables and IoT in health and fitness tracking and discuss how they are shaping the future of personal health management. like Fitbit, Garmin, and the Apple Watch are equipped with accelerometers and sensors that track steps, distance, and calories burned, offering users a detailed view of their daily physical activity levels. Many wearables also offer advanced features such as heart rate monitoring(Junglas & Watson, 2003), GPS tracking for outdoor exercises like running or cycling, and cadence tracking for more precise data on specific workouts.These devices encourage users to stay active by providing real-time feedback and nudges, such as reminders to move if they have been inactive for too long or goals to meet a target number of steps. By collecting and analyzing activity data, . Heart Rate and Cardiovascular Health Monitoring-Heart rate monitoring is one of the most common features of wearables, providing users with valuable insights into their cardiovascular health. Many fitness trackers continuously measure heart rate throughout the day and during exercise to assess the intensity of physical activity. This feature can be particularly Some advanced wearables, such as the Apple Watch and Fitbit Charge series, also offer features like ECG (electrocardiogram) readings, which can detect irregular heart rhythms, such as atrial fibrillation (AFib). Early detection of irregular heart rhythms can be crucial for preventing serious health issues, making these wearables an important tool in proactive health management.(Kees et al., 2015)Wearables and IoT technologies are also making significant strides in tracking nutrition and hydration, two essential elements for maintaining overall health. While many wearables do not directly track food intake, some devices allow users to manually log their meals or sync with third-party nutrition apps to keep track of caloric intake, macronutrients, and other essential nutrients.In addition, smart hydration trackers like the Hydro Coach and the Level app track water consumption throughout the day, reminding users to drink water based on their activity level, weather conditions, and personal hydration goals.(Lee & Lee, 2015) These wearables play a crucial role in helping users stay on top of their dietary and hydration needs, supporting their overall fitness and health goals.

Stress is a major factor affecting both mental and physical health, and wearables are increasingly being designed to help users manage and reduce stress. Many wearables measure heart rate variability (HRV), which can serve as an indicator of stress levels. Low HRV has been associated with increased stress and anxiety, while higher HRV is often linked to better relaxation and recovery.Some wearables, like the Apple Watch and Garmin devices, also feature guided breathing exercises to help users manage stress. These devices may prompt users to take deep breaths or perform mindfulness exercises when they detect high stress levels. Moreover, some wearables offer features to track mood or provide reminders for mental health practices such as meditation, improving users' ability to manage their emotional well-being.For individuals with chronic conditions such as diabetes, hypertension, or asthma, wearables can provide valuable real-time data for managing their health. For instance, continuous glucose monitoring (CGM) systems, such as the Dexcom G6, allow people with diabetes to track their blood sugar levels throughout the day without the need for regular finger pricks. These devices are part of a broader IoT network, sending data to smartphones or healthcare providers to monitor glucose trends and make timely adjustments to medication or diet.Wearables are also being used to monitor other conditions like hypertension, with devices like the Omron HeartGuide providing users with the ability to measure blood pressure on the go. By empowering Wearables can be incredibly helpful for individuals recovering from surgery or injury. Devices that track mobility, muscle activity, and physical progress during rehabilitation exercises can aid in recovery by providing data that allows healthcare providers to adjust rehabilitation plans. Wearables can also track adherence to physical therapy routines and provide feedback on performance, ensuring that individuals stay on track with their recovery goals.Benefits of Wearables and IoT in Health and Fitness Tracking Wearables and IoT technologies offer numerous benefits for health and fitness enthusiasts, individuals with chronic health conditions, and anyone looking to improve their overall well-being. Some of the key benefits include: These devices collect and analyze a wide range of data, offering users customized recommendations based on their unique health and fitness profiles. Whether it's setting personalized fitness goals, managing stress, or improving sleep quality, behaviors in real time, improving motivation and helping them stay on track with their health and fitness goals. high blood pressure, or sleep apnea. (Lee et al., 2011).

Early detection can lead to more timely medical intervention, reducing the risk of serious health complications. For example, wearables that monitor heart rate and ECG can help detect atrial fibrillation (AFib) or other arrhythmias, prompting users to seek medical attention before these conditions become life-threatening. Improved Motivation and Accountabilit which encourage users to stay motivated and engaged with their health goals. By providing users with concrete data on their progress, wearables create a sense of accountability, pushing individuals to maintain or improve their fitness levels. For individuals with chronic conditions or those recovering from surgery, wearables can assist in the ongoing management of their health. By continuously monitoring vital signs, wearables help users and healthcare providers track health trends and make adjustments as needed. This reduces the need for frequent visits to the doctor and provides a more convenient and cost-effective way to manage chronic health conditions.While wearables have become increasingly accurate, there are still concerns about the reliability of the data they collect. For example, heart rate monitors and step counters may not always provide 100% accurate readings, which can impact the effectiveness of the health insights provided. It is important for users to understand that wearables are tools for tracking trends and should not be solely relied upon for making medical decisions. rely on wearables for continuous health monitoring, frequent recharging can be an inconvenience. Additionally, wearables may require software updates or maintenance to ensure optimal performance, adding to the complexity of device management. tracking features can still be costly. This limits access to these technologies for some individuals, especially those in lower-income groups or in developing countries. Making wearables more affordable and accessible is essential for widespread adoption and for ensuring that everyone has the opportunity to benefit from the health and fitness tracking capabilities they offer.

IOT IN TRANSPORTATION: CONNECTED CARS, SMART TRAFFIC MANAGEMENT, AND AUTONOMOUS VEHICLES

This analysis explores how IoT is impacting transportation, with a focus on connected cars, smart traffic management systems, and the rapidly developing field of autonomous vehicles. Additionally, Connected Cars: Enhancing Driver Experience and SafetyConnected cars, or vehicles equipped with IoT technologies, and exchange data with other vehicles, infrastructure, and cloud-based platforms. This connectivity enables a wide range of functionalities, from real-time diagnostics to enhanced safety features and personalized driving experiences.refers to the ability of a vehicle to communicate with various entities,(Ma et al., 2017) including other vehicles (V2V), infrastructure (V2I), pedestrians (V2P), and even cloud platforms (V2C). This communication helps reduce traffic accidents, improve road safety, and enhance traffic flow.. These sensors collect data on the car's performance, allowing for predictive maintenance. For example, if the system detects an issue with the brake pads or low tire pressure, it will send a notification to the driver, prompting timely repairs and preventing breakdowns or accidents.This capability not only increases the safety and longevity of vehicles but also enhances the overall user experience by reducing unexpected mechanical failures. Moreover, predictive maintenance reduces repair costs by addressing issues before they become more serious, offering convenience and cost savings to car owners. enabling a range of connected services, including navigation, entertainment, and communication. Through seamless integration with smartphones, cloud services, and other IoT devices, connected cars offer personalized in-car experiences, such as real-time traffic updates, personalized music playlists, and voice-activated commands for hands-free operation. This connectivity allows drivers to interact with their vehicles and external environments more intuitively, making the driving experience safer and more enjoyable. This information allows traffic controllers to make data-driven decisions to adjust traffic signal timings, manage lane usage, and direct vehicles to alternative routes when congestion is high. By analyzing traffic patterns, smart traffic systems can predict congestion before it occurs, helping to prevent gridlocks and improving overall traffic efficiency. (Madgule et al., 2023)For instance, adaptive traffic signals can adjust the likelihood of traffic jams and shortens travel times, contributing to more efficient and sustainable transportation networks., IoT technologies are reshaping transportation are immense. As these technologies continue to evolve, the future of transportation looks poised to be more interconnected, sustainable, and user-centric than ever before.

ARTIFICIAL INTELLIGENCE (AI) AND MACHINE LEARNING (ML) IN IOT: ENHANCING DECISION-MAKING AND AUTOMATION

We will also look at how AI and ML enable automation, predictive analytics, and enhanced decision-making, while addressing the key obstacles that businesses must overcome to effectively leverage this powerful combination.(Nan et al., 2017) in IoT can be broken down into several key areas: In healthcare, IoT devices monitoring patient vitals can feed data into AI algorithms that assess health risks, providing doctors with real-time insights for better decision-making. speed and accuracy are crucial., without the need for human intervention.can use AI and ML to analyze traffic patterns and adjust signal timings in real time, optimizing traffic flow and reducing congestion.r greater personalization of products and services.(Oberländer et al., 2018) By continuously learning from user behaviors and preferences, IoT devices can offer tailored experiences. For example, IoT-powered wearables like fitness Based on this data, the devices can recommend personalized fitness plans, track progress, and provide health insights, all of which contribute to improving the user's overall well-being. reaping the benefits of these technologies. Below are some of the key areas where AI and ML in IoT are making a significant impact.AI and ML can also improve public safety by analyzing data surveillance cameras and sensors. can detect anomalies or unusual patterns, such as detecting accidents, fires, or criminal activity in real time, enabling authoritiesferent health factors, offering doctors more accurate and data-driven diagnoses. AI-powered tools, such as diagnostic imaging analysis, can assist radiologists in detecting conditions like tumors or fractures, improving the accuracy of medical imaging In addition to predictive maintenance, AI-powered IoT systems in manufacturing can optimize production processes by identifying inefficiencies, predicting demand, and improving quality control through real-time data analysis(Porter & Heppelmann, 2014).AI and ML integrated into IoT can revolutionize retail experiences by offering more personalized services to customers. recommend personalized products, and offer tailored discounts based on individual shopping habits., improving the customer shopping experience. Furthermore, AI and ML can help retailers optimize store layouts, pricing strategies, and marketing campaigns by analyzing consumer behavior patterns.

5G AND IOT: THE IMPACT OF NEXT-GENERATION WIRELESS NETWORKS ON IOT APPLICATIONS

The unprecedented improvements in connectivity, speed, reliability, and scalability. As IoT devices proliferate across industries, 5G's high-speed, low-latency network is positioned to address the limitations of previous wireless technologies, such as 4G and Wi-Fi, creating new opportunities for IoT applications that were previously constrained by bandwidth, coverage, or reliability. With 5G, IoT networks will become more intelligent, agile, and capable of supporting a much higher density of connected devices, paving the way for smarter cities,(Pousttchi et al., 2015) autonomous vehicles, advanced industrial systems, and next-generation consumer applications. However, this transformation also brings with it a range of challenges that need to be addressed in order to fully capitalize on the potential of 5G and IoT., which improve signal strength and capacity.The key differences between communication for applications that require instant feedback, which can handle only a fraction of that. Reliability: 5G offers more reliable connectivity in areas with high device density, ensuring consistent service even in crowded environments.5G is poised to play a transformative role in IoT applications across a wide range of industries, offering benefits that enhance performance, scalability, and efficiency. Below are some key areas where 5G will have a profound impact on IoT. can support large-scale IoT networks, such as those deployed in smart cities or industrial environments.

This increase in device density allows for more IoT applications to be deployed in crowded environments without and environmental sensors. These devices can collect and transmit data to central systems in real-time, enabling smarter city management and improving urban living standards.Similarly, in industrial environments, 5G's support for large device densities will enable the deployment of thousands of sensors on manufacturing floors, providing detailed insights into equipment performance, production line status, and supply chain operations.Reliability and coverage are critical factors for IoT applications, especially in remote or hard-to-reach areas. 5G networks provide more reliable connections and broader coverage, particularly in densely populated environments. This enhanced reliability ensures that IoT devices can maintain stable connectivity even in challenging conditions, such as underground, indoors, or in areas with poor traditional network coverage. For example, in agriculture, 5G can be used to deploy IoT devices in rural areas for precision farming, where reliable connectivity is needed to monitor soil moisture, track crop health, and automate irrigation systems. Similarly, in logistics, 5G can enhance the tracking of shipments in remote locations, ensuring that real-time updates are always available., 5G-connected traffic management systems can dynamically adjust signal timings in real-time based on traffic conditions, reducing congestion and improving traffic flow. Additionally, 5G-powered environmental sensors can monitor air and water quality, providing real-time data that can be used to tackle pollution and improve public health.The use of higher-frequency millimeter-wave spectrum, which is essential for 5G's ultra-fast speeds, is limited and requires careful management. Governments and telecom companies must work together to ensure that sufficient spectrum is available for 5G networks and that it is licensed effectively to avoid interference between different wireless services.these devices create more opportunities for cyberattacks. Securing IoT networks and protecting user data will be crucial to the success of 5G-powered IoT applications.

EDGE COMPUTING AND IOT: REDUCING LATENCY, IMPROVING PERFORMANCE, AND ENHANCING SECURITY

This analysis explores the role of edge computing in IoT, including its benefits, challenges, and opportunities, as well as how it is by enabling faster processing, improved security, and more scalable IoT solutions. Edge computing alleviates these challenges by enabling local processing of data on edge devices or nearby edge servers, minimizing the need for long-distance communication with the cloud.In an IoT context, edge computing helps address several key challenges, including centralized servers, significantly lowering latency and allowing for faster decision-making. Bandwidth: As to the cloud. With data being processed locally, edge computing minimizes the risk of data breaches during transmission, as sensitive data can be kept within local networks instead of being exposed during long-distance communication to cloud servers. and LIDAR systems, enabling the vehicle to make immediate decisions, such as avoiding obstacles or adjusting its route. Similarly, in industrial IoT (IIoT) environments, edge computing enables machines to monitor their own health and performance, detecting potential issues and triggering preventive maintenance actions before they lead to costly downtime (Xiao & Benbasat, 2007). This local data processing ensures that the network is not overwhelmed with raw data, allowing IoT systems to operate more efficiently and scale effectively. various security risks, including hacking, data breaches, and interception during transmission.Edge computing mitigates these risks privacy regulations like HIPAA, while avoiding the risks of sending sensitive data to remote cloud servers. data processing workload across a network of edge devices, gateways, and local servers, ensuring that the system can scale effectively as the number of devices grows.For example, in smart manufacturing, edge computing allows the deployment of thousands of connected sensors across a factory floor, each processing its own data locally.(Wan, 2015).

As production lines expand or new machines are added, Managing and maintaining a distributed network of edge devices and edge servers can be more complex than relying on centralized cloud infrastructure. Since edge computing involves deploying hardware at the edge of the network, managing these devices, ensuring their proper functioning, and keeping them updated can become a logistical challenge, particularly in large-scale deployments across multiple locations.For instance, in industrial settings where edge devices are located on factory floors, maintenance personnel must ensure that devices are functioning properly, software is up-to-date, and security vulnerabilities are addressed. Without proper monitoring tools and maintenance protocols, the risk of device failure or security breaches increases.careful balance between what data should be processed locally at the edge and what should be sent to the cloud for further processing. operate on different communication protocols, and ensuring that these devices can communicate seamlessly with edge computing systems requires standardization and collaboration across manufacturers. Without common protocols and interfaces, the deployment of edge computing in IoT environments can become fragmented and difficult to scale.While edge computing can reduce operational costs by minimizing bandwidth and improving efficiency, the initial cost of deploying and maintaining edge devices and infrastructure can be significant. This is particularly true for industries . However, as edge computing technology evolves and becomes more affordable, the cost of deployment is expected to decrease, making it more accessible for a wider range of industries.

CYBERSECURITY AND IOT: MANAGING RISKS, THREATS, AND VULNERABILITIES

However, as IoT devices become increasingly integral to everyday life, they also present new and complex cybersecurity risks. With the growing number of connected devices, ranging from simple household appliances to sophisticated industrial systems, the attack surface for potential cyber threats has expandedfocusing on managing risks,s.(Vijayakumar et al., 2024) One of the core reasons cybersecurity is so challenging in IoT environments is the sheer complexity of IoT ecosystems. Unlike traditional IT networks, IoT networks consist of numerous interconnected devices that often communicate in real time,, wearables, and even autonomous vehicles, and they can be deployed in various settings such as homes, factories, cities, and hospitals.The heterogeneous nature of IoT devices introduces significant security challenges because not all devices are built with the same level of security in mind. Some IoT devices may be low-cost or resource-constrained, meaning they lack the processing power or memory to implement robust security measures. and the broader IoT ecosystem. Understanding these threats is essential to managing and mitigating risks. a compromised smart thermostat or security camera could provide attackers with access to the home's network and sensitive personal information.For instance, in a smart healthcare system, if the communication between wearable devices and medical databases is not properly encrypted, attackers could intercept patient data or even manipulate it, leading to erroneous diagnoses or compromised patient privacy. execute arbitrary code, or take control of the deviceMany IoT manufacturers do not provide regular security updates for their devices, leaving them exposed to known vulnerabilities for extended periods. The lack of a standard for patching and updating IoT devices exacerbates the problem. Additionally, if an attacker gains access to a vulnerable device's firmware, they can potentially modify it to create persistent backdoors that allow them to maintain control over the device even after it is rebooted or reset.. This makes them susceptible to physical tampering. Attackers can directly access the devices to extract sensitive data, plant malicious software, or replace the device with a compromised one. Physical security threats are particularly concerning in critical infrastructure settings, where attackers can disrupt operations by tampering with IoT sensors, actuators, or controllers.Given the variety of cybersecurity threats that IoT systems face, a proactive and layered approach to risk management is essential for protecting (Vaithianathan, 2010) Device Authentication and Access Control The variety of IoT devices—ranging from consumer devices to industrial systems—makes it difficult to establish a universal approach to security. Different devices have different hardware capabilities, software architectures, and communication protocols, all of which may require tailored security measures. This diversity increases the complexity of securing IoT environments.(Uckelmann et al., 2011) continuous monitoring. This resource constraint makes it challenging to protect these devices from evolving threats while maintaining their functionality. IoT manufacturers vary widely in their security practices. While some invest heavily in robust security features, others may prioritize cost over security, leading to devices with weak or inadequate protection. The lack of industry-wide standards for security practices exacerbates this issue, leaving consumers and organizations vulnerable to attacks.

DATA ANALYTICS AND IOT: TURNING DATA INTO INSIGHTS AND ACTION

IoT devices continuously generate data through sensors and other technologies that measure variables such as temperature, humidity, location, speed, health metrics, and more. This data is often unstructured, large in volume, and highly dynamic, which presents challenges for traditional data processing systems. As a result, the need for sophisticated data analytics tools and techniques is crucial to convert raw data into meaningful insights.(Schierz et al., 2010)Analytics can be applied to IoT data at various stages of the data lifecycle, including real-time analysis, batch processing, predictive modeling, and historical analysis. Each of these analytics approaches plays a unique role in helping businesses and organizations achieve specific objectives, whether that's making real-time decisions, predicting future trends, or analyzing long-term performance. in a smart manufacturing facility, descriptive analytics can analyze data collected from sensors on machinery to determine how often equipment has broken down, the average time between failures, or the frequency of maintenance activities. By aggregating and visualizing this data, organizations can identify patterns that help in understanding operational performance and areas that may require improvement.Common tools for descriptive analytics include dashboards, data visualization techniques, and basic statistical analysis. These tools allow businesses to look back at performance metrics and gain insights into operational efficiency, system reliability, and customer behavior, setting the foundation for more advanced analytics. examining "why" something happened (Sreenivasulu et al., 2022). This type of analytics focuses on identifying the root causes of trends or anomalies within the data. For example, diagnostic analytics in an IoT-enabled supply chain might look at factors contributing to delays, such as breakdowns in machinery, delays in transportation, or stock shortages.By using advanced statistical techniques such as correlation analysis, regression analysis, and root cause analysis, a particular region are lower than expected, diagnostic analytics could identify whether supply chain disruptions, marketing inefficiencies, or product quality issues are contributing to the decline in sales.. This type of analytics is particularly valuable for anticipating challenges, opportunities, and potential risks before they occur. nagement in smart buildings to forecast energy consumption patterns, helping facilitymanagers optimize heating, cooling, and lighting systems and reduce costs.Machine learning models, time series forecasting, and anomaly detection a. In the context of IoT, prescriptive analytics analyzes IoT data alongside external variables to generate actionable recommendations for decision-makers.For instance, in a smart grid system, prescriptive analytics can recommend optimal energy distribution strategies can suggest optimal routes for delivery trucks, considering factors such as traffic, Prescriptive analytics leverages advanced optimization algorithms, simulation models, and artificial intelligence (AI) to evaluate various scenarios and provide recommendations that align with business goals and objectives.

CASE STUDY: IOT IN INDUSTRIAL AUTOMATION - A SUCCESS STORY

Industrial automation has solutions were implemented, the benefits they achieved, and the broader implications for industrial automation. Background and ChallengesThe company in focus is a global leader in the manufacturing of automotive components, with production facilities located across multiple regions. The company was facing several operational challenges that were impacting its overall efficiency. These included frequent equipment breakdowns, suboptimal machine utilization, delays in production schedules, and a lack of real-time data for decision-making. The traditional maintenance approach, which was largely reactive, led to costly downtime and repairs, and the company was struggling to meet the increasing demand for its products.Additionally, the company's existing infrastructure lacked the ability to integrate data across multiple production lines and provide real-time insights into machine performance, energy consumption, and inventory management. Without access to real-time data, it was difficult to predict maintenance needs, optimize production workflows, or identify inefficiencies in the manufacturing process. These challenges created a strong business case for adopting IoT technologies to modernize the company's operations and improve its competitive edge.IoT Implementation and Solution DesignTo address these challenges, the company partnered with an IoT solutions provider to implement a comprehensive industrial automation system based on IoT technologies. The first step in the process was to deploy sensors and smart devices across various machines and production lines. These sensors were designed to collect real-time data on parameters such as temperature, vibration, pressure, humidity, energy usage, and machine speed. The data was then transmitted to a centralized cloud-based platform, where it could be analyzed and processed in real time.The system also included real-time dashboards and visualization tools, which provided operators and managers with easy-to-understand insights into the performance of machines and the overall production process.

The dashboards offered information on production output, equipment efficiency, energy consumption, and other key performance indicators (KPIs). This enabled managers to make more informed decisions and take corrective actions immediately if any issues arose.(Turban et al., 2015). This integration helped optimize inventory management, supply chain logistics, and production planning.The implementation of IoT in the company's industrial automation system led to a wide range of tangible benefits, . Reduced Downtime and Improved Equipment UtilizationOne of the most significant outcomes of the IoT implementation was the reduction in machine downtime. The predictive maintenance system, by over 15%, and production schedules were more predictable, leading to higher overall throughput. By monitoring energy consumption in real time, the company was able to identify energy-intensive processes and implement strategies to reduce waste. For example, the company used the data to optimize machine settings, reduce idle time, and identify areas where energy savings could be achieved. This led to a 12% reduction in energy costs, contributing to both cost savings and sustainability efforts.The real-time dashboards and data visualization tools provided managers with immediate access to critical information on machine performance, production status, and energy consumption. This enabled faster decision-making and more effective management of production lines. Managers were able to make adjustments to production schedules, order supplies, and address issues before they escalated, improving overall operational efficiency. accommodate additional production lines, facilities, and machines. As the company's operations grew, the IoT infrastructure could be easily scaled to handle the increased volume of data and devices. This flexibility positioned the company to continue reaping the benefits of IoT as it expanded into new markets and increased its production capacity. in efficiency, cost savings, and productivity. The combination of real-time data collection, predictive analytics, and machine learning allows companies to make smarter decisions, reduce operational risks, and enhance their competitive advantage.

CONCLUSION

This case study provides a comprehensive overview of how Barcelona has integrated IoT into its infrastructure, the applications that have been deployed, the benefits realized by the city and its residents, and the challenges encountered during implementation.Background and Vision for Smart Cities Barcelona's vision of becoming a smart city began with a commitment to improving the quality of life for its citizens while making its urban infrastructure more sustainable, efficient, and responsive. The city wanted to leverage digital technologies to optimize resource management, reduce environmental impact, and enhance civic engagement. With a rapidly growing population and increased urbanization, the city faced challenges related to traffic congestion, energy consumption, waste management, water supply, and public safety. The integration of IoT was seen as a way to address these issues in a smart, data-driven manner.Barcelona's approach to creating a smart city focused on collecting real-times that would improve the city's overall managementt. For instance, if traffic congestion is detected at a particular intersection, the system can extend the green light for vehicles in the high-density area, preventing bottlenecks and minimizing delays.. (Xu & Gutierrez, 2006)The city's parking management system is integrated with mobile apps, allowing users to find and reserve parking spaces remotely, reducing traffic in densely populated areas.Energy consumption and sustainability are critical challenges for cities worldwide, and Barcelona has adopted IoT-enabled smart lighting to address these issues. The city has deployed iFor instance, streetlights automatically dim when no pedestrians or vehicles are detected in the area, saving energy and reducing the city's carbon footprint. During peak hours, or in busy areas with high foot traffic, the lights brighten to ensure safety and visibility. Additionally, the smart lighting system is connected to a central management platform that enables city officials to monitor energy consumption and perform maintenance more effectively. IoT has also played a, sensors, and monitoring systems throughout public spaces to ensure the safety of its residents and visitors. These systems are designed to detect unusual activity, such as accidents, crowding, or incidents of violence, and send real-time alerts to law enforcement agencies. resources for crime prevention or emergency response.. For example, the city can issue air quality alerts when pollution levels exceed safe thresholds, helping citizens make informed decisions about outdoor activities. Additionally, the data collected by environmental sensors can guide urban planning decisions aimed at improving the quality of life and minimizing environmental impacts.

REFERENCES

Adolphs, C., & Winkelmann, A. (2010). Personalization research: A rigorous literature review on personalization in e-commerce (2000-2008). *Journal of Electronic Commerce Research, 11*(4), 326–341.

Al-Obeidat, F., Spencer, B., & Kafeza, E. (2018). The opinion management framework: Identifying and addressing customer concerns extracted from online product reviews. *Electronic Commerce Research and Applications, 27*, 52–64. DOI: 10.1016/j.elerap.2017.11.003

Allen, D. K., Brown, A., Karanasios, S., & Norman, A. (2013). How should technology-mediated organizational change be explained? A comparison of the contributions of critical realism and activity theory. *Management Information Systems Quarterly, 37*(3), 835–854. DOI: 10.25300/MISQ/2013/37.3.08

Bærentsen, K. B., & Trettvik, J. (2002). An activity theory approach to affordance. In *Proceedings of the 2nd Nordic conference on Human-computer interaction (NordiCHI 2002)* (pp. 51–60). DOI: 10.1145/572020.572028

Baethge, C., Klier, J., & Klier, M. (2016). Social commerce: State-of-the-art and future research directions. *Electronic Markets, 26*(3), 269–290. DOI: 10.1007/s12525-016-0225-2

Barbosa, J. L. V. (2015). Ubiquitous computing: Applications and research opportunities. In *Proceedings of the IEEE International Conference on Computational Intelligence and Computing Research (ICCIC 2015)*. DOI: 10.1109/ICCIC.2015.7435625

Chua, C., Khoo, H., Straub, D., Kadiyala, S., & Kuechler, D. (2005). The evolution of e-commerce research: A stakeholder perspective. *Journal of Electronic Commerce Research, 6*(4), 262–280.

Chunxia, Q., Zhenzhong, Z., & Litao, Z. (2010). A shopping model in ubiquitous media environment. In *Proceedings of the International Forum on Information Technology and Applications (IFITA 2010)* (pp. 319–322). DOI: 10.1109/IFITA.2010.119

Clarke, I. I.III. (2008). Emerging value propositions for m-commerce. *The Journal of Business Strategy, 25*(2), 41–57. DOI: 10.54155/jbs.25.2.41-57

Deloitte. (2016). Switch on to the connected home: The Deloitte Consumer Review. Retrieved December 20, 2018, from https://www2.deloitte.com/content/dam/Deloitte/uk/Documents/consumer-business/deloitte-uk-consumer-review-16.pdf

Evans, M. (2017, January 24). 5 Ways the internet of things will influence commerce. Forbes. Retrieved January 30, 2019, from https://www.forbes.com/sites/michelleevans1/2017/01/24/5-ways-the-internet-of-things-will-influence-commerce

Fox, P., Rezania, D., Wareham, J., & Christiaanse, E. (2006). Will mobiles dream of electric sheep? Expectations of the new generation of mobile users: Misfits with practice and research. In Proceedings of the International Conference on Mobile Business (ICMB 2006). Copenhagen.

Frambach, R. T., Roest, H. C. A., & Krishnan, T. V. (2007). The impact of consumer internet experience on channel preference and usage intentions across the different stages of the buying process. *Journal of Interactive Marketing*, *21*(2), 26–41. DOI: 10.1002/dir.20079

Gaur, A., Scotney, B., Parr, G., & McClean, S. (2015). Smart city architecture and its applications based on iot. *Procedia Computer Science*, *52*, 1089–1094. DOI: 10.1016/j.procs.2015.05.122

Hartson, H. R. (2003). Cognitive, physical, sensory, and functional affordances in interaction design. *Behaviour & Information Technology*, *22*(5), 315–338. DOI: 10.1080/01449290310001592587

Hasan, H., & Kazlauskas, A. (2014). Activity theory: Who is doing what, why and how. In Hasan, H. (Ed.), *Being practical with theory. A window into business research* (pp. 9–14). THEORI.

Junglas, I., & Watson, R. (2003). U-commerce: A conceptual extension of e-commerce and m-commerce. In Proceedings of the International Conference on Information Systems (ICIS 2003) (Article 55).

Kees, A., Oberländer, A. M., Röglinger, M., & Rosemann, M. (2015). Understanding the internet of things: A conceptualisation of business-to-thing (b2t) interactions. In Proceedings of the 23th European Conference on Information Systems (ECIS 2015) (article 92).

Lee, I., & Lee, K. (2015). The internet of things (iot): Applications, investments, and challenges for enterprises. *Business Horizons*, *58*(4), 431–440. DOI: 10.1016/j.bushor.2015.03.008

Lee, S. M., Hwang, T., & Lee, D. H. (2011). Evolution of research areas, themes, and methods in electronic commerce. *Journal of Organizational Computing and Electronic Commerce*, *21*(3), 177–201. DOI: 10.1080/10919392.2011.590095

Ma, Y., Chen, G., & Wei, Q. (2017). Finding users preferences from large-scale online reviews for personalized recommendation. *Electronic Commerce Research, 17*(1), 3–29. DOI: 10.1007/s10660-016-9240-9

Madgule, M., Vinayaka, N., Sonkhaskar, Y. M., Patel, D. R., Karthikeyan, R., & Selvakumar, P. (2023). Mechanical properties and microstructure of activated TIG welded similar joints of Inconel alloys by desirability approaches. *Materials Today: Proceedings, 77*, 528–533.

Nan, G., Yang, J., & Dou, R. (2017). Do only review characteristics affect consumers' online behaviours? A study of relationship between reviews. *Journal of Electronic Commerce Research, 18*(4), 330–345.

Oberländer, A. M., Röglinger, M., Rosemann, M., & Kees, A. (2018). Conceptualizing business-to-thing interactions: A sociomaterial perspective on the internet of things. *European Journal of Information Systems, 27*(4), 486–502. DOI: 10.1080/0960085X.2017.1387714

Porter, M. E., & Heppelmann, J. E. (2014). How smart, connected products are transforming companies. Harvard Business Review. Retrieved December 20, 2018, from https://hbr.org/2014/11/how-smart-connected-products-are-transforming-competition

Pousttchi, K., Tilson, D., Lyytinen, K., & Hufenbach, Y. (2015). Introduction to the special issue on mobile commerce: Mobile commerce research yesterday, today, tomorrow - what remains to be done? *International Journal of Electronic Commerce, 19*(4), 1–20. DOI: 10.1080/10864415.2015.1029351

Schierz, P. G., Schilke, O., & Wirtz, B. W. (2010). Understanding consumer acceptance of mobile payment services: An empirical analysis. *Electronic Commerce Research and Applications, 9*(3), 209–216. DOI: 10.1016/j.elerap.2009.07.005

Sreenivasulu, A., & Manimozhi, T. Satheesh kumar P., and Singh P.,(2022). "The Model of Smart Sensing Device For Sensitive Nanoclusters Modification in Sensing Properties," 2022 2nd International Conference on Advance Computing and Innovative Technologies in Engineering (ICACITE), Greater Noida, India, 2022, pp. 1043-1047, DOI: 10.1109/ICACITE53722.2022.9823846

Turban, E., King, D., Lee, J. K., Liang, T.-P., & Turban, D. C. (2015). *Electronic commerce: A managerial and social networks perspective* (8th ed.). Springer. DOI: 10.1007/978-3-319-10091-3

Uckelmann, D., Harrison, M., & Michahelles, F. (2011). *Architecting the internet of things*. Springer. DOI: 10.1007/978-3-642-19157-2

Vaithianathan, S. (2010). A review of e-commerce literature on India and research agenda for the future. *Electronic Commerce Research*, *10*(1), 83–97. DOI: 10.1007/s10660-010-9046-0

Vijayakumar, G., Rajkumar, M., Rajiv Chandar, N., Selvakumar, P., & Duraisamy, R. (2024). Muniyandi Rajkumar, Rajiv Chandar N, Selvakumar P and Ramesh Duraisamy, (2024). Environmentally friendly TDS removal from waste water by electrochemical ion exchange batch-type recirculation (EIR) technique. *Environmental Science. Water Research & Technology*, *10*(4), 826–835. DOI: 10.1039/D3EW00793F

Wan, Y. (2015). The matthew effect in social commerce. *Electronic Markets*, *25*(4), 313–324. DOI: 10.1007/s12525-015-0186-x

Xiao, B., & Benbasat, I. (2007). E-commerce product recommendation agents: Use, characteristics, and impact. *Management Information Systems Quarterly*, *31*(1), 137–209. DOI: 10.2307/25148784

Xu, G., & Gutierrez, J. A. (2006). An exploratory study of killer applications and critical success factors in m-commerce. *Journal of Electronic Commerce in Organizations*, *4*(3), 63–79. DOI: 10.4018/jeco.2006070104

Chapter 11

Trust in the Future:
Building Brand Confidence for IoT Consumer Adoption

Md Mehedi Hasan Emon
http://orcid.org/0000-0002-6224-9552
American International University-Bangladesh, Bangladesh

Abid Aziz
http://orcid.org/0009-0002-1582-9113
Uttara University, Bangladesh

Kamal Hossain
World University of Bangladesh, Bangladesh

Md. Adnan Rahman
http://orcid.org/0000-0003-3378-0958
Uttara University, Bangladesh

Abu Bakar Abdul Hamid
http://orcid.org/0009-0007-5177-8145
Infrastructure University Kuala Lumpur, Malaysia

ABSTRACT

As the Internet of Things (IoT) increasingly permeates everyday life, consumer trust has emerged as the decisive factor in adoption. This chapter explores the psychological and behavioral economic dimensions that shape consumer attitudes toward IoT, emphasizing how perceived risks and cognitive biases hinder engagement. It examines how brands can build trust through ethical transparency, effective positioning, and data-responsible personalization. Drawing on case studies from leading firms across industries, the chapter highlights strategic storytelling, omnichannel

DOI: 10.4018/979-8-3373-3441-7.ch011

coherence, and value-driven marketing as vital tools for fostering long-term brand confidence. By integrating insights from consumer psychology, digital strategy, and real-world practices, the chapter offers a comprehensive framework for navigating the trust economy that defines the future of IoT adoption.

INTRODUCTION

The development of Internet of Things (IoT) technology offers moving change in the way customers relate themselves to their products, services and to their environment. The Internet has unique opportunities for personalization as they also convert smart home devices along with connected vehicles and intelligent retail solutions and automated wearables (Assimakopoulos et al., 2024; Saxena et al., 2022). Users question the revolutionary nature of these inventions everywhere. Consumers typically voice powerful fears concerning data security, surveillance and exploitative practices (Emon & Mazid-Ul-Haque, 2025; Panahi Rizi et al., 2022). An absence of customer confidence concerning these devices would be the main cause of dislike that institutions must reduce with 'technical evidence' as well as strategic messaging strategies. The chapter explores trust as an important contributor that motivates consumer acceptance of IoT technology. Research applies consumer psychological and behavioral economic tools to research the mental and emotional aspect that causes consumer doubt (Emon & Chowdhury, 2025). The research goes beyond the analysis of technology to examine business approaches of establishing trust, genuineness when the data is at once an asset and a liability.

This chapter offers a detailed and practical manual for scholars and marketers and business executives. The study begins with the assessment of psychological adoption impediments to IoT, such as risk perceptions in combination with cognitive biases and privacy behavioral paradoxes. Brand trust is, therefore, identified as the most important issue in contemporary IoT branding due to the fact of transparency and responsibility, together with an ethical standpoint are the four corners which form the foundation towards building trust among consumers today. These chapters examine strategic brand differentiation through the implementation of digital storytelling and brand ambassador impact on associated technology validation. This chapter examines the functions of AI based digital marketing and omnichannel strategies in both advertisement for IoT products and development of reliable consumer-brand engagement. A vast part of the discussion is oriented towards IoT's ability of offering personalized interactions, whereas there is also a discussion of the moral predicaments from data-centric promotional activities. The chapter ends by demonstrating how large enterprises implement outstanding branding operations for IoT solutions. The provided examples provide necessary knowledge on how to establish trust relationships whilst increasing more market acceptability and ensuring the viability of brand in a connected economic framework. Branded technologies capable of living up to their potential cannot unless they deliver on their basic mandate of building trust as is this chapter. Organizations derive the revolutionary power of IoT when they marry ethical tenets into the corporate image and cater for their market engagement with the customers.

CONSUMER PSYCHOLOGY AND BEHAVIORAL ECONOMICS IN IOT ADOPTION

Ambivalence of customers towards the exceptional IoT technology requires an intensive insight into the psychological aspect of trust to be satisfactorily described. The Internet of technologies introduce convenience and adaptation and automated solutions with them come the massive privacy-related related security concerns and user independence issues. The mechanism through which the products of IoT differentiate themselves with the regular consumer products is that they gather and process the data used by users and even provide personal information that turns the product consumption process into a data-oriented active process. The heightened complexity in the brand-consumer relations transforms trust into a vital success factor in the market by changing the psychological contractual interactions.

The Privacy Paradox and Bounded Rationality

The behavior of consumers who express privacy worries yet keep using linked devices stands as the most discussed mystery in IoT literature. The "privacy paradox" demonstrates how customers express privacy concerns in one way through words but demonstrate different actions in real life (Chhabra et al., 2023; Gotsch & Schögel, 2023). People who feel concerned about smart speakers listening to fitness trackers collecting health data never take serious precautions to protect themselves mainly because they either have no better options or are unclear about potential risks (Md Al Amin et al., 2024). The paradoxes of the IoT get clarity through behavioral economics analytical instruments. According to Yamini, (2020), bounded rationality demonstrates that people do not make fully rational choices since their awareness and mental capacity and timespan create performance limitations. The lack of customer knowledge about data practices in IoT occurs together with their difficulty in understanding complex privacy documents because they lack time or analytical skills. The demand for simple mental shortcuts known as heuristics leads customers to choose immediate ease over doing thorough cost-versus-benefit evaluations along with understanding unknown risks. When people judge the probability of events through examples that easily come to mind, they might develop inaccurate risk assessments. Individuals who lack direct exposure to data breaches and friends who have not disclosed these incidents tend to underestimate the likelihood of such incidents. People perceive risks from adopting IoT technologies to be lower for themselves than for others because of the optimism bias (Chen et al., 2022).

Loss Aversion and the Fear of Losing Control

People resist adopting IoT because of loss aversion which Malhotra et al. (2021) developed from their prospect theory (Koh & Chin, 2022). According to the hypothesis human beings feel substantially stronger discomfort from losses than satisfaction from equivalent gains. In IoT environments individuals experience more fear from privacy loss and data confidentiality risks than they expect to achieve through efficiency gains and customized services (Zhang et al., 2020). The emotional connection between consumers and data protection risks outweighs their irrationality because they do not fully trust the entities requesting sensitive information. The implementation of IoT technology systems often challenges what people believe about their ownership rights and their ability to make decisions independently. The automatic temperature controls based on consumer pattern data are viewed by some users as devices that both intrude on personal space and act paternalistically. The underlying concern goes beyond data retrieval because people fear their autonomy is gradually shutting down when it comes to controlling their environment and actions. Because people who experience psychological discomfort marketers must implement methods to explain how IoT technology functions and demonstrate that users maintain their control over information. To overcome consumers' reluctance against loss. Binary messages should connect the above technical information with human emotional responses. People feel more autonomous when providers explain specific data protection features such as the ability to cancel data sharing or erase obtained information. Brands which combine effective communication of empathy alongside reliability and accountability can better overcome this major barrier.

Status Quo Bias and Ambiguity Aversion

People often prefer things they are already familiar with which scientists classify as status quo bias (Oschinsky et al., 2021). The IoT requires special attention to this behavioral pattern since behavioral modifications through new technology learning and infrastructure transformation are often necessary for IoT adoption. Establishing and maintaining smart devices demands considerable work which acts as a significant obstacle especially when the benefits are not obvious to users. Before implementing changes people compare their learning effort to the system advantages to maintain their current operational methods. Ambiguity aversion based on the behavior of individuals towards unknown or insufficiently understood outcomes hinders the adoption of Internet of Things technology (Emon, 2025; FakhrHosseini et al., 2024). People without expert knowledge find it hard to understand the many unknown algorithms and backend processes and third-party data dealings found in most IoT technology systems. People who fail to predict how their data will be used or what consequences might arise will tend to reject the technology altogether. The reduction of these biases requires brands to create simpler operations while providing complete system transparency to their customers. Transparent delivery of data collection and use understanding along with intuitive user interfaces and step-by-step user access training should become part of this approach.

Trust as a Psychological Construct

The concept of trust on the Internet of Things operates at a sophisticated level. Users form three types of trust regarding technology performance and brand ethics and bond between brand and user: competence trust, integrity trust and affective trust (Yang & Wibowo, 2022). Time sculpts these components since they grow based on public opinion towards the product and the brand over the company's consumers' input. New users who embrace technology tend to base their primary initial confidence on their knowledge of brand reputation in combination with all the perceptions from social influence. The study by Hooda et al., (2022) proves that trust acts as a mediator bridging the gap between perceived utility and adoption intentions experienced by people in technological environments. The first user-to-device contacts either in Advertisements or Testimonials or social recommendations become of utmost value in influencing long-term perception assessments. The first interactions between users and devices either through advertisements or testimonials or social recommendations become vital for shaping long-term perception evaluations (Emon & Khan, 2025). Irrelevant companies that write negative media about data exploitation make the entire IoT market ostracizes consumer trust (Tan & Saraniemi, 2023). A trustworthy brand requires brands to deliver reliable performance standards alongside reflecting moral principles in their marketing approach. The establishment of institution-based trust depends on proactive customer-related trust-building through privacy-centric principles, ethical data management and transparent communication.

The Role of Social Proof and Peer Influence

Social verification maintains its influence as one of the major factors determining adoption decisions. Individuals frequently make decisions about ambiguous actions by observing others' behaviors in social proof theory (Erjavec & Manfreda, 2022; Naeem, 2021). Endorsements of IoT technologies by peer groups or influencers help users recognize linked technologies as safe and reduce adoption risks. When people see trusted individuals and experts use smart home products their connections to safety and operational performance immediately improves. The solutions from behavioral science show that customers often lack specific confidence rather than having fundamental disagreements. Positive reports from trustworthy people tend to erase doubts from others regarding new technologies.

BUILDING BRAND TRUST IN IOT PRODUCTS AND SERVICES

Trust now encompasses the leading factor which determines competitive success in digital brand management specifically within IoT environments. The reliability of brands proves essential in determining how customers accept and continue using IoT products which have connected them to their homes and bodies as well as vehicle technology (Korneeva et al., 2021). The continuous data exchange and behavioral monitoring aspects of IoT technologies adjust the customer choice elements since they stagnate from conventional product pricing and quality-based selection methods. On the Internet of Things period a brand must demonstrate performance guarantees alongside ethical management and personal data protection and extended responsibility.

Transparency as a Strategic Imperative

The ability of the IoT industry to remain fully transparent is the key to building trust in the industry. According to Wang et al., (2022), the way data gathers and processes and disseminates information will dictate the level of consumer trust in digital services.. The privacy information traditional product disclosures present in fine print must be avoided by IoT brands. Users need essential information through transparent communication which involves delivering data through easy interfaces at appropriate times in an understandable manner. The essential aspect of developing trust-rich user experiences is proactive disclosure methods also known as "privacy by design" concepts (Bu et al., 2020). Every smart home device during its setup process must display a direct interactive data policy which explains what data it collects with its use purposes and permission authorization details. The privacy procedure needs continuous implementation instead of happening once. Brands show true ethical transparency when they keep customers well informed about data practice changes and give easy access to privacy settings even though they meet regulatory standards. Aldossari & Sidorova, (2020) demonstrated in their study that

IoT technology permeation increases significantly when consumers feel capable of making data choices and are actively involved in these choices according to their findings. Brands ought to know clear guidelines about where transparency is a strategic value since it has an influence on customer flow of trust.

Operationalizing Accountability and Autonomy

Transparency helps in creation of trust, but accountability supports its existence. The operating conditions made by the interconnected IoT systems result in creating an imbalance of power between businesses and their customers. This difference in data leads to disempowerment of users since they are not aware of how they can regulate or restrict the exposure of their personal data. The solution to this problem is that the IoT brands should develop accountability mechanisms that enhance user control functions. The use of real-time data utilization dashboards is also an efficient solution to users that require monitoring data collection and processing and external sharing operations. The user-centric design of the-dashboards is useful in converting the suspicion of surveillance into a reality that the user can attain. It gives the user more confidence to be able to control systems without sacrificing the functionality of the systems when Apple and other companies of the same nature provide control mechanisms. The key to success in operation is authorization configurations with details. The marketers are expected to do away with generalized and broadest permission groups and offer their clients distinct choices to approve individual services and related data flows. Decisions are given priority and a perpetual process of consent that disapproves of a momentary agreement. According to Buck & Reith, (2020) found that consumer-managed data environment yields outcomes in terms of improved brand trust which in turn yields in-depth analysis of services. As an operating principle, data minimization proves beneficial as a means-to showcase brand integrity since it entails gathering of information required in the operation. The custom of not overpopulating the data collection represents brand respect of the markers between users and data institutions. The decisions made by companies should result in accumulating brand equity and achieving consumer loyalty even though they need to allocate funds in the beginning (Nobar et al., 2020).

Ethical Branding and Corporate Social Responsibility

The IoT sector allows brands to build trust through two interconnected components: dedicated work with individual products as well as an overall organizational ethical framework. The marketplace now demands responsible self-regulation from companies that exceed technological progress because consumers want brands to set ethical standards for sensitive matters linked to data monitoring and algorithmic bias and digital environmental impacts. Every corporate entity needs to emphasize Corporate Social Responsibility (CSR) to build trust among its stakeholders. Companies which engage the public with discussions about data ethics and AI ethics and environmental sustainability become ethical leaders in addition to product providers within the social fabric. This trend is essential because the increasing popularity of value-based purchasing trends among consumers is focused on younger market segments (Essiz & Senyuz, 2024). Google Nest together with other companies now address these matters through AI principles and third-party audits and open-source projects that support community surveillance. Smaller firms in IoT space demonstrate sustainability through their production choices while also promising data independence to their customers. The decisions show willingness toward following established social criteria which results in better brand reputation and stronger emotional bonds with consumers. The organizational responsibility must exist genuinely instead of being limited to superficial displays. People today are more skilled at detecting bogus ethical practices which mask harmful business behavior. According to Halkos & Nomikos, (2021) the validity of CSR gets evaluated through both the transmitted message and consistent action adherence across multiple customer interfaces. A brand needs its marketing story to match its internal operational activities for validity.

The Role of Reputation and Third-Party Endorsements

Brands in the IoT space need reputation as a key foundation for credibility because customers face limited product awareness combined with tough assessment obstacles. Since consumers find backend operations difficult to comprehend their decisions about trust depend heavily on independent validations through certifications and expert verifications (Lee et al., 2021). Brand legitimacy regarding trust assertions receives support from data protection organizations and privacy-focused non-governmental organizations and security firms. The European Data Protection Seal together with the IoT Security Foundation Compliance Framework act as trust intermediary systems which bridge business statements to customer doubt. Public dialogue about the brand as well as consumer feedback directly affects how credible the brand is perceived to be. When privacy management fails or when data breaches occur, they lead to severe damage of consumer trust both in an individual product along with the entire brand portfolio. The management of reputation requires predictive awareness together with continuous risk appraisal and prepared crisis communication plans as well as a strong focus on customer feedback.

Co-Creation and Participatory Design

Trust building through co-creation requires consumers to participate actively in the development of IoT products starting from design to enhancement. The participative method changes brand relationships from one-way transactions into collaborative partnerships. Product quality and relational trust develop through consumer participation in product beta tests and interface creation and feature selection processes (Guo et al., 2021). Co-creation helps build contextual trust by establishing trust between people through shared experiences rather than broad assumptions. Users perceive even a brand as caring and polite if they feel that their notion of what needs improving prompts immediate changes to products.

BRANDING AND POSITIONING STRATEGIES FOR IOT BUSINESSES

The IoT technological development has brought about a total revolution in the way value has been communicated by brands. Modern branding methods do not meet the requirements of current markets because they are developed in the era of network connectivity and data intimacy and have shifted customers' expectations. The marketplace of the IoT branding is characterized by dual difficulty since it is an area of disruptive innovation opportunities, but at the same time, it has established monitoring complexities, and this poses the dilemma of diminished control. Exceptional customers should be provided by the IoT industry with branding and positioning approaches beyond typical technology greatness to compete with profound emotional and thinking as well as ethical dilemmas (Vassallo et al., 2023). The mark is not merely a title, but it provides narration opportunities that govern relationships and provide a model to beliefs to gain trust.

Emotional Differentiation and Cognitive Salience

Brand isolation in the IoT business thrives due to the fact-that they outperform technology specifications only. The customers do not normally have the technical expertise required to recognize the difference between the architecture of devices as well as protocol and interoperability standards. The ability of the brands to engage with customers emotionally and intellectually is the key to defining the brand choice (Mostafa & Kasamani, 2020). The firm should transform their technological capabilities into experience value through developing proper positioning strategies. The brand messages should also include functional explanation as well as demonstration of product utility to the daily routines of the consumer. The Ecobee smart device company develops advertising messages based on the promise of comfort and savings of money with the environment together with the stewardship of the environment as these are the core values that help to establish the emotional bonds among the consumers. In terms of positioning, the brand can be used to entrench itself in the personal ambitions as well as individual identities that the consumers have. The products can be positioned based on emotional and achievement-oriented values of the target markets, which build long-term brand differentiation of IoT brands (Rajaram, 2022).

The Power of Digital Storytelling

Digital storytelling would be the best branding instrument in the IoT market. Storytelling in digital form is better than a normal list of features, and it creates emotional narratives that resonate with settings and emphasize social significance. The tools help users to determine their involvement in the increasing technological trend. Determine the success that Fitbit has had in the sale of the wearable technology devices. The company prefers to show real life examples of how its devices assist individuals in losing weight as they manage their illnesses as well as form friendships with their products which are health oriented (Chakra Bortty et al., 2025). These creative tales ensure that technology is relatable to the audience to ensure that a viewer can both experience its functionality and have an emotional connection. Kang et al., (2020) explain that when individuals become so engaged with a narrative, they are transported to the narrative which enhances their feelings to the brands and their future behaviors. The approach of storytelling is simple to use because it establishes the connection between the complex IoT technology and practical use by the consumers. The educational medium avoids condescending attitudes when teaching the public. Nest uses thermometers to adapt to household energy use patterns in stories that boost brand identity while simplifying the understanding of embedded AI technology as a cost-reducing system. Digital platforms promote the spread of narratives between users through enhanced distribution of content originating from users. The sharing of authentic experiences by IoT device users through reviews and testimonials and social media allows the creation of an ecological brand perception system that depends on authenticity more than advertising.

Influencer Alignment and Authenticity

IoT branding requires influencer marketing because various markets exhibit different levels of technological understanding. Regular users receive support from influencers who act as communication channels to explain complicated technological concepts. This approach is affected mainly by how genuine the information seems to recipients. Specialized micro-influencers consistently produce better return on investment than celebrity influencers do in the Internet of Things marketplace. Their apparent proficiency and proximity to the audience develop trust. The evaluation of a smart kitchen device provided by a home chef influencer tends to be more influential than generalized reviews from lifestyle stars. Influencers achieve maximum impact when demonstrating authentic product usage along with seamless integration and extended satisfaction because these factors strongly appeal to critical buyers who prioritize personal privacy (Kim et al., 2025). Proper ethical conduct has evolved into an imperative necessity for all operators in the market. The promotional brands become more ethical when influencers demonstrate serious consideration about data protection and environment-friendly practices and social impact. Brands that work with entities focused on social principles will gain better trust with customers because the public becomes more aware of IoT's negative aspects including surveillance capitalism and algorithmic discrimination (Shams et al., 2025).

Anticipating Consumer Expectations and Ethical Positioning

A successful IoT brand strategy requires demonstration of technological superiority together with predicting consumer demands that will emerge in the future. Brand-linking to social values and lifestyle objectives and ethical stances has become more essential as the market develops. Customers require evidence that device-makers pursue goals which support social well-being because their devices compile large amounts of individual data while becoming inside personal residence and physical structure frameworks. Fairphone stands as a compelling example of IoT even though it is not singularly focused on IoT because it places ethical sourcing and device sustainability at the core of its corporate philosophy. IoT companies who incorporate ethical AI policies and promote sustainable materials and enhance data protection laws create themselves as innovative value-based organizations rather than just product producers. Research by Farhad, (2024) reveals that a global number of 69% of customers would trust brands because they defend data privacy rights regardless of how it impacts business performance. Dedication to digital ethics as the main brand focus will generate business advantage when the market increases value ethics. The brand needs to monitor post-purchase positioning, which describes how it behaves and communicates after finalizing sales. The way companies update their services and utilize data and handle their customers post-sale goes beyond functional requirements to form lasting brand impressions that customers remember. The continuous evolution of an IoT product along with its capability to accept feedback and maintain transparent communication helps build both value and trustworthiness for an extended period.

Platform Synergy and Ecosystem Positioning

Brand value development in IoT environments occurs most frequently through platform combination and system interoperability. A smart device operates independently yet depends completely on its connections with other hardware and platform operations and support services. A brand must demonstrate its capability to work in ecosystems for successful customer positioning. The Alexa ecosystem from Amazon exercises substantial power that pushes IoT products from different companies to implement "Alexa compatibility" for enhanced brand recognition. Open standards stand as an obstacle for brands in their efforts to scale their operations because they operate through isolated systems. Product quality becomes irrelevant because these brands face difficulties. Companies that establish partnerships through co-branding and display flawless integration with established platforms create valuable improvements to their perceived usefulness and customer attraction (Paydas Turan, 2021). Organizations that take part in open-source ecological programs or lead standards-setting undertakings like the Matter protocol initiated by Apple, Google, Amazon and others establish themselves as dependable entities able to withstand imminent changes. The activities function as collaborative practices instead of exploitative approaches while establishing lasting confidence from consumers.

Cultural Sensitivity and Localization

A position tactic must maintain relevance according to specific situations. A well-told brand narrative together with ethical standpoint that succeed in one culture may produce opposite results in another cultural setting. Markets in the West respond favorably to privacy-driven stories but emerging markets focus on practical benefits and affordable pricing. Companies need to have different branding according to their cultural practices, and the economic situation and digital awareness, which they need to have during the investment with different markets. The companies that adopt the concept of glocalization that combines such global brand ideas with the local value effectively acquire larger and more varied user bases. Xiaomi has made South Asia an important region since the Milanese company discovered the low-cost electronics mixed with advertisements that are sensitive to local culture needs.

The IoT industry requires branding as well as positioning strategies that can affect the way the consumers view the products and how they adopt them and remain loyal. The defying variable of this group of interchangeable products is its brand to achieve emotional meaning as well as ethical values and trust in people. Companies that plan to become successful in IoT need to create marketing roles that bring emotional and ethical and narrative value to the client. The importance of focusing on the cognitive and emotional domains should not be pushed aside as the companies present technological excellence but should also provide visions on how digital life should be made better. Such endeavors build enduring relationships, convert users to armies of heroes and make new ventures into established confidence.

EFFECTIVE DIGITAL MARKETING AND OMNICHANNEL STRATEGIES

The current marketing tactics will need to be realigned to the rising consumer demand along with similar attributes of the emerging technologies in the dynamic digital world. The use of traditional linear marketing funnels is ineffective in the digital world as the non-linear interactions that are multi-platform and are usually automated based. The success of digital marketing and omnichannel strategies in the IoT domains demand individualized approach to be undertaken through predictive analysis of the real-time data gathered in an ethical manner to deliver the platform-based value-added messages uniformly.

The Imperative of Integration in the IoT Age

The uses of digital marketing in the IoT world go beyond simple communication of messages to uninfluenced masses. The system strives to generate immediate content that is relevant and cut across several endpoint technologies. Individuals are currently consuming brands via smart appliances, wearable technology and mobile applications and web portals in addition to voice assistant systems and augmented reality interfaces. The interactions are dynamic as the streams of data interact with each other and cause the users to implement their behaviors (Acquisti et al., 2020). Marketing should be intrinsically integrated since it demands the connection between brand communications and data analytics and user experience provisions into an omnichannel strategic perspective. Omnichannel strategy will facilitate a smooth brand interaction since it must create a consistent data integration between and among channels and touchpoints (Neslin, 2022). The devices of home automation should employ the same messaging that is both social media-style and retail location we and mobile application content to ensure brand continuity.

AI-Driven Personalization and Contextual Marketing

The present IoT marketing basis is present due to the ability to personalize through AI technological capabilities. Machine learning capability gives marketers access to real-time information that helps to create elaborate personalized customer experiences to a large number-of people simultaneously. IoT devices send context-based signals with the information about the position of the users as well as their pattern behavior and environmental information and bodily reactions that allow predicting preferences of the individuals to develop highly personalized content (Emon et al., 2025). The monitoring system picks up an increased stress level among the patients automatically transmitting notification material such as meditation instructions or advert offers of supplements. The pace of timely interventions depicts the fundamental aspects of relevance and responsiveness on which trust is built between the consumers and the IoT networks (Khan & Hasan Emon, 2024).

Social Media as a Platform for Community and Trust

Brand equity has the basis of interaction with people despite the complex IoT technologies. The rightful use of each of the social media platforms facilitates both promotion and ethical debates and societal building. Organizations should use these platforms to present consumer stories instead of only focusing on product launches while collecting visitors' suggestions about ethical matters regarding data and sustainability or inclusivity. User engagement increases while transparency builds when content such as engineer Q&As and products shown live and behind-the-scenes footages are provided. Testimonials in user-generated content led to increased legitimacy and confidence specifically within sectors that the American Medical Association (AMA) defines as high involvement such as health technology and home security (Chakraborty et al., 2025; Crigger et al., 2022). Social media proved to be a valuable opportunity for brands to show their readiness to respond on various occasions. The brand becomes more responsive when its representatives provide quick replies to consumer questions and concerns. According to Macheka et al., (2024) research 76% of customers demonstrate greater inclination for purchasing from companies that activate meaningful social media connections because interacting creates stronger relationships than mere one-way content sharing.

Ensuring Cross-Channel Consistency and Cohesion

The achievement of omnichannel success relies on creating standardized user experience. Customers should move between different devices and platforms seamlessly without facing any differences in marketing elements or service delivery or functional capabilities. The customer interface must unify experience through continuous presentation of similar brand elements and personalization and functional standards no matter how the customer engages (Hoyer et al., 2020). Centralized customer data platforms (CDPs) which merge data from numerous touchpoints should be the main investment for IoT brands to achieve this goal. Marketers gain full customer insight and deploy standard promotion messages and support systems by using these integrated systems which function equally well regardless of customer entry points. Social media product inquiries by consumers enable apps to deliver customized recommendations alongside appropriate communications that do not force users to restart their preference specifications. Standardization of user experience design elements along with user interface design elements needs to occur consistently across all platforms. Interfaces which differ from each other through opposing branding features and functionalities reduce system confidence while making them less beneficial to users. Design standardization enables users to work with complex connected systems because it strengthens brand recognition and minimizes system complexity.

Ethical Marketing and Responsible Data Governance

Digital marketing faces growing ethical challenges because both personalization power and predictive technology's prediction capabilities rise in strength. Customers are developing heightened awareness about the data collection methods alongside analysis processes and usage in IoT devices because surveillance concerns increase in this area. Insufficient recognition of such issues by marketing strategies will drive customers away and might face legal consequences (Dwivedi et al., 2022). For IoT device multichannel marketing to succeed it needs a base of granted permission alongside complete transparency. The methods that obtain user consent need to provide clear information which must not stand in the way of users' experience. A brand that will show its status as a data steward to consumers will be the one where customers can choose how their data is used and allow them to monitor their data with the ability to explicitly control their data usage. The marketing message must be able to position itself based on the ethical perspective. The company has already established itself as an ethical company beyond being a vendor of the product, with initiatives on data protection and sustainability practices and digital equity and accessibility. The brand marketing of ethical diversity, manifested in various consumer and energy savings and ensuring environmental sustainability makes companies successful in the market since this approach attracts ethically conscious clients to the brand and provides long-term brand value creation (Moghrabi et al., 2023).

Seamless Integration with Physical Retail and Support Channels

Physical environment is one of the critical parameters in marketing IoT since it influences consumer products that are based on touch like smart appliances and wearable devices. The physical touch experience is usually relied upon by the consumers because it is what dictates what they purchase. The integration between physical and digital environment should be a phygital one, which would address the needed requirements. The use of mobile tools to make contactless actions enhances product displays and customers receive deals based on their location with the help of retail facilities with IoT kiosks and augmented reality stations. Post-sale support should be provided to customers, and this includes the AI chatbots alongside live diagnostic services and remote update functionalities that will allow keeping the brand cohesive and keep customers satisfied at all stages of using their products.

Measuring Effectiveness and Closing the Feedback Loop

When working with omnichannel systems, business performance metrics should advance beyond the mere conversion of data. Cross-channel attribution systems are warranted by a proper conception of the influence of the number of customer touchpoints on purchasing choices. The metrics that will be included include CLV, depth of interaction, and sentiment analysis that can be considered a complete picture. Internet of Things devices provide market response through operational feedback in terms of usage patterns and malfunctions and user behavior of devices. The data that is returned can be optimally adjusted on a constant basis with-regard to marketing content and timing and the channel to be used in marketing systems. The responsiveness of companies to customer needs will change as they offer their market with such tools as marketing dashboards, AI suggestions and natural language processing of social media engagement.

IoT companies digital marketing will be successful in-the event that they establish single and individualist ethical solutions that will accommodate all consumer touchpoints. Electronic devices are still in the process of a profound infusion with daily-life routine of individuals however it necessitates the shift of marketing practices towards less transactional sales and more contextual value-delivery systems. Compared to the linking of different platforms, an effective omnichannel strategy goes a step further and integrates personal relationships between individuals and their core values and where they meet. The strategy encourages customers to feel connected and appreciated and not people that are just targeted. Personalization driven by AI, predictive analytics and ethical engagement strategies facilitate IoT companies develop profitable but meaningful relationships to transform simple messaging to important interactions.

PERSONALIZED CUSTOMER EXPERIENCES ENABLED BY IOT

Internet of Things vendors receive a myriad of opportunities to create personalized customer engagements that improve user pleasure that strengthens brand-interactions. Enterprise IoT empowers organizations to collect huge real time data from connected devices which they can employ to deliver personalized experiences depending on individual consumers activities, preferences and environment. Such exciting ideas of personalized IoT experiences require the brands to carry their activities out by balancing the privacy conflicts against relevance but giving priority to the personal consent. Upcoming IoT-supported personalization will be successful when industries appropriately use data ethically to create consumer value by leaving users with self-determinacies.

The Promise and Potential of IoT for Personalization

Companies enjoy unmatched access to large and serial customer information streams available from IoT devices from the market. Scannable household devices and wearable technology together with fitness monitors and vehicle connectivity systems collect habitual user-oriented data of preferences and actions and physical manifestations and routine procedures. The unique advantage of this data enables fast prediction and delivers highly specific products to customers. A fitness smartwatch uses its tracking features to measure heart rate together with activity and sleep patterns for providing relevant feedback such as customized fitness programs and water consumption alerts. Smart IoT thermostats understand household schedules to adjust settings in ways that increase comfort while conserving energy. These devices consolidate fundamental capabilities into a single user experience, but at the same time create the greatest difficulty to the IoT brands, which would provide customized solutions to their customer without at the same time encroaching on the user privacy criteria.

The Double-Edged Sword of Personalization

Personalization in IoT has a number-of advantages to users but also poses risks to the users. Today clients are gaining awareness of how enormous amounts of data facilitate individual offers, thus, they have cultivated concerns over monitoring and data abuse that is one of the biggest challenges to trust. Deloitte developed their 2023 research and determined that over 60 percent of the respondents were cautious about IoT firms utilizing their data following the prevalence of personal data (Abedin & Hajek, 2023). Marketers are also faced with a trade-off of providing personalized comfortable services to consumers since they remain concerned with the way their personal information is processed. Merging agreement-based and accurate offerings is the main idea of successful IoT personalization. Consumer sale terms should include clear data consent that the brands should include alongside clear means of control that allow the users manage their preferences and access data records (Sivakumar et al., 2024). A personalized strategy should be implemented as a mutual collaboration between brands and the customer who will retain control of their data records but will see a real value in giving it away. The customers are expected to get the tools to appropriately control their access to the data and personal options and attain clear knowledge regarding the use of the data.

Real-Time Personalization and Contextual Relevance

Real-time user customization becomes possible through IoT because it processes the latest information in dynamic conditions. IoT-enabled personalization differs from traditional customer profiling through data collection because it makes quick changes to match user behavior variations. The ability to adapt delivers brands the power to supply highly relevant recommendations or interventions that match the exact moment when they are needed. A smart health monitor tracks user vital indications that include blood pressure and heart rate. The device will automatically furnish the tailored relaxation exercise instructions or the contact clinical healthcare staff whenever the device identifies significant changes in measurements (Joy Chakra Bortty et al., 2024). By gathering information on the activity of the user, the smart appliance allows customers to view energy-saving preference suggestions regarding how they used them in the past thereby extending its credibility as being a green brand (Waris & Hameed, 2020). The primary advantage of IoT customization is the ability to develop predictive maintenance warning. The intelligent washing machines identify key component malfunctions before incidents of the same hence sending alerts to users along with suggested solutions or designated service reservations. These proactive solutions help companies to better satisfy their consumers as they reduce disruption, and build long-lasting brand relationships (Rego et al., 2022). The IoT device also evolves with the users in real time via recommendations. The device is driven by user wants and situations which interactively change its behavior as it adapts to changing conditions rather than relying on user inputs to get its responses.

The Role of Data Analytics in Dynamic Segmentation

Data analysis is the key process that will enable personalization with the improvement of IoT. The dynamic segmentation of consumers into groups based on their current activities and the interests and environment factors is possible because of the time-sensitive nature of the data captured by the IoT devices, which are grouped based on these factors rather than the traditional static categories. This approach allows the marketers to deliver information that resonates with the individual consumers in a specific manner. The smart home system employs the habit analysis program that creates automatic preferences that anticipate the needs of the user in advance.

Fitness applications differentiate their users by exercise patterns to deliver specific workout plans and applicable health guidance adapted to individual progress goals (Wackerhage & Schoenfeld, 2021). Programs using analytic data techniques help businesses determine micro-interaction periods which represent brief windows where users prefer receiving personalized material. The smart wearable system determines the completion point of exercise sessions to deliver recovery methods and discount offers toward relevant products including protein shakes. Quick adaptive recommendations make the products of the brand more relevant thus enhancing the entire experience of the user.

Ethical Considerations and Consumer Trust

Along with significant ethical issues, which are bound to emerge with the implementation of the IoT, the opportunities that this customization imposes come with significant issues. The primary challenge that brands have to meet is to sustain consumers trust and offer them worthy services. Consumer rights to data control accompany the need of transparency in business in the process of collecting storing and use of their data. Clear privacy regulations should also be given to users and consent forms are also suggested that will allow them to amend or remove their data (Andreotta et al., 2022). The security of data in IoT enterprises is an issue that needs to be implemented. As a result of such intensive information sharing between devices, a brand needs to make sure that the information about the user remains intact when the device sends personal and sensitive data due to the nature of the information sharing. Consumer confidence underlies the basis of business encrypted data with a heavy-handed data encryption approach along with secure authentication systems and a complete adherence to information protection regulations such as GDPR. The value system of data sharing should be developed in businesses to regulate the way in which consumer information is managed. Customers are supposed to consider themselves creating value with brands rather than being considered an asset whose information is used without their permission. By providing information on data-driven product improvement related to their contributions and compensation opportunities in the form of discounts or awards, customers will increase the mutual value of information-sharing relationship (Akkaş & Sahoo, 2020).

The Future of Personalized IoT Experiences

IoT technology will be improved in new ways, which will facilitate developing more specialized encounters with clients. The use of advanced artificial intelligence (AI) machine learning and natural language processing features built into IoT devices win more opportunities with regard-to customization. Smart assistants, which are voice-activated, can facilitate human conversations, during which they can make suggestions that appear more and-more natural to the needs of the chosen person. The further development of personalized technology may be more thorough integration of VR and AR so that the devices of IoT could be adapted to the environmental conditions and create new digital surroundings around people. The entertainment options of a smart house system will be triggered by emotional data of sensor reading or behavioral sequence information used to control the light of the house and the indoor climate. The ethical rules of these technologies should also be altered when the development of the technologies takes place. Businesses operating on the IoT ought to carefully understand the fact that its personalization policies must focus on three essential areas. absolute openness, full security and freedom of control by the user. Businesses successful in the market will introduce IoT and custom services to build close relationships with clients in the spirit of mutual trust and extra services.

CROSS-INDUSTRY INSIGHTS: LESSONS FROM SUCCESSFUL IOT ADOPTION CAMPAIGNS

Good organizations in the IoT space also exist and use the technology to create standardizing frameworks of which others can replicate. The viability of IoT functions outside the technical provision as it depends on strategic story in conjunction of ethical information management as well as cooperative ecology in different sectors. The case of the success of companies like Nest, Fitbit and Tesla enables us to investigate typical IoT approaches; whereby-trust in conjunction to transparency and constant innovation establishes long-lasting consumer connections over our connected era.

Nest: Transparency and User-Centric Design

Before Google acquired Nest Labs in 2014, the IoT design thinking concept is evident in the way the company was designed. The Nest Labs smart thermostat was a paradigm shifter when it came to home automation since the product provided not only an advanced, but also simple interface that could be easily accommodated in modern interior design. Nest managed to succeed because it delivered design excellence combined with meticulous user-centered standards and absolute data transparency (Hauser et al., 2023). Nest succeeded by winning market confidence through complete transparency of data collection practices as well as usage purposes during their first profitable period. Through extensive efforts in consumer education the company provided easy-to-understand access to their privacy policies. Nest implemented choices featuring user-control over their information alongside data-sharing consent processes known as "informed consent architecture" (Mettler, 2024). Customer trust became vital for successful IoT branding because of the ethical design approach which emphasized empowerment rather than monitoring the users.

Fitbit: Community, Wellness, and Social Proof

Similar-to Nest's activity in home automation, Fitbit established itself as an IoT company for personal health tracking with wearable technology. The company's adoption initiative experienced significant influence from its ability to build social relationships that served as marketing proof (Alaba, 2024). Through its platform users could track their fitness metrics while interacting with friends through social activities and competition to earn status updates that they shared on Facebook. This was a really- strategic approach. Fitbit was able to transcend the business of the devices by introducing wellness content and game features and thereby became an active lifestyle brand. By partnering with influencers and health practitioners and public personalities Fitbit was able to create its image and its aspirational position in the marketplace. The firm has always maintained an attitude with regard to the ownership of data and privacy of the users by playing a dual role as a safeguard of the data rather than the owner (Alaba, 2024).

Tesla: Open Innovation and Ethical Branding

Thirdly Tesla applies the IoT technology in electric cars as an adoption channel due to its efforts in the adoption of radical representational approaches and moral management standards. The vehicles of Tesla act as portable data centers of the IoT that broadcast telemetry data to enhance driving efficiency and enhance security and introduce computer-based amendments to the system. The technical skills possessed by Tesla enabled the company to develop a long message that conveyed environmental protection and technological innovation and software autonomy. By releasing its open-source patent initiative in 2014, Tesla had also signaled its desire to work towards sustainable transport development by foregoing the traditional competitive business strengths. This move was described by critics as a somewhat of a publicity gesture but as a symbolic gesture it saw Tesla become a visionary company that wanted to spearhead universal progress before it would fall into proprietary hands. Tesla strengthened its customers' trust because it shared its patents, and this showed its credibility in the IoT as it demonstrated a moral urge to create solutions that would help society.

Key Cross-Industry Patterns

Based on these cases, different strategic patterns are formed, which are rather universal for all industries:

1. **Trust through Transparency**: Each brand gave very clear reasons for how much data their services used. The doubt of consumers and regulatory control levels force brands to have open communication about their data because transparency serves to be an essential business need.
2. **Narrative as Strategy**: Every brand created compelling stories that focused on the advantages to humans rather than description of technology. All these companies articulated messages of how their products united elegance with control (Nest), health partnerships (Fitbit) and reached future mobilities overflow (Tesla) with varied tales. The technological products of the companies had human elements supplied via their stories which made it easier for the consumers to relate to IoT devices.
3. **Ecosystem Thinking**: Multi- vendor integration is generally a success factor of IoT initiatives. Three examples of fitness between IoT products and their partners include Fitbits app interface with third parties also Tesla has partnered with solar and energy providers and Nest supports the Google smart home eco-system service ties. Strategic collaborations between brands create combined operational capability and the consumer obstacles are lowered at the same time the customer perceptions are increased of brand worth.
4. **Ethical Clarity**: Effective collection of sensitive information through IoT products demands full understanding of ethical standards. Companies that speak about ethical guidelines in a proper communication tone and act on them appropriately have a better chance of responding to consumer concerns and building long term customer relationships.

Looking Ahead: Emerging Frontiers

IoT adoption patterns in the future will grow via multiple emerging technological advances. Modern connected devices will change the consumer's interaction due to the progress of voice-first interfaces as well as ambient computing and AI empowered personalization services for context. The convergence between the real and the virtual will soar to greater heights, and this translates to the brands making more visible the need to provide safe and secure design which will provide security to human needs. The digital revolution builds trust as the value that is important in shaping the future. The succeeding organizations must incorporate technology, actual transparency and upright moral standing to create necessary interactions that consequently meet genuine human requirements. Nest, Fitbit and Tesla cases represent crucial points which should be noticed and pursued by future IoT strategists.

CONCLUSION

The IoT of modern life innovation needs more than operational effectiveness and functional innovation of IoT brands. The trust is the most important factor in customer adoption success because it comprises of data transparency dimensions coupled with ethical transparency and technology reliability and emotional attachment. The modern interconnected devices covertly control the houses and watch over health systems, and tracking movement patterns and behavioral practices in order-to win and keep consumers loyal is a key business need, not to mention that it is a moral necessity. In the chapter, the author describes that trust is not just mere marketing exercise that is required to generate it. Brand confidence must trickle down to the brand construction guidelines and governance procedures and the channels of communication within the brand. The current customers are insisting on both transparency in the use of data and responsible business practice in privacy maintenance and decision-making based on algorithms which would otherwise disrupt the traditional method of conventional branding. The development of brand trust emanates from important actions such as enabling users to give approvals of terms explicitly while having direct tracking interfaces and setting brand engagement in the public deputations regarding surveillance and equity and sustainability.

The existing IoT brands which have succeeded prove through their practices that the development of brand confidence cannot be achieved without active involvement with customers going beyond reputation management approaches. Manufacturers of ICT must keep constant dialogue with their consumers and justify their commitment to values, which outgo economic self-interest. Three key aspects of this process are storytelling and ethical leadership combined with ecosystem integration. The growth of vulnerabilities concerning the trust of IoT technology will continually increase during the forecast period. People will be more passionately engaged in invisible perpetuating systems as technologies such as ambient computing with AI based personalization and voice command interfaces go from being experimental to common. Trust in such conditions will change from being static to a state of constant evolution which people will advance step by step but which they may unwittingly destroy forever. Trust is vital as a necessary design basis for IoT brands because, every policy and consumer interaction or the use of each interface requires trust as a key design philosophy. The underlying necessity for brand confidence of IoT age concerns the ethical ways in which companies manage customer data. IoT calls for brands to move from basic compliance lists to an integrated approach of caring for users and their data and all the social consequences of technological adoption. The next IoT infrastructure will not be sufficient with code sensors as well as connectivity because it must build lasting consumer trust as a foundation. Digital transformation relies on brands' need to understand these ethical concerns since these organizations will achieve the adoption rate while aligning to higher ethical standards.

REFERENCES

Abedin, M. Z., & Hajek, P. (2023). *Cyber Security and Business Intelligence*. Routledge., DOI: 10.4324/9781003285854

Acquisti, A., Brandimarte, L., & Loewenstein, G. (2020). Secrets and Likes: The Drive for Privacy and the Difficulty of Achieving It in the Digital Age. *Journal of Consumer Psychology*, *30*(4), 736–758. DOI: 10.1002/jcpy.1191

Akkaş, A., & Sahoo, N. (2020). Reducing Product Expiration by Aligning Salesforce Incentives: A Data-driven Approach. *Production and Operations Management*, *29*(8), 1992–2009. DOI: 10.1111/poms.13191

Al Amin, M., Liza, I. A., Hossain, S. F., Hasan, E., Haque, M. M., & Bortty, J. C. (2024). Predicting and Monitoring Anxiety and Depression: Advanced Machine Learning Techniques for Mental Health Analysis. *British Journal of Nursing Studies*, *4*(2), 66–75. DOI: 10.32996/bjns.2024.4.2.8

Alaba, F. A. (2024). *The Evolution of the IoT*., DOI: 10.1007/978-3-031-67984-1_1

Aldossari, M. Q., & Sidorova, A. (2020). Consumer Acceptance of Internet of Things (IoT): Smart Home Context. *Journal of Computer Information Systems*, *60*(6), 507–517. DOI: 10.1080/08874417.2018.1543000

Andreotta, A. J., Kirkham, N., & Rizzi, M. (2022). AI, big data, and the future of consent. *AI & Society*, *37*(4), 1715–1728. DOI: 10.1007/s00146-021-01262-5 PMID: 34483498

Assimakopoulos, F., Vassilakis, C., Margaris, D., Kotis, K., & Spiliotopoulos, D. (2024). Artificial Intelligence Tools for the Agriculture Value Chain: Status and Prospects. *Electronics (Basel)*, *13*(22), 4362. DOI: 10.3390/electronics13224362

Bortty, J. C., Bhowmik, P. K., Reza, S. A., Liza, I. A., Mohammed, N. I. M., Muhammad, S. R. C., & Al Amin, M. (2024). Optimizing Lung Cancer Risk Prediction with Advanced Machine Learning Algorithms and Techniques. *Journal of Medical and Health Studies*, *5*(4), 35–48. DOI: 10.32996/jmhs.2024.5.4.7

Bu, F., Wang, N., Jiang, B., & Liang, H. (2020). “Privacy by Design” implementation: Information system engineers’ perspective. *International Journal of Information Management*, *53*, 102124. DOI: 10.1016/j.ijinfomgt.2020.102124

Buck, C., & Reith, R. (2020). Privacy on the road Evaluating German consumers’ intention to use connected cars. *International Journal of Automotive Technology and Management*, *20*(3), 297. DOI: 10.1504/IJATM.2020.110408

Chakra Bortty, J., Chakraborty, G. S., Noman, I. R., Batra, S., Das, J., Bishnu, K. K., Tarafder, M. T. R., & Islam, A. (2025). A Novel Diagnostic Framework with an Optimized Ensemble of Vision Transformers and Convolutional Neural Networks for Enhanced Alzheimer's Disease Detection in Medical Imaging. *Diagnostics (Basel), 15*(6), 789. DOI: 10.3390/diagnostics15060789 PMID: 40150131

Chakraborty, G. S., Bortty, J. C., Das, J., Noman, I. R., Bishnu, K. K., & Islam, A. (2025). Efficient multi-modal fusion framework with advanced AI-driven approaches for automated Parkinson's disease detection. *Intelligence-Based Medicine, 12*, 100310. DOI: 10.1016/j.ibmed.2025.100310

Chen, H., Turel, O., & Yuan, Y. (2022). E-waste information security protection motivation: The role of optimism bias. *Information Technology & People, 35*(2), 600–620. DOI: 10.1108/ITP-09-2019-0458

Chhabra, S., Mukherjee, J., & Agarwal, N. (2023). UNDERSTANDING PRIVACY PARADOX: AN EXPERIMENTAL APPROACH TO STUDY PRIVACY CONCERNS AND ACTUAL DISCLOSURE AMONG APP USERS. *Journal of Organizational Computing and Electronic Commerce, 33*(3–4), 97–116. DOI: 10.1080/10919392.2023.2251328

Crigger, E., Reinbold, K., Hanson, C., Kao, A., Blake, K., & Irons, M. (2022). Trustworthy Augmented Intelligence in Health Care. *Journal of Medical Systems, 46*(2), 12. DOI: 10.1007/s10916-021-01790-z PMID: 35020064

Dwivedi, Y. K., Hughes, L., Baabdullah, A. M., Ribeiro-Navarrete, S., Giannakis, M., Al-Debei, M. M., Dennehy, D., Metri, B., Buhalis, D., Cheung, C. M. K., Conboy, K., Doyle, R., Dubey, R., Dutot, V., Felix, R., Goyal, D. P., Gustafsson, A., Hinsch, C., Jebabli, I., & Wamba, S. F. (2022). Metaverse beyond the hype: Multidisciplinary perspectives on emerging challenges, opportunities, and agenda for research, practice and policy. *International Journal of Information Management, 66*, 102542. DOI: 10.1016/j.ijinfomgt.2022.102542

Emon, M. M. H. (2025). Circularity Meets AI: Revolutionizing Consumer Engagement Through Green Marketing. In *Transforming Business Practices With AI-Powered Green Marketing* (pp. 169–208). IGI Global Scientific Publishing. DOI: 10.4018/979-8-3373-3017-4.ch007

Emon, M. M. H., & Chowdhury, M. S. A. (2025). AI and IoT-Powered Smart Logistics: Transforming Supply Chains for Efficiency and Sustainability. In *Emerging Trends in Smart Logistics Technologies* (A. Hlali, pp. 45–72). IGI Global Scientific Publishing. DOI: 10.4018/979-8-3373-2434-0.ch002

Emon, M. M. H., & Khan, T. (2025). Exploring the mediating role of green logistics in enhancing green supply chain performance: Evidence from Bangladesh. *Journal of Engineering Research*. Advance online publication. DOI: 10.1016/j.jer.2025.10.003

Emon, M. M. H., & Mazid-Ul-Haque, M. (2025). Balancing Usability and Security: Enhancing User Experience Without Compromising Privacy. In *User-Centric Cybersecurity Implications for Sustainable Digital Transformation* (pp. 309–342). IGI Global Scientific Publishing. DOI: 10.4018/979-8-3373-3171-3.ch010

Emon, M. M. H., Rahman, K. M., Nath, A., Mahsin-Ul-Islam, M., Rifat, H. H., & Kutub, J. (2025). Exploring Drivers of Sustainable E-Commerce Adoption among SMEs in Bangladesh: A TOE Framework Approach for Industry 5.0 Transformation. *2025 IEEE 7th International Conference on Sustainable Technologies For Industry 5.0 (STI)*, 1–6. DOI: 10.1109/STI69347.2025.11367600

Erjavec, J., & Manfreda, A. (2022). Online shopping adoption during COVID-19 and social isolation: Extending the UTAUT model with herd behavior. *Journal of Retailing and Consumer Services*, *65*, 102867. DOI: 10.1016/j.jretconser.2021.102867

Essiz, O., & Senyuz, A. (2024). Predicting the value-based determinants of sustainable luxury consumption: A multi-analytical approach and pathway to sustainable development in the luxury industry. *Business Strategy and the Environment*, *33*(3), 1721–1758. DOI: 10.1002/bse.3569

FakhrHosseini, S., Chan, K., Lee, C., Jeon, M., Son, H., Rudnik, J., & Coughlin, J. FakhrHosseini. (2024). User Adoption of Intelligent Environments: A Review of Technology Adoption Models, Challenges, and Prospects. *International Journal of Human-Computer Interaction*, *40*(4), 986–998. DOI: 10.1080/10447318.2022.2118851

Farhad, M. A. (2024). Consumer data protection laws and their impact on business models in the tech industry. *Telecommunications Policy*, *48*(9), 102836. DOI: 10.1016/j.telpol.2024.102836

Gotsch, M. L., & Schögel, M. (2023). Addressing the privacy paradox on the organizational level: Review and future directions. *Management Review Quarterly*, *73*(1), 263–296. DOI: 10.1007/s11301-021-00239-4

Guo, L., Hu, X., Lu, J., & Ma, L. (2021). Effects of customer trust on engagement in live streaming commerce: Mediating role of swift guanxi. *Internet Research*, *31*(5), 1718–1744. DOI: 10.1108/INTR-02-2020-0078

Halkos, G., & Nomikos, S. (2021). Corporate social responsibility: Trends in global reporting initiative standards. *Economic Analysis and Policy*, *69*, 106–117. DOI: 10.1016/j.eap.2020.11.008

Hauser, S., Redström, J., & Wiltse, H. (2023). The widening rift between aesthetics and ethics in the design of computational things. *AI & Society*, *38*(1), 227–243. DOI: 10.1007/s00146-021-01279-w

Hooda, A., Gupta, P., Jeyaraj, A., Giannakis, M., & Dwivedi, Y. K. (2022). The effects of trust on behavioral intention and use behavior within e-government contexts. *International Journal of Information Management*, *67*, 102553. DOI: 10.1016/j.ijinfomgt.2022.102553

Hoyer, W. D., Kroschke, M., Schmitt, B., Kraume, K., & Shankar, V. (2020). Transforming the Customer Experience through New Technologies. *Journal of Interactive Marketing*, *51*(1), 57–71. DOI: 10.1016/j.intmar.2020.04.001

Kang, J., Hong, S., & Hubbard, G. T. (2020). The role of storytelling in advertising: Consumer emotion, narrative engagement level, and word-of-mouth intention. *Journal of Consumer Behaviour*, *19*(1), 47–56. DOI: 10.1002/cb.1793

Khan, T., & Hasan Emon, M. M. (2024). Determinants of AI Image Generator Adoption Among Marketing Agencies: The Mediating Effects of Perceived Usefulness. *2024 IEEE 3rd International Conference on Robotics, Automation, Artificial-Intelligence and Internet-of-Things (RAAICON)*, 177–182. DOI: 10.1109/RAAICON64172.2024.10928548

Kim, J., Kim, M., & Lee, S.-M. (2025). Unlocking Trust Dynamics: An Exploration of Playfulness, Expertise, and Consumer Behavior in Virtual Influencer Marketing. *International Journal of Human-Computer Interaction*, *41*(1), 378–390. DOI: 10.1080/10447318.2023.2300018

Koh, W. P., & Chin, K. K. (2022). The applicability of prospect theory in examining drivers' trip decisions, in response to Electronic Road Pricing (ERP) rates adjustments - a study using travel data in Singapore. *Transportation Research Part A, Policy and Practice*, *155*, 115–127. DOI: 10.1016/j.tra.2021.11.012

Korneeva, E., Olinder, N., & Strielkowski, W. (2021). Consumer Attitudes to the Smart Home Technologies and the Internet of Things (IoT). *Energies*, *14*(23), 7913. DOI: 10.3390/en14237913

Lee, C.-H., Yang, H.-C., Wei, Y.-C., & Hsu, W.-K. (2021). Enabling Blockchain Based SCM Systems with a Real Time Event Monitoring Function for Preemptive Risk Management. *Applied Sciences (Basel, Switzerland)*, *11*(11), 4811. DOI: 10.3390/app11114811

Macheka, T., Quaye, E. S., & Ligaraba, N. (2024). The effect of online customer reviews and celebrity endorsement on young female consumers' purchase intentions. *Young Consumers*, *25*(4), 462–482. DOI: 10.1108/YC-05-2023-1749

Malhotra, P., Singh, Y., Anand, P., Bangotra, D. K., Singh, P. K., & Hong, W.-C. (2021). Internet of Things: Evolution, Concerns and Security Challenges. *Sensors (Basel)*, *21*(5), 1809. DOI: 10.3390/s21051809 PMID: 33807724

Mettler, T. (2024). The connected workplace: Characteristics and social consequences of work surveillance in the age of datification, sensorization, and artificial intelligence. *Journal of Information Technology*, *39*(3), 547–567. DOI: 10.1177/02683962231202535

Moghrabi, I. A. R., Bhat, S. A., Szczuko, P., AlKhaled, R. A., & Dar, M. A. (2023). Digital Transformation and Its Influence on Sustainable Manufacturing and Business Practices. *Sustainability (Basel)*, *15*(4), 3010. DOI: 10.3390/su15043010

Mostafa, R. B., & Kasamani, T. (2020). Brand experience and brand loyalty: Is it a matter of emotions? *Asia Pacific Journal of Marketing and Logistics*, *33*(4), 1033–1051. DOI: 10.1108/APJML-11-2019-0669

Naeem, M. (2021). The role of social media to generate social proof as engaged society for stockpiling behaviour of customers during Covid-19 pandemic. *Qualitative Market Research*, *24*(3), 281–301. DOI: 10.1108/QMR-04-2020-0050

Neslin, S. A. (2022). The omnichannel continuum: Integrating online and offline channels along the customer journey. *Journal of Retailing*, *98*(1), 111–132. DOI: 10.1016/j.jretai.2022.02.003

Nobar, H. B. K., Kalejahi, H. K., & Rostamzadeh, R. (2020). Impact of social media marketing activities on brand equity and brand commitment in the leather industry. *International Journal of Business Excellence*, *20*(2), 191. DOI: 10.1504/IJBEX.2020.105346

Oschinsky, F. M., Stelter, A., & Niehaves, B. (2021). Cognitive biases in the digital age – How resolving the status quo bias enables public-sector employees to overcome restraint. *Government Information Quarterly*, *38*(4), 101611. DOI: 10.1016/j.giq.2021.101611

Panahi Rizi, M. H., Hosseini Seno, S. A., Rizi, M. H. P., & Seno, S. A. H. (2022). A systematic review of technologies and solutions to improve security and privacy protection of citizens in the smart city. *Internet of Things : Engineering Cyber Physical Human Systems*, *20*, 100584. DOI: 10.1016/j.iot.2022.100584

Paydas Turan, C. (2021). Success drivers of co-branding: A meta-analysis. *International Journal of Consumer Studies*, *45*(4), 911–936. DOI: 10.1111/ijcs.12682

Rajaram, K. (2022). *Leading and Transforming Organizations*. Routledge., DOI: 10.4324/9781003286288

Rego, L., Brady, M., Leone, R., Roberts, J., Srivastava, C., & Srivastava, R. (2022). Brand response to environmental turbulence: A framework and propositions for resistance, recovery and reinvention. *International Journal of Research in Marketing*, *39*(2), 583–602. DOI: 10.1016/j.ijresmar.2021.10.006

Saxena, A., Singh, R., Gehlot, A., Akram, S. V., Twala, B., Singh, A., Montero, E. C., & Priyadarshi, N. (2022). Technologies Empowered Environmental, Social, and Governance (ESG): An Industry 4.0 Landscape. *Sustainability (Basel)*, *15*(1), 309. DOI: 10.3390/su15010309

Shams, S. M. R., Brown, D. M., & Hardcastle, K. (2025). *Brand Management*. Marketing Communication, and Promotion Management for People, Planet, and Profit., DOI: 10.1007/978-3-031-79130-7_4

Sivakumar, C. L. V., Mone, V., & Abdumukhtor, R. (2024). Addressing privacy concerns with wearable health monitoring technology. *Wiley Interdisciplinary Reviews. Data Mining and Knowledge Discovery*, *14*(3), e1535. Advance online publication. DOI: 10.1002/widm.1535

Tan, T. M., & Saraniemi, S. (2023). Trust in blockchain-enabled exchanges: Future directions in blockchain marketing. *Journal of the Academy of Marketing Science*, *51*(4), 914–939. DOI: 10.1007/s11747-022-00889-0

Vassallo, J. P., Banerjee, S., Zaman, H., & Prabhu, J. C. (2023). Design thinking and public sector innovation: The divergent effects of risk-taking, cognitive empathy and emotional empathy on individual performance. *Research Policy*, *52*(6), 104768. DOI: 10.1016/j.respol.2023.104768

Wackerhage, H., & Schoenfeld, B. J. (2021). Personalized, Evidence-Informed Training Plans and Exercise Prescriptions for Performance, Fitness and Health. *Sports Medicine (Auckland, N.Z.)*, *51*(9), 1805–1813. DOI: 10.1007/s40279-021-01495-w PMID: 34143410

Wang, Z., Li, M., Lu, J., & Cheng, X. (2022). Business Innovation based on artificial intelligence and Blockchain technology. *Information Processing & Management*, *59*(1), 102759. DOI: 10.1016/j.ipm.2021.102759

Waris, I., & Hameed, I. (2020). Promoting environmentally sustainable consumption behavior: An empirical evaluation of purchase intention of energy-efficient appliances. *Energy Efficiency*, *13*(8), 1653–1664. DOI: 10.1007/s12053-020-09901-4

Yamini, S. (2020). Behavioral perspective of newsvendor ordering decisions: Review, analysis and insights. *Management Decision*, *59*(2), 240–257. DOI: 10.1108/MD-07-2019-0975

Yang, R., & Wibowo, S. (2022). User trust in artificial intelligence: A comprehensive conceptual framework. *Electronic Markets*, *32*(4), 2053–2077. DOI: 10.1007/s12525-022-00592-6

Zhang, H., Zhang, M., Lu, J., Zhao, L., Zhao, D., Xiao, C., Gu, R., & Luo, W. (2020). Interpersonal relationships modulate outcome evaluation in a social comparison context: The pain and pleasure of intimacy. *Cognitive, Affective & Behavioral Neuroscience*, *20*(1), 115–127. DOI: 10.3758/s13415-019-00756-6 PMID: 31823210

KEY TERMS AND DEFINITIONS

Behavioral Economics: The field of the combination of psychology and economics treats the decisions made by people in uncertain conditions even though they are not logical.

Brand Positioning: Brands are strategically created with communication strategies to secure an individual mental position which stands out as meaningful to consumers.

Consumer Trust: Trust of customers in brands in their reliability and ethical practices as far as personal data protection is concerned in technology-based services is the brand's authenticity.

Digital Storytelling: Brands are formed by deliberate measures put in by the experience of communication strategies with a purpose of winning an individual mental position that is notable to consumers.

Ethical Data Practices: The digital ecosystem must have a list of principles; the principles of data responsibility (transparency, user consent), empowering the customers throughout all data routine.

Internet of Things (IoT): Embedded physical objects called Internet of Things devices use sensors along with software components and network connection to transfer data in real-time for automated purposes.

Omnichannel Strategy: Integrated customer experience demands the organizations accept online and offline and mobile and in-store channels as one continuum approach to uniform brand touch.

Privacy Paradox: Consumers come out to the open to voice their concerns over data privacy; yet they use technology that will capture private data.

Compilation of References

Abbas, T., Khan, V.-J., & Markopoulos, P. (2020). Investigating the Crowd's Creativity for Creating On-Demand IoT Scenarios. *International Journal of Human-Computer Interaction*, *36*(11), 1022–1049. DOI: 10.1080/10447318.2019.1709331

Abedin, M. Z., & Hajek, P. (2023). *Cyber Security and Business Intelligence*. Routledge., DOI: 10.4324/9781003285854

Abiodun, K. (2025). Digital infrastructure & sustainable data centers investment in Africa: Role of Tier III & Tier IV. *International Journal of Multidisciplinary Research and Growth Evaluation*, *6*(1), 1878–1888. DOI: 10.54660/.IJMRGE.2025.6.1-1878-1888

Abrahams, T., Farayola, O., Kaggwa, S., Uwaoma, P., Hassan, A., & Dawodu, S. (2024). Cybersecurity Awareness and Education Programs: A Review of Employee Engagement and Accountability. Computer Science and IT Research Journal. Vol 5. page (100-119).

Accenture. (2020). *Technology Vision 2020: We, the post-digital people*. Accenture.

Acquisti, A., Brandimarte, L., & Loewenstein, G. (2020). Secrets and Likes: The Drive for Privacy and the Difficulty of Achieving It in the Digital Age. *Journal of Consumer Psychology*, *30*(4), 736–758. DOI: 10.1002/jcpy.1191

Adolphs, C., & Winkelmann, A. (2010). Personalization research: A rigorous literature review on personalization in e-commerce (2000-2008). *Journal of Electronic Commerce Research*, *11*(4), 326–341.

Adomako, S., Shenkar, O., Liu, X., Amankwah-Amoah, J., & Ahsan, M. (2024). Editorial on doing business in Africa: Navigating opportunities and challenges in Africa's emerging markets. *Journal of International Management*, *30*(101189), 1–20. DOI: 10.1016/j.intman.2024.101189

African Development Bank. (2023). *African economic outlook 2023: Mobilizing private sector financing for climate and green growth in Africa*. African Development Bank Group. https://www.afdb.org/en/documents/african-economic-outlook-2023

Agarwal, V., Purwar, S., & Agrawal, S. (2024, November). IoT-Driven Environmental Surveillance to Foster Sustainable Development. In *2024 3rd Edition of IEEE Delhi Section Flagship Conference (DELCON)* (pp. 1-6). IEEE. DOI: 10.1109/DELCON64804.2024.10866673

Aggarwal, N., & Singh, S. (2025). Embracing the future by unlocking the door to smart living: A systematic review of consumers' adoption and acceptance of smart home devices. *The Journal of Consumer Research*, *42*(3), 123–145. DOI: 10.1177/09711023241310286

Ahmad, I., Anyanwu, A., Onwusinkwue, S., Dawodu, S., Akagha, O., & Ejairu, E. (2024). Cybersecurity Challenges in Smart Cities: A Case Review of African Metropolises. *Computer Science and IT Research Journal.*, *5*(2), 254–269. DOI: 10.51594/csitrj.v5i2.756

Ahmad, K., Maabreh, M., Ghaly, M., Khan, K., Qadir, J., & Al-Fuqaha, A. (2022). Developing future human-centered smart cities: Critical analysis of smart city security, Data management, and Ethical challenges. *Computer Science Review*, *43*, 100452. DOI: 10.1016/j.cosrev.2021.100452

Ahmad, T., Madonski, R., Zhang, D., Huang, C., & Mujeeb, A. (2022). Data-driven probabilistic machine learning in sustainable smart energy/smart energy systems: Key developments, challenges, and future research opportunities in the context of smart grid paradigm. *Renewable & Sustainable Energy Reviews*, *160*, 112128. DOI: 10.1016/j.rser.2022.112128

Ahmad, W., Rasool, A., Javed, A. R., Baker, T., & Jalil, Z. (2021). Cyber Security in IoT-Based Cloud Computing: A Comprehensive Survey. *Electronics (Basel)*, *11*(1), 16. DOI: 10.3390/electronics11010016

Ahmed, M., & Ahmed, M. J. (2026). Sustainable Industrial Operations Through IoT-Generated Big Data Insights. In *Sustainable Operations in the Age of AI and Big Data* (pp. 37–82). DOI: 10.4018/979-8-2600-0216-2.ch002

Ahmed, M., Al Amareen, O. S., & Arafat, Y. (2026). Harnessing Big Data for Reverse Logistics and Waste Management: Pathways to Sustainable Supply Chains. In *Enhancing Sustainability in Global Supply Chains With Big Data Analytics* (pp. 175–210). IGI Global Scientific Publishing. DOI: 10.4018/979-8-3373-6896-2.ch006

Ahmetoglu, S., Che Cob, Z., & Ali, N. A. (2022). A systematic review of Internet of Things adoption in organizations: Taxonomy, benefits, challenges and critical factors. *applied sciences, 12*(9), 4117.

Ahmetoglu, S., Che Cob, Z., & Ali, N. (2023). Internet of Things adoption in the manufacturing sector: A conceptual model from a multi-theoretical perspective. *Applied Sciences (Basel, Switzerland), 13*(3856), 1–21. DOI: 10.3390/app13063856

Ahsan, M., Adomako, S., & Mole, K. F. (2021). Perceived institutional support and small venture performance: The mediating role of entrepreneurial persistence. *International Small Business Journal, 39*(1), 18–39. DOI: 10.1177/0266242620943194

Ajzen, I. (2020). The theory of planned behavior: Frequently asked questions. Human Behavior and Emerging Technologies. https://www.researchgate.net/publication/342077056

Ajzen, I. (1991). The theory of planned behavior. *Organizational Behavior and Human Decision Processes, 50*(2), 179–211. DOI: 10.1016/0749-5978(91)90020-T

Akkaş, A., & Sahoo, N. (2020). Reducing Product Expiration by Aligning Salesforce Incentives: A Data-driven Approach. *Production and Operations Management, 29*(8), 1992–2009. DOI: 10.1111/poms.13191

Al Amin, M., Liza, I. A., Hossain, S. F., Hasan, E., Haque, M. M., & Bortty, J. C. (2024). Predicting and Monitoring Anxiety and Depression: Advanced Machine Learning Techniques for Mental Health Analysis. *British Journal of Nursing Studies, 4*(2), 66–75. DOI: 10.32996/bjns.2024.4.2.8

Alabadi, M., Habbal, A., & Wei, X. (2022). Industrial Internet of Things: Requirements, Architecture, Challenges, and Future Research Directions. *IEEE Access : Practical Innovations, Open Solutions, 10*, 66374–66400. DOI: 10.1109/ACCESS.2022.3185049

Alaba, F. A. (2024). *The Evolution of the IoT.*, DOI: 10.1007/978-3-031-67984-1_1

Alam, S. M. I. (2022). *Behavioral Economics: Concepts.* History, and Evolution.

Aldossari, M. Q., & Sidorova, A. (2020). Consumer Acceptance of Internet of Things (IoT): Smart Home Context. *Journal of Computer Information Systems, 60*(6), 507–517. DOI: 10.1080/08874417.2018.1543000

Alenizi, A. S., & Al-Karawi, K. A. (2022, July). Internet of things (IoT) adoption: challenges and barriers. In *Proceedings of Seventh International Congress on Information and Communication Technology: ICICT 2022, London,* Volume 3 (pp. 217-229). Singapore: Springer Nature Singapore.

Alhassan, I., & Islam, K. A. (2021). Credit management strategies and financial performance of industrial goods sector in Nigeria. *Indian Journal of Finance and Banking*, *8*(1), 59–74.

AlHogail, A. (2018). Improving IoT technology adoption through improving consumer trust. *Technologies*, *6*(64), 64. Advance online publication. DOI: 10.3390/technologies6030064

Alkhamery, N., Zainol, F. A., & Al-Nashmi, M. (2020). Conceptualizing the role of organizational capabilities in enhancing firms readiness for digital business transformation. *International Journal of Management*, *11*(12), 785–797. DOI: 10.34218/IJM.11.12.2020.072

Allen, D. K., Brown, A., Karanasios, S., & Norman, A. (2013). How should technology-mediated organizational change be explained? A comparison of the contributions of critical realism and activity theory. *Management Information Systems Quarterly*, *37*(3), 835–854. DOI: 10.25300/MISQ/2013/37.3.08

Allioui, H., & Mourdi, Y. (2023). Exploring the Full Potentials of IoT for Better Financial Growth and Stability: A Comprehensive Survey. *Sensors (Basel)*, *23*(19), 8015. DOI: 10.3390/s23198015 PMID: 37836845

Al-Moaid, N. A. A., & Almarhdi, S. G. (2024). Developing dynamic capabilities for successful digital transformation projects: The mediating role of change management. *Journal of Innovation and Entrepreneurship*, *13*(85), 1–26. DOI: 10.1186/s13731-024-00446-9

Almusaed, A., Yitmen, I., & Almssad, A. (2023). Enhancing Smart Home Design with AI Models: A Case Study of Living Spaces Implementation Review. *Energies*, *16*(6), 2636. DOI: 10.3390/en16062636

AlNuaimi, B. K., Kumar Singh, S., Ren, S., Budhwar, P., & Vorobyev, D. (2022). Mastering digital transformation: The nexus between leadership, agility, and digital strategy. *Journal of Business Research*, *145*, 636–648. DOI: 10.1016/j.jbusres.2022.03.038

Al-Obeidat, F., Spencer, B., & Kafeza, E. (2018). The opinion management framework: Identifying and addressing customer concerns extracted from online product reviews. *Electronic Commerce Research and Applications*, *27*, 52–64. DOI: 10.1016/j.elerap.2017.11.003

Alqudhaibi, A., Krishna, A., Jagtap, S., Williams, N., Afy-Shararah, M., & Salonitis, K. (2024). Cybersecurity 4.0: Safeguarding trust and production in the digital food industry era. *Discover Food*, *4*(1), 2. DOI: 10.1007/s44187-023-00071-7

Alrawais, A., Alhothaily, A., Hu, C., & Cheng, X. (2017). Fog computing for the Internet of Things: Security and privacy issues. *IEEE Internet Computing*, *21*(2), 34–42. DOI: 10.1109/MIC.2017.37

Al-Rawashdeh, M., Keikhosrokiani, P., Belaton, B., Alawida, M., & Zwiri, A. (2022). IoT adoption and application for smart healthcare: A systematic review. *Sensors (Basel)*, *22*(14), 5377. DOI: 10.3390/s22145377 PMID: 35891056

Alrub, Y. A., & Sánchez-Cañizares, S. M. (2025). Dynamic capabilities and digital transformation: Toward strategic planning in the digital age—Evidence from Palestine. *Administrative Sciences*, *15*(1), 21. Advance online publication. DOI: 10.3390/admsci15010021

Alshar'e, M. (2023). Cyber Security Framework Selection: Comparision of NIST and ISO27001. Applied computing Journal, Volume 3, Issue 1, (pp. 245-255).

Amin, M. S., Kim, S., Rishat, M. A. S. A., Tang, Z., & Ahn, H. (2024). A Systematic Literature Review of Privacy Information Disclosure in AI-Integrated Internet of Things (IoT) Technologies. *Sustainability (Basel)*, *17*(1), 8. DOI: 10.3390/su17010008

Amofah, D. O., & Chai, J. (2022). Sustaining Consumer E-Commerce Adoption in Sub-Saharan Africa: Do Trust and Payment Method Matter? *Sustainability (Basel)*, *2022*(14), 8466. DOI: 10.3390/su14148466

Andreotta, A. J., Kirkham, N., & Rizzi, M. (2022). AI, big data, and the future of consent. *AI & Society*, *37*(4), 1715–1728. DOI: 10.1007/s00146-021-01262-5 PMID: 34483498

Antonakakis, M., April, T., & Bailey, M.. (2017). Understanding the Mirai botnet. In *USENIX Security Symposium*.

Arafat, Y., Pk, M. K., Hossen, A., & Sarker, M. N. (2025). Adaptive Temporal Convolution Framework for Multi-Channel Sales Forecasting Through Dynamic EMA-XGBoost. *International Journal of Research. Innovation and Commercialisation*, *6*(1), 10073445. Advance online publication. DOI: 10.1504/IJRIC.2025.10073445

Arthurs, P., Gillam, L., Krause, P., Wang, N., Halder, K., & Mouzakitis, A. (2022). A Taxonomy and Survey of Edge Cloud Computing for Intelligent Transportation Systems and Connected Vehicles. *IEEE Transactions on Intelligent Transportation Systems*, *23*(7), 6206–6221. DOI: 10.1109/TITS.2021.3084396

Ashrafi, A., Zareravasan, A., Trkman, P., & Afshari, S. (2019). The role of business analytics capabilities in bolstering firms' agility and performance. *International Journal of Information Management*, *47*, 1–15. DOI: 10.1016/j.ijinfomgt.2018.12.005

Asir, T. R. G., & Manohar, H. L. (2023). Variations on Internet of Things adoption factors between India and the USA. *South African Journal of Business Management, 54*(1), a3810. DOI: 10.4102/sajbm.v54i1.3810

Asongu, S. A., Nwachukwu, J. C., & Orim, S.-M. I. (2018). Mobile phones, institutional quality and entrepreneurship in Sub-Saharan Africa. *Technological Forecasting and Social Change, 131*, 183–203. DOI: 10.1016/j.techfore.2017.08.007

Assimakopoulos, F., Vassilakis, C., Margaris, D., Kotis, K., & Spiliotopoulos, D. (2024). Artificial Intelligence Tools for the Agriculture Value Chain: Status and Prospects. *Electronics (Basel), 13*(22), 4362. DOI: 10.3390/electronics13224362

Atayero, A. A., Oluwatobi, S. O., & Alege, P. O. (2016). An assessment of the Internet of Things (IoT) adoption readiness of Sub-Saharan Africa. *Journal of South African Business Research, 2016*, 321563. Advance online publication. DOI: 10.5171/2016.321563

Atetedaye, J. (2024). *Cybersecurity in the Internet of Things (IoT).* Challenges and Solutions.

Attah, R. U., Garba, B. M. P., Gil-Ozoudeh, I., & Iwuanyanwu, O. (2024). Strategic frameworks for digital transformation across logistics and energy sectors: Bridging technology with business strategy. *Open Access Res J Sci Technol, 12*(02), 070-80.

Atzori, L., Iera, A., & Morabito, G. (2010). The Internet of Things: A survey. *Computer Networks, 54*(15), 2787–2805. DOI: 10.1016/j.comnet.2010.05.010

Bærentsen, K. B., & Trettvik, J. (2002). An activity theory approach to affordance. In *Proceedings of the 2nd Nordic conference on Human-computer interaction (NordiCHI 2002)* (pp. 51–60). DOI: 10.1145/572020.572028

Baethge, C., Klier, J., & Klier, M. (2016). Social commerce: State-of-the-art and future research directions. *Electronic Markets, 26*(3), 269–290. DOI: 10.1007/s12525-016-0225-2

Balaji, S., Nathani, K., & Santhakumar, R. (2019). IoT technology, applications and challenges: A contemporary survey. *Wireless Personal Communications, 108*(1), 363–388. DOI: 10.1007/s11277-019-06407-w

Barbosa, J. L. V. (2015). Ubiquitous computing: Applications and research opportunities. In *Proceedings of the IEEE International Conference on Computational Intelligence and Computing Research (ICCIC 2015)*. DOI: 10.1109/ICCIC.2015.7435625

Barney, J. B. (1986). Organizational culture: Can it be a source of sustained competitive advantage? *Academy of Management Review, 11*(3), 656–665. DOI: 10.2307/258317

Barth, S., & de Jong, M. D. T. (2017). The privacy paradox – Investigating discrepancies between expressed privacy concerns and actual online behavior – A systematic literature review. *Telematics and Informatics*, *34*(7), 1038–1058. DOI: 10.1016/j.tele.2017.04.013

Basu, R., Lim, W. M., Kumar, A., & Kumar, S. (2023). Marketing analytics: The bridge between customer psychology and marketing decision-making. *Psychology and Marketing*, *40*(12), 2588–2611. DOI: 10.1002/mar.21908

Bedewy, S. F. (2024). The Impact of Data Security and Privacy Concerns on the Implementation of Integrated Systems in Smart Cities. https://www.intechopen.com/chapters/89615#:~:text=DOI%3A%2010.5772/intechopen.115076

Behera, R. K., Bala, P. K., & Rana, N. P. (2024). Assessing the intention to adopt computational intelligence in interactive marketing. *Journal of Retailing and Consumer Services*, *78*, 103765. DOI: 10.1016/j.jretconser.2024.103765

Belanger, F., & Crossler, R. E. (2011). Privacy in the digital age: A review of information privacy research in information systems. *Management Information Systems Quarterly*, *35*(4), 1017–1041. DOI: 10.2307/41409971

Beldad, A., de Jong, M., & Steehouder, M. (2010). How shall I trust the faceless and the intangible? *Computers in Human Behavior*, *26*(5), 857–869. DOI: 10.1016/j.chb.2010.03.013

Bentalha, B., & Hmioui, A. (2022). *Smart Service Supply Chain and Just Walk Out Technology: A Netnographic Approach* (pp. 223–236). DOI: 10.1007/978-3-030-94191-8_18

Berte, D.-R. (2018). Defining the IoT. *Proceedings of the International Conference on Business Excellence*. 12. 118-128. DOI: 10.2478/picbe-2018-0013

Bertino, E., & Islam, N. (2017). Botnets and internet of things security. *Computer*, *50*(2), 76–79. DOI: 10.1109/MC.2017.62

Bhatt, V., & Chakraborty, S. (2023). Improving service engagement in healthcare through internet of things based healthcare systems. *Journal of Science and Technology Policy Management*, *14*(1), 53–73. DOI: 10.1108/JSTPM-03-2021-0040

Bhor, P. P., Mishra, J. R., Valvi, P. R., Thale, R. J., & Dodia, S. (2024, December). A systematic review on the application of IoT in agriculture. In *IET Conference Proceedings CP900* (Vol. 2024, No. 23, pp. 12-18). Stevenage, UK: The Institution of Engineering and Technology.

Blythe, J. M., Johnson, S. D., & Manning, M. (2020). What is security worth to consumers? Investigating willingness to pay for secure Internet of Things devices. *Crime Science*, *9*(1), 1. DOI: 10.1186/s40163-019-0110-3

Borgia, E. (2014). Internet of Things vision: Key features, applications and open issues. *Computer Communications*, *54*, 1–31. DOI: 10.1016/j.comcom.2014.09.008

Bortty, J. C., Bhowmik, P. K., Reza, S. A., Liza, I. A., Mohammed, N. I. M., Muhammad, S. R. C., & Al Amin, M. (2024). Optimizing Lung Cancer Risk Prediction with Advanced Machine Learning Algorithms and Techniques. *Journal of Medical and Health Studies*, *5*(4), 35–48. DOI: 10.32996/jmhs.2024.5.4.7

Bouteska, A., & Regaieg, B. (2020). Loss aversion, overconfidence of investors and their impact on market performance evidence from the US stock markets. *Journal of Economics, Finance and Administrative Science*, *25*(50), 451–478. DOI: 10.1108/JEFAS-07-2017-0081

Bridhikitti, A., Kaewsuk, J., Karaket, N., Friend, R., Sallach, B., Chong, J. P. J., & Redeker, K. R. (2023). Balancing Agriculture and Industry through Waste Utilization for Sugarcane Sustainability. *Sustainability (Basel)*, *15*(20), 14711. DOI: 10.3390/su152014711

Brinkley, J. (2020). Designing inclusive IoT devices. *Journal of Information Technology & Politics*, *17*(2), 112–128.

Brouns, N., Tata, S., Ludwig, H., Asensio, E. S., & Grefen, P. (2018). Modeling IoT-aware business processes - A state of the art report. *arXiv*. https://arxiv.org/abs/1811.00652

Buck, C., & Reith, R. (2020). Privacy on the road Evaluating German consumers' intention to use connected cars. *International Journal of Automotive Technology and Management*, *20*(3), 297. DOI: 10.1504/IJATM.2020.110408

Bu, F., Wang, N., Jiang, B., & Liang, H. (2020). "Privacy by Design" implementation: Information system engineers' perspective. *International Journal of Information Management*, *53*, 102124. DOI: 10.1016/j.ijinfomgt.2020.102124

Bukhari, S. M. S., Zafar, M. H., Abou Houran, M., Qadir, Z., Moosavi, S. K. R., & Sanfilippo, F. (2024). Enhancing cybersecurity in Edge IIoT networks: An asynchronous federated learning approach with a deep hybrid detection model. *Internet of Things : Engineering Cyber Physical Human Systems*, *27*, 101252. DOI: 10.1016/j.iot.2024.101252

Burkhardt, G., Boy, F., Doneddu, D., & Hajli, N. (2023). Privacy Behaviour: A Model for Online Informed Consent. *Journal of Business Ethics, 186*(1), 237–255. DOI: 10.1007/s10551-022-05202-1

Butt, U., & Gutappa, B. shaheer, Pendlebury, G., Hassan, B., Butt, W., & Davelis, A. (2023). *IoT Privacy by Design* (pp. 270–300). DOI: 10.4018/978-1-6684-6403-8.ch015

Bzai, J., Alam, F., Dhafer, A., Bojović, M., Altowaijri, S. M., Niazi, I. K., & Mehmood, R. (2022). Machine Learning-Enabled Internet of Things (IoT): Data, Applications, and Industry Perspective. *Electronics (Basel), 11*(17), 2676. DOI: 10.3390/electronics11172676

Caputo, F., Scuotto, V., Carayannis, E., & Cillo, V. (2018). Intertwining the internet of things and consumers' behaviour science: Future promises for businesses. *Technological Forecasting and Social Change, 136*, 277–284. DOI: 10.1016/j.techfore.2018.03.019

Caso, J., Cole, Z., Patel, M., & Zhu, W. (2023). Cybersecurity for the IoT: How trust can unlock value. *McKinsey & Company, 7.*

Caven, P., Zhang, Z., Abbott, J., Ma, X., & Camp, L. (2024, May). Comparing the Use and Usefulness of Four IoT Security Labels. In *Proceedings of the 2024 CHI Conference on Human Factors in Computing Systems* (pp. 1-31). DOI: 10.1145/3613904.3642951

Cavoukian, A. (2011). *Privacy by design: The 7 foundational principles.* Information and Privacy Commissioner of Ontario.

Cavoukian, A. (2012). Privacy by design: Origins, meaning, and prospects. In *Privacy protection measures and technologies in business organizations* (pp. 170–208). IGI Global. DOI: 10.4018/978-1-61350-501-4.ch007

Çeken, C. (2024). *Design and Implementation of a Scalable IoT-Based Real-Time Environmental Monitoring and Alarm System: An Experimental Study. Vestnik of M.* Kozybayev North Kazakhstan University. DOI: 10.54596/2958-0048-2024-3-155-164

Chakra Bortty, J., Chakraborty, G. S., Noman, I. R., Batra, S., Das, J., Bishnu, K. K., Tarafder, M. T. R., & Islam, A. (2025). A Novel Diagnostic Framework with an Optimized Ensemble of Vision Transformers and Convolutional Neural Networks for Enhanced Alzheimer's Disease Detection in Medical Imaging. *Diagnostics (Basel), 15*(6), 789. DOI: 10.3390/diagnostics15060789 PMID: 40150131

Chakrabarty, A., Zavitsanou, S., Sowrirajan, T., Doyle, F. J., III, & Dassau, E. (2019). Getting IoT-ready: The face of next generation artificial pancreas systems. In *The Artificial Pancreas* (pp. 29-57). Academic Press.

Chakraborty, G. S., Bortty, J. C., Das, J., Noman, I. R., Bishnu, K. K., & Islam, A. (2025). Efficient multi-modal fusion framework with advanced AI-driven approaches for automated Parkinson's disease detection. *Intelligence-Based Medicine, 12*, 100310. DOI: 10.1016/j.ibmed.2025.100310

Chandra, S., Verma, S., Lim, W.M., Kumar, S. & Donthu, N. (2022). Personalization in personalized marketing: Trends and ways forward. DOI: DOI: 10.1002/mar.21670

Chaudhary, P., Kiran, P., Kate, N., & Pandey, S. (2022). Experiential tourism – role and application of micro-targeting in enhancing customer experience, engagement and loyalty. *Journal of Information and Optimization Sciences*, *43*(6), 1463–1473. DOI: 10.1080/02522667.2022.2139929

Chen, C. C., Shu, D., Ravishankar, H., Li, X., Agarwal, Y., & Cranor, L. F. (2024, May). Is a Trustmark and QR code enough? The effect of IoT security and privacy label information complexity on consumer comprehension and behavior. In *Proceedings of the 2024 CHI Conference on Human Factors in Computing Systems* (pp. 1-32). DOI: 10.1145/3613904.3642011

Chen, H., Turel, O., & Yuan, Y. (2022). E-waste information security protection motivation: The role of optimism bias. *Information Technology & People*, *35*(2), 600–620. DOI: 10.1108/ITP-09-2019-0458

Chhabra, S., Mukherjee, J., & Agarwal, N. (2023). UNDERSTANDING PRIVACY PARADOX: AN EXPERIMENTAL APPROACH TO STUDY PRIVACY CONCERNS AND ACTUAL DISCLOSURE AMONG APP USERS. *Journal of Organizational Computing and Electronic Commerce*, *33*(3–4), 97–116. DOI: 10.1080/10919392.2023.2251328

Choe, E. K., Jung, J., Lee, B., & Fisher, K. (2018). The role of privacy and personalization in IoT. [TOCHI]. *ACM Transactions on Computer-Human Interaction*, *25*(1), 1–29.

Christidis, K., & Devetsikiotis, M. (2016). Blockchains and smart contracts for the Internet of Things. *IEEE Access : Practical Innovations, Open Solutions*, *4*, 2292–2303. DOI: 10.1109/ACCESS.2016.2566339

Chua, C., Khoo, H., Straub, D., Kadiyala, S., & Kuechler, D. (2005). The evolution of e-commerce research: A stakeholder perspective. *Journal of Electronic Commerce Research*, *6*(4), 262–280.

Chunxia, Q., Zhenzhong, Z., & Litao, Z. (2010). A shopping model in ubiquitous media environment. In *Proceedings of the International Forum on Information Technology and Applications (IFITA 2010)* (pp. 319–322). DOI: 10.1109/IFITA.2010.119

CISA. (2021, May 27). Advisory: Colonial Pipeline Incident. Cybersecurity and Infrastructure Security Agency. https://www.cisa.gov/news-events/cybersecurity-advisories/aa21-147a

Clarke, I. I.III. (2008). Emerging value propositions for m-commerce. *The Journal of Business Strategy*, *25*(2), 41–57. DOI: 10.54155/jbs.25.2.41-57

Conti, M., Dehghantanha, A., Franke, K., & Watson, S. (2018). Internet of Things security and forensics: Challenges and opportunities. *Future Generation Computer Systems*, *78*, 544–546. DOI: 10.1016/j.future.2017.07.060

Cozzolino, A., Verona, G., & Rothaermel, F. T. (2018). Unpacking the disruption process: New technology, business models, and incumbent adaptation. *Journal of Management Studies*, *55*(7), 1166–1202. DOI: 10.1111/joms.12352

Crespo Márquez, A. (2022). *Digital Maintenance Management*. Springer International Publishing., DOI: 10.1007/978-3-030-97660-6

Creswell, J. W., & Creswell, J. D. (2018). *Research design: Qualitative, quantitative, and mixed methods approaches* (5th ed.). SAGE Publications.

Crigger, E., Reinbold, K., Hanson, C., Kao, A., Blake, K., & Irons, M. (2022). Trustworthy Augmented Intelligence in Health Care. *Journal of Medical Systems*, *46*(2), 12. DOI: 10.1007/s10916-021-01790-z PMID: 35020064

Cruz, M. (Ed.). (2024). International Finance Corporation Research Series *Digital opportunities in African businesses*. World Bank Publications.

Cui, L., Gao, M., Dai, J., & Mou, J. (2022). Improving supply chain collaboration through operational excellence approaches: An IoT perspective. *Industrial Management & Data Systems*, *122*(3), 565–591. DOI: 10.1108/IMDS-01-2020-0016

Daramola, O., & Etim, E. (2022). Affordances of digital platforms in sub-Saharan Africa: An analytical review. *The Electronic Journal on Information Systems in Developing Countries*, *88*(4), 1–21. DOI: 10.1002/isd2.12213

Davis, F. D. (1985). A technology acceptance model for empirically testing new end-user information systems: Theory and results [Doctoral dissertation, Massachusetts Institute of Technology]. MIT Libraries. http://hdl.handle.net/1721.1/15192

Davis, F. D., Bagozzi, R. P., & Warshaw, P. R. (1989). User acceptance of computer technology: A comparison of two theoretical models. *Management Science*, *35*(8), 982–1003. DOI: 10.1287/mnsc.35.8.982

De Vaus, D. A. (2014). *Research design in social research.* SAGE Publications.

De Waal, C. (2021). *Introducing pragmatism: a tool for rethinking philosophy.* Routledge. DOI: 10.4324/9781003199731

Dehghanpouri, H., Soltani, Z., & Rostamzadeh, R. (2020). The impact of trust, privacy and quality of service on the success of E-CRM: The mediating role of customer satisfaction. *Journal of Business and Industrial Marketing*, *35*(11), 1831–1847. DOI: 10.1108/JBIM-07-2019-0325

Deloitte. (2016). Switch on to the connected home: The Deloitte Consumer Review. Retrieved December 20, 2018, from https://www2.deloitte.com/content/dam/Deloitte/uk/Documents/consumer-business/deloitte-uk-consumer-review-16.pdf

Dhaigude, S. A., & Mohan, B. C. (2023). Customer experience in social commerce: A systematic literature review and research agenda. *International Journal of Consumer Studies*, *47*(5), 1629–1668. DOI: 10.1111/ijcs.12954

Dhanawade, M., Nikam, P., & Mane, S. T. (2024). Role of Internet of Things (IOT) in Revolutionizing Digital Marketing. ShodhKosh. *Journal of Visual and Performing Arts*, *5*(6), 767–784.

Dhirani, L. L., Armstrong, E., & Newe, T. (2021). Industrial IoT, cyber threats, and standards landscape: Evaluation and roadmap. *Sensors (Basel)*, *21*(11), 3901. DOI: 10.3390/s21113901 PMID: 34198727

Díaz-Arancibia, J., Hochstetter-Diez, J., Bustamante-Mora, A., Sepúlveda-Cuevas, S., Albayay, I., & Arango-López, J. (2024). Navigating digital transformation and technology adoption: A literature review from small and medium-sized enterprises in developing countries. *Sustainability (Basel)*, *16*(5946), 5946. Advance online publication. DOI: 10.3390/su16145946

Ding, S., Tukker, A., & Ward, H. (2023). Opportunities and risks of internet of things (IoT) technologies for circular business models: A literature review. *Journal of Environmental Management*, *336*, 117662. DOI: 10.1016/j.jenvman.2023.117662

Ding, Y., Jin, M., Li, S., & Feng, D. (2021). Smart logistics based on the Internet of Things technology: An overview. *International Journal of Logistics*, *24*(4), 323–345. DOI: 10.1080/13675567.2020.1757053

Din, I. U., Guizani, M., Hassan, S., Kim, B. S., Khan, M. K., Atiquzzaman, M., & Ahmed, S. H. (2018). The Internet of Things: A review of enabled technologies and future challenges. *IEEE Access : Practical Innovations, Open Solutions, 7*, 7606–7640. DOI: 10.1109/ACCESS.2018.2886601

Dirwan, D., & Latief, F. (2023). Understanding the Psychology Behind Consumer Behavior. *Advances in Business & Industrial Marketing Research, 3*(1), 130–145. DOI: 10.60079/abim.v1i3.201

Dorri, A., Kanhere, S. S., Jurdak, R., & Gauravaram, P. (2017, March). *Blockchain for IoT security and privacy: The case study of a smart home. In 2017 IEEE international conference on pervasive computing and communications workshops (PerCom workshops)*. IEEE.

Dosumu, O. S., Mahame, C., Niyitegeka, S., & Hahiirwuwambaza, J. A. (2023). Applications and challenges of adopting the Internet of Things (IoT) in the Rwandan construction industry. *Journal of Construction in Developing Countries, 28*(2), 81–100. DOI: 10.21315/jcdc-05-22-0098

Dubey, R., Gunasekaran, A., Childe, S. J., Blome, C., & Papadopoulos, T. (2019). Big data and predictive analytics and manufacturing performance: Integrating institutional theory, resource-based view and big data culture. *British Journal of Management, 30*(2), 341–361. DOI: 10.1111/1467-8551.12355

Dutta, A., & Hammad, E. (2020, September). 5G security challenges and opportunities: A system approach. In *2020 IEEE 3rd 5G world forum (5GWF)* (pp. 109-114). IEEE.

Dwivedi, Y. K., Hughes, L., Baabdullah, A. M., Ribeiro-Navarrete, S., Giannakis, M., Al-Debei, M. M., Dennehy, D., Metri, B., Buhalis, D., Cheung, C. M. K., Conboy, K., Doyle, R., Dubey, R., Dutot, V., Felix, R., Goyal, D. P., Gustafsson, A., Hinsch, C., Jebabli, I., & Wamba, S. F. (2022). Metaverse beyond the hype: Multidisciplinary perspectives on emerging challenges, opportunities, and agenda for research, practice and policy. *International Journal of Information Management, 66*, 102542. DOI: 10.1016/j.ijinfomgt.2022.102542

Dwork, C. (2006). Differential privacy. *International Colloquium on Automata, Languages, and Programming*, 1–12.

Ebrahim, A. Q., & van den Berg, C. L. (2024). The barriers to technology adoption among businesses in the informal economy in Cape Town. *South African Journal of Information Management, 26*(1), 1–13. DOI: 10.4102/sajim.v26i1.1872

Edje, A. E., Abd Latiff, M. S., & Chan, W. H. (2023). IoT data analytic algorithms on edge-cloud infrastructure: A review. *Digital Communications and Networks*, *9*(6), 1486–1515. DOI: 10.1016/j.dcan.2023.10.002

Edquist, H., Goodridge, P., & Haskel, J. (2021). The Internet of Things and economic growth in a panel of countries. *Economics of Innovation and New Technology*, *30*(3), 262–283. DOI: 10.1080/10438599.2019.1695941

Egbuhuzor, N. S., Ajayi, A. J., Akhigbe, E. E., & Agbede, O. O. (2024). Leveraging AI and cloud solutions for energy efficiency in large-scale manufacturing. *International Journal of Science and Research Archive*, *13*(2), 4170–4192. DOI: 10.30574/ijsra.2024.13.2.2314

El-Afifi, M. I., Sedhom, B. E., Padmanaban, S., & Eladl, A. A. (2024). A review of IoT-enabled smart energy hub systems: Rising, applications, challenges, and future prospects. *Renewable Energy Focus*, *51*, 100634. DOI: 10.1016/j.ref.2024.100634

Ellström, D., Holtström, J., Berg, E., & Josefsson, C. (2022). Dynamic capabilities for digital transformation. *Journal of Strategy and Management*, *15*(2), 272–286. DOI: 10.1108/JSMA-04-2021-0089

Elmalaki, S. (2021, May). Fair-IoT: Fairness-aware human-in-the-loop reinforcement learning for harnessing human variability in personalised IoT. In *Proceedings of the International Conference on Internet-of-Things Design and Implementation* (pp. 119-132). DOI: 10.1145/3450268.3453525

Emami-Naeini, P., Dheenadhayalan, J., Agarwal, Y., & Cranor, L. F. (2023). Are Consumers Willing to Pay for Security and Privacy of {IoT} Devices. In *32nd USENIX Security Symposium (USENIX Security 23)* (pp. 1505-1522).

Emon, M. M. H. (2025). Circularity Meets AI: Revolutionizing Consumer Engagement Through Green Marketing. In *Transforming Business Practices With AI-Powered Green Marketing* (pp. 169–208). IGI Global Scientific Publishing. DOI: 10.4018/979-8-3373-3017-4.ch007

Emon, M. M. H. (2025a). Ethical Intelligence in Motion: Leveraging AI for Responsible Sourcing in Supply Chain and Logistics. In *Navigating Responsible Business Practices Through Ethical AI* (pp. 207–240). DOI: 10.4018/979-8-3373-3104-1.ch008

Emon, M. M. H. (2025b). Overcoming Hurdles: Navigating Challenges in the Adoption of Smart Logistics. In *Emerging Trends in Smart Logistics Technologies* (A. Hlali, pp. 197–228). IGI Global Scientific Publishing. DOI: 10.4018/979-8-3373-2434-0.ch007

Emon, M. M. H. (2025c). Navigating the Digital Labyrinth: Personal Data Privacy and Security at Individual and Organizational Levels. In *User-Centric Cybersecurity Implications for Sustainable Digital Transformation* (pp. 257–288). IGI Global Scientific Publishing. DOI: 10.4018/979-8-3373-3171-3.ch008

Emon, M. M. H., & Chowdhury, M. S. A. (2025). AI and IoT-Powered Smart Logistics: Transforming Supply Chains for Efficiency and Sustainability. In *Emerging Trends in Smart Logistics Technologies* (A. Hlali, pp. 45–72). IGI Global Scientific Publishing. DOI: 10.4018/979-8-3373-2434-0.ch002

Emon, M. M. H., & Chowdhury, M. S. A. (2025). Safeguarding Student Data: Privacy and Security Challenges in AI-Powered Education Tools. In *Enhancing Student Support and Learning Through Conversational AI* (pp. 191–228). IGI Global Scientific Publishing. DOI: 10.4018/979-8-3373-3316-8.ch008

Emon, M. M. H., & Mazid-Ul-Haque, M. (2025). Balancing Usability and Security: Enhancing User Experience Without Compromising Privacy. In *User-Centric Cybersecurity Implications for Sustainable Digital Transformation* (pp. 309–342). IGI Global Scientific Publishing. DOI: 10.4018/979-8-3373-3171-3.ch010

Emon, M. M. H., Rahman, K. M., Nath, A., Mahsin-Ul-Islam, M., Rifat, H. H., & Kutub, J. (2025). Exploring Drivers of Sustainable E-Commerce Adoption among SMEs in Bangladesh: A TOE Framework Approach for Industry 5.0 Transformation. *2025 IEEE 7th International Conference on Sustainable Technologies For Industry 5.0 (STI)*, 1–6. DOI: 10.1109/STI69347.2025.11367600

Emon, M. M. H. (2025a). Digital transformation in emerging markets: Adoption dynamics of AI image generation in marketing practices. *Telematics and Informatics Reports*, *20*, 100267. DOI: 10.1016/j.teler.2025.100267

Emon, M. M. H. (2025b). Leveraging AI on Social Media & Digital Platforms to Enhance English Language Teaching and Learning. In *AI-Powered English Teaching* (pp. 211–238). IGI Global Scientific Publishing., DOI: 10.4018/979-8-3373-1952-0.ch007

Emon, M. M. H., & Khan, T. (2025). Exploring the mediating role of green logistics in enhancing green supply chain performance: Evidence from Bangladesh. *Journal of Engineering Research*. Advance online publication. DOI: 10.1016/j.jer.2025.10.003

Erhueh, O. V., Elete, T., Akano, O. A., Nwakile, C., & Hanson, E. (2024). Application of Internet of Things (IoT) in energy infrastructure: Lessons for the future of operations and maintenance. *Comprehensive Research and Reviews in Science and Technology*, *2*(2), 28–54. DOI: 10.57219/crrst.2024.2.2.0036

Erjavec, J., & Manfreda, A. (2022). Online shopping adoption during COVID-19 and social isolation: Extending the UTAUT model with herd behavior. *Journal of Retailing and Consumer Services*, *65*, 102867. DOI: 10.1016/j.jretconser.2021.102867

Eslami, E., Razi, N., Lonbani, M., & Rezazadeh, J. (2024). Unveiling IoT Customer Behaviour: Segmentation and Insights for Enhanced IoT-CRM Strategies: A Real Case Study. *Sensors (Basel)*, *24*(4), 1050. DOI: 10.3390/s24041050

Essiz, O., & Senyuz, A. (2024). Predicting the value-based determinants of sustainable luxury consumption: A multi-analytical approach and pathway to sustainable development in the luxury industry. *Business Strategy and the Environment*, *33*(3), 1721–1758. DOI: 10.1002/bse.3569

Etemad, H. (2023). The need for strategic redirection and business model change: The impact of evolving influential forces of change on international entrepreneurship environment. *Journal of International Entrepreneurship*, *21*(4), 441–463. DOI: 10.1007/s10843-024-00348-7

European Commission. (2021). *Industry 5.0: Towards a sustainable, human-centric and resilient European industry*. Publications Office of the European Union.

Evans, M. (2017, January 24). 5 Ways the internet of things will influence commerce. Forbes. Retrieved January 30, 2019, from https://www.forbes.com/sites/michelleevans1/2017/01/24/5-ways-the-internet-of-things-will-influence-commerce

Fagan, M., Marron, J., Brady, K. G.Jr, Cuthill, B. B., Megas, K. N., Herold, R., & Hoehn, B. (2021). Iot device cybersecurity guidance for the federal government. *NIST Special Publication*, *800*, 213.

FakhrHosseini, S., Chan, K., Lee, C., Jeon, M., Son, H., Rudnik, J., & Coughlin, J. FakhrHosseini. (2024). User Adoption of Intelligent Environments: A Review of Technology Adoption Models, Challenges, and Prospects. *International Journal of Human-Computer Interaction*, *40*(4), 986–998. DOI: 10.1080/10447318.2022.2118851

Faraj, S., & Leonardi, P. M. (2022). Strategic organization in the digital age: Rethinking the concept of technology. *Strategic Organization*, *20*(4), 771–785. DOI: 10.1177/14761270221130253

Farhad, M. A. (2024). Consumer data protection laws and their impact on business models in the tech industry. *Telecommunications Policy*, *48*(9), 102836. DOI: 10.1016/j.telpol.2024.102836

Ferreira, J. J., Fernandes, C. I., Rammal, H. G., & Veiga, P. M. (2021). Wearable technology and consumer interaction: A systematic review and research agenda. *Computers in Human Behavior*, *118*, 106710. DOI: 10.1016/j.chb.2021.106710

Ferro-Escobar, R., Vacca-González, H., & Gómez-Castillo, H. (2022). Smart and sustainable cities in collaboration with IoT: the Singapore success case. In *Machine learning for smart environments/cities: An IoT approach* (pp. 213–243). Springer International Publishing. DOI: 10.1007/978-3-030-97516-6_12

Fink, A. (2019). *Conducting research literature reviews: From the Internet to paper* (5th ed.). SAGE Publications.

Floridi, L., Cowls, J., Beltrametti, M., Chatila, R., Chazerand, P., Dignum, V., & Schafer, B. (2018). AI4People—An ethical framework for a good AI society: Opportunities, risks, principles, and recommendations. *Minds and Machines*, *28*(4), 689–707. DOI: 10.1007/s11023-018-9482-5

Fortino, G., Guerrieri, A., Pace, P., Savaglio, C., & Spezzano, G. (2022). IoT Platforms and Security: An Analysis of the Leading Industrial/Commercial Solutions. *Sensors (Basel)*, *22*(6), 2196. DOI: 10.3390/s22062196 PMID: 35336368

Fox, P., Rezania, D., Wareham, J., & Christiaanse, E. (2006). Will mobiles dream of electric sheep? Expectations of the new generation of mobile users: Misfits with practice and research. In Proceedings of the International Conference on Mobile Business (ICMB 2006). Copenhagen.

Frambach, R. T., Roest, H. C. A., & Krishnan, T. V. (2007). The impact of consumer internet experience on channel preference and usage intentions across the different stages of the buying process. *Journal of Interactive Marketing*, *21*(2), 26–41. DOI: 10.1002/dir.20079

Fuller, A., Fan, Z., Day, C., & Barlow, C. (2020). Digital twin: Enabling technologies, challenges and open research. *IEEE Access : Practical Innovations, Open Solutions*, *8*, 108952–108971. DOI: 10.1109/ACCESS.2020.2998358

Gadre, M., & Deoskar, A. (2020). Industry 4.0–digital transformation, challenges and benefits. *International Journal of Future Generation Communication and Networking*, *13*(2), 139–149.

Gaiseb, R. (2025) N$120m to bridge the digital divide. New Era Publication. https://neweralive.na/n120m-to-bridge-digital-divide/

Garczarek-Bak, U., Szymkowiak, A., Jaks, Z., & Jansto, E. (2024). Impact of product vs brand storytelling on online customer experience. *International Journal of Wine Business Research*, *36*(3), 370–405. DOI: 10.1108/IJWBR-07-2023-0041

Garrity, J. (2015). Harnessing the Internet of Things for global development. In SSRN *Electronic Journal* (pp. 1–61). DOI: 10.2139/ssrn.2588129

Gartner. (2021). *Consumer perceptions of IoT and privacy.*

Gartoumi, K. I., & Tekouabou, S. C. K. (2024). Exploring African skills 4.0 required for 4IR industry: A systematic literature review. *Data & Policy*, *6*(36), e36. Advance online publication. DOI: 10.1017/dap.2024.28

Gaur, A., Scotney, B., Parr, G., & McClean, S. (2015). Smart city architecture and its applications based on iot. *Procedia Computer Science*, *52*, 1089–1094. DOI: 10.1016/j.procs.2015.05.122

Gefen, D. (2000). E-commerce: The role of familiarity and trust. *Omega*, *28*(6), 725–737. DOI: 10.1016/S0305-0483(00)00021-9

Gefen, D., Karahanna, E., & Straub, D. W. (2003). Trust and TAM in online shopping. *Management Information Systems Quarterly*, *27*(1), 51–90. DOI: 10.2307/30036519

Gerli, P., Clement, J., Esposito, G., Mora, L., & Crutzen, N. (2022). The hidden power of emotions: How psychological factors influence skill development in smart technology adoption. *Technological Forecasting and Social Change*, *180*, 121721. Advance online publication. DOI: 10.1016/j.techfore.2022.121721

Gfrerer, A., Hutter, K., & Ströhle, T. (2021). Ready or not: Managers' and employees' different perceptions of digital readiness. *California Management Review*, *63*(2), 94–117. DOI: 10.1177/0008125620977487

Gilbert, M. A. (2024). *Disrupting Marketing*., DOI: 10.4018/979-8-3693-4361-6.ch002

Gokhale, P., Bhat, O., & Bhat, S. (2018). Introduction to IOT. *International Advanced Research Journal in Science. Engineering and Technology*, *5*(1), 41–44.

Gotsch, M. L., & Schögel, M. (2023). Addressing the privacy paradox on the organizational level: Review and future directions. *Management Review Quarterly*, *73*(1), 263–296. DOI: 10.1007/s11301-021-00239-4

Govinda, K., & Saravanaguru, R. A. K. (2016). Review on IOT technologies. *International Journal of Applied Engineering Research: IJAER*, *11*(4), 2848–2853.

Goyal, P., Sahoo, A. K., & Sharma, T. K. (2021). Internet of things: Architecture and enabling technologies. *Materials Today: Proceedings*, *34*, 719–735. DOI: 10.1016/j.matpr.2020.04.678

Granić, A. (2022). Technology acceptance and adoption in education. In *Handbook of open, distance and digital education* (pp. 1–15). Springer Singapore. DOI: 10.1007/978-981-19-0351-9_11-1

Greenberg, A. (2015, July 21). Hackers Remotely Kill a Jeep on the Highway—With Me in It. Wired. https://www.wired.com/2015/07/hackers-remotely-kill-jeep-highway/

Greenhalgh, T., Thorne, S., & Malterud, K. (2018). Time to challenge the spurious hierarchy of systematic over narrative reviews? *European Journal of Clinical Investigation*, *48*(6), 1–13. DOI: 10.1111/eci.12931

Greenleaf, G. (2020). California's CCPA 2.0: Does the US Finally Have a Data Privacy Act?.

GSMA. (2022). *The Mobile Gender Gap Report 2022*. GSMA.

Gubbi, J., Buyya, R., Marusic, S., & Palaniswami, M. (2013). Internet of Things (IoT): A vision, architectural elements, and future directions. *Future Generation Computer Systems*, *29*(7), 1645–1660. DOI: 10.1016/j.future.2013.01.010

Guhr, N., Werth, O., Blacha, P. P. H., & Breitner, M. H. (2020). Privacy concerns in the smart home context. *SN Applied Sciences*, *2*(247), 247. Advance online publication. DOI: 10.1007/s42452-020-2025-8

Guido, G. (2025). Godfather Marketing: Offering favors before products. *Review of Managerial Science*, *19*(4), 1095–1129. DOI: 10.1007/s11846-024-00785-7

Gunning, D. (2017). *Explainable artificial intelligence (XAI)*. Defense Advanced Research Projects Agency (DARPA).

Guo, L., Hu, X., Lu, J., & Ma, L. (2021). Effects of customer trust on engagement in live streaming commerce: Mediating role of swift guanxi. *Internet Research*, *31*(5), 1718–1744. DOI: 10.1108/INTR-02-2020-0078

Gupta, S., Leszkiewicz, A., Kumar, V., Bijmolt, T., & Potapov, D. (2020). Digital analytics: Modeling for insights and new methods. *Journal of Interactive Marketing*, *51*(1), 26–43. DOI: 10.1016/j.intmar.2020.04.003

Gyrard, A., Zimmermann, A., & Sheth, A. (2018). Building IoT-based applications for smart cities: How can ontology catalogs help. *IEEE Internet of Things Journal*, *5*(5), 3978–3990. DOI: 10.1109/JIOT.2018.2854278 PMID: 34734100

Haleem, A., Javaid, M., Pratap Singh, R., & Suman, R. (2023). Exploring the revolution in healthcare systems through the applications of digital twin technology. *Biomedical Technology*, *4*, 28–38. DOI: 10.1016/j.bmt.2023.02.001

Halkos, G., & Nomikos, S. (2021). Corporate social responsibility: Trends in global reporting initiative standards. *Economic Analysis and Policy*, *69*, 106–117. DOI: 10.1016/j.eap.2020.11.008

Hammi, B., Zeadally, S., Khatoun, R., & Nebhen, J. (2022). Survey on smart homes: Vulnerabilities, risks, and countermeasures. *Computers & Security*, *117*, 102677. DOI: 10.1016/j.cose.2022.102677

Hamukwaya, P. S., & Nautwima, J. P. (2019). Does microfinance really eradicate poverty in Africa? *Africa Growth Agenda, 16*(2).

Harkin, D., Mann, M., & Warren, I. (2022). Consumer IoT and its under-regulation: Findings from an Australian study. *Policy and Internet*, *14*(1), 96–113. DOI: 10.1002/poi3.285

Hartl, E., & Hess, T. (2017). The role of cultural values for digital transformation: Insights from a delphi study. *Twenty-Third Americas Conference on Information Systems, 23*, 1–10.

Hartson, H. R. (2003). Cognitive, physical, sensory, and functional affordances in interaction design. *Behaviour & Information Technology*, *22*(5), 315–338. DOI: 10.1080/01449290310001592587

Hasan, H., & Kazlauskas, A. (2014). Activity theory: Who is doing what, why and how. In Hasan, H. (Ed.), *Being practical with theory. A window into business research* (pp. 9–14). THEORI.

Hassan El-Annan, S., & Hassoun, R. (2024). *Enhancing Consumer Trust Through Transparent Data Practices and Ethical Data Management in Business.*, DOI: 10.4018/979-8-3693-8357-5.ch005

Hassan, M. M., Fahim Abrar, M., Kakon, S., Hossen, A., & Arafat, Y. (2024). Improving Loan Approval Decisions: The Impact of Data Balancing on the Classifier's Performance in Predicting Borrower Reliability. *2024 27th International Conference on Computer and Information Technology (ICCIT)*, 1690–1695. DOI: 10.1109/ICCIT64611.2024.11022094

Hassan, M. M., Hossen, A., Arafat, Y., Sarker, M. N., Jamil, M. H., & Siddika, A. (2025). Exploratory Analysis of the Impact of Data Balancing on the Classifier's Performance in Predicting Creditworthiness Reliability. [IJEEI]. *Indonesian Journal of Electrical Engineering and Informatics*, *13*(3). Advance online publication. DOI: 10.52549/ijeei.v13i3.6667

Hassan, M. M., Hossen, A., Sarker, M. N., Arafat, Y., Khan, A., Talukder, S. I., & Roy, B. K. S. (2025). An Empirical Analysis on Renewable Energy: Biogas Production Prediction Using Machine Learning. *Journal of Power and Energy Engineering*, *13*(07), 40–59. DOI: 10.4236/jpee.2025.137002

Hauser, S., Redström, J., & Wiltse, H. (2023). The widening rift between aesthetics and ethics in the design of computational things. *AI & Society*, *38*(1), 227–243. DOI: 10.1007/s00146-021-01279-w

Hautamäki, J., & Kokkonen, T. (2020, June). Model for cyber security information sharing in healthcare sector. In *2020 International Conference on Electrical, Communication, and Computer Engineering (ICECCE)* (pp. 1-5). IEEE. DOI: 10.1109/ICECCE49384.2020.9179175

Hay, N. A., Chien, P. M., & Ruhanen, L. (2022). Tell me your story: Branding destinations through residents' (place) stories. *Journal of Vacation Marketing*, *28*(3), 319–334. DOI: 10.1177/13567667211060567

Hildebrandt, G., Dittler, D., Habiger, P., Drath, R., & Weyrich, M. (2024). Data integration for digital twins in industrial automation: A systematic literature review. *IEEE Access : Practical Innovations, Open Solutions*, *12*, 139129–139153. DOI: 10.1109/ACCESS.2024.3465632

Hill, K. (2012, February 16). How Target figured out a teen girl was pregnant before her father did. Forbes. Available at: https://www.forbes.com/sites/kashmirhill/2012/02/16/how-target-figured-out-a-teen-girl-was-pregnant-before-her-father-did/

Hooda, A., Gupta, P., Jeyaraj, A., Giannakis, M., & Dwivedi, Y. K. (2022). The effects of trust on behavioral intention and use behavior within e-government contexts. *International Journal of Information Management*, *67*, 102553. DOI: 10.1016/j.ijinfomgt.2022.102553

Hossen, A., Arafat, Y., Sarker, M. N., Jamil, M. H., Islam, M. A., & Hasan, R. (2024). A Predictive Framework for Financial Crashes Using Advanced Time Series Techniques. *2024 International Conference on Progressive Innovations in Intelligent Systems and Data Science (ICPIDS)*, 476–483. DOI: 10.1109/ICPIDS65698.2024.00080

Hoyer, W. D., Kroschke, M., Schmitt, B., Kraume, K., & Shankar, V. (2020). Transforming the Customer Experience through New Technologies. *Journal of Interactive Marketing*, *51*(1), 57–71. DOI: 10.1016/j.intmar.2020.04.001

Hsu, C. W., & Yeh, C. C. (2017). Understanding the factors affecting the adoption of the Internet of Things. *Technology Analysis and Strategic Management*, *29*(9), 1089–1102. DOI: 10.1080/09537325.2016.1269160

Ikpe, A. & Ohwoekevwo, J. (2024). Intelligent Transportation Systems as a Pivotal Instrument in the Development of Smart Cities in the 21st Century.

International Telecommunication Union (ITU). (2023). Measuring digital development: Facts and figures 2023.

International Telecommunication Union. (2023). Measuring digital development. https://demo.ifgict.org/wp-content/uploads/2024/09/ITU-Report-on-Measuring-digital-development.pdf

Israr, A., Yang, Q., Li, W., & Zomaya, A. Y. (2021). Renewable energy powered sustainable 5G network infrastructure: Opportunities, challenges and perspectives. *Journal of Network and Computer Applications*, *175*(102910), 1–24. DOI: 10.1016/j.jnca.2020.102910

Issa, A., Hatiboglu, B., Bildstein, A., & Bauernhansl, T. (2018). Industrie 4.0 roadmap: Framework for digital transformation based on the concepts of capability maturity and alignment. *Procedia CIRP*, *72*, 973–978. DOI: 10.1016/j.procir.2018.03.151

Issock Issock, P. B., Roberts-Lombard, M., & Mpinganjira, M. (2020). The importance of customer trust for social marketing interventions: A case of energy-efficiency consumption. *Journal of Social Marketing*, *10*(2), 265–286. DOI: 10.1108/JSOCM-05-2019-0071

ITU Publication Africa. (2021). Digital trends in Africa 2021: Information and communication technology trends and developments in the Africa region 2017-2020. In *International Telecommunication Union Publication* (Vols. 2017–2020). https://elibrary.acbfpact.org/acbf/collect/acbf/index/assoc/HASH0146/faa3ee36/f864265c/9547.dir/Digital trends in Africa 2021.pdf

Iwayemi, A. (2018). Internet of Things: Implementation challenges in Nigeria. *American Journal of Engineering Research (AJER*, *7*(12), 105–115. www.ajer.org

Jaffrin, L. C., Nithya, T., & Divya, J. (2025, April). IoT for Sustainable Development: Enhancing Environmental Efficiency and Resource Optimization. In *2025 5th International Conference on Trends in Material Science and Inventive Materials (ICTMIM)* (pp. 1224-1230). IEEE.

Jamil, M. H., Hossen, A., Talukder, S. I., Arafat, Y., & Sozib, H. M. (2025). Big Data Analytics and Its Usage on Financial Fraud Detection in the USA. *Advances in Machine Learning IoT and Data Security*, *1*, amlid25001. Advance online publication. DOI: 10.63471/amlid25001

Javaid, M., Haleem, A., Singh, R. P., Rab, S., & Suman, R. (2021). Internet of Behaviours (IoB) and its role in customer services. *Sensors International*, *2*, 100122. DOI: 10.1016/j.sintl.2021.100122

Jayashankar, P., Nilakanta, S., Johnston, W. J., Gill, P., & Burres, R. (2018). IoT adoption in agriculture: The role of trust, perceived value and risk. *Journal of Business and Industrial Marketing*, *33*(6), 804–821. Advance online publication. DOI: 10.1108/JBIM-01-2018-0023

Jinxuan, T., Tianjun, M., & Qianwen, L. (2020). Trends Prediction of Big Data: A Case Study based on Fusion Data, Procedia Computer Science, Volume 174, Pages 181-190, ISSN 1877-0509, https://doi.org/DOI: 10.1016/j.procs.2020.06.073

Johnson, S. D., Blythe, J. M., Manning, M., & Wong, G. T. (2020). The impact of IoT security labelling on consumer product choice and willingness to pay. *PLoS One*, *15*(1), e0227800. DOI: 10.1371/journal.pone.0227800 PMID: 31978096

Joshi, A., Moschetta, G., & Winslow, E. (2025). Global cybersecurity outlook 2025. In *World Economic Forum (WEF), Geneva, Switzerland, Tech. Rep* (Vol. 1).

Judijanto, L., Triwiyatno, A., & Sofyan, S. (2024). The influence of Internet of Things (IoT) on operational efficiency and competitive advantage in the information technology industry in Indonesia. *The Eastasouth Journal of Information System and Computer Science, 1*(3), 155–166. arXiv+1BW Journal+1DOI: 10.58812/esiscs.v1i03.240

Junglas, I., & Watson, R. (2003). U-commerce: A conceptual extension of e-commerce and m-commerce. In Proceedings of the International Conference on Information Systems (ICIS 2003) (Article 55).

Kahneman, D., & Tversky, A. (1979). Prospect theory: An analysis of decision under risk. *Econometrica*, *47*(2), 263–291. DOI: 10.2307/1914185

Kala, E. (2023). Challenges of Technology in African Countries: A Case Study of Zambia. *Open Journal of Safety Science and Technology*, *13*(4), 202–230. DOI: 10.4236/ojsst.2023.134011

Kamutuezu, E.U., Winschiers-Tehophilus, H. & Peters, A. (2021). AN exploration of factors influencing the adoption of ictenabled entrepreneurship applications in Namibian ruralcommunities.

Kang, J., Hong, S., & Hubbard, G. T. (2020). The role of storytelling in advertising: Consumer emotion, narrative engagement level, and word-of-mouth intention. *Journal of Consumer Behaviour*, *19*(1), 47–56. DOI: 10.1002/cb.1793

Kang, M. J., & Hwang, Y. C. (2022). Exploring the Factors Affecting the Continued Usage Intention of IoT-Based Healthcare Wearable Devices Using the TAM Model. *Sustainability (Basel)*, *14*(19), 12492. DOI: 10.3390/su141912492

Karie, N. M., Sahri, N. M., Yang, W., Valli, C., & Kebande, V. R. (2021). A review of security standards and frameworks for IoT-based smart environments. *IEEE Access : Practical Innovations, Open Solutions*, *9*, 121975–121995. DOI: 10.1109/ACCESS.2021.3109886

Kashyap, R. (2019). Machine Learning, data mining for IOT-based systems. In *Handbook of Research on Big Data and the IoT* (pp. 314–338). IGI Global. DOI: 10.4018/978-1-5225-7432-3.ch018

Kees, A., Oberländer, A. M., Röglinger, M., & Rosemann, M. (2015). Understanding the internet of things: A conceptualisation of business-to-thing (b2t) interactions. In Proceedings of the 23th European Conference on Information Systems (ECIS 2015) (article 92).

Khalid, H. G., Abbas, H. H., Hussein, M. J., Abu-AlShaeer, M. J., Mukhlif, S. K., & Khlaponin, D. (2024). Unveiling the Next Frontier: The Future of Connected Technologies. *2024 36th Conference of Open Innovations Association (FRUCT)*, 207–218. DOI: 10.23919/FRUCT64283.2024.10749851

Khalifa, M., & Albadawy, M. (2024). AI in diagnostic imaging: Revolutionising accuracy and efficiency. *Computer Methods and Programs in Biomedicine Update*, *5*, 100146. DOI: 10.1016/j.cmpbup.2024.100146

Khan, T., & Emon, M. M. H. (2025a). Preparing for the Next Disruption: Lessons Learned From Past Crises and Building a Playbook for Future Supply Chain Shocks. In *Supply Chain Disruptions and Impact on Global Inflation* (pp. 253–286). IGI Global Scientific Publishing. DOI: 10.4018/979-8-3373-1982-7.ch010

Khan, T., & Emon, M. M. H. (2025b). Resilient Supply Chains: Lessons From Past Crisis Strategies Companies Can Adopt to Create More Resilient Supply Chains. In *Mass Media and Impact of Fake News on Supply Chains* (pp. 285–318). IGI Global. DOI: 10.4018/979-8-3373-2175-2.ch011

Khan, T., & Hasan Emon, M. M. (2024). Determinants of AI Image Generator Adoption Among Marketing Agencies: The Mediating Effects of Perceived Usefulness. *2024 IEEE 3rd International Conference on Robotics, Automation, Artificial-Intelligence and Internet-of-Things (RAAICON)*, 177–182. DOI: 10.1109/RAAICON64172.2024.10928548

Khan, T., Emon, M. M. H., & Nath, A. (2024). Quantifying the Effects of AI-Driven Inventory Management on Operational Efficiency in Online Retail. *2024 27th International Conference on Computer and Information Technology (ICCIT)*, 2092–2097. DOI: 10.1109/ICCIT64611.2024.11021996

Khan, T., Emon, M. M. H., Rahman, M. A., Hamid, A. B. A., Yaakub, N. I., Abdul Hamid, A. B., & Ya'akub, N. I. B. (2024). Bridging the Gap: Realizing Green-Tech Potential. *AI and Green Technology Applications in Society*, 91–121. DOI: 10.4018/979-8-3693-9879-1.ch004

Khan, P. W., Byun, Y.-C., & Park, N. (2020). IoT-Blockchain Enabled Optimized Provenance System for Food Industry 4.0 Using Advanced Deep Learning. *Sensors (Basel)*, *20*(10), 2990. DOI: 10.3390/s20102990 PMID: 32466209

Khan, S., Parkinson, S., Grant, L., Liu, N., & Mcguire, S. (2020). Biometric systems utilising health data from wearable devices: Applications and future challenges in computer security. *ACM Computing Surveys*, *53*(4), 1–29. DOI: 10.1145/3400030

Khan, T., & Emon, M. M. H. (2025). The role of digital supply chain practices in enhancing firm performance: Insights from the manufacturing sector of Bangladesh. *Brazilian Journal of Operations & Production Management*, *22*(2), 2493. DOI: 10.14488/BJOPM.2493.2025

Khan, T., Emon, M. M. H., Rahman, K. M., Nipa, M. N., & Fuad, M. N. (2025). The Role of AI in Driving Customer Engagement Through Technological, Organizational and Environmental Enablers in E-Commerce. *2025 International Conference on Quantum Photonics, Artificial Intelligence, and Networking (QPAIN)*, 1–6. DOI: 10.1109/QPAIN66474.2025.11171949

Khan, W. U.Waseem Ullah Khan. (2025). The business value of IoT and big data analytics. *Journal of Business and Management Studies*, *7*(1), 279–283. DOI: 10.32996/jbms.2025.7.1.23

Kim, H. J., Park, S. Y., & Park, H. Y. (2018). A study on the effect of storytelling marketing on brand image and brand attitude. *Journal of Economics, Marketing, and Management*, *6*(4), 1–16. DOI: 10.20482/jemm.2018.6.4.1

Kim, J., Kim, M., & Lee, S.-M. (2025). Unlocking Trust Dynamics: An Exploration of Playfulness, Expertise, and Consumer Behavior in Virtual Influencer Marketing. *International Journal of Human-Computer Interaction*, *41*(1), 378–390. DOI: 10.1080/10447318.2023.2300018

Kim, K. J., & Wang, S. (2021). Understanding the acceptance of the Internet of Things: An integrative theoretical approach. *Aslib Journal of Information Management*, *73*(5), 754–771. DOI: 10.1108/AJIM-03-2021-0073

Kim, M., & Cho, I. (2024). Navigating user discontent in wearable tech: An in-depth study of Fitbit reviews. *Technology Analysis and Strategic Management*, •••, 1–15. DOI: 10.1080/09537325.2024.2408727

Kindervag, J. (2010). *No more chewy centers: Introducing the zero trust model of information security*. Forrester Research.

Kingdon, A. (2024). *Socio-Technical and Multi-stakeholder Approaches to Countering Online Propaganda*., DOI: 10.1007/978-3-031-75393-0_8

King, R. (2022). The utility of pragmatism in educational research. *Creative Education, 13*(10), 3153–3161. DOI: 10.4236/ce.2022.1310199

Kioufi, N., & Chen, W. (2023). Exploring IoT adoption and operational efficiency within the international chilled beverages industry. *Journal of Industrial and Production Engineering, 41*(2), 158–181. DOI: 10.1080/21681015.2023.2270994

Koh, W. P., & Chin, K. K. (2022). The applicability of prospect theory in examining drivers' trip decisions, in response to Electronic Road Pricing (ERP) rates adjustments - a study using travel data in Singapore. *Transportation Research Part A, Policy and Practice, 155*, 115–127. DOI: 10.1016/j.tra.2021.11.012

Kolias, C., Kambourakis, G., Stavrou, A., & Voas, J. (2017). DDoS in the IoT: Mirai and other botnets. *Computer, 50*(7), 80–84. DOI: 10.1109/MC.2017.201

Korneeva, E., Olinder, N., & Strielkowski, W. (2021). Consumer Attitudes to the Smart Home Technologies and the Internet of Things (IoT). *Energies, 14*(23), 7913. DOI: 10.3390/en14237913

Kortjan, N., & Solms, R. (2014). A conceptual framework for cyber security awareness and education in SA. *South African Computer Journal = Suid-Afrikaanse Rekenaartydskrif, 52*(52), 29–41. DOI: 10.18489/sacj.v52i0.201

Krebs, B. (2016). Who makes the IoT Things Attacking https://www.google.com/search?q=BrianKrebs.com? KrebsOnSecurity. https://krebsonsecurity.com/2016/10/who-makes-the-iot-things-attacking-briankrebs-com/

Kronlid, C., Brantnell, A., Elf, M., Borg, J., & Palm, K. Sociotechnical analysis of factors influencing IoT adoption in healthcare: A systematic review. *Technology in Society* 78 (2024) 102675. ISSN 0160-791X, https://doi.org/DOI: 10.1016/j.techsoc.2024.102675

Kuaban, G. S., Nkemeni, V., Nwobodo, O. J., Czekalski, P., & Mieyeville, F. (2024). Internet of Things adoption in technology ecosystems within the Central African Region: The case of Silicon Mountain. *Future Internet, 16*(10), 376. Advance online publication. DOI: 10.3390/fi16100376

Kuiler, E. W., & McNeely, C. L. (2023). Panopticon implications of ethical AI: equity, disparity, and inequality in healthcare. In *AI Assurance* (pp. 429–451). Elsevier., DOI: 10.1016/B978-0-32-391919-7.00026-3

Kumar, A., Dhingra, S., & Falwadiya, H. (2023). Adoption of internet of things: A systematic literature review and future research agenda. *International Journal of Consumer Studies*, *47*(6), 2553–2582. DOI: 10.1111/ijcs.12964

Kumar, A., Saudagar, A. K. J., & Khan, M. B. (2024). Enhanced medical education for physically disabled people through integration of IoT and digital twin technologies. *Systems*, *12*(9), 325. DOI: 10.3390/systems12090325

Kumar, K. V. R., Kumar, K. D., Poluru, R. K., Basha, S. M., & Reddy, M. P. K. (2020). Internet of things and fog computing applications in intelligent transportation systems. In *Architecture and security issues in fog computing applications* (pp. 131–150). IGI Global. DOI: 10.4018/978-1-7998-0194-8.ch008

Kumar, S., & Mallipeddi, R. R. (2022). Impact of cybersecurity on operations and supply chain management: Emerging trends and future research directions. *Production and Operations Management*, *31*(12), 4488–4500. DOI: 10.1111/poms.13859

Kumo, W. (2023). Leveraging consumer behavior research for effective marketing strategies. *Advances in Business & Industrial Marketing Research*, *1*(3), 117–129. DOI: 10.60079/abim.v1i3.196

Kwakye, E. (2023). Unraveling the Privacy Paradox: Smart Home IoT Adoption Dynamics in Saudi Arabia. DOI: 10.13140/RG.2.2.25471.21923

La Diega, N. (2023). *Internet of things and the law: legal strategies for consumer-centric smart technologies*. Taylor & Francis.

Ladeira, W. J., Lim, W. M., de Oliveira Santini, F., Rasul, T., Frantz, B., de Oliveira Rosa, J. C., & Azhar, M. (2025). Consumer adoption of internet of things. *Journal of Consumer Behaviour*, *24*(2), 673–693. DOI: 10.1002/cb.2427

Lau, J., Zimmerman, B., & Schaub, F. (2018). Alexa, are you listening? Privacy perceptions, concerns and privacy-seeking behaviors with smart speakers. *Proceedings of the ACM on Human-Computer Interaction, 2*(CSCW), 1–31.

Lee, A. T., Ramasamy, R. K., & Subbarao, A. (2025). Understanding Psychosocial Barriers to Healthcare Technology Adoption: A Review of TAM Technology Acceptance Model and Unified Theory of Acceptance and Use of Technology and UTAUT Frameworks. *Healthcare (Basel)*, *13*(3), 250. DOI: 10.3390/healthcare13030250

Lee, C.-H., Yang, H.-C., Wei, Y.-C., & Hsu, W.-K. (2021). Enabling Blockchain Based SCM Systems with a Real Time Event Monitoring Function for Preemptive Risk Management. *Applied Sciences (Basel, Switzerland), 11*(11), 4811. DOI: 10.3390/app11114811

Lee, I., & Lee, K. (2015). The Internet of Things (IoT): Applications, investments, and challenges for enterprises. *Business Horizons, 58*(4), 431–440. DOI: 10.1016/j.bushor.2015.03.008

Lee, M. L., & Kobsa, A. (2016). Understanding user privacy in IoT. *IEEE Security and Privacy, 14*(2), 36–44.

Lee, S. M., Hwang, T., & Lee, D. H. (2011). Evolution of research areas, themes, and methods in electronic commerce. *Journal of Organizational Computing and Electronic Commerce, 21*(3), 177–201. DOI: 10.1080/10919392.2011.590095

Leoneti, A. B., & Gomes, L. F. A. M. (2021). A novel version of the TODIM method based on the exponential model of prospect theory: The ExpTODIM method. *European Journal of Operational Research, 295*(3), 1042–1055. DOI: 10.1016/j.ejor.2021.03.055

Liang, W., Rajuroy, A., Chaudhary, P., Cai, M., & Johnson Mary, B. (2025). IoT and Cultural Knowledge in Transforming Healthcare Operations.

Li, J.-Y., Lee, Y., Tao, W., Xu, D., & Dong, E. (2024). Organizations with True Heart: The Role of Organizational Identity in Shaping Consumer Attributions of Corporate Responsibility to Race (CRR) Motives. *Journal of Public Relations Research, 36*(4), 320–340. DOI: 10.1080/1062726X.2023.2298864

Lin, D., Lee, C. K. M., & Lin, K. (2016). Research on effect factors evaluation of internet of things (IOT) adoption in Chinese agricultural supply chain. *IEEE International Conference on Industrial Engineering and Engineering Management (IEEM)*, Bali, Indonesia, 2016, pp. 612-615, DOI: 10.1109/IEEM.2016.7797948

Liu, A., Urquía-Grande, E., López-Sánchez, P., & Rodríguez-López, Á. (2024). The power of play in microfinance: Examining the effect of gamification on customer relationship management performance. *Journal of Behavioral and Experimental Finance, 44*, 100972. Advance online publication. DOI: 10.1016/j.jbef.2024.100972

Liu, S. (2023). Digital transformation of enterprises in the mode of IoT - A case study of Haier. *Proceedings of the 2nd International Conference on Financial Technology and Business Analysis, 2*(1), 52–61. DOI: 10.54254/2754-1169/64/20231488

Lizhen, S.H.I, Huang, X., Abbas, S., Yang, Z. & Huang, L. (2022). The Relationships Between Perceived Usefulness and Fitness Wearable Technology User Adoption Mediated by Culture, Gender, and COVID-19: A Meta-Analysis. Quality in Sport. 2022;8(1):55-69. eISSN 2450-3118. DOI http://dx.doi.org/DOI: 10.12775/QS.2021.08.01.005

Lokare, A., Bankar, S., & Mhaske, P. (2025). Integrating Cybersecurity Frameworks into IT Security: A Comprehensive Analysis of Threat Mitigation Strategies and Adaptive Technologies.

Lorenz, F., & Buchwald, A. (2023). Chief digital officers' social construction of and coping with digital transformation. *Academy of Management Proceedings, 2023*(1). DOI: 10.5465/AMPROC.2023.11220abstract

Luiz, J., Stringfellow, D., & Jefthas, A. (2017). Institutional complementarity and substitution as an internationalization strategy: The emergence of an African multinational giant. *Global Strategy Journal*, *7*(1), 83–103. DOI: 10.1002/gsj.1143

Luo, H., Luo, J., & Vasilakos, A. V. (2024). BC4LLM: A perspective of trusted artificial intelligence when blockchain meets large language models. *Neurocomputing*, *599*, 128089. DOI: 10.1016/j.neucom.2024.128089

Lupton, D. (2016). *The quantified self.* John Wiley & Sons.

Macheka, T., Quaye, E. S., & Ligaraba, N. (2024). The effect of online customer reviews and celebrity endorsement on young female consumers' purchase intentions. *Young Consumers*, *25*(4), 462–482. DOI: 10.1108/YC-05-2023-1749

Madden, M. (2014), Public perceptions of privacy and security in the age of smart devices. Pew Research Center. https://www.pewresearch.org/internet/2014/11/12/public-privacy-perceptions/

Madgule, M., Vinayaka, N., Sonkhaskar, Y. M., Patel, D. R., Karthikeyan, R., & Selvakumar, P. (2023). Mechanical properties and microstructure of activated TIG welded similar joints of Inconel alloys by desirability approaches. *Materials Today: Proceedings*, *77*, 528–533.

Madhavaram, S. (2024). Chartering marketing strategy and marketing management research toward greater relevance and impact. *Journal of Business Research*, *178*, 114667. Advance online publication. DOI: 10.1016/j.jbusres.2024.114667

Ma, G., Ma, J., Li, H., Wang, Y., Wang, Z., & Zhang, B. (2022). Customer behavior in purchasing energy-saving products: Big data analytics from online reviews of e-commerce. *Energy Policy*, *165*, 112960. DOI: 10.1016/j.enpol.2022.112960

Maio, R., Araújo, T., Marques, B., Santos, A., Ramalho, P., Almeida, D., Dias, P., & Santos, B. S. (2024). Pervasive Augmented Reality to support real-time data monitoring in industrial scenarios: Shop floor visualization evaluation and user study. *Computers & Graphics*, *118*, 11–22. DOI: 10.1016/j.cag.2023.10.025

Malatji, M. (2023, January). Management of enterprise cyber security: A review of ISO/IEC 27001: 2022. In *2023 International conference on cyber management and engineering (CyMaEn)* (pp. 117-122). IEEE. DOI: 10.1109/CyMaEn57228.2023.10051114

Malhotra, P., Singh, Y., Anand, P., Bangotra, D. K., Singh, P. K., & Hong, W.-C. (2021). Internet of Things: Evolution, Concerns and Security Challenges. *Sensors (Basel)*, *21*(5), 1809. DOI: 10.3390/s21051809 PMID: 33807724

Malik, S. (2024). Data-driven decision-making: Leveraging the IoT for real-time sustainability in organizational behavior. *Sustainability (Basel)*, *16*(15), 6302. DOI: 10.3390/su16156302

Malodia, S., Kaur, P., Ractham, P., Sakashita, M., & Dhir, A. (2022). Why do people avoid and postpone the use of voice assistants for transactional purposes? A perspective from decision avoidance theory. *Journal of Business Research*, *146*, 605–618. DOI: 10.1016/j.jbusres.2022.03.045

Manoharan, G., Ashtikar, S. P., Nivedha, M., & Dutta, P. K. (2024). *Tailoring the Future—The Ascendancy of Artificial Intelligence in the Fashion Industry* (pp. 503–520). DOI: 10.1007/978-3-031-71052-0_20

Mansilla, D. C., Irizar, A. M., Garaizar, P., & Ipina, D. L. (2019). On the Side Effects of Automation in IoT: Complacency and Comfort vs. *Relapse and Distrust. CHI Workshop*, Glasgow, UK

Marikyan, D., & Papagiannidis, S. (2024). Technology Acceptance Model: A review. In Papagiannidis, S. (Ed.), *TheoryHub Book*., Available at https://open.ncl.ac.uk /

Martin, K., & Murphy, P. E. (2017). The role of data privacy in marketing. *Journal of the Academy of Marketing Science*, *45*(2), 135–155. DOI: 10.1007/s11747-016-0495-4

Marx, C., de Paula, D., & Uebernickel, F. (2021). Dynamic capabilities & digital transformation: A quantitative study on how to gain a competitive advantage in the digital age. *European Conference on Information Systems (ECIS)*. https://aisel.aisnet.org/ecis2021_rp/58

Ma, S., Ding, W., Liu, Y., Ren, S., & Yang, H. (2022). Digital twin and big data-driven sustainable smart manufacturing based on information management systems for energy-intensive industries. *Applied Energy*, *326*, 119986. DOI: 10.1016/j.apenergy.2022.119986

Mashinini, T., & Sethibe, T. (2025). A model of the interplay between leadership styles, culture and digital transformation. *South African Journal of Information Management*, *27*(1), 1–9. DOI: 10.4102/sajim.v27i1.1959

Masoodi, F. S., Bamhdi, A., Manocha, A., Teli, T. A., Masoodi, Z. S., & Reegu, F. A. (2024). *Internet of Things Applications and Technology*. Auerbach Publications., DOI: 10.1201/9781003458401

Matos, J. F., Piedade, J., Freitas, A., Pedro, N., Dorotea, N., Pedro, A., & Galego, C. (2023). Teaching and learning research methodologies in education: A systematic literature review. *Education Sciences*, *13*(2), 173. DOI: 10.3390/educsci13020173

MAY. P. M. A., Savitha, V., Gayathri, S., & Mahalakshmi, S. (2025, April). Exploring Sustainable Computing: IoT, Big Data, and Energy-Efficient Solutions. In *2025 5th International Conference on Trends in Material Science and Inventive Materials (ICTMIM)* (pp. 1218-1223). IEEE.

Ma, Y., Chen, G., & Wei, Q. (2017). Finding users preferences from large-scale online reviews for personalized recommendation. *Electronic Commerce Research*, *17*(1), 3–29. DOI: 10.1007/s10660-016-9240-9

Mayeke, N. R. (2025). *Evaluating the Cost-Benefit Dynamics of Cybersecurity Compliance Investments: A Multi-Sectoral Analysis Across Financial*. Educational, and Ecommerce Industries.

Mayer, R. C., Davis, J. H., & Schoorman, F. D. (1995). An integrative model of organizational trust. *Academy of Management Review*, *20*(3), 709–734. DOI: 10.2307/258792

Mbewe, E. S., & Chavula, J. (2021, December). Security mental models and personal security practices of Internet users in Africa. In *International Conference on e-Infrastructure and e-Services for Developing Countries* (pp. 47-68). Cham: Springer International Publishing.

McCarthy, P., Sammon, D., & Alhassan, I. (2022). Digital transformation leadership characteristics: A literature analysis. *Journal of Decision Systems*, *32*(1), 79–109. DOI: 10.1080/12460125.2021.1908934

Mckinsey & Company. (2024) What is the Internet of Things (IoT)? Accessed 27 April 2024, https://www.mckinsey.com/featured-insights/mckinsey-explainers/what-is-the-internet-of-things#/

McKnight, D. H., & Chervany, N. L. (2002). What trust means in e-commerce customer relationships. *International Journal of Electronic Commerce*, *6*(2), 35–59. DOI: 10.1080/10864415.2001.11044235

McKnight, D. H., Choudhury, V., & Kacmar, C. (2002). Developing and validating trust measures for e-commerce: An integrative typology. *Information Systems Research*, *13*(3), 334–359. DOI: 10.1287/isre.13.3.334.81

Medical Device Cybersecurity. (2019). *FDA's Role and Public Health Mission*. U.S. Food and Drug Administration.

Mettler, T. (2024). The connected workplace: Characteristics and social consequences of work surveillance in the age of datification, sensorization, and artificial intelligence. *Journal of Information Technology*, *39*(3), 547–567. DOI: 10.1177/02683962231202535

Mhangara, P., Mudau, N., Mboup, G., & Mwaniki, D. (2016). Transforming the City of Cape Town from an Apartheid City to an Inclusive Smart City: The Long March to a Sustainable, Inclusive and Prosperous City. In *Smart Economy in Smart Cities: International Collaborative Research: Ottawa, St. Louis, Stuttgart, Bologna, Cape Town, Nairobi, Dakar, Lagos, New Delhi, Varanasi, Vijayawada, Kozhikode, Hong Kong* (pp. 951–983). Springer Singapore.

Michelotto, F., & Joia, L. A. (2024). Organizational digital transformation readiness: An exploratory investigation. *Journal of Theoretical and Applied Electronic Commerce Research*, *19*(4), 3283–3304. DOI: 10.3390/jtaer19040159

Millnert, V., & Eker, J. (2020, December). HoloScale: Horizontal and vertical scaling of cloud resources. In *2020 IEEE/ACM 13th International Conference on Utility and Cloud Computing (UCC)* (pp. 196-205). IEEE.

Miltgen, C. L., & Smith, H. J. (2015). Exploring information privacy regulation, risks, trust, and behavior. *Information & Management*, *52*(6), 741–759. DOI: 10.1016/j.im.2015.06.006

Mineraud, J., Mazhelis, O., Su, X., & Tarkoma, S. (2015). A gap analysis of Internet-of-Things platforms. *arXiv*. https://arxiv.org/abs/1502.01181

Mirsch, T., Lehrer, C., & Jung, R. (2017). *Digital nudging: Altering user behavior in digital environments. Proceedings der 13.* Internationalen Tagung Wirtschaftsinformatik.

Mittelstadt, B. D., Allo, P., Taddeo, M., Wachter, S., & Floridi, L. (2016). The ethics of algorithms: Mapping the debate. *Big Data & Society*, *3*(2), 1–21. DOI: 10.1177/2053951716679679

Moeti, M. N., Mokwena, S. N., & Selape, M. (2024). Factors influencing the adoption of Internet of Things in the agricultural sector in Limpopo province. *South African Journal of Information Management*, *26*(1), 1–8. DOI: 10.4102/sajim.v26i1.1669

Moghrabi, I. A. R., Bhat, S. A., Szczuko, P., AlKhaled, R. A., & Dar, M. A. (2023). Digital Transformation and Its Influence on Sustainable Manufacturing and Business Practices. *Sustainability (Basel)*, *15*(4), 3010. DOI: 10.3390/su15043010

Mohanty, S. N., Chatterjee, J. M., & Satpathy, S. (Eds.). (2022). *Internet of Things and Its Applications*. Springer. DOI: 10.1007/978-3-030-77528-5

Möller, D. P. (2023). NIST cybersecurity framework and MITRE cybersecurity criteria. In *Guide to Cybersecurity in Digital Transformation: Trends, Methods, Technologies, Applications and Best Practices* (pp. 231–271). Springer Nature Switzerland. DOI: 10.1007/978-3-031-26845-8_5

More, A. B. (2023). *Implementing Digital Age Experience Marketing to Make Customer Relations More Sustainable.*, DOI: 10.1007/978-3-031-20443-2_5

Morić, Z., Dakic, V., Djekic, D., & Regvart, D. (2024). Protection of Personal Data in the Context of E-Commerce. *Journal of Cybersecurity and Privacy*, *4*(3), 731–761. DOI: 10.3390/jcp4030034

Mortenson, M. J., & Vidgen, R. (2016). A computational literature review of the technology acceptance model. *International Journal of Information Management*, *36*(6), 1248–1259. DOI: 10.1016/j.ijinfomgt.2016.07.007

Mostafa, R. B., & Kasamani, T. (2020). Brand experience and brand loyalty: Is it a matter of emotions? *Asia Pacific Journal of Marketing and Logistics*, *33*(4), 1033–1051. DOI: 10.1108/APJML-11-2019-0669

Mouha, R. A. (2021). Internet of Things (IoT). *Journal of Data Analysis and Information Processing*, *9*(2), 77–101. https://www.scirp.org/journal/jdaip. DOI: 10.4236/jdaip.2021.92006

Moyo, A., Makota, J., & Kabote, F. (2024). Changes in the Data and Information Systems in Zimbabwe: Lessons from Legislation and Policy Post 2018. *Lighthouse: The Zimbabwe Ezekiel Guti University Journal of Law, Economics and Public Policy*, 1-15.

Mphale, O., Gorejena, K. N., & Nojila, O. H. (2024). IoT adoption in Botswana's SMEs: Technological readiness and government initiatives. *Journal of Information Systems and Informatics*, *6*(4), 2419–2446. DOI: 10.51519/journalisi.v6i4.885

Mubarik, M. S., & Khan, S. A. (2024). Digital Supply Chain and Industry 4.0 Technologies. In *The Theory, Methods and Application of Managing Digital Supply Chains* (pp. 121–132). Emerald Publishing Limited. DOI: 10.1108/978-1-80455-968-020241008

Muinga, N., Magare, S., Monda, J., English, M., Fraser, H., Powell, J., & Paton, C. (2020). Digital health Systems in Kenyan Public Hospitals: A mixed-methods survey. *BMC Medical Informatics and Decision Making*, *20*(1), 2. DOI: 10.1186/s12911-019-1005-7 PMID: 31906932

Mukherjee, S., Baral, M. M., Chittipaka, V., Nagariya, R., & Patel, B. S. (2024). Achieving organizational performance by integrating industrial Internet of things in SMEs: A developing country perspective. *The TQM Journal*, *36*(1), 265–287. DOI: 10.1108/TQM-07-2022-0221

Munara, K. J., Kamil, U. S. A., Rizki, M., Pahala, I., & Handaru, A. W. (2025). Strategic technology adaptation framework: AI, IoT, and the shift in strategic paradigms. *JEMSI (Jurnal Ekonomi, Manajemen, dan Akuntansi, 11*(3), 1575–1582. DOI: 10.35870/jemsi.v11i3.4154

Munongo, S., & Pooe, D. (2022). Small and medium enterprises' adoption of 4IR technologies for supply chain resilience during the COVID-19 pandemic. *Journal of Transport and Supply Chain Management*, *16*(1), 1–11. DOI: 10.4102/jtscm.v16i0.747

Musa, H. G., Fatmawati, I., Nuryakin, N., & Suyanto, M. (2024). Marketing research trends using technology acceptance model (TAM): A comprehensive review of researches (2002–2022). *Cogent Business & Management*, *11*(1), 2329375. DOI: 10.1080/23311975.2024.2329375

Muteba, F., Djouani, K., & Olwal, T. (2019). A comparative survey study on LPWA IoT technologies: Design, considerations, challenges and solutions. *Procedia Computer Science*, *155*, 636–641. DOI: 10.1016/j.procs.2019.08.090

Mu, X., & Antwi-Afari, M. F. (2024). The applications of Internet of Things (IoT) in industrial management: A science mapping review. *International Journal of Production Research*, *62*(5), 1928–1952. DOI: 10.1080/00207543.2023.2290229

Nachanuya, S., & Itabitha-Patience, J. (2025). IoT as a managerial tool for effective business management. *BW Academic Journal*. Retrieved from https://bwjournal.org/index.php/bsjournal/article/view/2626

Nadal, C., Sas, C., & Doherty, G. (2020). Technology Acceptance in Mobile Health: Scoping Review of Definitions, Models, and Measurement J Med. *Journal of Medical Internet Research*, *22*(7), e17256. https://www.jmir.org/2020/7/e17256. DOI: 10.2196/17256

Naeem, M. (2021). The role of social media to generate social proof as engaged society for stockpiling behaviour of customers during Covid-19 pandemic. *Qualitative Market Research*, *24*(3), 281–301. DOI: 10.1108/QMR-04-2020-0050

Nain, G., Pattanaik, K. K., & Sharma, G. K. (2022). Towards edge computing in intelligent manufacturing: Past, present and future. *Journal of Manufacturing Systems*, *62*, 588–611. DOI: 10.1016/j.jmsy.2022.01.010

Nair, A. J., & Manohar, S. (2024). Green Service Consumption: Unlocking Customer Expectations on Technological Transformations Enhancing Purchase Experience in Retail Store. *International Journal of Information Management Data Insights*, *4*(2), 100277. DOI: 10.1016/j.jjimei.2024.100277

Nan, G., Yang, J., & Dou, R. (2017). Do only review characteristics affect consumers' online behaviours? A study of relationship between reviews. *Journal of Electronic Commerce Research*, *18*(4), 330–345.

Narayanan, S., & Singh, G. A. (2023). Consumers' willingness to pay for corporate social responsibility: Theory and evidence. *International Journal of Consumer Studies*, *47*(6), 2212–2244. DOI: 10.1111/ijcs.12910

Narciandi-Rodriguez, D., Aveleira-Mata, J., Garcia-Ordas, M. T., Alfonso-Cendon, J., Benavides, C., & Alaiz-Moreton, H. (2025). A cybersecurity review in IoT 5G networks. *Internet of Things : Engineering Cyber Physical Human Systems*, *30*, 101478. DOI: 10.1016/j.iot.2024.101478

Nasir, F., & Sultani, H. (n.d.). IoT in Healthcare: Advanced Remote Monitoring and Telemedicine Solutions. *International Journal of Advanced Engineering Technologies and Innovations*, *10*(2), 604048.

Nautwima, J. P., & Asa, A. R. (2021). The impact of microfinance support on the development of manufacturing SMEs operating in Windhoek, Namibia. *Archives of Business Research*, *9*(12), 250–272. DOI: 10.14738/abr.912.11417

Nautwima, J. P., Asa, A. R., & Nendongo, V. P. (2022). Integrating gamification into middle school Mathematics curriculum : Game-based learning approach in Namibia. *International Journal of Operations Management*, *2*(4), 7–19. DOI: 10.18775/ijom.2757-0509.2020.24.4001

Nautwima, J. P., Obrenovic, B., Asa, A. R., Johannes, H. N., & Abueva, N. (2025). Determinants of technology adoption in small and medium-sized enterprises. *Sustainable Futures : An Applied Journal of Technology, Environment and Society*, *10*(100919), 100919. DOI: 10.1016/j.sftr.2025.100919

Ndubuaku, M., & Okereafor, D. (2015). Internet of things for Africa: Challenges and opportunities. *2015 International Conference on Cyberspace Governance - CyberAbuja2015, 9*, 23–31. DOI: 10.1007/978-3-319-04223-7_1

Neal Joshua, E. S., Bhattacharyya, D., & Rao, N. T. (2022). Managing information security risk and Internet of Things (IoT) impact on challenges of medicinal problems with complex settings. In *Multi-Chaos, Fractal and Multi-Fractional Artificial Intelligence of Different Complex Systems* (pp. 291–310). Elsevier. DOI: 10.1016/B978-0-323-90032-4.00007-9

Negm, E. (2022). Internet of Things (IoT) acceptance model – assessing consumers'behavior toward the adoption intention of IoT. *Arab Gulf Journal of Scientific Research*, *41*(4), 539–556. Advance online publication. DOI: 10.1108/AGJSR-09-2022-0183

Nepomuceno, T., Carneiro, T., Maia, P. H., Adnan, M., Nepomuceno, T., & Martin, A. (2020, March). AutoIoT: A framework based on user-driven MDE for generating IoT applications. In *Proceedings of the 35th Annual ACM Symposium on Applied Computing* (pp. 719-728). DOI: 10.1145/3341105.3373873

Neslin, S. A. (2022). The omnichannel continuum: Integrating online and offline channels along the customer journey. *Journal of Retailing*, *98*(1), 111–132. DOI: 10.1016/j.jretai.2022.02.003

Ngepah, N., Saba, C., & Kajewole, D. (2024). The impact of industry 4.0 on South Africa's manufacturing sector. *Journal of Open Innovation*, *10*(1), 1–23. DOI: 10.1016/j.joitmc.2024.100226

Ngwenya, M., & Ngoepe, M. (2022). Data trust in Consumer Internet of Things assemblages in the mobile and fixed telecommunication operators in South Africa. *South African Journal of Information Management*, *24*(1), a1426. DOI: 10.4102/sajim.v24i1.1426

Nimigan, S. (2019). The Malabo Protocol, the ICC, and the idea of 'regional complementarity'. *Journal of International Criminal Justice*, *17*(5), 1005–1029. DOI: 10.1093/jicj/mqz040

NIST. (2020). *Considerations for managing Internet of Things (IoT) cybersecurity and privacy risks (NISTIR 8228)*. National Institute of Standards and Technology.

Nizetic, S., Soli, P., & Patrono, L. (2020). Internet of Things (IoT): Opportunities, issues and challenges towards a smart and sustainable future. *Journal of Cleaner Production*, *274*, 1–32. DOI: 10.1016/j.jclepro.2020.122877

Nobar, H. B. K., Kalejahi, H. K., & Rostamzadeh, R. (2020). Impact of social media marketing activities on brand equity and brand commitment in the leather industry. *International Journal of Business Excellence*, *20*(2), 191. DOI: 10.1504/IJBEX.2020.105346

Norbu, T., Park, J. Y., Wong, K. W., & Cui, H. (2024). Factors Affecting Trust and Acceptance for Blockchain Adoption in Digital Payment Systems: A Systematic Review. *Future Internet*, *16*(3), 106. DOI: 10.3390/fi16030106

Oberländer, A. M., Röglinger, M., Rosemann, M., & Kees, A. (2018). Conceptualizing business-to-thing interactions: A sociomaterial perspective on the internet of things. *European Journal of Information Systems*, *27*(4), 486–502. DOI: 10.1080/0960085X.2017.1387714

Ojubanire, O. A., Kolapo, A. G., Berbain, S., & Sebti, H. (2025). Awareness and perceived readiness of Industry4.0 in Africa: A case study of SMMEs in Nigeria. *Supply Chain Forum, 26*(2), 165–179. DOI: 10.1080/16258312.2024.2418794

Okorie, G. N., Egieya, Z. E., Ikwue, U., Udeh, C. A., & Adaga, E. M. (2024). Leveraging big data for personalized marketing campaigns: A review. *International Journal of Management & Entrepreneurship Research*, *6*(1), 216–242. DOI: 10.51594/ijmer.v6i1.778

Omol, E., Mburu, L., & Abuonji, P. (2024). Pioneering digital transformation in African: The path to maturity amidst unique challenges and opportunities. *Canadian Journal of Business and Information Studies*, *6*(2), 35–48. DOI: 10.34104/cjbis.024.035048

Omoseebi, A., Jayson, A., and Winston, W. (2025). Skill Development: Training Programs to Equip Employees with Digital Skills.

Oncioiu, I., Căpu neanu, S., Topor, D., Tama , A., Solomon, A.-G., & Dănescu, T. (2021). Fundamental Power of Social Media Interactions for Building a Brand and Customer Relations. *Journal of Theoretical and Applied Electronic Commerce Research, 16*(5), 1702–1717. DOI: 10.3390/jtaer16050096

Oon Ling, L., Tay, R., Too, S., & Gorod, A. (2019). A Smart City Transportation System of Systems Governance Framework: A Case Study of Singapore. page 37-42.

Oredo, J., Njihia, J., & Iraki, X. N. (2019). Institutional pressures and cloud computing adoption: The moderating effect of organizational mindfulness. *2019 IST-Africa Week Conference. IST-Africa, 2019*, 1–9. DOI: 10.23919/ISTAFRICA.2019.8764832

Oschinsky, F. M., Stelter, A., & Niehaves, B. (2021). Cognitive biases in the digital age – How resolving the status quo bias enables public-sector employees to overcome restraint. *Government Information Quarterly, 38*(4), 101611. DOI: 10.1016/j.giq.2021.101611

Osseiran, A., Boccardi, F., Braun, V., Kusume, K., Marsch, P., Maternia, M., Queseth, O., Schellmann, M., Schotten, H., Taoka, H., Tullberg, H., Uusitalo, M. A., Timus, B., & Fallgren, M. (2014). Scenarios for 5G mobile and wireless communications: The vision of the METIS project. *IEEE Communications Magazine, 52*(5), 26–35. DOI: 10.1109/MCOM.2014.6815890

Padyab, A., Habibipour, A., Rizk, A., & Ståhlbröst, A. (2019). Adoption barriers of IoT in large scale pilots. *Information (Basel), 11*(1), 23. DOI: 10.3390/info11010023

Palanisamy, R., & Wu, Y. (2021). Users' attitude on perceived security of enterprise systems mobility: An empirical study. *Information and Computer Security, 29*(1), 159–186. DOI: 10.1108/ICS-05-2020-0069

Palmié, M., Miehé, L., Mair, J., & Wincent, J. (2024). Valuation entrepreneurship through product-design and blame-avoidance strategies: How Tesla managed to change the public perception of sustainable innovations. *Journal of Product Innovation Management, 41*(3), 644–676. DOI: 10.1111/jpim.12732

Panahi Rizi, M. H., Hosseini Seno, S. A., Rizi, M. H. P., & Seno, S. A. H. (2022). A systematic review of technologies and solutions to improve security and privacy protection of citizens in the smart city. *Internet of Things : Engineering Cyber Physical Human Systems, 20*, 100584. DOI: 10.1016/j.iot.2022.100584

Pandey, S., Singh, R. K., Gunasekaran, A., & Kaushik, A. (2020). Cyber security risks in globalized supply chains: Conceptual framework. *Journal of Global Operations and Strategic Sourcing, 13*(1), 103–128. DOI: 10.1108/JGOSS-05-2019-0042

Paré, G., & Kitsiou, S. (2016). Methods for literature reviews. In Lau, F., & Kuziemsky, C. (Eds.), *Handbook of eHealth evaluation: An evidence-based approach* (pp. 157–179). University of Victoria., DOI: 10.1515/9781503604513-004

Park, E., Chung, K., & Lee, S. (2021). Understanding the acceptance of IoT in households. *Technological Forecasting and Social Change*, *173*, 121108.

Park, M., Kayuni, M., Manda, T., & Kim, H. (2020). Modeling secure home area network based on IoT for resource constraints environment. *Journal of Computer and Communications*, *8*(1), 45–70. DOI: 10.4236/jcc.2020.81004

Park, S., Chung, K., & Jayaraman, P. P. (2017). Trust in IoT: Understanding trustworthiness of IoT systems. *IEEE Access : Practical Innovations, Open Solutions*, *5*, 23416–23425.

Patel, M., Shangkuan, J., & Thomas, C. (2017). What's new with the Internet of Things. *McKinsey & Company*, 1-8.

Patwa, N., Gupta, M., & Mittal, A. (2024). Social proof: Empowering social commerce through social validation. *Global Knowledge, Memory and Communication*. Advance online publication. DOI: 10.1108/GKMC-06-2023-0188

Paul, J., & Barari, M. (2022). Meta-analysis and traditional systematic literature reviews—What, why, when, where, and how? *Psychology and Marketing*, *39*(6), 1099–1115. DOI: 10.1002/mar.21657

Paul, K., Chatterjee, S. S., Pai, P., Varshney, A., Juikar, S., Prasad, V., Bhadra, B., & Dasgupta, S. (2022). Viable smart sensors and their application in data driven agriculture. *Computers and Electronics in Agriculture*, *198*, 107096. DOI: 10.1016/j.compag.2022.107096

Paydas Turan, C. (2021). Success drivers of co-branding: A meta-analysis. *International Journal of Consumer Studies*, *45*(4), 911–936. DOI: 10.1111/ijcs.12682

Perera, C., Liu, C. H., Jayawardena, S., & Chen, M. (2015). Context-aware computing in the Internet of Things: A survey on IoT from industrial market perspective. *International Journal of Distributed Sensor Networks*. Advance online publication. DOI: 10.1155/2015/967415

Peter, O., Pradhan, A., & Mbohwa, C. (2022). Industrial internet of things (IIoT): Opportunities, challenges, and requirements in manufacturing businesses in emerging economies. *Procedia Computer Science*, *217*, 856–865. DOI: 10.1016/j.procs.2022.12.282

Pingali, S. R., Singha, S., Arunachalam, S., & Pedada, K. (2023). Digital readiness of small and medium enterprises in emerging markets: The construct, propositions, measurement, and implications. *Journal of Business Research, 164*(1139), 113973. DOI: 10.1016/j.jbusres.2023.113973

Porter, M. E., & Heppelmann, J. E. (2014). How smart, connected products are transforming companies. Harvard Business Review. Retrieved December 20, 2018, from https://hbr.org/2014/11/how-smart-connected-products-are-transforming-competition

Porter, M. E., & Heppelmann, J. E. (2014). How smart, connected products are transforming competition. *Harvard Business Review, 92*(11), 64–88.

Pousttchi, K., Tilson, D., Lyytinen, K., & Hufenbach, Y. (2015). Introduction to the special issue on mobile commerce: Mobile commerce research yesterday, today, tomorrow - what remains to be done? *International Journal of Electronic Commerce, 19*(4), 1–20. DOI: 10.1080/10864415.2015.1029351

Protick, T. I., Sabir, A., Abhinaya, S., Bartlett, A., & Das, A. (2024). Unveiling Users' Security and Privacy Concerns Regarding Smart Home IoT Products from Online Reviews. *ACM Journal on Computing and Sustainable Societies, 2*(4), 1–41. DOI: 10.1145/3685929

Purnima, F. H., Mosaddek, N., Chanchal, M. A. U., & Khan, B. (2024). Integration of IoT in strategic management: A review of current trends, future possibilities, and challenges. *International Journal of Science and Research Archive, 12*(2), 2634–2645. DOI: 10.30574/ijsra.2024.12.2.1565

Putra, R. H., Sutjipto, M. R., Widodo, A., & Kuntadi, S. (2024). Business ecosystem architecture development: A case study of IoT business in the transportation industry. *Journal of Asian Multicultural Research for Economy and Management Study, 5*(3), 25–41. DOI: 10.47616/jamrems.v5i3.536

PwC. (2022). 2022 Global Digital Trust Insights. Available at: https://www.pwc.com/gx/en/issues/cybersecurity/digital-trust-insights.html

Qalati, S. A., Ostic, D., Sulaiman, M. A. B. A., Gopang, A. A., & Khan, A. (2022). Social media and SMEs' performance in developing countries: Effects of Technological-Organizational-Environmental factors on the adoption of social media. *SAGE Open, 12*(2), 1–13. DOI: 10.1177/21582440221094594

Quach, S., Thaichon, P., Martin, K. D., Weaven, S., & Palmatier, R. W. (2022). Digital technologies: Tensions in privacy and data. *Journal of the Academy of Marketing Science, 50*(6), 1299–1323. DOI: 10.1007/s11747-022-00845-y

Quartey, P., Turkson, E., Abor, J. Y., & Iddrisu, A. M. (2017). Financing the growth of SMEs in Africa: What are the contraints to SME financing within ECOWAS? *Review of Development Finance, 7*(1), 18–28. DOI: 10.1016/j.rdf.2017.03.001

Quaye, W., Akon-Yamga, G., Akuffobea-Essilfie, M., & Onumah, J. A. (2024). Technology adoption, competitiveness and new market access among SMEs in Ghana: What are the limiting factors? *African Journal of Science, Technology, Innovation and Development, 16*(7), 1023–1037. DOI: 10.1080/20421338.2024.2414949

Quinones, M., Gomez-Suarez, M., Cruz-Roche, I., & Díaz-Martín, A. M. (2023). Technology: A strategic imperative for successful retailers. *International Journal of Retail & Distribution Management, 51*(4), 546–566. DOI: 10.1108/IJRDM-03-2022-0088

Radanliev, P. (2024). Integrated cybersecurity for metaverse systems operating with artificial intelligence, blockchains, and cloud computing. *Frontiers in Blockchain, 7*, 1359130. DOI: 10.3389/fbloc.2024.1359130

Rahayu, R., & Day, J. (2015). Determinant factors of E-commerce adoption by SMEs in developing country: Evidence from Indonesia. *Procedia: Social and Behavioral Sciences, 195*, 142–150. DOI: 10.1016/j.sbspro.2015.06.423

Raheja, N., & Kumar Manocha, A. (2022). IoT based ECG monitoring system with encryption and authentication in secure data transmission for clinical health care approach. *Biomedical Signal Processing and Control, 74*, 103481. DOI: 10.1016/j.bspc.2022.103481

Rai, K., Sahana, B., Pai, A. N., Gautham, S., & Dhanush, U. (2021, August). Vertical scaling of virtual machines in cloud environment. In *2021 International Conference on Recent Trends on Electronics, Information, Communication & Technology (RTEICT)* (pp. 458-462). IEEE. DOI: 10.1109/RTEICT52294.2021.9573715

Rajabzadeh, M., & Fatorachian, H. (2023). Modelling factors influencing IoT adoption: With a focus on agricultural logistics operations. *Smart Cities, 6*(6), 3266–3296. DOI: 10.3390/smartcities6060145

Rajaram, K. (2022). *Leading and Transforming Organizations*. Routledge., DOI: 10.4324/9781003286288

Raji, I. D., Smart, A., White, R. N., Mitchell, M., Gebru, T., Hutchinson, B., & Barnes, P. (2020, January). Closing the AI accountability gap: Defining an end-to-end framework for internal algorithmic auditing. In *Proceedings of the 2020 conference on fairness, accountability, and transparency* (pp. 33-44). DOI: 10.1145/3351095.3372873

Raji, I. D., Xu, P., Honigsberg, C., & Ho, D. (2022). Outsider Oversight: Designing a Third Party Audit Ecosystem for AI Governance. *Proceedings of the 2022 AAAI/ACM Conference on AI, Ethics, and Society*, 557–571. DOI: 10.1145/3514094.3534181

Rane, N. L. (2023). Enhancing Customer Loyalty through Artificial Intelligence (AI), Internet of Things (IoT), and Big Data Technologies: Improving Customer Satisfaction, Engagement, Relationship, and Experience. http://dx.doi.org/DOI: 10.2139/ssrn.4616051

Rashid, A., Rasheed, R., Amirah, N. A., Yusof, Y., Khan, S., & Agha, A. A. (2021). A Quantitative Perspective of Systematic Research: Easy and Step-by-Step Initial Guidelines. *Turkish Online Journal of Qualitative Inquiry, 12*(9).

Rath, K. C., Khang, A., & Roy, D. (2024). The role of Internet of Things (IoT) technology in Industry 4.0 economy. In *Advanced IoT technologies and applications in the industry 4.0 digital economy* (pp. 1–28). CRC Press. DOI: 10.1201/9781003434269-1

Ray, P. P. (2018). A survey on Internet of Things architectures. *Journal of King Saud University. Computer and Information Sciences*, *30*(3), 291–319. DOI: 10.1016/j.jksuci.2016.10.003

Rego, L., Brady, M., Leone, R., Roberts, J., Srivastava, C., & Srivastava, R. (2022). Brand response to environmental turbulence: A framework and propositions for resistance, recovery and reinvention. *International Journal of Research in Marketing*, *39*(2), 583–602. DOI: 10.1016/j.ijresmar.2021.10.006

Rehman, M. H. ur., Yaqoob, I., Salah, K., Imran, M., Jayaraman, P. P., & Perera, C. (2019). The role of big data analytics in industrial Internet of Things. *arXiv*. https://arxiv.org/abs/1904.05556

Ren, G., Chen, Y., & Yang, M. (2024). Customer perception, integration behavior, and loyalty of internet of things enterprises. *Technology in Society*, *78*, 102600. DOI: 10.1016/j.techsoc.2024.102600

Reyes, P. M. (2023). Radio Frequency Identification (RFID) and Supply Chain Management. In *The Palgrave Handbook of Supply Chain Management* (pp. 1–35). Springer International Publishing. DOI: 10.1007/978-3-030-89822-9_109-1

Richard Bevis, R. B. (2023, April 19). *7 Examples of IoT in Everyday Life.*

Rimbeck, M., Stumpf-Wollersheim, J., & Richter, A. (2024). Unfolding IoT Adoption: A status quo bias perspective. *Business & Information Systems Engineering*, •••, 1–18.

Rimbeck, M., Stumpf-Wollersheim, J., & Richter, A. (2024). Unfolding IoT Adoption: A Status Quo Bias Perspective. *Business & Information Systems Engineering*. Advance online publication. DOI: 10.1007/s12599-024-00891-6

Roffarello, A. M. (2018, June). End user development in the IoT: a semantic approach. In *2018, 14th International Conference on Intelligent Environments (IE)* (pp. 107-110). IEEE. DOI: 10.1109/IE.2018.00026

Roman, R., Zhou, J., & Lopez, J. (2013). On the features and challenges of security and privacy in distributed Internet of Things. *Computer Networks*, *57*(10), 2266–2279. DOI: 10.1016/j.comnet.2012.12.018

Rosário, A. T., & Dias, J. C. (2023). How has data-driven marketing evolved: Challenges and opportunities with emerging technologies. *International Journal of Information Management Data Insights*, *3*(2), 100203. DOI: 10.1016/j.jjimei.2023.100203

Roy, C., Pandey, M., & Rautaray, S. S. (2018). An approach for optimal horizontal scaling in big data scenario. In Advances in Data and Information Sciences: Proceedings of ICDIS-2017, Volume 1 (pp. 223-230). Springer Singapore

Sadeeq, M. M., Abdulkareem, N. M., Zeebaree, S. R., Ahmed, D. M., Sami, A. S., & Zebari, R. R. (2021). IoT and Cloud computing issues, challenges and opportunities: A review. *Qubahan Academic Journal*, *1*(2), 1–7. DOI: 10.48161/qaj.v1n2a36

Sadeghi, M., Carenini, A., Corcho, O., Rossi, M., Santoro, R., & Vogelsang, A. (2024). Interoperability of heterogeneous Systems of Systems: From requirements to a reference architecture. *The Journal of Supercomputing*, *80*(7), 8954–8987. DOI: 10.1007/s11227-023-05774-3

Sahoo, S. K., & Goswami, S. S. (2023). A comprehensive review of multiple criteria decision-making (MCDM) methods: Advancements, applications, and future directions. *Decision Making Advances*, *1*(1), 25–48. DOI: 10.31181/dma1120237

Sakib, N., Veeramalla, H. S. J., Naidu, N. A. R., Anik, F. I., Vanga, L. R., Valero, M., & Hossain, E. (2023). *Unpacking Privacy Calculus and Interplay of Data Privacy and Healthcare: Paths Towards Safeguarding Patient Empowerment* (pp. 137–171). DOI: 10.1007/978-3-031-42112-9_7

Sallam, K., Mohamed, M., & Mohamed, A. W. (2023). Internet of Things (IoT) in supply chain management: Challenges, opportunities, and best practices. *Sustainable Machine Intelligence Journal*, *2*, 3–1. DOI: 10.61185/SMIJ.2023.22103

Sanctorum, A., & Lujan, B. O. (2024, June). Towards End-User-Driven Generation of IoT Applications. In *Companion Proceedings of the 16th ACM SIGCHI Symposium on Engineering Interactive Computing Systems* (pp. 66-73). DOI: 10.1145/3660515.3661332

Santos, Z. R., Cheung, C. M. K., Coelho, P. S., & Rita, P. (2022). Consumer engagement in social media brand communities: A literature review. *International Journal of Information Management, 63*, 102457. DOI: 10.1016/j.ijinfomgt.2021.102457

Sarker, A., Jesser, A., & Speidel, M. (2024, April). Enhancing Decentralized Federated Learning with User Feedback Loops: A Novel Approach for Personalized and Adaptive Learning in IoT Environments. In *2024 IEEE 3rd International Conference on Computing and Machine Intelligence (ICMI)* (pp. 1-5). IEEE. DOI: 10.1109/ICMI60790.2024.10585926

Satar, S. B. A., Hussin, A. R. C., & Ali, Y. S. (2018). Drivers of internet of things adoption in oil and gas industry. *Advanced Science Letters, 24*(10), 7364–7370. DOI: 10.1166/asl.2018.12943

Sathya, U., Hashini, S., Lakshmipriya, C., Varun, C. M., & Nalini, M. (2024, December). Emerging Trends and Future Prospects in Internet of Things (IoT) Technology. In *2024 International Conference on Sustainable Communication Networks and Application (ICSCNA)* (pp. 79-85). IEEE.

Saunders, M., Lewis, P., & Thornhill, A. (2019). *Research methods for business students* (8th ed.). Pearson Education.

Savoury, R. D., & Burchell, J. M. (2021). Exploring the influential determinants of IoT adoption in the U.S. manufacturing sector. *International Journal of Applied Management and Technology, 20*(1), 183–193. DOI: 10.5590/IJAMT.2021.20.1.10

Saxena, A., Singh, R., Gehlot, A., Akram, S. V., Twala, B., Singh, A., Montero, E. C., & Priyadarshi, N. (2022). Technologies Empowered Environmental, Social, and Governance (ESG): An Industry 4.0 Landscape. *Sustainability (Basel), 15*(1), 309. DOI: 10.3390/su15010309

Schierz, P. G., Schilke, O., & Wirtz, B. W. (2010). Understanding consumer acceptance of mobile payment services: An empirical analysis. *Electronic Commerce Research and Applications, 9*(3), 209–216. DOI: 10.1016/j.elerap.2009.07.005

Schorr, A. (2023). The technology acceptance model (TAM) and its importance for digitalization research: A review. *Proceedings TecPsy, 2023*, 55–65. DOI: 10.2478/9788366675896-005

Seele, P., Dierksmeier, C., Hofstetter, R., & Schultz, M. D. (2021). Mapping the Ethicality of Algorithmic Pricing: A Review of Dynamic and Personalized Pricing. *Journal of Business Ethics, 170*(4), 697–719. DOI: 10.1007/s10551-019-04371-w

Seetharaman, K. M. R.Karthika Murugandi Reddiar Seetharaman. (2021). Internet of Things (IoT) Applications in SAP: A Survey of Trends, Challenges, and Opportunities. *Int. J. Adv. Res. Sci. Commun. Technol, 3*(2), 499–508. DOI: 10.48175/IJARSCT-6268B

Sendjaja, T., Prastiawan, E., Suryani, Y., & Fatmawati, E. (2024). Cybersecurity In the Digital Age: Developing Robust Strategies to Protect Against Evolving Global Digital Threats and Cyber Attacks. *The International Journal of Science in Society, 6*(1), 1008–1019. DOI: 10.54783/ijsoc.v6i1.1098

Šerić, M., Vernuccio, M., & Pastore, A. (2024). Revising the basic principles of integrated marketing communications during a health-related crisis: The case of Croatian tourism and hospitality industry. *Corporate Communications, 29*(2), 257–278. DOI: 10.1108/CCIJ-05-2023-0081

Shafique, K., Khawaja, B. A., Sabir, F., Qazi, S., & Mustaqim, M. (2020). Internet of things (IoT) for next-generation smart systems: A review of current challenges, future trends and prospects for emerging 5G-IoT scenarios. *IEEE Access : Practical Innovations, Open Solutions, 8*, 23022–23040. DOI: 10.1109/ACCESS.2020.2970118

Shameli-Sendi, A., Aghababaei-Barzegar, R., & Cheriet, M. (2016). Taxonomy of information security risk assessment (ISRA). *Computers & Security, 57*, 14–30. DOI: 10.1016/j.cose.2015.11.001

Shams, S. M. R., Brown, D. M., & Hardcastle, K. (2025). *Brand Management.* Marketing Communication, and Promotion Management for People, Planet, and Profit., DOI: 10.1007/978-3-031-79130-7_4

Shandilya, S. K., Datta, A., Kartik, Y., & Nagar, A. (2024). *Navigating the Regulatory Landscape.*, DOI: 10.1007/978-3-031-53290-0_3

Shan, Z., & Wang, Y. (2024). Strategic talent development in the knowledge economy: A comparative analysis of global practices. *Journal of the Knowledge Economy, 15*(4), 19570–19596. DOI: 10.1007/s13132-024-01933-w

Shaukat, K., Alam, T. M., Hameed, I. A., Khan, W. A., Abbas, N., & Luo, S. (2021, September). A review on security challenges in internet of things (IoT). In 2021 26th international conference on automation and computing (ICAC) (pp. 1-6). IEEE.

Sheoran, S., & Vij, S. (2023). A consumer-centric paradigm shifts in business environment with the evolution of the Internet of Things: A literature review. *Vision (Basel)*, *27*(4), 431–442. DOI: 10.1177/09722629211033944

Sheth, J. N. (2011). Impact of emerging markets on marketing: Rethinking existing perspectives and practices. *Journal of Marketing*, *75*(4), 166–182. DOI: 10.1509/jmkg.75.4.166

Shin, D. (2010). The effects of trust, security and privacy in social networking: A security-based approach to understand the pattern of adoption. *Interacting with Computers*, *22*(5), 428–438. DOI: 10.1016/j.intcom.2010.05.001

Shin, D., & Park, Y. J. (2019). Role of fairness, accountability, and transparency in algorithmic affordance. *Computers in Human Behavior*, *98*, 277–284. DOI: 10.1016/j.chb.2019.04.019

Shi, W., Cao, J., Zhang, Q., Li, Y., & Xu, L. (2016). Edge computing: Vision and challenges. *IEEE Internet of Things Journal*, *3*(5), 637–646. DOI: 10.1109/JIOT.2016.2579198

Sicari, S., Rizzardi, A., Grieco, L. A., & Coen-Porisini, A. (2015). Security, privacy and trust in Internet of Things: The road ahead. *Computer Networks*, *76*, 146–164. DOI: 10.1016/j.comnet.2014.11.008

Sim, J., Kim, B., Jeon, K., Joo, M., Lim, J., Lee, J., & Choo, K.-K. R. (2023). Technical Requirements and Approaches in Personal Data Control. *ACM Computing Surveys*, *55*(9), 1–30. DOI: 10.1145/3558766

Siva, S. R., Bushra, S. N., Maheswari, B., & Prabukumar, M. K. (2022, April). Performance Analysis of Different Machine Learning in Customer Prediction. In *2022 6th International Conference on Trends in Electronics and Informatics (ICOEI)* (pp. 1425-1430). IEEE. DOI: 10.1109/ICOEI53556.2022.9776714

Sivakumar, C. L. V., Mone, V., & Abdumukhtor, R. (2024). Addressing privacy concerns with wearable health monitoring technology. *Wiley Interdisciplinary Reviews. Data Mining and Knowledge Discovery*, *14*(3), e1535. Advance online publication. DOI: 10.1002/widm.1535

Snyder, H. (2019). Literature review as a research methodology: An overview and guidelines. *Journal of Business Research*, *104*, 333–339. DOI: 10.1016/j.jbusres.2019.07.039

Soeker, I., Lusinga, S., & Chigona, W. (2021). Readiness of the South African agricultural sector to implement IoT. *arXiv*. https://arxiv.org/abs/2108.10081

Soumyalatha, S. G. H. (2016, May). Study of IoT: Understanding IoT architecture, applications, issues and challenges. In *1st International Conference on Innovations in Computing & Net-working (ICICN16), CSE, RRCE. International Journal of Advanced Networking & Applications*, *478*, 14.

Sreenivasulu, A., & Manimozhi, T. Satheesh kumar P., and Singh P.,(2022). "The Model of Smart Sensing Device For Sensitive Nanoclusters Modification in Sensing Properties," 2022 2nd International Conference on Advance Computing and Innovative Technologies in Engineering (ICACITE), Greater Noida, India, 2022, pp. 1043-1047, DOI: 10.1109/ICACITE53722.2022.9823846

Statista. (2023). Consumer IoT - Namibia. https://www.statista.com/outlook/tmo/internet-of-things/consumer-iot/namibia

Statista. (2023). *Internet of Things (IoT) connected devices installed base worldwide from 2015 to 2030*. Retrieved from https://www.statista.com/

Sturm, M., Weking, J., Böhm, M., & Krcmar, H. (2023). How two leading partners learn to tango: The case of IoT-based business model co-innovation between a retailer and an electronics supplier. *Electronic Markets*, *33*(1), 34. DOI: 10.1007/s12525-023-00645-4

Tagscherer, F., & Carbon, C. C. (2023). Leadership for successful digitalization: A literature review on companies' internal and external aspects of digitalization. *Sustainable Technology and Entrepreneurship*, *2*(100039), 1–15. DOI: 10.1016/j.stae.2023.100039

Talib, Y. Y. A., & Saat, R. M. (2017). Social proof in social media shopping: An experimental design research. SHS Web of Conferences 34, shsconf/20173402005

Tan, T. M., & Saraniemi, S. (2023). Trust in blockchain-enabled exchanges: Future directions in blockchain marketing. *Journal of the Academy of Marketing Science*, *51*(4), 914–939. DOI: 10.1007/s11747-022-00889-0

Tawalbeh, L. A., Muheidat, F., Tawalbeh, M., & Quwaider, M. (2020). IoT privacy and security: Challenges and solutions. *Applied Sciences (Basel, Switzerland)*, *10*(12), 4102. DOI: 10.3390/app10124102

Tedeschi, S., Rodrigues, D., Emmanouilidis, C., Erkoyuncu, J., Roy, R., & Starr, A. (2018). A cost estimation approach for IoT modular architectures implementation in legacy systems. *Procedia Manufacturing*, *19*, 103–110. DOI: 10.1016/j.promfg.2018.01.015

Teece, D. J. (2007). Explicating dynamic capabilities: The nature and microfoundations of (sustainable) enterprise performance. *Strategic Management Journal, 28*(13), 1319–1350. DOI: 10.1002/smj.640

Telukdarie, A., Dube, T., Matjuta, P., & Philbin, S. (2022). The opportunities and challenges of digitalization for SME's. *Procedia Computer Science, 217*, 689–698. DOI: 10.1016/j.procs.2022.12.265

Tewera, D., Zhou, M., & Gavai, P. V. (2024, November). Enhancing IoT Security for Socio-Economic Development in the Mirror of Challenges, Emerging Technologies, and Holistic Solutions. In *2024 3rd Zimbabwe Conference of Information and Communication Technologies (ZCICT)* (pp. 1-8). IEEE.

Thaler, R. H., & Sunstein, C. R. (2021). *Nudge: The final edition*. Penguin Books.

Tiwari, M., & Waoo, A. A. (2024). *Transforming Healthcare: The Synergistic Fusion of AI and IoT for Intelligent*. Personalized Well-Being., DOI: 10.1007/978-3-031-65022-2_7

Tondro, M., Jahanbakht, M., & Ozay, D. (2025). Enhancing IoT technology acquisition in emerging economies: Insights and recommendations using analytical case study review of IoT startups. *Businesses, 5*(20), 1–25. DOI: 10.3390/businesses5020020

Torraco, R. J. (2005). Writing integrative literature reviews: Guidelines and examples. *Human Resource Development Review, 4*(3), 356–367. DOI: 10.1177/1534484305278283

Torre, D., Chennamaneni, A., & Rodriguez, A. (2022). *IoT security standards and certifications. Institute of Electrical and Electronics Engineers*. IEEE Transactions and Journals., DOI: 10.1109/ACCESS.2023.3245524

Tripathy, B. K., & Anuradha, J. (Eds.). (2017). *Internet of things (IoT): technologies, applications, challenges and solutions*. CRC press. DOI: 10.1201/9781315269849

Tufekci, Z. (2015). Algorithmic harms beyond Facebook and Google: Privacy, big data and the internet of things. *Colorado Technology Law Journal*, 13(2).

Turban, E., King, D., Lee, J. K., Liang, T.-P., & Turban, D. C. (2015). *Electronic commerce: A managerial and social networks perspective* (8th ed.). Springer. DOI: 10.1007/978-3-319-10091-3

Uckelmann, D., Harrison, M., & Michahelles, F. (2011). *Architecting the internet of things*. Springer. DOI: 10.1007/978-3-642-19157-2

Ullah, R., Yahya, M., Mostarda, L., Alshammari, A., Alutaibi, A. I., Sarwar, N., Ullah, F., & Ullah, S. (2024). Intelligent decision making for energy efficient fog nodes selection and smart switching in the IOT: A machine learning approach. *PeerJ. Computer Science*, *10*, e1833. DOI: 10.7717/peerj-cs.1833 PMID: 38660213

University of Southern Califonia. (2024) What is Consumer Psychology https://appliedpsychologydegree.usc.edu/blog/what-is-consumer-psychology

Vaithianathan, S. (2010). A review of e-commerce literature on India and research agenda for the future. *Electronic Commerce Research*, *10*(1), 83–97. DOI: 10.1007/s10660-010-9046-0

Valdez-de-Leon, O. (2016). A Digital maturity model for telecommunications service providers. *Technology Innovation Management Review*, *6*(8), 19–32. DOI: 10.22215/timreview/1008

van Dinter, R., Tekinerdogan, B., & Catal, C. (2022). Predictive maintenance using digital twins: A systematic literature review. *Information and Software Technology*, *151*, 107008. DOI: 10.1016/j.infsof.2022.107008

Van Zoonen, L. (2016). Privacy concerns in smart cities. *Government Information Quarterly*, *33*(3), 472–480. DOI: 10.1016/j.giq.2016.06.004

VanDeWiele, M. D., Hastings, A. M., Evans, M. D., O'Connell, M. S., & Flynn, P. M. (2025). Using the Unified Theory of Acceptance and Use of Technology (UTAUT) to predict the behavioral intent of teledentistry utilization amongst United States adults. *Journal of Telemedicine and Telecare*, *31*(2), 286–296. DOI: 10.1177/1357633X231182405

Vassallo, J. P., Banerjee, S., Zaman, H., & Prabhu, J. C. (2023). Design thinking and public sector innovation: The divergent effects of risk-taking, cognitive empathy and emotional empathy on individual performance. *Research Policy*, *52*(6), 104768. DOI: 10.1016/j.respol.2023.104768

Vassilakos, A., & Martin, R. (2023). Understanding the Challenge of Cybersecurity in Africa: A Holistic Analysis of Southern African Development Community (SADC) and Foundation for Future Research. HOLISTICA - Journal of Business and Public Administration. Volume 14, Issue 1, 162-172.

Vecchiato, R. (2012). Environmental uncertainty, foresight and strategic decision making: An integrated study. *Technological Forecasting and Social Change*, *79*(3), 436–447. DOI: 10.1016/j.techfore.2011.07.010

Venkatesh, V. (2022). Adoption and use of AI tools: A research agenda grounded in UTAUT. *Annals of Operations Research, 308*(1–2), 641–652. DOI: 10.1007/s10479-020-03918-9

Vijayakumar, G., Rajkumar, M., Rajiv Chandar, N., Selvakumar, P., & Duraisamy, R. (2024). Muniyandi Rajkumar, Rajiv Chandar N, Selvakumar P and Ramesh Duraisamy, (2024). Environmentally friendly TDS removal from waste water by electrochemical ion exchange batch-type recirculation (EIR) technique. *Environmental Science. Water Research & Technology, 10*(4), 826–835. DOI: 10.1039/D3EW00793F

Vinoth, S., & Srivastava, N. (2024). Unveiling the Power of Omni-channel Retail Strategies. In *Augmenting Retail Reality, Part B: Blockchain, AR, VR, and AI* (pp. 85–112). Emerald Publishing Limited. DOI: 10.1108/978-1-83608-708-320241014

Vishwakarma, N. K., Singh, R. K., & Sharma, R. R. K. (2020). Internet of things architectures: Do organizational strategies matter? *Business Process Management Journal, 26*(1), 102–131. DOI: 10.1108/BPMJ-03-2018-0092

Voigt, P., & Von dem Bussche, A. (2017). *The EU General Data Protection Regulation (GDPR): A practical guide*. Springer International Publishing. DOI: 10.1007/978-3-319-57959-7

Volberda, H. W., Khanagha, S., Baden-Fuller, C., Mihalache, O. R., & Birkinshaw, J. (2021). Strategizing in a digital world: Overcoming cognitive barriers, reconfiguring routines and introducing new organizational forms. *Long Range Planning, 54*(5), 102110. DOI: 10.1016/j.lrp.2021.102110

Wachter, S. (2018). The GDPR and the Internet of Things: A three-step transparency model. *Law, Innovation and Technology, 10*(2), 266–294. DOI: 10.1080/17579961.2018.1527479

Wackerhage, H., & Schoenfeld, B. J. (2021). Personalized, Evidence-Informed Training Plans and Exercise Prescriptions for Performance, Fitness and Health. *Sports Medicine (Auckland, N.Z.), 51*(9), 1805–1813. DOI: 10.1007/s40279-021-01495-w PMID: 34143410

Waiganjo, I., Osakwe, J., & Azeta, A. (2025). Cybersecurity in Namibia: Challenges, strategies and prospects. *Global Journal of Engineering and Technology Advances., 22*(3), 1–008. DOI: 10.30574/gjeta.2025.22.3.0048

Wang, J., Shahzad, F., & Ashraf, S. F. (2023). Elements of information ecosystems stimulating the online consumer behavior: A mediating role of cognitive and affective trust. *Telematics and Informatics, 80*, 101970. DOI: 10.1016/j.tele.2023.101970

Wang, M., Wei, Y., Azumah, G., & Wang, C. L. (2024). African returnees in international knowledge transfer: A social capital perspective. *Journal of International Management, 30*(101118), 1–26. DOI: 10.1016/j.intman.2023.101118

Wang, Q., Peng, C. H., Jin, Y., & Jiang, S. (2025). Impact of Data Breach on IT Investment: Embracing Both Failure Learning and Threat Rigidity. *Production and Operations Management, 34*(6), 1256–1275. DOI: 10.1177/10591478241277455

Wang, S. (2024). The role of IoT in transforming marketing strategies for a connected era. *Journal of Business and Future Economy, 1*(2), 41–49.

Wang, W. X., Kim, K. S., & Kim, J. K. (2023). Investigating the determinants of IoT device continuance intentions: An empirical study of smart speakers through the lens of expectation-confirmation theory. *SAGE Open, 10*(3), 21582440231197067. DOI: 10.1177/21582440231197067

Wang, Y., & Wang, K. Y. (2017). How do firms tackle strategic change? A theoretical model of the choice between dynamic capability-based and ad hoc problem-solving approaches. *Journal of Organizational Change Management, 30*(5), 725–743. DOI: 10.1108/JOCM-03-2016-0045

Wang, Z., Li, M., Lu, J., & Cheng, X. (2022). Business Innovation based on artificial intelligence and Blockchain technology. *Information Processing & Management, 59*(1), 102759. DOI: 10.1016/j.ipm.2021.102759

Wan, Y. (2015). The matthew effect in social commerce. *Electronic Markets, 25*(4), 313–324. DOI: 10.1007/s12525-015-0186-x

Waris, I., & Hameed, I. (2020). Promoting environmentally sustainable consumption behavior: An empirical evaluation of purchase intention of energy-efficient appliances. *Energy Efficiency, 13*(8), 1653–1664. DOI: 10.1007/s12053-020-09901-4

Weber, R. H. (2010). Internet of Things – New security and privacy challenges. *Computer Law & Security Review, 26*(1), 23–30. DOI: 10.1016/j.clsr.2009.11.008

Weber, R. H. (2015). Internet of things: A review of privacy concerns. *Computer Law & Security Review, 31*(5), 618–627. DOI: 10.1016/j.clsr.2015.07.002

Weber, S. (2017). Coercion in cybersecurity: What public health models reveal. *Journal of Cybersecurity, 3*(3), 173–183. DOI: 10.1093/cybsec/tyx005

Wessel, L., Baiyere, A., Ologeanu-Taddei, R., Cha, J., & Jensen, T. B. (2021). Unpacking the difference between digital transformation and it-enabled organizational transformation. *Journal of the Association for Information Systems, 22*(1), 102–129. DOI: 10.17705/1jais.00655

Westergren, U. H., Mähler, V., & Jadaan, T. (2024). Enabling digital transformation: Organizational implementation of the internet of things. *Information & Management*, *61*(103996), 103996. Advance online publication. DOI: 10.1016/j.im.2024.103996

Westerman, G., Bonnet, D., & McAfee, A. (2014). *Leading digital: Turning technology into business transformation*. Harvard Business Press.

Whitmore, A., Agarwal, A., & Da Xu, L. (2015). The Internet of Things—A survey of topics and trends. *Information Systems Frontiers*, *17*(2), 261–274. DOI: 10.1007/s10796-014-9489-2

Willis, B., Jai, T., & Lauderdale, M. (2021). Trust and commitment: Effect of applying consumer data rights on U.S. Consumers' attitudes toward online retailers in big data era. *Journal of Consumer Behaviour*, *20*(6), 1575–1590. DOI: 10.1002/cb.1968

Winkelhake, U. (2022). Vision Digitised Automotive Industry 2030. In *The Digital Transformation of the Automotive Industry* (pp. 85–145). Springer International Publishing. DOI: 10.1007/978-3-030-83826-3_5

Wohlin, C., Kalinowski, M., Romero Felizardo, K., & Mendes, E. (2023). Successful combination of database search and snowballing for identification of primary studies in systematic literature studies. arXiv. https://arxiv.org/abs/2307.02612

Xiao, B., & Benbasat, I. (2007). E-commerce product recommendation agents: Use, characteristics, and impact. *Management Information Systems Quarterly*, *31*(1), 137–209. DOI: 10.2307/25148784

Xiao, J., Zhen, Z., Tian, L., Su, B., Chen, H., & Zhu, A. X. (2021). Green behavior towards low-carbon society: Theory, measurement and action. *Journal of Cleaner Production*, *278*, 123765. DOI: 10.1016/j.jclepro.2020.123765

Xi, Y. (2024). Navigating Technological Shifts: An Examination of User Inertia and Technology Prestige in Large-Language-Model AI Chatbot Transition. *International Journal of Human-Computer Interaction*, ●●●, 1–17. DOI: 10.1080/10447318.2024.2405786

Xu, G., & Gutierrez, J. A. (2006). An exploratory study of killer applications and critical success factors in m-commerce. *Journal of Electronic Commerce in Organizations*, *4*(3), 63–79. DOI: 10.4018/jeco.2006070104

Xu, L., & Mehta, R. (2022). Technology devalues luxury? Exploring consumer responses to AI-designed luxury products. *Journal of the Academy of Marketing Science*, *50*(6), 1135–1152. DOI: 10.1007/s11747-022-00854-x

Xu, T., Wendt, J., & Potkonjak, M. (2014). Security of IoT Systems: *Design Challenges and Opportunities. IEEE/ACM International Conference on Computer-Aided Design (ICCAD)*. 417-423.

Yadav, N., Gupta, V., & Garg, A. (2024). Industrial Automation Through AI-Powered Intelligent Machines—Enabling Real-Time Decision-Making. In *Recent Trends in Artificial Intelligence Towards a Smart World: Applications in Industries and Sectors* (pp. 145–178). Springer Nature Singapore. DOI: 10.1007/978-981-97-6790-8_5

Yamini, B., Ramana, K. V., Nalini, M., Devi, D. C., Maheswari, B., & Siva, S. R. (2024). Customer churn prediction model in enterprises using machine learning. *International Journal of Advanced Technology and Engineering Exploration*, *11*(110), 94.

Yamini, S. (2020). Behavioral perspective of newsvendor ordering decisions: Review, analysis and insights. *Management Decision*, *59*(2), 240–257. DOI: 10.1108/MD-07-2019-0975

Yang, R., & Wibowo, S. (2022). User trust in artificial intelligence: A comprehensive conceptual framework. *Electronic Markets*, *32*(4), 2053–2077. DOI: 10.1007/s12525-022-00592-6

Yavari, A., & Georgakopoulos, D. (2021). Privacy-preserving mechanisms for IoT data collection. *Future Generation Computer Systems*, *115*, 230–246.

Yerpude, S., & Singhal, T. K. (2019). Custolytics. *International Journal of Emerging Markets*, *16*(1), 92–112. DOI: 10.1108/IJOEM-05-2018-0250

Zahra, S. A., Sapienza, H. J., & Davidsson, P. (2006). Entrepreneurship and dynamic capabilities: A review, model and research agenda. *Journal of Management Studies*, *43*(4), 917–955. DOI: 10.1111/j.1467-6486.2006.00616.x

Zeng, E., Mare, S., & Roesner, F. (2017). End user security and privacy concerns with smart homes. In *Thirteenth Symposium on Usable Privacy and Security (SOUPS 2017)* (pp. 65–80).

Zengeya, T., Sambo, P., & Mabika, N. (2021). The adoption of the internet of things for smart agriculture In Zimbabwe. *Computer Science and Information Technology*, *2021*, 99–106.

Zhang, H., Hou, L., Yang, H., Bai, Y., Lu, Z., & Liu, Y. (2024, May). Intelligent Defect Detection System Based on Cloud-edge Synergy Technology. In *2024 IEEE 9th International Conference on Smart Cloud (SmartCloud)* (pp. 103-108). IEEE Computer Society. DOI: 10.1109/SmartCloud62736.2024.00026

Zhang, H., Zhang, M., Lu, J., Zhao, L., Zhao, D., Xiao, C., Gu, R., & Luo, W. (2020). Interpersonal relationships modulate outcome evaluation in a social comparison context: The pain and pleasure of intimacy. *Cognitive, Affective & Behavioral Neuroscience, 20*(1), 115–127. DOI: 10.3758/s13415-019-00756-6 PMID: 31823210

Zhang, J., Zhang, S., Tan, X., & Zhao, H. (2025). The impact of digitalization on organizational agility: Evidence from the enterprise survey for innovation and entrepreneurship in China. [OPEN]. *Humanities & Social Sciences Communications, 12*(917), 1–15. DOI: 10.1057/s41599-025-05256-2

Zhang, W., Siyal, S., Riaz, S., Ahmad, R., Hilmi, M. F., & Li, Z. (2023). Data Security, Customer Trust and Intention for Adoption of Fintech Services: An Empirical Analysis From Commercial Bank Users in Pakistan. *SAGE Open, 13*(3), 21582440231181388. Advance online publication. DOI: 10.1177/21582440231181388

Zhan, X., Xu, Y., & Liu, Y. (2024). Personalized UI layout generation using deep learning: An adaptive interface design approach for enhanced user experience. *International Journal of Engineering and Management Research, 14*(5), 134–147.

Zheng, S., Apthorpe, N., Chetty, M., & Feamster, N. (2018). User perceptions of smart home IoT privacy. *arXiv*. https://arxiv.org/abs/1802.08182

Zhou, Z. (2024). Data extraction in dockless bikeshare: An analysis from users' perspective. *Big Data & Society, 11*(4), 20539517241299724. Advance online publication. DOI: 10.1177/20539517241299724

Zikria, Y., Ali, R., Afzal, M. K., & Kim, S. W. (2021). Next-Generation Internet of Things (IoT): Opportunities, Challenges, and Solutions. *Sensors (Basel), 21*(4), 1174. DOI: 10.3390/s21041174 PMID: 33562343

Zuboff, S. (2019). *The age of surveillance capitalism: The fight for a human future at the new frontier of power*. PublicAffairs.

About the Contributors

Asa Romeo Asa is an accomplished academic and industry expert with extensive experience in management science, logistics, and entrepreneurship. He earned his PhD in Management Science (Management Strategy) from Wuhan University of Technology, China. He also holds an MSc in International Business Law from the University of Salford, UK, and an MBA from Wuhan University of Technology. Prof. Asa is the Director of the Namibian-German Institute for Logistics and an Associate Professor of Business Management at the Namibia University of Science and Technology. He has held several leadership roles in academia, including Head of Department and Associate Dean, where he played a pivotal role in research development, curriculum innovation, and institutional strategy. His research focuses on logistics, sustainability, entrepreneurship, and business strategy. He has supervised numerous master's and PhD students and has contributed to scholarly publications, academic reviews, and policy discussions in these fields. Prof. Asa is also an experienced consultant, advising businesses and institutions on strategic management, process improvement, and research-driven decision-making. With a passion for business research, data analytics, and lifelong learning, Prof. Asa continues to shape the discourse on sustainable business practices and technological advancements in logistics and supply chain management.

Johanna Pangeiko Nautwima is an accomplished economist and business strategist with a strong background in international economics, trade policy, regional integration, and business development. She holds a Doctor of Business Administration from the Namibia Business School, University of Namibia, where she investigated the impact of blue ocean strategy on the sustainable business performance of manufacturing SMEs. She is currently pursuing a PhD in Economics at Nelson Mandela University, South Africa, focusing on the impact of trade liberalisation and renewable energy consumption on industrial development and carbon emissions in Namibia. Dr. Nautwima is a Consultant - Economist and Trade

Data Analyst at the African Development Bank Group, where she contributes to regional development and integration initiatives. Her work includes producing key knowledge products such as the Africa Visa Openness Index and the Africa Regional Integration Index, as well as engaging in policy formulation, trade, and investment strategy. With a strong academic background spanning Africa, Europe, and Asia, Dr. Nautwima has earned multiple degrees, including an MA in Economics from Savitribai Phule Pune University (India) and an MSc in Energy Policy from the Pan African University Institute of Water and Energy Sciences (Algeria). Her expertise extends to research in financial integration, entrepreneurship, and industrial development. Dr. Nautwima has published extensively in peer-reviewed journals, contributing to the fields of economic policy, sustainability, and strategic management. She has also been recognised with various academic scholarships and awards for her excellence in research and higher education. Her commitment to data-driven decision-making and policy analysis continues to shape discussions on regional economic growth and business innovation.

***

Prema A is an Assistant Professor in the Department of Artificial Intelligence and Data Science at Velammal Engineering College, Chennai. Her academic interests include data analytics, machine learning, and intelligent systems. She is committed to delivering quality education and promoting research-driven learning.

Abu Bakar Bin Abdul Hamid chose academia as his profession in 1992, beginning as a lecturer and later rising to a Professor of Marketing and Supply Chain Management. He holds a BBA and an MBA from Northrop University (USA) and a PhD from the University of Derby, UK. He has demonstrated an excellent record of teaching and supervision for more than 25 years in the academic field, at both undergraduate and postgraduate levels. Above all, his achievement in graduating more than 35 PhD candidates proves his ability, capability, and passion in postgraduate supervisions. He has also produced impactful research and publications which directly strengthen his expertise in his area of interest. In particular, he has published more than 300 articles in competitive international journals, proceedings, books, and book chapters. He also managed to secure several competitive national grants and consultancies for various projects. Such commitment is truly a landmark of an academician. His accolades, academic recognition, and leadership demonstrate his level of professorship. His notable contributions are recognized locally and internationally, as proven by the multiple invitations he has received to be an invited speaker, reviewer, editor in journals, external assessor, and internal or external examiner. With such calibre, he has much to contribute to any academic institution in the world.

Dinesh Aleria is a Research Scholar in the field of Management, specializing in content marketing and consumer behavior. His research focuses on the role of content marketing tools in shaping purchase intentions among rural consumers in India. He has authored and co-authored several research papers published in reputed national and international journals indexed in Scopus and other recognized academic databases. Dinesh actively participates in academic conferences and research activities, contributing to the advancement of knowledge in content marketing and consumer engagement.

Abid Aziz is serving as a Trustee on the Board of Uttara University Trust in Bangladesh. He has a BSc in Business from Birkbeck College, University of London, United Kingdom, as well as an MBA and an MS in Economics. His work towards smart tech deployment and dissemination, digitization of majority or the administrative business processes, integration of Ai into academics and Smart Campus transition, future-proofing Uttara University with digital transformation is the first of its kind in the country that has been setting benchmarks, fostering innovation, ensuring efficiency, and generating socioeconomic impact within the community. He has a robust research background with expertise in corporate strategy as well. Mr Aziz had previously served as the Director of the Fintech Research Group and is presently steering the Office of the Future, leading the transformation project in partnership with top industries. This project team is actively working on improving the tech-led academic experience, which is at par with global forces.

Nabid Aziz is a Doctoral Researcher at the University of Hull in the East Riding of Yorkshire, located in the United Kingdom. Additionally, in Bangladesh he has been serving as an Assistant Professor at Gopalganj Science and Technology University (formerly BSMRSTU) and as a member of the governing body of Uttara University he heads it's Planning and Development Committee ensuring growth of the institutions. His work in academia and educational administration is concentrated on the areas such as inclusive technology deployment, campus infrastructure and capacity building, faculty development, internationalisation and business innovation. With a long term association with the education sector, he continues to contribute towards institutional sustainability.

Inos Chibidi is a Lecturer in the Department of Mathematics and Computer Science within the School of Natural Sciences at Great Zimbabwe University, Zimbabwe. Holding a Master of Commerce Degree in Information Systems from the same institution, Mr. Chibidi is an emerging voice in artificial intelligence and emerging technologies. His passion lies in the adoption of AI and its transformative impact across various facets of human life. Driven by a keen interest in researching AI and such technologies as IoT, he explores their potential to revolutionize operations within both academic and business environments. Mr. Chibidi advocates for the responsible utilization of AI in sectors such as education, business, and healthcare. He is also interested in research on cybersecurity. Currently, his research focuses on leveraging AI to enhance efficiency in businesses, specifically Small and Medium Enterprises (SMEs) and academic institutions, with several articles in progress.

Clainos Chidoko is a Senior Lecturer in the Department of Economics and Finance, School of Business Sciences at Great Zimbabwe University, Zimbabwe. He holds a PhD in Economics from the University of Zimbabwe. Dr Chidoko has a passion for economic development and trade issues. He is a keen researcher and has published various articles and books with leading publishing houses. He has over the years taught various courses that include International Trade, International Economics, Industrial Economics and Development Economics, among many.

Cyril Crasto is a distinguished Associate Professor at the Balaji Institute of Management and Human Resource Development (BIMHRD), under Sri Balaji University, Pune. With extensive academic and industry experience, Dr. Crasto has made significant contributions to the fields of management and human resource development. His teaching and research focus on enhancing organizational performance, leadership development, and employee engagement. Known for his dynamic teaching style and commitment to academic excellence, he strives to bridge the gap between theoretical knowledge and practical application. Dr. Crasto's dedication to shaping competent management professionals makes him a respected and influential figure in the field of business education.

Md Mehedi Hasan Emon is an SDG-focused research practitioner with expertise in Artificial Intelligence (AI), digital transformation, supply chain management, sustainability, marketing analytics, and Educational Technology (EduTech). With an interdisciplinary foundation bridging Management Information Systems, Marketing, and Operations & Supply Chain Management, he contributes to AI-driven Industry 4.0 and 5.0, digital innovation, and sustainable business ecosystems in emerging economies. His research aligns with the United Nations Sustainable Development Goals (SDGs), reflecting a commitment to sustainable industrial transformation and green innovation. He has been involved in multiple UGC-funded research projects through the Centre for Higher Studies and Research (CHSR) and the BUP Research Centre (BRC) at Bangladesh University of Professionals, contributing to project coordination, research design, data analysis, and reporting on AI adoption, digital supply chains, sustainability practices, and consumer behavior. He has also contributed to European Union-funded collaborative research initiatives. His scholarly contributions include journal articles, conference papers, book chapters, and edited books such as Sustainable Operations in the Age of AI and Big Data and Enhancing Sustainability in Global Supply Chains With Big Data Analytics. He focuses on AI adoption, digital supply chain integration, sustainability performance, green innovation, cybersecurity behavior, and AI-enabled marketing systems, and serves as a peer reviewer for international journals and publishers. His research interests span AI, sustainable supply chains, digital transformation, green marketing, consumer trust, cybersecurity adoption, and technology acceptance, with a focus on how AI reshapes organizational capabilities, enhances sustainability outcomes, influences consumer behavior, and transforms strategic decision-making. Through academic excellence, grant-funded research, industry analytics expertise, and international collaboration, he advances evidence-based, technology-enabled, and innovation-driven development in Bangladesh and beyond.

Sammy F is an Assistant Professor in the Department of Computing Technologies, School of Computing, at SRM Institute of Science and Technology, Kattankulathur. He is actively involved in teaching and mentoring students in the field of computing and technology. His academic interests include software development, data analytics, and emerging computing paradigms

Manisha G is an Assistant Professor in the Department of Computer Science and Engineering at R.M.D Engineering College. Her academic interests focus on teaching and research in computer science and engineering disciplines.

Kamal Hossain is an Assistant Professor of Management at the World University of Bangladesh, Dhaka. He holds a PhD from the University of Malaya, Malaysia. His research interests include Business and Management, the Digital Transformation of Business, Innovation Management, Strategic Management, Human Resource Management (HRM), and International Entrepreneurship. Dr. Hossain is committed to advancing scholarly and practical understanding in these fields, with a focus on addressing contemporary challenges in an increasingly dynamic and technology-driven business environment.

Subramaniam Iyer is a distinguished faculty member in the Department of MBA at the Datta Meghe Institute of Management Studies (DMIMS), located in Nagpur, Maharashtra. With a strong academic background and extensive experience in management education, Dr. Iyer has been instrumental in shaping future business leaders through his expertise in strategic management, organizational behavior, and leadership development. Known for his dedication to academic excellence and research, he actively contributes to the institute's vision of fostering innovation and professional growth among students. His commitment to quality education and his passion for mentoring make him a respected figure in the field of management studies.

Sharmin Jahan, an Assistant Professor at Daffodil International University in Bangladesh, with having a strong research background including 15 years of teaching experiences. She holds a BBA and an MBA in Marketing from the University of Dhaka in Bangladesh, where she achieved outstanding academic results & Currently pursuing her PhD in Marketing at the same institution.

Sucheta Kanchi is a dedicated Assistant Professor at the Institute of Management and Entrepreneurship Development (IMED), Bharati Vidyapeeth (Deemed to be University), Pune. With a strong academic foundation and a passion for teaching, she has been actively engaged in shaping the academic and professional growth of management students. Dr. Kanchi's expertise spans various areas of business and management, and she is known for her innovative teaching methods and research-oriented approach. Her commitment to academic excellence and her ability to inspire students make her a valued member of the IMED faculty. Through her work, she continues to contribute meaningfully to the field of management education and research.

Suman Lata is associated in Department of Tourism and Travel Management Central University of Jammu

Mohana M is an Assistant Professor in the Department of Artificial Intelligence and Data Science at Vel Tech Multi Tech Dr. Rangarajan Dr. Sakunthala Engineering College. Her academic interests include machine learning, data analytics, and intelligent systems. She is committed to delivering quality education and fostering research-oriented learning.

Dinesh M. G. is a faculty member at EASA College of Engineering and Technology, Coimbatore, Tamil Nadu, India. He specializes in engineering education and research, contributing to advancements in his field.

Mercy Nyasha Magoso is a full-time lecturer in the Department of Mathematics and Computer Science at Great Zimbabwe University. She holds a Master of Science Degree in Information Systems Management at Midlands State University (MSU), Bachelor of Science Honours Degree in Information Technology at Chinhoyi University of Technology (CUT). She is currently studying a Doctor of Philosophy in Computer and Information Sciences with Computer Science and Information

Systems at North West University, South Africa. She is an upcoming researcher, and her research and teaching interests include Artificial intelligence, Machine Learning, Cybersecurity as well as Information Systems Management.

T.C. Manjunath was born on 6th February 1967. He did his B.E. from RV College of Engg. in 1989 (B'lore Univ), M.E. in Robotics & Automation from Govt.'s LD College of Engg., (Gujarat Univ., Ahmedabad) in 1992 with FCD-First Rank & PhD in Systems & Control Engg. from IIT Bombay in the year 2007, got best research scholar award for the entire IITB. He is currently working as the Dean Research (R & D) and as Professor in Dept. of Computer Science & Engg. with specialization in IoT, Cyber Security, Blockchain Technology in Rajarajeswari College of Engineering, Bengaluru, Karnataka. He has got a teaching (academic), research & administrative experience of more than 35+ years (10 years as Principal & 8 years as HoD, 1 year as Dean Research & rest as faculty) and has published more than 1500+ research papers in various national & international journals & conferences, with 175+ patents, 100+ book-chapters, 25 awards, 100s of Keynote talks and also published 25 text books in various field of science, engineering & technology, completed projects worth Rs. 9 Crores till date & guided 10 PhD scholars in VTU. He is a member of 30 Professional Society Chapters and is a fellow of IE, IETE, AMIEE, Sr. Member of IEEE and a chartered engineer.

P. Selvakumar is currently an Associate Professor in the Department of Science and Humanities at Nehru Institute of Technology, Coimbatore, Tamil Nadu, India. Prior to joining Nehru Institute of Technology, he held positions as an Assistant Professor in the Department of Science and Humanities various engineering colleges in Coimbatore, Tamil Nadu, India, spanning from 2011 to 2023. Dr.P. Selvakumar's academic and research interests lie primarily in the field of phytochemistry. He has made significant contributions to his field, with an impressive record that includes 30 journal publications, 12 patents, and 20 conference papers. Additionally, he has organized 5 seminars and conferences, further demonstrating his commitment to academic and scientific exchange. Throughout his career, Dr. P.Selvakumar has been recognized for his dedication and excellence in teaching, having been honored with several awards, including the Best Teacher Awards. He holds a prominent position in the academic community, contributing actively to research.

Ruchika Paidalwar is a dedicated student pursuing her Master of Business Administration (MBA) at the Datta Meghe Institute of Management Studies (DMIMS), located in Nagpur, Maharashtra – 440022. She is passionate about developing her skills in management, leadership, and strategic decision-making to build a successful career in the business world. With a strong academic foundation and a keen interest in learning about modern business practices, Ruchika strives to excel both academically and professionally. Her commitment to continuous growth and her enthusiasm for innovation make her a promising future leader in the field of management.

Usha Prabhu, is a senior academician having 23+ years of teaching experience – at UG & PG levels, aware of new changes in the education sector like the implementation of the National Education Policy, a member of the Syllabus Revision Committee -PG Level MBA at Bangalore University. She holds three Master degrees - MA, M. Phil, MBA, UGC- NET qualified and holds Ph.D from Bangalore University, presently working at Jain(Deemed-to-be University.· She has authored 2 books - Organization Behaviour for MBA and Entrepreneurship Skill for III semester B. Com published by Sapna Book House. She has published 12 research papers in International Journals, presented 9 research papers at International Conferences and 3 research Book Chapters(Scopus indexed).

Md. Adnan Rahman is an Associate Professor of Digital Marketing and MIS at Uttara University, Dhaka, Bangladesh. Additionally, he is the Director of the Office of Brand & Communication and Public Relations of this university. Dr. Adnan is a postdoctoral researcher at Infrastructure University Kuala Lumpur (IUKL), Malaysia. Dr. Adnan holds a PhD in Marketing from Putra Business School (AACSB-Accredited), UPM, Malaysia; an MSc in MIS; and an MA in IHRM from the University of Bedfordshire, United Kingdom.

Varanasi Rahul is an Assistant Professor at JAIN University (Bangalore), a semi-qualified Cost Accountant, holding three postgraduate degrees: M.Com (Accounting & Taxation), M.Com (Management), and an MA (History). He has cleared the UGC NET in Commerce twice and has also cleared the AP SET in Commerce, History, and Management, as well as the TS SET in Commerce. With 3 years of experience as an Assistant Professor and 6 months as a Corporate Tax Associate for Australian Taxation at PwC (Big 4), he brings both academic and professional expertise to his field. Additionally, he is a freelance archaeologist, practicing epigraphist in Brahmi script, and a numismatist. His scholarly and creative contributions include over 30 newspaper articles published in Deccan Chronicle, Times of India, and other local newspapers. He has presented and participated in 25 national and international seminars and has published 2 research articles in ABDC Journals, 7 in SCOPUS-indexed journals, 2 in Web of Science and 4 in peer-reviewed journals. As a story writer, 5 of his stories have been published in top magazines of Andhra Pradesh. Furthermore, he has authored 3 books. He has also contributed 13 book chapters to various academic publications. In addition to his extensive achievements, he has applied for 17 patents, of which 2 has been granted in India, 3 in UK and 11 have been published.

Njodzi Ranganai is a holder of Master of Commerce degree in Information Systems, Great Zimbabwe University (2014), BSc Honours degree in Information systems (2010) Midlands State University, Zimbabwe and Post graduate diploma in education PGDE (2016) (Zimbabwe Open University). He is currently a lecturer at Great Zimbabwe University in the Department of Mathematics and Computer Science, teaching Artificial intelligence, Communication skills for Computer Science, Management Information Systems, and Applied Research Methods. He has published several papers in reputable journals in areas like Machine Learning, Digital Inclusion, Applications of Computer Science in agriculture and tourism.

Shivangi Rapria is a Senior Research Fellow of Marketing at the Institute of Management Studies and Research, Maharshi Dayanand University, Rohtak, India. Her doctoral research focuses on the topic "Role of Sensory Marketing Cues and Brand Experience in Building Customer Loyalty: A Study of Personal Care Products." She has published various research papers in Scopus-indexed journals, Web of Science, UGC care-listed journals as well as ABDC ranked peer-reviewed journals, in addition she contributed several book chapters to edited book volumes. Moreover, Shivangi has actively engaged with the academic community by presenting her research at national and international conferences. She has also participated in various seminars and workshops, demonstrating her continued commitment to scholarly development and academic research.

N Sathyanarayana has over 15 years of teaching experience at both undergraduate and postgraduate levels. He holds a Master of Business Administration degree from VTU and a Master of Commerce degree from Periyar University. He has completed his Ph.D. in Banking and Finance from Dayananda Sagar University. Currently, he serves as an Assistant Professor in the School of Commerce at Jain (Deemed-to-be University), Bangalore. He has published 24 research papers in international journals, including three indexed in Scopus, and seven papers in national journals. Additionally, he has presented 14 research papers at international conferences and 11 at national conferences. He has co-authored two books at the national level and contributed 13 Scopus-indexed book chapters.

Madireddi Srikumar is presently associated with Global Business School, Koneru Lakshmaiah Education Foundation (KLEF), Deemed to be university, in Hyderabad. He has done his Masters degree in Commerce, Business administration and he was awarded Ph. D from Acharya Nagarjuna University. He has 27 years of research and Academic experience and has held various positions in leading academic institutions like Jain Deemed to be University, Bangalore, Avanthi's Postgraduate and Research Academy, Hyderabad, Vision P.G. College, Hyderabad, St. Xaviour P.G College Hyderabad etc. as Faculty, Assistant Professor, Associate Professor, Head of the Department and Principal. He is an external project evaluator for different universities. He is guiding two scholars for Ph.D scholars and guiding many projects in different management disciplines and conducted management and faculty development programs in the area of Management. He has attended many national seminars and International conferences and has also published many research papers and his articles got published in leading management international and national journals.

G Srividhya, M.Com, M.Phil, Ph.D., is currently an Assistant Professor in the Department of Commerce at the School of Commerce, Jain (Deemed-to-be University), Bangalore. With a career spanning since 2005, she has accumulated 19 years of teaching experience and 10 years of research experience across various institutions. She has published papers in reputed journals and contributed book chapters to various national and international conferences. She is a life member of professional bodies such as IARA and IAA. She also possesses expertise in accounting and finance.

Anish T. P is a faculty member in the Department of Computer Science and Engineering at R.M.K. College of Engineering and Technology, Tamil Nadu. He is dedicated to advancing research and education in computing technologies. His areas of expertise include artificial intelligence, machine learning, and software engineering.

Zerin Tasnim is an Assistant Professor of Supply Chain Management at North South University, Dhaka, Bangladesh, where she also serves as the Course Coordinator for the MBA program. She holds a PhD in Management from Putra Business School, Universiti Putra Malaysia (UPM), and a BSc in Mechanical Engineering from Bangladesh University of Engineering and Technology (BUET). Dr. Tasnim brings an interdisciplinary academic background and a global research perspective to her work, with research interests spanning digital supply chains, healthcare logistics, and sustainable and green operations.

Index

Symbols

A

B

C

D

S

T

V

www.ingramcontent.com/pod-product-compliance
Lightning Source LLC
LaVergne TN
LVHW081537300926
849161LV00006B/1472